WOR
HISTORY
ENCYCLOPEDIA

WORLD HISTORY ENCYCLOPEDIA

4 million years ago to the present day

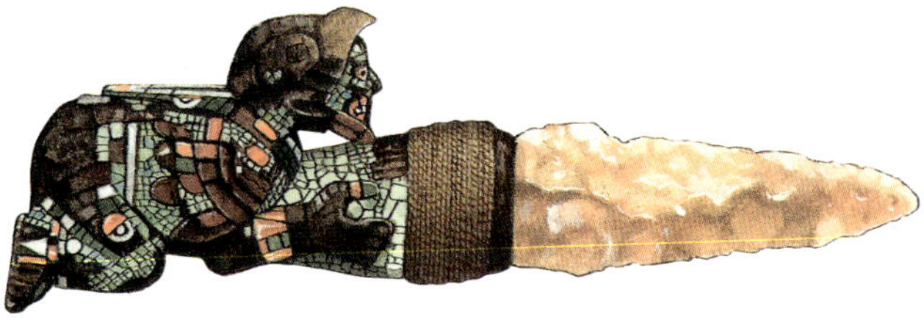

This is a Parragon Book
This edition published in 2001

Parragon
Queen Street House
4 Queen Street
BATH, BA1 1HE, UK

2468109753 1

Produced by Miles Kelly Publishing Ltd
Unit 11, Bardfield Centre, Great Bardfield, Essex CM7 4SL

British Library Cataloguing-in-Publication Data
A catalogue record for this book is available from the British Library

Hardback ISBN 0-75256-596-6
Paperback ISBN 0-75256-579-6

Printed in China

AUTHORS
Anita Ganeri, Hazel Mary Martell, Brian Williams

GENERAL EDITOR
Charlotte Hurdman

DESIGN AND ART DIRECTION
Full Steam Ahead Ltd

SENIOR EDITOR
Rosie Alexander

ARTWORK COMMISSIONING
Branka Surla

PICTURE RESEARCH
Rosie Alexander, Kate Miles, Elaine Willis, Yannick Yago

EDITORIAL ASSISTANT
Lynne French

CONSULTANTS
Theodore Rowland-Entwistle, John Sherman

ADDITIONAL EDITORIAL HELP FROM
Suzanne Airey, Hilary Bird, Jenni Cozens, Pat Crisp, Paul Kilgour, Joanne Murray

EDITORIAL DIRECTOR
Jim Miles

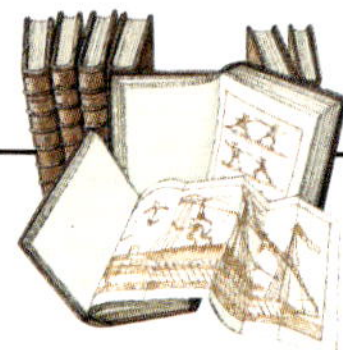

Contents

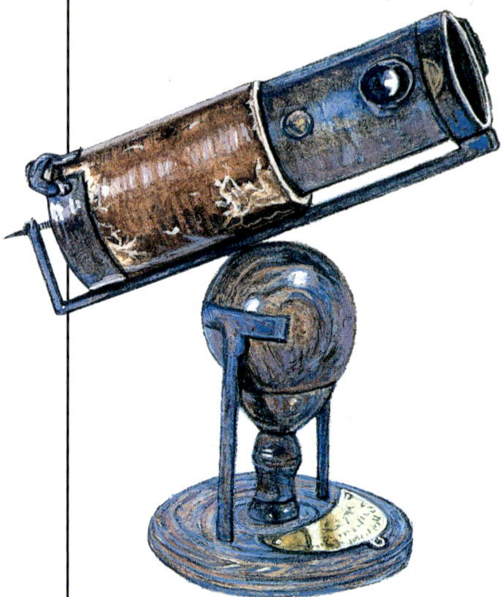

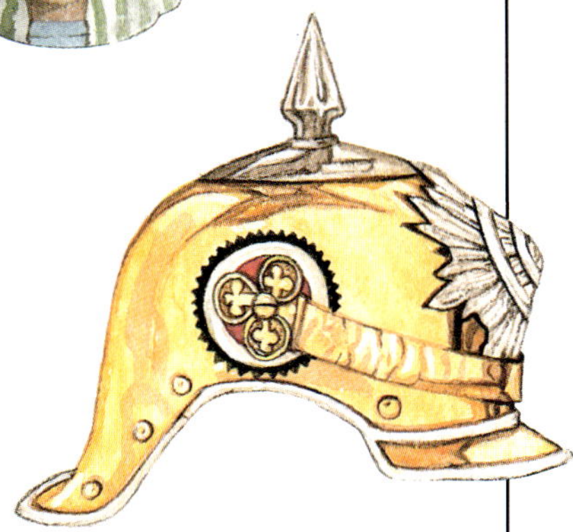

Discovering the Past

△ ***A cuneiform writing tablet****. Cuneiform was the first system of writing and the oldest tablets date from about 5500 years ago. Ancient written records like this are the raw materials of history. Before writing was invented, history was passed on by word of mouth.*

▽ ***Alabaster canopic jars*** *from the tomb of an ancient Egyptian. We can find out a lot about ancient people because of their belief in an afterlife. The Egyptians firmly believed in life after death and filled their tombs with the things they needed in the afterlife.*

What is history? In its broadest sense, history is the story of people – the study of our past. Some historians look at important events, such as wars, revolutions and governments, while others are interested in ordinary people's lives.

Henry Ford, the American car manufacturer, once famously said "History is bunk", but most people would disagree. Our lives today are shaped by decisions and actions made decades, centuries or even thousands of years ago. By understanding the past we may be able to gain a more balanced view of the present.

The basic aims of history are to record and explain our past. Historians study a range of written and oral (spoken) evidence. Combined with archaeology (the study of the things people have left behind them, such as buildings and objects), historians interpret the facts to build up a picture of the past. The first people to study history seriously were the ancient Greeks. In the 5th century BC, the Greek historian Herodotus (called the Father of History) set out to write a true and systematic record of the wars between the Greeks and the Persians. He hoped to preserve the memory of past events and show how two peoples came into conflict with one another. The study of archaeology, however, is a much more recent development. True archaeological investigation only began in the 18th century. Archaeologists today try to preserve even the tiniest fragments left behind by our ancestors to help create a more complete picture of the past.

Interpreting the evidence is the most fascinating part of an historian's or archaeologist's job. Historians, however, must always be aware of bias or prejudice in the things that they read or write. Bias means being influenced by a particular point of view, while prejudice means "judging before" – before you have all the facts. All accounts are an interpretation of the events, sometimes unknowingly. Histories written by the ancient Egyptians, for example, record and praise the deeds of their kings with little concern for accuracy.

When historians read a text, they must ask themselves what was the attitude of the writer to the people or events being described? How close was the writer to the event? These questions must also be asked of oral history, when people's memories fade and can become exaggerated or distorted over time. Historians themselves are influenced by the times they live in and modern historians try to avoid applying the values and beliefs of the present to their interpretations of the past.

History is not just concerned with the long distant past. History is the story of our lives – what is news today will be history tomorrow. Change can be sudden and dramatic, with ideas and systems thought to be fixed quickly overturned.

△ ***A miniature painting*** *from the Duc de Berry's* Très Riches Heures. *Pictures like this tell a great deal about life in medieval Europe, such as the clothes people wore, the jobs that they did and the food that they ate. They also reveal how society was organized.*

◁ ***Krak des Chevaliers****, a Crusader castle in what is now Syria. Castles were built for defence as well as to provide accommodation for lords and their families. A historian studying the life of a medieval knight would look at the buildings of the time.*

◁ ▷ ***Navigational instruments*** *like these were used in the 15th century by explorers in search of new lands. New inventions can change the world and objects like these reveal the type of technology people used in the past.*

▷ ***This carved ivory mask*** *was worn as an ornament by the oba, or king, of Benin. Benin was a powerful empire in West Africa that was at its height between the 14th and 17th centuries. The wealth and sophistication of Benin was expressed in its art.*

Historical Evidence

△ ***The Domesday Book** was a nationwide survey of England (except the far north). It was divided into two volumes, one covering the richest counties of Essex, Suffolk and Norfolk, the other covering the remaining counties. Citizens had to answer officials' questions under oath.*

△ ***Viking runes** carved on a stone. The letters of the Viking alphabet, called runes, were used to carve everyday messages on wood, metal and stone. Some rune stones tell stories from Viking history recalling battles and heroic deeds.*

Before historians can interpret the past, they must first establish the facts about the events they are studying. Historians look for evidence by researching a wide range of documents and records, called historical sources.

Primary sources are accounts written by people involved in the events, and include government and legal papers, wills, maps, business agreements, letters and diaries. Historians read a wide range of texts, not just actual accounts of past events, but also texts, such as prayer books, that show the interests and beliefs of people in the past. Historians also look for evidence from government census returns, and birth, death and marriage registers. Possibly the most famous census ever carried out was the Domesday Book, compiled in 1086 by order of William the Conqueror, King of England. This was the first thorough survey of part of the British Isles, detailing who owned the land, who lived there and how much it was worth. No survey of the British Isles was conducted again until 1801.

Historians also look for secondary sources – these are studies of primary sources made at a later date. Secondary sources include such documents as newspaper reports, or the books of previous historians. Newspapers are an especially important resource for modern historians. They enable historians to read as many accounts of an event as possible, thus helping them to get an overview of many different opinions.

Texts are not always written in books or on paper. Over the centuries, people have written on clay, bone, silk, metal, stone and wood. Even cultures that never developed a system of writing invented their own ways of keeping records. The Incas of Peru, for example, were a very advance civilization that never developed writing. They worked out a way or recording information using knotted lengths of string, called quipus.

Oral history is also often a vital source of information. For thousands of years people have passed on their history by word of mouth from generation to generation. Stories, songs and poems telling of migrations, battles and power struggles were composed, their verses and music making it easier for people to remember the words. Today, historians make films and tape recordings as a record of events.

△ ***Julius Caesar*** *(c. 101–44 BC) was a great general and dictator of Rome. He also wrote an account of his conquest of Gaul (France), perhaps to show that his actions were not done for personal glory. History is sometimes written by those who take a major part in it.*

▽ ***Churchill, Roosevelt and Stalin*** *meet togther at the Yalta conference in February 1945. Photographs like this one have provided superb and sometimes dramatic documentary evidence of key historical events.*

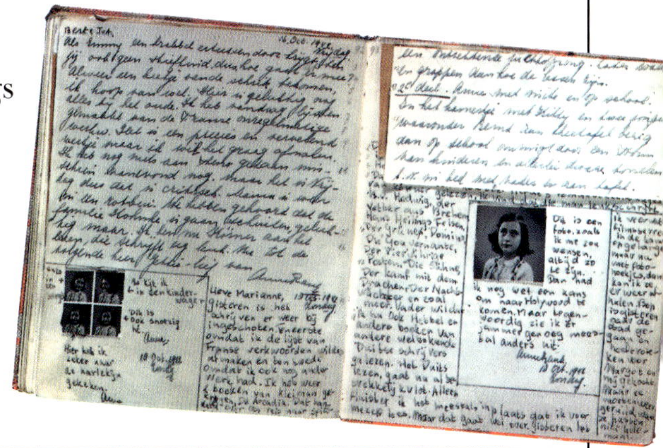

▷ ***Anne Frank's diary*** *is a vivid account of life for Jews living in Nazi occupied Europe during World War II. Diaries provide invaluable sources of information as eye-witness accounts of everyday life.*

△ ***Nicolaus Copernicus*** *(1473–1543) was the first person to suggest that the Earth went round the Sun. This is an illustration of his idea. Illustrations and maps like this can show us how much people knew about the world and what they considered important.*

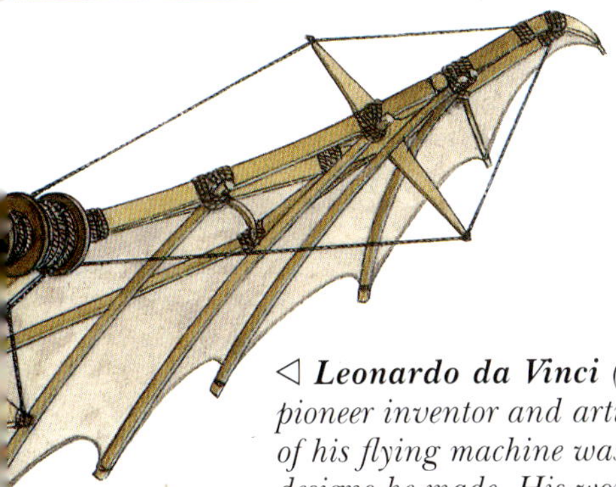

◁ ***Leonardo da Vinci*** *(1452–1519) was a pioneer inventor and artist. This reconstruction of his flying machine was taken from detailed designs he made. His work, although ahead of its time, shows an explosion of interest in science.*

Archaeological Evidence

▽ ***This wall painting*** *is from the Lascaux Caves in France. It was painted by prehistoric hunters in about 15,000 BC. Paintings like this show the animals people hunted for food.*

△ ***Howard Carter*** *(on the left) breaking into Tutankhamun's tomb in 1922. The discovery of the tomb caused a sensation in archaeology, as it was filled with fabulous 3500-year-old treasures.*

▽ ***Stonehenge****, in England, was built between about 2800 and 1100 BC. No one is exactly sure what it was used for, but it may have been an astronomical observatory or a giant calendar.*

Archaeology is the study of the physical remains of the past – everything from a priceless statue to a rubbish tip. Archaeology can tell us about societies that existed before written records were made, as well as adding to our knowledge of literate societies. In the past, archaeologists were little better than treasure-seekers. Today, however, they use scientific methods to analyse their finds and build a picture of the past.

Archaeologists study objects (artefacts), features (buildings) and ecofacts (seeds or animal bones). Artefacts such as pottery, glass and metal survive well, although often broken into many fragments. Objects made of organic materials, such as wood, leather and fabric, rarely survive – they quickly rot away leaving little or no trace for us to find. Organic materials survive best in waterlogged conditions, such as rivers or bogs. They also survive well in very dry, desert-like areas, or freezing conditions.

By studying the remains of human skeletons, experts can tell how tall people were, what age they lived to and what diseases they suffered from. Burials often reveal a lot about the social structure of an ancient society as well as their beliefs. Remains such as animal bones and shells can tell us about people's diets, while seeds, pollen and insect remains can build up a picture of their environment.

When archaeologists discover a site they want to examine, they set up an excavation, or dig. Most archaeologists today work on rescue digs, attempting to record a site before it is completely destroyed, often by building work. Other sites for a dig are identified by archaeologists by looking at maps, documents or unusual features in the landscape. Aerial photography is used to reveal traces of buildings, fields and ditches that are impossible to see on the ground, while special techniques, such as geophysics, can help indicate underground remains without having to dig them up.

◁ ***A vast army of terracotta soldiers*** *guards the tomb of the first emperor of China. Emperor Shi Huangdi died in 210 BC and the life-like rows of silent soldiers, archers and horses buried with him were discovered with real weapons and chariots.*

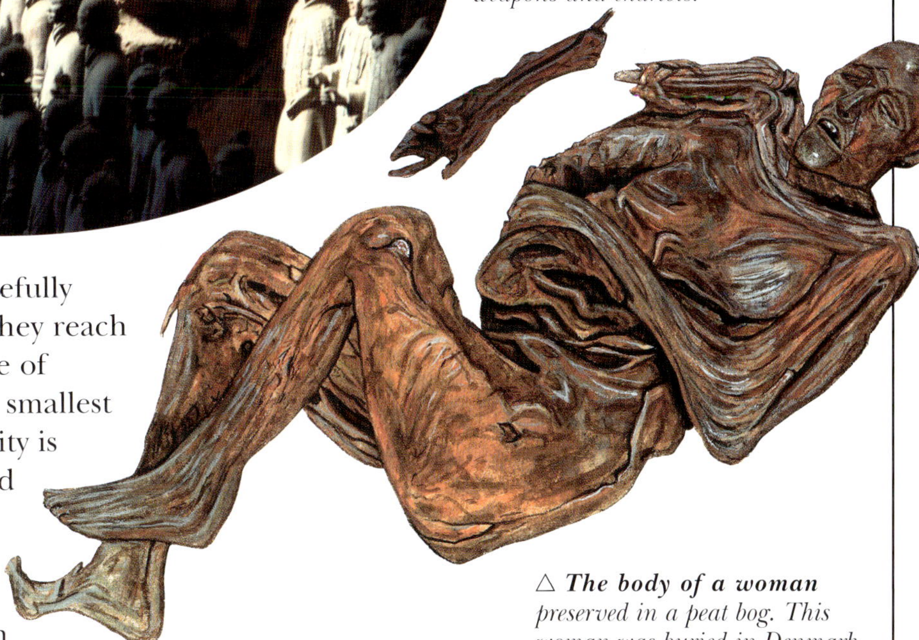

△ ***The body of a woman*** *preserved in a peat bog. This woman was buried in Denmark in AD 95. The peat tanned her flesh, which prevented it rotting away unlike most dead bodies.*

At a dig, archaeologists carefully remove layers of earth until they reach undisturbed soil with no trace of human occupation. Even the smallest evidence of past human activity is recorded. Many sites have had different inhabitants at different times, building up layers of occupation. A technique called stratification is used to determine the relative age of the objects found. At its simplest, this uses the principle that the most recent layers will occur at the top of a site.

The specific date of an object may be found by examining historical records or by comparing it with other similar finds whose date is known. There are also scientific techniques, such as dendrochronology – the study of tree rings. Tree growth is affected by climate and patterns build up in a tree's growth rings. House timbers or wooden objects can be compared with other timbers that have already been dated. This method is accurate for objects as old as 3000 BC in Europe. Radiocarbon dating is another technique. All living things contain some radioactive carbon, or C14. After a living thing dies, C14 decays (its atoms break down) at a known rate. If the amount of C14 in an organic find is known, its age can be estimated. This technique is used to date objects between about 40,000 years ago and AD 1500.

◁ ***The Colosseum*** *in Rome. The architecture, arrangement of seats, animal cages and cells for the gladiators in the Colosseum can tell us much about life in ancient Rome.*

▽ ***An archaeological dig in Peru.*** *The position and location of objects found in a dig can provide important clues to their age and use. Every find must be carefully recorded.*

The Ancient World

4 million years ago to AD 500

The period from about 4 million years ago to AD 500 covers a vast sweep of the world's history, from the appearance of the first human beings to the fall of the Roman empire.

Our earliest ancestors appeared in Africa some 2.5 million years ago, having evolved from man-apes who came down from the trees and learned to walk upright on two legs. Over thousands of years, they learned how to make fire to keep themselves warm and to cook their food, how to hunt and how to make tools. The first ever metal tools and weapons were made in the Near East about 7000 years ago.

Throughout the world, early people lived by hunting animals and gathering wild fruit, roots and nuts to eat. Then, about 10,000 years ago, an extraordinary change took place. People learned how to grow their own crops on patches of land and to raise their own animals for food. For the first time in history, people began to build permanent homes, followed by towns and cities.

By about 5000 BC, the world's first civilizations began to emerge along the banks of rivers where the land was extremely rich for farming. The Sumerians, Assyrians and Babylonians built magnificent cities and temples on the fertile plains between the Tigris and Euphrates rivers. The ancient Egyptians flourished along the river Nile. By about 500 BC, important civilizations had also appeared in India, China,

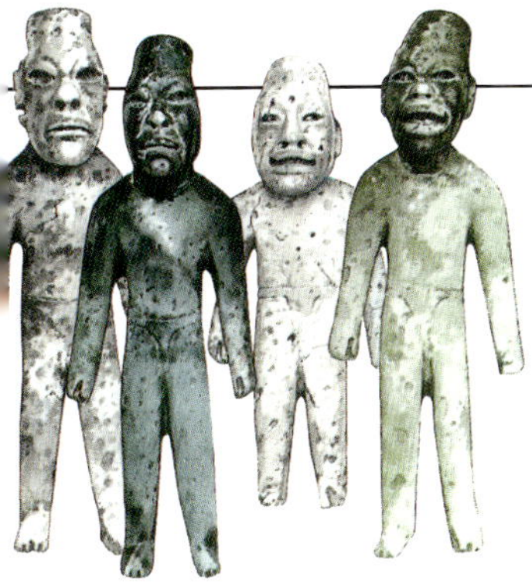

Persia and in North and South America.

The great age of ancient Greece and Rome is known as the classical world. Between them, these two mighty civilizations played a major role in shaping the modern world. From Greece came discoveries in politics, philosophy and science. These were spread farther afield by the Greek conqueror, Alexander the Great, and by the Romans, who were great admirers of Greek culture and knowledge. The Romans added many achievements of their own and, by the 1st century AD, they ruled over the most powerful empire ever seen. By AD 500, the empire had fallen and the ancient world was in decline. The Middle Ages had begun.

THE ANCIENT WORLD

c. **2.5–2 million years BC** *Homo habilis* appears in Africa. They are the first people ever to make tools.

c. **40,000 BC** Our direct ancestors, *Homo sapiens sapiens*, appear in many parts of the world.

c. **10,000 BC** The last Ice Age comes to an end.

c. **8000 BC** Farming begins and the first towns are built in the Near East.

c. **5000 BC** The first ever metal tools (made from copper) are made in the Near East.

c. **3500 BC** The Sumerians of Mesopotamia invent writing and the wheel.

c. **3100 BC** King Menes unites Upper and Lower Egypt.

c. **2800 BC** Building begins at Stonehenge, England.

c. **2580 BC** The Great Pyramid at Giza, Egypt, is built.

c. **2500 BC** Indus civilization in ancient India is at its height.

c. **1600–1100 BC** The Mycenaeans dominate mainland Greece.

c. **1200–900 BC** Olmec civilization flourishes in western Mexico.

c. **1200–200 BC** Chavin culture flourishes in northern Peru.

c. **1000–612 BC** The New Assyrian empire flourishes.

776 BC The first Olympic Games are held in ancient Greece.

753 BC Traditional date for the founding of Rome.

c. **605–562 BC** Reign of King Nebuchadnezzar II who rebuilds the city of Babylon.

c. **600 BC** Nok culture begins in Nigeria, West Africa.

479–431 BC The Golden Age of Athens, Greece.

323 BC Alexander the Great dies.

269–232 BC Reign of Emperor Ashoka Maurya in India.

221 BC Shi Huangdi unites China; he is its first emperor.

27 BC–AD 14 Augustus rules as the first Roman emperor.

c. **AD 200** Kingdom of Axum rises to power in northeast Africa.

AD 286 The Roman empire is divided into west and east.

c. **AD 350–550** The Gupta empire flourishes in India.

AD 476 The last western emperor of Rome is deposed.

The First Humans

THE FIRST HUMANS

c. **4 million years BC** *Australopithecus* (meaning southern ape) appears in Africa. They walk on two legs instead of on all fours.

c. **2.5–2 million years BC** *Homo habilis* (handy man) appears in Africa. They are the first people to make tools.

c. **1.5 million years BC** *Homo erectus* (upright man) appears in Africa. They were the first people to learn how to use fire and the first to spread out of Africa.

c. **120,000 BC** The Neanderthals, a sub-species of *Homo sapiens* (wise man), appear in Africa, Asia and Europe. They are the first humans to bury their dead.

c. **40,000 BC** By this date, *Homo sapiens sapiens* (modern humans) are living in many parts of the world, including Australia.

c. **33,000 BC** The Neanderthals die out as modern humans appear in Asia and Europe.

c. **13,000 BC** By this date, modern humans have crossed from Asia into the Americas for the first time.

△ ***The hand axe*** *was one of the earliest tools ever made. Homo erectus invented the hand axe around 2 million years ago. This multi-purpose tool was used to dig up roots, to chop wood and bone, to butcher meat and to cut up animal skins. Hand axes were being used by modern humans until about 13,000 BC.*

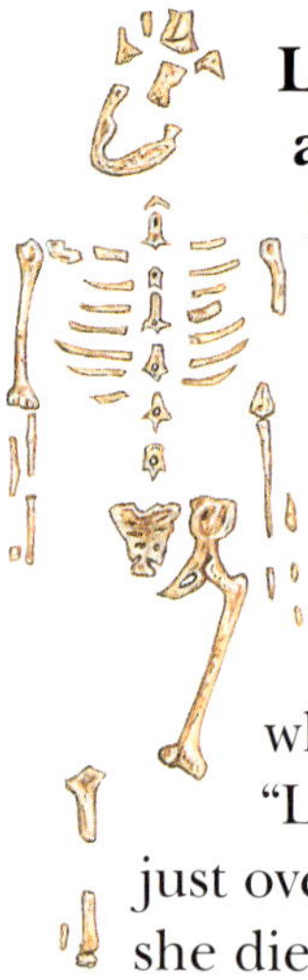

Life on our planet began some 3200 million years ago, with tiny cells that lived in the sea. But the first human-like creatures did not appear until about 4 million years ago, in Africa. These "man-apes" came down from the trees they lived in and began to walk on two legs.

The most complete man-ape (*Australopithecus*) skeleton was found in Ethiopia, East Africa, in 1974. She was nicknamed "Lucy" because the archaeologists who discovered her were listening to the Beatles' song "Lucy in the Sky with Diamonds" at the time. Lucy stood just over a metre tall, about as tall as a 10-year-old girl. When she died, 3 million years ago, she was 40 years old.

The first true human beings, called Homo habilis, or "handy man", appeared about 2.5 million years ago. They had bigger brains and were more intelligent than the man-apes. A million years later another species, Homo erectus, or "upright man", appeared. Over the next 2 million years, these early humans, or hominids, learned to make tools, to hunt and gather food, to make shelters and fire and to communicate. Homo erectus was the first hominid to spread from Africa to Asia and later Europe.

Modern humans, Homo sapiens sapiens, our own direct ancestors, first lived about 100,000 years ago. They were skilful tool makers and hunters. By about 35,000 years ago, they had spread all over Europe and had reached Australia.

▷ ***As early people evolved,*** *they gradually became less like apes and more like humans. They developed larger brains and bodies designed for walking upright, with longer legs than arms – the reverse of apes. Standing upright left their hands free for holding and using tools and weapons.*

Australopithecus
(Southern ape)
4–1.5 million years ago
Africa

Homo habilis
(Handy man)
2.5–1.5 million years ago
Africa

20,000 BC 15,000 BC 10,000 BC 5,000 BC

△ ***Fires were made*** *by striking two flints together. They provided people with heat, light, protection from wild animals and cooked food.*

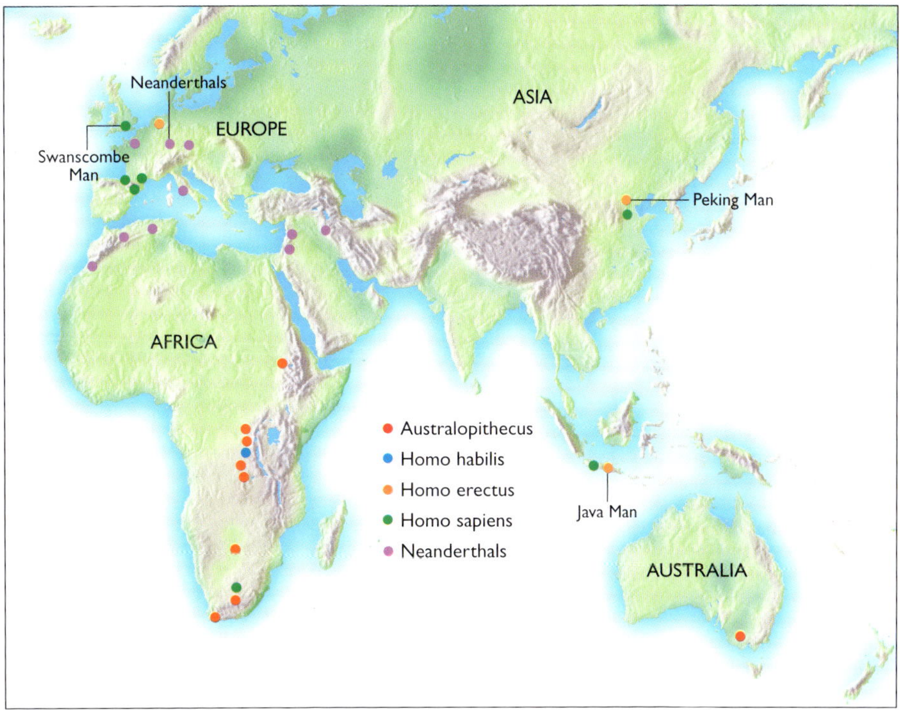

△ ***This map shows*** *where important fossil remains of early people have been found. So far, Africa is the only continent where the remains of* Australopithecus *and* Homo habilis *have been found.*

▽ ***When Mary Leakey*** *found these 2.5 million-year-old footprints made by two* Australopithecines *in volcanic ash, she helped prove the first hominids walked upright. The Leakey family have spent many years in Africa, searching for fossils of early humans.*

Homo erectus
(Upright man)
.5 million–200,000 years ago
Africa, Asia, Europe

Homo sapiens neanderthalensis
(Neanderthal man)
120,000–30,000 years ago
Africa, Asia, Europe

Homo sapiens sapiens
(Modern man)
From 15,000 years ago
worldwide

MAKING TOOLS

***c.* 2 million years–10,000 BC** The Old Stone Age (or Palaeolithic Age). The first stone tools are made.

From *c.* 10,000 BC The Middle Stone Age (or Mesolithic Age). People make a greater variety of stone tools.

From *c.* 8000 BC The New Stone Age (or Neolithic Age). People make stone tools, such as sickles and hoes.

***c.* 5000 BC** The Copper Age begins in the Near East. Metal tools are made for the very first time. (Copper is used from *c.* 3000 BC in Europe.)

***c.* 3000 BC** The Bronze Age begins in the Near East. Bronze is an alloy, or mixture, of copper and tin. (Bronze is used from *c.* 2000 BC in Europe.)

***c.* 1000 BC** The Iron Age begins in Europe. (Iron is used from *c.* 700 BC in the Near East and Africa.)

CAVE ART

***c.* 40,000 BC** Rock engravings carved in Australia – may be oldest artworks found so far.

***c.* 27,000 BC** Mammoth hunters make figures of people and animals out of clay.

***c.* 24,000 BC** Cave paintings drawn in Namibia, Africa.

***c.* 22,000 BC** The Venus of Willendorf carved in Austria.

***c.* 17,000 BC** Animals are painted on cave walls at Lascaux, France, and Altamira, Spain.

▽ ***This bison cave painting*** *is from the Altamira Caves in Spain. It dates from about 12,000 BC and is painted almost life-sized on the ceiling.*

Making Tools

The first known tools were made by *Homo habilis* more than 2 million years ago. These were very simple tools made from pebbles. Gradually tools became more advanced. People soon discovered that flint was one of the best tool-making materials. Not only was it very hard, but it could also be chipped into many different shapes and sizes.

Using a pebble as a hammer, early people shaped flints into sharp-edged hand axes, knives, scrapers and choppers. When the edges became blunt, they could easily be resharpened by further chipping. Hand axes are among the oldest known tools ever made, with some examples dating from around 2 million years ago. These were made from hand-sized lumps of stone, pointed at one end and used for cutting plants, meat and skins.

Cave Art

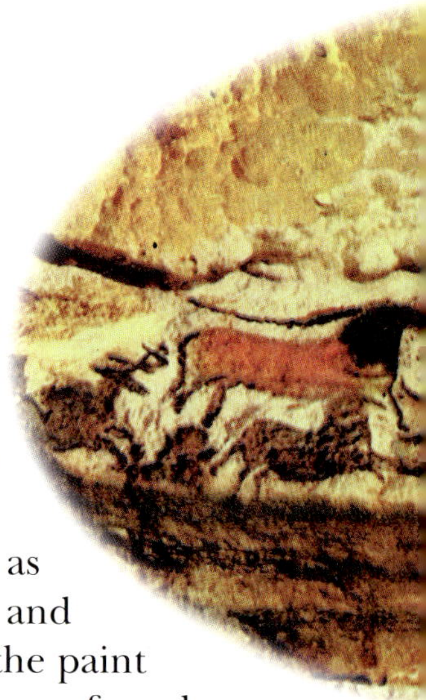

The earliest works of art were created some 40,000 years ago. During the last Ice Age, early artists painted pictures of the animals they hunted – bulls, reindeer and bison – on the walls of the caves they sheltered in.

They used paints made from minerals, such as clay, lime and charcoal, ground into a powder and mixed with water or animal fat. They applied the paint with brushes made of animal fur, feathers, moss or frayed twigs. Their paintings were not simply for decoration. It is thought that they may have had some religious or magical meaning. Perhaps the painters thought they would bring them better luck in the hunt. Cave paintings have been found in various parts of Europe, Africa, Asia and Australia. The most famous

20,000 BC 15,000 BC 10,000 BC 5000 BC

Flints, bones and antlers were also used for making weapons, including sharp stone spearheads and arrowheads. Bows and arrows were first used about 15,000 years ago – the first shooting weapons ever made. About 7000 years ago, people in the Near East learned how to make metal tools and weapons from copper. By 3000 BC they were using a stronger alloy of copper – the Bronze Age had begun.

▷ ***Stone Age tools** included knife blades, axes, scrapers, harpoons, needles, spearheads and arrowheads. For 98 per cent of the time people have lived on Earth they have made all their tools from stone, bone, wood, ivory and antler.*

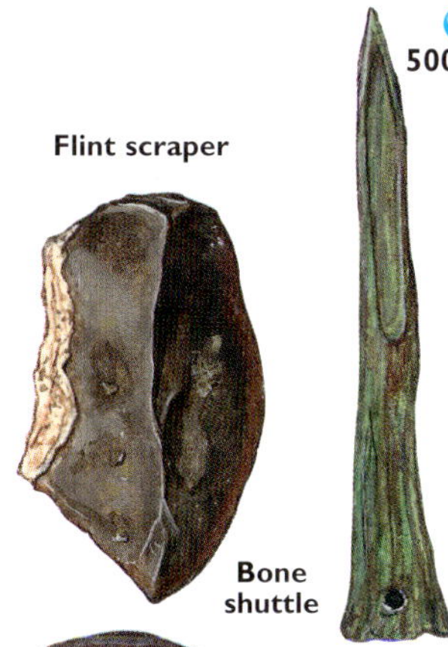

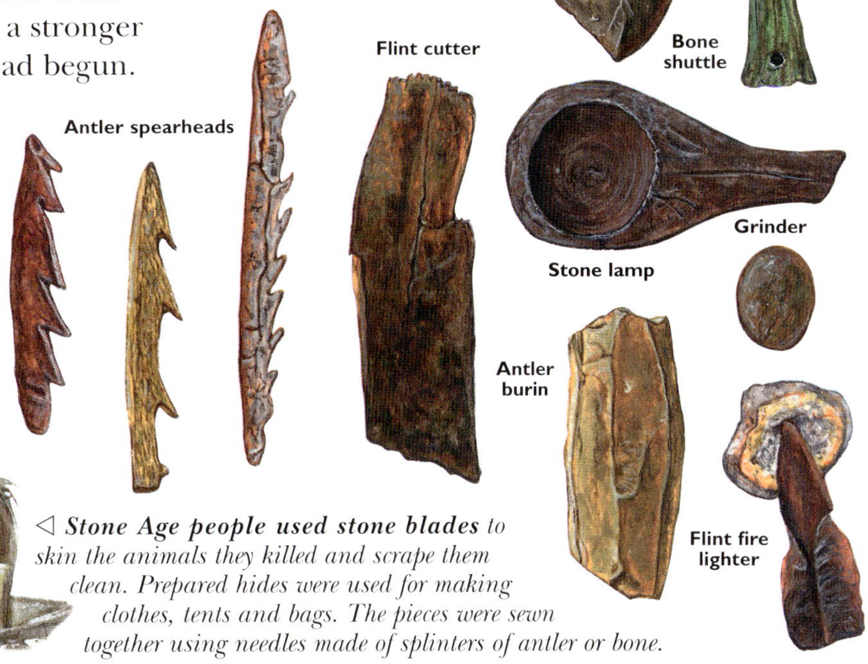

◁ ***Stone Age people used stone blades** to skin the animals they killed and scrape them clean. Prepared hides were used for making clothes, tents and bags. The pieces were sewn together using needles made of splinters of antler or bone.*

paintings in Europe cover the walls of the Lascaux Caves in southern France. Dating from about 15,000 BC to 10,000 BC, they consist of hundreds of animal drawings, including woolly mammoths, bison, reindeer, horses and four huge white bulls. The caves were rediscovered in 1940 by accident, when four local schoolboys stumbled into them while looking for their lost dog. Next day, they returned with ropes and lamps and saw the paintings for the first time. To prevent damage to the paintings, the caves are now closed to the public but a full-sized model (using the same techniques) has been opened so people can view copies of these prehistoric masterpieces.

△ ***The Great Hall of the Bulls** provides a dramatic entrance to the Lascaux Caves. The walls are covered with painted and engraved animals moving in herds or files.*

◁ ***This bison** was carved from an antler around 27,000 BC. Its detail shows that the artist closely observed the animal he portrayed.*

STONE SCULPTURE

The figure above is one of the oldest pieces of sculpture ever found. Discovered in Austria, it is called the Venus of Willendorf. It is carved from sandstone, stands 10.5 cm high and dates from about 22,000 BC. Several similar statues have been found across Europe. They may represent mother goddesses, carved to bring good luck. Mammoth ivory, reindeer antlers and animal bones were also used by prehistoric sculptors and carvers.

Life in the Ice Age

About 24,000 years ago, temperatures across the world plummeted and the Earth was gripped by freezing, icy weather. A huge sheet of ice, more than 200 m thick in places, covered about a third of the Earth's surface and enormous icebergs floated in half its seas. Remnants of this ancient ice still cover Greenland and Antarctica.

The very cold climate is called the Ice Age and 18,000 years ago it was at its height. In fact, there have been many "ice ages", the first known occurring some 2300 million years ago. We are now living in the Quarternary ice age, which began about 2 million years ago. Since then, there have been 17 glacial (cold) periods and 17 interglacial (warm periods). What we often call the "Ice Age" was actually the last glacial period, which ended about 10,000 years ago. Experts think that ice ages are caused by changes in the path taken by the Earth as it orbits the Sun. Even the slightest difference can drastically affect the amount of heat reaching the Earth.

As the seas froze over during the Ice Age, sea level fell by over 100 m in some places, exposing bridges of land between the continents. The Bering Strait between Siberia and Alaska became dry land, creating a bridge between Asia and North America up to 1000 km wide. The first people to reach North America probably walked across this land bridge.

HOW ANIMALS ADAPTED

This baby mammoth was found, perfectly preserved, in the frozen ground of Siberia, Russia. Animals had to adapt to survive the cold of the Ice Age. Some, such as mammoths and rhinoceroses, grew larger in size because a bigger body is better at conserving heat. They also grew warm, woolly coats.

▽ ***Men hunted mammoths*** *in groups. They used pits dug across their migration routes to trap an animal, then spears and stones to fatally wound it. Where trees were scarce, hunters used tusks and bones as frameworks for their huts, then covered them with skins. Skins were also made into clothes and shoes. Ornaments and tools were carved from bones and tusks.*

Conditions were extremely harsh for the people who lived near the ice sheets. Woolly mammoths were a valuable source of meat, skins for clothes and bones for weapons and carvings, but mammoth hunting was tough, dangerous work. The men hunted in groups, driving the mammoth into a corner or up against a cliff. Then they closed in for the kill, attacking the mammoth with sharp spears made of flint and wood and large stones. One mammoth could provide enough meat to feed a group for many months. Any extra meat was stored in holes dug in the frozen ground. The bones and tusks were used for building homes, with turf, moss and hides used to cover the cracks for warmth. Other Ice Age animals included woolly rhinoceros and giant reindeer.

LIFE IN THE ICE AGE

c. **2 million BC** The Quaternary ice age begins. It consists of 17 glacials (cold periods) separated by 17 interglacials (warmer periods).

c. **22,000 BC** The Ice Age enters its latest glacial. Ice covers about a third of the Earth. Sea levels fall by over 100 m.

c. **16,000 BC** The last Ice Age reaches its coldest point. People living at Mezhirich in the Ukraine build huts from mammoth bones and tusks.

c. **13,000 BC** Hunter-gatherers cross from Asia into North America via the now exposed Bering Strait.

c. **12,000 BC** The Bering Strait floods over again, as the ice starts to melt and sea level rises.

c. **10,000 BC** In Europe, the glaciers begin to retreat and the Ice Age ends.

c. **6000 BC** Rising sea level separates Britain from the continent of Europe.

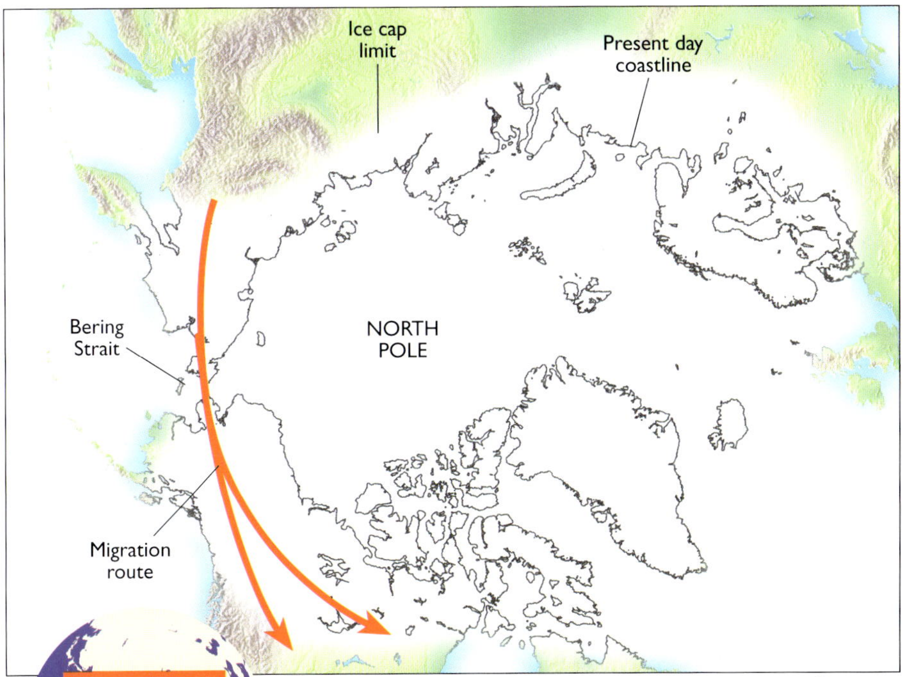

◁ ***This map shows*** *the extent of the ice cover in the Northern Hemisphere during the last Ice Age. The land bridges exposed by the drop in sea level allowed people and animals to migrate from Asia into North America.*

The First Farmers

THE FIRST FARMERS

c. **10,500 BC** The first clay pots are made in Japan.

c. **8000 BC** Farming begins in the Near East in an area known as the Fertile Crescent, and in Southeast Asia. Sheep are domesticated in Iraq.

c. **7000 BC** Farming develops in Central and South America.

c. **7000 BC** Clay pots are made in the Near East and Africa to store grain and water.

c. **6500 BC** The oldest known textiles are woven at Çatal Hüyük in Turkey.

c. **6000 BC** Beer is made in the Near East.

c. **5000 BC** Farming is adopted in China and Egypt and spreads to Europe. Farming also begins in India, along the Indus and Ganges river valleys.

c. **4400 BC** Horses are domesticated in Eastern Europe and used for riding for the first time.

c. **4000 BC** The first ploughs are used in the Near East. They are made of sharply pointed, forked sticks. The earliest marks made by a plough have been discovered in Mesopotamia.

For the great majority of human history, people have found their food by hunting and gathering. They hunted wild animals, such as mammoths, bison and deer, and gathered berries, nuts and roots to eat.

Meat made up about a third of prehistoric people's diet and because they had to follow the herds of animals they hunted, they were not based in one place, but lived as nomads, moving from camp to camp with the changing seasons. Then, about 10,000 years ago, a massive change occurred in the way people lived. People learned how to grow their own crops and to rear animals for their meat, milk and skins. Instead of having to roam farther and farther afield to find enough food to eat, people found they could grow enough food on a small patch of land to feed their families. This meant, in turn, that they had to settle in one place all year round and build permanent homes. These people were the first farmers. Their farming settlements became the first villages, which grew to become the first towns.

Plants and animals that are grown or raised by people are known as domesticated, or tamed. The first domesticated plants and animals were developed from plants and animals found in the wild.

▽ ***Life on a farm*** *in Europe around 3000 BC was very hard work. People made pots from clay and fired them in a kiln to store grain and water. They used stone axes to fell trees and clear the ground and stone sickles to harvest their crops. They spun wool into thread and wove it into cloth.*

20,000 BC 15,000 BC 10,000 BC 5000 BC

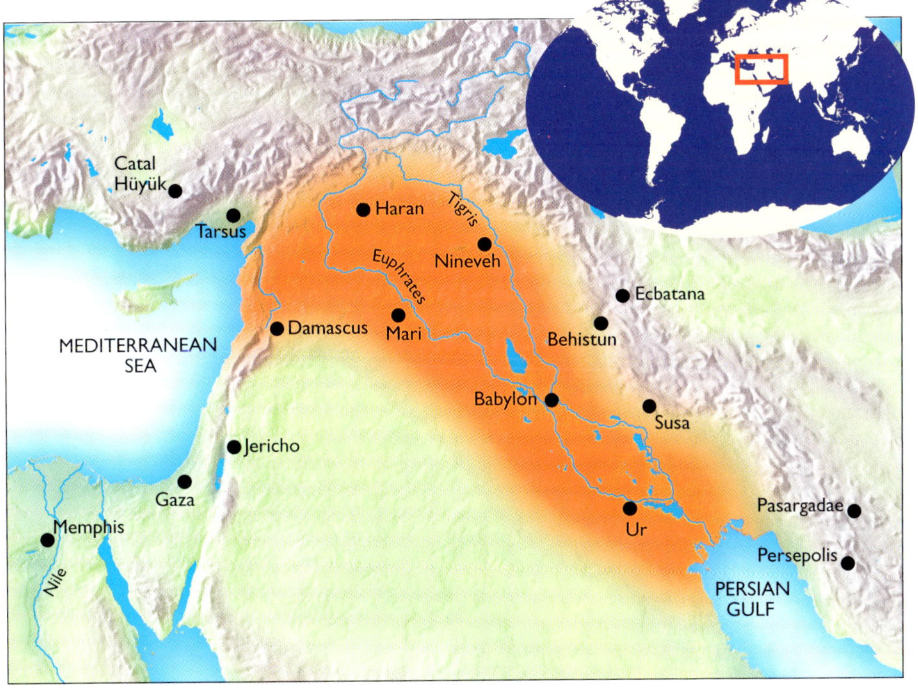

◁ ***This map shows*** *some important towns in the ancient world. Many of these grew up as farming settlements. The first farms developed in the Near East and Europe in a region known as the Fertile Crescent (shaded on the map). Crops, such as wheat and barley, were grown and animals, such as goats and sheep, raised. Farming spread throughout Europe and western Asia. It developed independently in the rest of Asia and in the Americas.*

Wheat and barley were two of the first crops to be domesticated. They had grown wild in parts of the Near East for thousands of years. The first farmers collected seeds from these wild plants and sowed them in ground dug over with deer antlers. (Ploughs were not invented until about 6000 years ago.) The following year, the crop was harvested and the grain used for grinding into flour. It was used to make bread, which was baked on hot stones. Grain was also made into beer. Farmers also learned how to tame wild animals and breed them in captivity. The first domesticated animals were sheep, goats and pigs. These animals are still among the most common domesticated animals in the world.

DESERT ROCK ART

Some 10,000 years ago, the Sahara Desert was much lusher and greener than it is today. Cave paintings from Tassili, in Algeria, which date from that time, show people hunting giraffe, hippopotamuses, rhinoceros and elephants. Later paintings show farmers tending herds of cattle. After about 3000 BC, the Sahara's climate became much drier. Many of these animals disappeared from the rock art, to be replaced by more traditional desert animals, such as camels.

The First Towns

Once people began to farm and to settle in permanent villages, the world's population grew rapidly. Towns grew up with a more complex way of life. More houses were built and services were established for the people of the town to use, such as roads, drainage systems and shops.

Trade also grew between the towns, as neighbouring farmers bought and sold any surplus produce. Specialist craft workers produced clay pots, jars and cooking vessels. Others carved figurines and fine jewellery for use by the town's people and for trade. Little is known about the first towns. The ruins of two ancient towns, however, have provided archaeologists with a fascinating glimpse into the past – Jericho in Jordan in the Near East, and Çatal Hüyük in Turkey.

Dating from about 8000 BC, Jericho was one of the oldest towns to be examined by archaeologists. The town was constructed near a natural spring, which was ideal for watering farmers' fields. Wheat and barley were grown, with sheep and goats raised for their meat. Jericho also stood on an important trade route and quickly grew wealthy. Among the goods traded were obsidian (a volcanic, glassy rock), shells and semi-precious stones used to make necklaces. To defend itself from envious neighbours, the town was surrounded by massive stone walls, some 3 m thick and more than 5 m high, with a great, circular watch tower 9 m tall. Inside the walls stood small, circular houses made of mud bricks, shaped by hand and left to bake hard in the sun. Jericho's walls

△ ***The ruins of Hisham's Palace in Jericho.*** *People have lived in the town of Jericho continuously since about 8000 bc to the present day. Hisham's Palace was a royal hunting lodge, built in the 8th century ad by the Arabic ruler, Caliph Hisham ibn Abd al-Malik. The palace was never completed and for many years, local people used it as a quarry of cut stones.*

were destroyed many times, but not by invading enemies. Instead they were toppled by a series of earthquakes. At one time, up to 2000 people lived in Jericho. The people of Çatal Hüyük were also successful farmers. Thanks to the town's position on a fertile river plain, its people grew wheat, barley and vegetables, although the town's wealth was also based on trade and cattle-breeding. The town controlled the trade in obsidian, for making tools and weapons, which was mined nearby. By 6500 BC, Çatal Hüyük was flourishing and some 5000 people lived there. For safety, they lived in interconnecting, rectangular houses, with no doors. People entered their houses through holes in the roofs, reached by long, wooden ladders. The rooftops also acted as streets. If the town was attacked, the ladders were quickly drawn up, leaving no obvious means of entry.

THE FIRST TOWNS

c. **9000 BC** A shrine stands on the site of ancient Jericho in the Near East.

c. **8000 BC** Jericho grows into a thriving town of some 2000 people. It is one of the oldest known towns, built on the west bank of the river Jordan. The first bricks are made by Jericho's people.

c. **7000 BC** Jericho is destroyed by an earthquake, but the town is later rebuilt. The Turkish town of Çatal Hüyük is founded. By 6500 BC, it is a flourishing place with a population of 5000 people.

c. **6500 BC** The oldest known textiles are made in Çatal Hüyük. They are linen, made from the fibres of the flax plant, and sewn into clothes.

◁ ***The buildings in Çatal Hüyük*** *around 6000 BC included houses and workshops, and also some that seem to have been religious shrines. The walls were painted with pictures of vultures and headless men, and decorated with plaster models of bulls' heads and statuettes of mother goddesses. At the funeral ceremony on the left of this picture, the priests are disguised as vultures. The people of Çatal Hüyük probably exposed their dead on platforms for the vultures to pick the bones clean.*

△ ***This skull*** *of a young woman was found in Jericho. The features have been modelled from painted plaster and the eyes set with cowrie shells. It may have been used in religious rituals, as part of some form of ancestor worship. The rest of the woman's skeleton was buried under the floor of a house.*

Mesopotamia and Sumer

One of the world's earliest civilizations grew up on the fertile plains between the rivers Tigris and Euphrates. Now situated in Iraq, this area became known as Mesopotamia, "the land between the two rivers". In about 5000 BC, a group of people called the Sumerians settled in the southern part of Mesopotamia.

Although the climate was hot and dry, the fertile land was ideal for growing crops and farmers soon learned how to build irrigation canals to bring water from the rivers to their fields. As more land was cultivated and more food produced, the population grew. By about 3500 BC, the original farming villages had grown into thriving towns and cities. Some of the larger settlements, such as Ur and Uruk, grew into cities, then into independent city-states. The cities were ruled by Councils of Elders.

In times of war, the Council appointed a *lugal*, or general, to lead the army. As wars between the rival cities became more frequent, so the lugals' powers grew. From about 2900 BC, the lugals became kings and ruled for life.

In the centre of each city stood a temple to the city's patron god or goddess. The Sumerians worshipped hundreds of gods and goddesses. They believed they controlled every aspect of nature and everyday life. It was vital to obey the gods and to keep them happy, with daily offerings in the temple. Otherwise, they might send wars, floods and disease to punish the people.

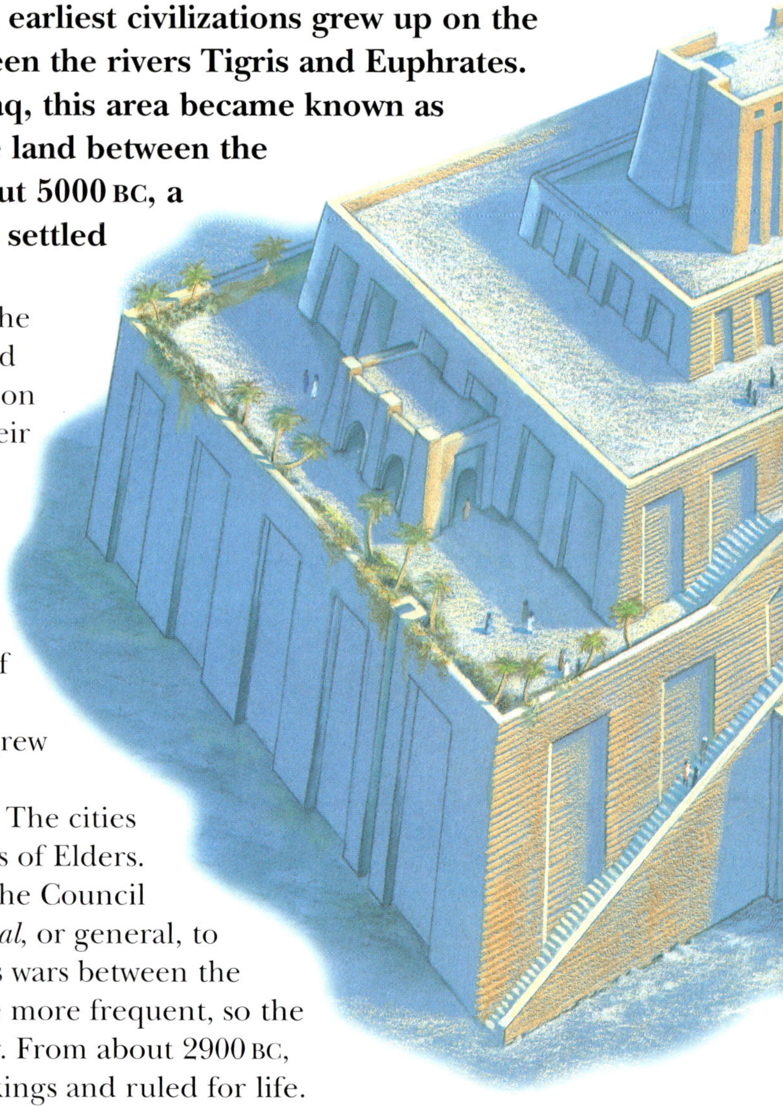

△ ***This great ziggurat****, or stepped temple, was built in the city of Ur by King Ur-Nammu in about 2100 BC. It was worshipped as the home of the Moon god, Nanna. Early temples were simple, mud-brick buildings on low platforms. As these fell into ruin, new temples were built on top, raising the platform higher and higher. The god's shrine was at the very top.*

◁ ***This Sumerian woman's*** *magnificent jewellery is made from gold and silver, inlaid with precious stones, such as lapis lazuli. Sumerian craft workers made many fabulous treasures, including furniture, wine cups and musical instruments. Treasures like these were discovered by archaeologists when they excavated the Royal Tombs at Ur.*

▷ ***These reed houses*** *were built by the Marsh Arabs who today live on the banks of the river Tigris in southern Iraq. Experts think they may be very similar to houses built by the Sumerians, who also used reeds to construct their homes. The reeds grew in the marshes around the rivers and the Sumerians made them into canoes and stables for their animals as well.*

The Sumerians were expert mathematicians and astronomers. They had two systems of counting. One was a decimal system, using the number 10, like the system we use today. The other used units of 60, for calculating time and the areas of circles. The Sumerians were the first to divide an hour into 60 seconds. They also devised a calendar, a complex legal system and adapted the potter's wheel for transport. Their most important breakthrough, however, was the invention of writing in about 3500 BC.

THE STORY OF GILGAMESH

The Sumerians had many myths and legends about their gods and heroes. The most famous is called the Epic of Gilgamesh. It tells the story of Gilgamesh, a Sumerian king, and his quest to find the secret of eternal life. After many adventures, Gilgamesh is told of a plant growing at the bottom of the sea that will bring immortality. Gilgamesh finds the plant, but, before he can use it, it is stolen by a snake.

MESOPOTAMIA AND SUMER

c. **5000 BC** Early Sumerians begin to farm in Ubaid, southern Mesopotamia (Iraq).

c. **4000 BC** The start of the Uruk Period. The Sumerians learn how to smelt metal and use sailing boats on the Tigris and Euphrates rivers.

c. **3500 BC** The Sumerians invent writing and the wheel. They discover how to make bronze from copper and tin.

c. **2900–2400 BC** The Early Dynastic Period. Kings are established in the main Sumerian cities.

c. **2400–2100 BC** Sumer is conquered by the Akkadians, then by the Gutians.

c. **2300 BC** Sumerian city of Agade dominates the region.

c. **2100 BC** City of Ur reaches the height of its power under King Ur-Nammu.

△ ***Writing was invented*** *in Sumer about 5500 years ago, as a way of keeping temple records and merchants' accounts. The Sumerian system of writing was called cuneiform, meaning 'wedge shaped', because it used symbols made up of wedge-shaped strokes, to represent words. These were impressed on to wet clay, using a reed pen. The clay was then baked hard in the sun. Hundreds of clay tablets were found in Sumerian libraries, giving an invaluable insight into their way of life.*

c. **2000 BC** Epic of Gilgamesh is first written down. The city of Ur is destroyed by the Elamites. The Sumerian civilization comes to an end.

Ancient Egypt

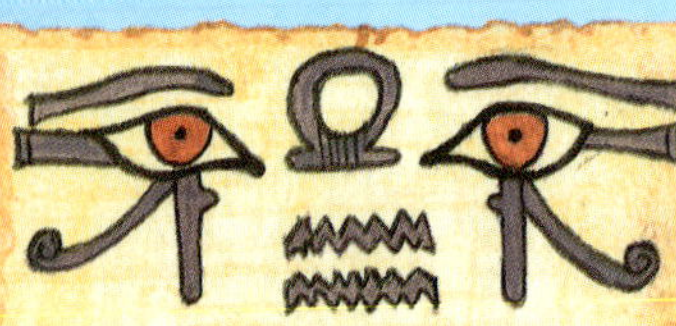

Without the life-giving waters of the river Nile, ancient Egypt would have been a barren desert, too dry for farming or living. The ancient Egyptians depended on the Nile river for drinking water and irrigation, and on its annual flooding that deposited rich, silty soil along its banks.

Here farmers cultivated wheat and barley (for bread and beer), flax (for linen), fruit and vegetables. They also raised cattle, sheep and goats. So vital was the river that the Greek historian, Herodotus, described ancient Egypt as the "gift of the Nile".

ANCIENT EGYPT

- ***c.* 5000–3100 BC** Predynastic Period in Egypt. Several different cultures appear along the Nile valley.
- ***c.* 4000 BC** Boats on the Nile use sails for the first time.
- ***c.* 3200 BC** Early hieroglyphs are used in Egypt.
- ***c.* 3100 BC** King Menes unites Lower and Upper Egypt.
- ***c.* 3100–2686 BC** Archaic Period (Dynasties 1 and 2).
- ***c.* 2686–2150 BC** The Old Kingdom (Dynasties 3 to 6). The first pyramids are built.
- ***c.* 2589–2566 BC** Reign of King Khufu (Dynasty 4).
- ***c.* 2580 BC** The Sphinx and Great Pyramid at Giza (a tomb for King Khufu) are built.
- ***c.* 2246–2150 BC** Reign of King Pepi II (Dynasty 6), the longest reign in history.

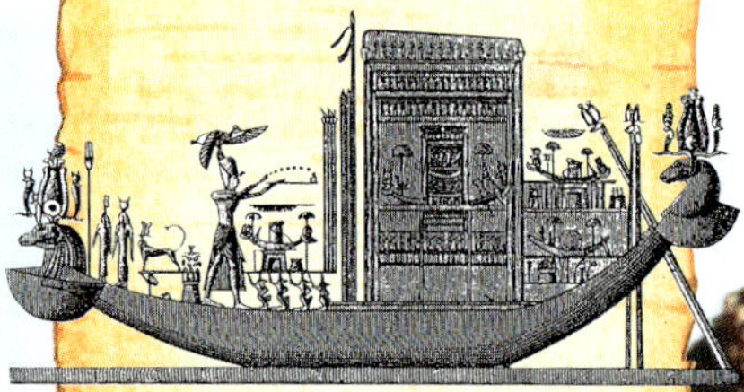

△ ***Boats*** *were the main form of transport in ancient Egypt, used for fishing, hunting, carrying cargo and passengers, and for leisure. Sturdy barges were used to carry huge blocks of stone for building palaces and pyramids. When a pharaoh died, his body was taken down the river to his tomb in a highly decorated funeral barge.*

- ***c.* 2150–2040 BC** First Intermediate Period (Dynasties 7 to 10).
- ***c.* 2040–1640 BC** The Middle Kingdom (Dynasties 11 to 13). King Mentuhotep II reunites Egypt and restores order under Dynasty 11.
- ***c.* 1640–1552 BC** The Second Intermediate Period (Dynasties 14 to 17). The Hyksos people from Asia overrun Egypt.

▷ ***Queen Nefertiti*** *was the chief wife of King Akhenaten who ruled Egypt from about 1364 BC to 1347 BC. Akhenaten and Nefertiti had six daughters, one of whom married King Tutankhamun* (*see page 31*).

The first villages of ancient Egypt were established some 7000 years ago. In time, these small settlements formed two kingdoms – Lower Egypt in the Nile delta and Upper Egypt along the river valley. In about 3100 BC, King Menes, the ruler of Upper Egypt, united the two kingdoms and built his capital at Memphis. He also established Dynasty 1, the first dynasty (line of kings) of ancient Egypt. The king was the most powerful person in ancient Egyptian society and was worshipped as the god Horus, in human form. From about 1554 BC, the king was given the honorary title of pharaoh, from the Egyptian words *per aa*, which mean "great house". To keep the royal blood pure, the pharaoh often married a close relation, such as his sister or half-sister. The pharaoh appointed two officials, called *viziers*, to help him govern and collect taxes. The country was also divided into 42 districts, called *nomes*, each governed on the pharaoh's behalf, by officials called *nomarchs*. Further officials were put in charge of the major state departments – the Treasury, the Royal Works (which supervised the building of pyramids and tombs), the Granaries, Cattle and Foreign Affairs. Every aspect of Egyptian life was under the pharaoh's control.

◁ ***The pyramids*** *were built as tombs for the early pharaohs. They housed not only the pharaoh's body but many priceless treasures – gold, jewellery and furniture – to accompany him into the next world. The Great Pyramid of Giza, built for King Khufu some 4600 years ago, was one of the Seven Wonders of the ancient world.*

▷ ***A farmer's year*** *was divided into three parts – the Inundation (July to November) when the river flooded, the Growing Season (December to March) and Harvest (March to July). During the Inundation, when no work on the farm was possible, farmers were sent to work on the royal buildings.*

PYRAMID CONSTRUCTION

The ancient Egyptians had no trucks or cranes and only the simplest tools to help them build the pyramids. No one knows exactly how the pyramids were built. It is thought that stone blocks, some as heavy as cars, were pulled to the site on wooden sledges dragged by teams of workers, then hauled up a series of spiral mud and brick ramps into place. Layer by layer, the ramp and the pyramid grew. Finally, the capstone (the top most stone) was added and the whole structure covered in white limestone casing blocks. Then the ramps were dismantled.

Egyptian Beliefs

Hermes

The ancient Egyptians believed firmly in life after death. When a person died, their soul was thought to travel to an underworld, called Duat. Here the soul had to pass a series of ordeals in order to progress to a better life in the next world.

The greatest test took place in the Judgement Hall of Osiris, god of the dead. Here the person's heart was weighed against the Feather of Truth. If the person had led a wicked life, their heart would be heavy and tip the balance. Then they were fed to a terrible monster. If their life had been virtuous, their heart would be light and balance with the feather. The person could then proceed to the next world, called the Kingdom of the West.

For a person's soul to prosper in the next world, their body had to survive intact. The ancient Egyptians discovered how to preserve bodies by using the process of mummification. After the internal organs had been removed, the body was dried out, oiled and wrapped in linen strips, then placed in its coffin. Animals were preserved in this way, too.

▷ ***The walls of tombs*** *were covered with paintings of gods and goddesses. Shown here are Osiris (on the left), the god of the dead, and Atum (on the right), the Sun god. Great importance was attached to proper burial in ancient Egypt. This ensured a happy afterlife and a place in Osiris' kingdom.*

c. **1552–1085 BC** The New Kingdom in Egypt(Dynasties 18 to 20).
c. **1479–1425 BC** Reign of King Tuthmosis III. The Egyptian empire is at the height of its power under his rule.
c. **1364–1347 BC** Reign of King Akhenaten.
c. **1347–1337 BC** Reign of King Tutankhamun.
c. **1289–1224 BC** Reign of King Ramesses II.
c. **1085–664 BC** Third Intermediate Period (Dynasties 21 to 25).
c. **664–332 BC** The Late Period (Dynasties 26 to 30).
c. **525–404 BC** The Persians invade Egypt and rule as Dynasty 27.
332 BC Alexander the Great takes control of Egypt. In 331 BC he founds the city of Alexandria.
323 BC Alexander dies. Egypt is ruled by the Ptolemies.
30 BC Cleopatra, the last of the Ptolemies, commits suicide. Egypt becomes a province of the Roman empire.

Hieroglyphics *was the system of picture writing used in ancient Egypt. Each picture, or hieroglyph, stood for a picture or sound. Hieroglyphs were extremely complicated so highly-trained scribes were employed to read and write them.*

▷ ***The Great Temple at Abu Simbel*** *was built by King Ramesses II who reigned from about 1289 BC to 1224 BC. Four gigantic seated statues of the king guard the entrance.*

2000 BC 1500 BC 1000 BC 500 BC AD 1 AD 500

Anubis Canop Osiris Amun Isis Horus

△ ***Tutankhamun's gold death mask*** *covered the face of the dead king. The king's body lay wrapped in linen inside a nest of three coffins, encased in a stone sarcophagus and protected by four wooden shrines.*

◁ ***Howard Carter*** *examining Tutankhamun's mummy. "Everywhere the glint of gold" was how he described what he saw inside the pharaoh's tomb.*

The kings of the New Kingdom in Egypt (*c.* 1552–1085 BC) were not buried in pyramids, but in tombs cut deep into the cliffs. The tombs were dug out of the sides of a valley near Thebes, called the Valley of the Kings. This was an attempt to deter the gangs of tomb-robbers who had stripped the pyramids bare of their treasures soon after they were sealed. Unfortunately, the idea did not work and most of these tombs were ransacked in their turn. In 1922, one of the last tombs to survive intact, that of the boy-king Tutankhamum, was discovered by British archaeologist Howard Carter. It had been sealed for over 3300 years. Inside, Carter found a dazzling collection of priceless treasures. But the greatest treasure of all was the spectacular coffin housing the mummy of King Tutankhamun himself.

CANOPIC JARS

When a body was mummified, the dead person's internal organs (liver, lungs, stomach and intestines) were removed through a slit near the left hip. They were then carefully wrapped and stored in four containers called canopic jars. The jars' stoppers were carved in the shape of the heads of protective gods, called the sons of Horus. The jars were then placed inside a special chest inside the tomb.

5000 BC 4500 BC 4000 BC 3500 BC 3000 BC 2500 BC

CARVED SEALS

Archaeologists have found a great many small, carved stone seals among the ruins of the Indus cities. These were used by merchants to seal their bundles of goods. Many show animals, such as bulls, tigers and elephants. Some also show religious scenes. Each has a written inscription, possibly the name of the merchant. No one has yet been able to decipher these inscriptions.

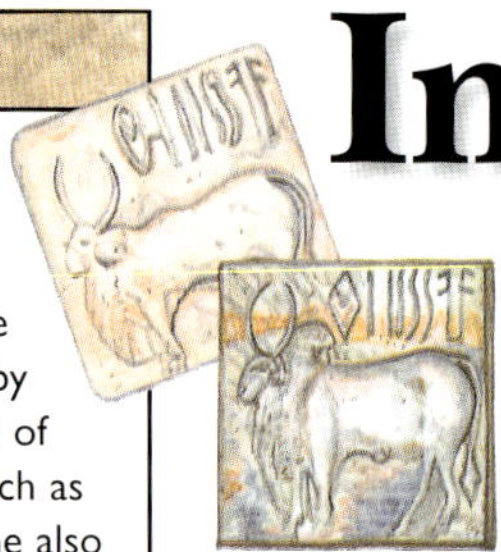

Indus Valley

Around 3000 BC, another great early civilization grew up along the banks of the river Indus in ancient India (present-day Pakistan). Called the Indus Valley civilization, by 2500 BC it had reached the height of its power.

The Indus Valley civilization was larger than either Sumer or ancient Egypt. Its two great centres were the cities of Harappa and Mohenjo Daro, each with a population of some 40,000 people. The Indus Valley civilization had a highly organized system of trade. Merchants traded grain and other agricultural produce, grown on the fertile river plains, as well as artefacts made by the cities' artists and craft workers, for precious metals and cloth. From about 2000 BC, however, this mighty civilization began to decline. This may have been caused by terrible flooding or by the river Indus changing course so that the fertile farmland dried up. Another theory is that the people over-grazed the land, leaving it too dry and poor to support crops.

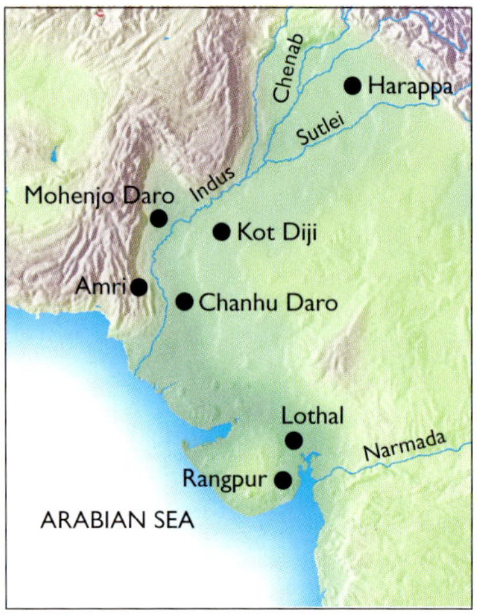

◁ ***This map shows*** *the extent and main cities of the Indus Valley civilization. This region now lies inside modern-day Pakistan.*

Megalithic Europe

From about 4500 BC, people in Europe began building monuments of massive, standing stones, called megaliths. These were placed in circles or upright one next to the other, with another stone laid horizontally on top.

Stones circles were laid out very carefully, according to strict mathematical rules, but no one is sure what they were used for. They may been have been early observatories for studying the Sun, Moon and stars, or temples where religious ceremonies were held. Experts also think that sacrifices, both human and animal, may have taken place inside these intriguing circles of stone.

▷ ***A mother goddess*** *figure made of clay and found at the Hypogeum, a megalithic monument on the island of Malta. The Hypogeum was built deep underground, carved out of the rock.*

▷ ***Stonehenge*** *in England is the most famous stone circle of all. Built in three stages, from about 2800 BC, the stones were positioned to align precisely with the rays of the Sun on Midsummer's Day. Other stones align with the phases of the Moon, which suggests that Stonehenge may have been a gigantic calendar.*

△ ***Mohenjo Daro**, like other cities in the Indus valley, was laid out on a grid pattern. The houses of mud brick had bathrooms and a drainage system. Each city also had a citadel, built on a hill, with important buildings, such as the Great Bath, used for religious rituals.*

Megalithic builders also constructed stone monuments over the graves of their dead. These often took the form of long, passage-like chambers, lined with megaliths, and buried under a mound of earth, called a barrow. One tomb contained over 40 skeletons, who might have been different generations of the same family. The bodies were not put immediately into the grave, but were exposed until most of the flesh had rotted away. Offerings of food and drink, pots and tools were left at the tomb entrance, for the dead to use in the next world.

INDUS VALLEY

c. **3000 BC** Farming settlements grow up along the valley of the river Indus in northwest India (now Pakistan).

c. **2500 BC** The Indus Valley civilization is at its height.

c. **2000 BC** Some Indus sites start to show signs of decline.

c. **1500 BC** The region is taken over by the Aryans, groups of Indo-Europeans from Iran. Their religious beliefs mix with those of the Indus cities to form the basis of the Hindu religion, which is still practised in India today.

◁ ***This stone statue** was found among the ruins of Mohenjo Daro. It may be the figure of a priest or a divine king. Many other figures made of clay have also been found, showing a mother goddess worshipped by the people of the Indus Valley civilization. Skilled craft workers also made many items of delicate jewellery from conch shells and metal.*

MEGALITHIC EUROPE

c. **4500 BC** People start building megaliths in western Europe.

c. **4000 BC** First passage graves are built at Carnac, France.

c. **3200 BC** Newgrange grave is built in Ireland.

c. **2800–2000 BC** Stonehenge, England, is built.

c. **2750–2000 BC** Megalithic temples are built in Malta.

▽ ***Druids** used megalithic stone circles hundreds of years after they were built. The druids were the religious leaders of the Celtic peoples of Europe.*

Minoans

THE MINOTAUR

According to Greek legend, a terrible monster, half-man, half-bull, lived in a labyrinth (maze) under the palace of Knossos on Crete. It was eventually killed by the Athenian prince, Theseus. The story may contain some truth, for bulls seem to have been sacred animals in Minoan society. It is thought that the king wore a bull's head mask during religious ceremonies.

The Minoan civilization was the first major civilization in Europe. It began on the island of Crete and was named after its legendary ruler, King Minos. It was at the height of its power from about 2000 BC.

The Minoans had a rich and glittering culture, with a highly organized society and flourishing economy. Merchants travelled far and wide throughout the Mediterranean, trading wine, grain and olive oil, grown by the island's farmers, for luxury goods, such as amber, ivory and precious metals. Each large Minoan town was built around a splendid palace, housing hundreds or even thousands of people. Apart from being royal residences, palaces acted as trading centres, where goods could be stored ready for export. They also contained shrines, workshops and living quarters for officials. By 1450 BC, however, most of the palaces had been destroyed, probably by earthquakes or volcanic eruptions, and Crete was taken over by the Mycenaeans.

Mycenaeans

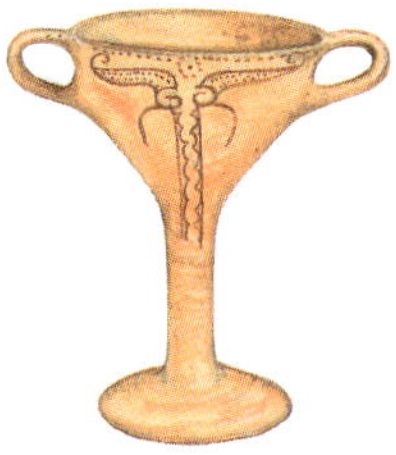

From about 1600 BC to 1100 BC the Mycenaeans dominated mainland Greece. They lived in separate, small kingdoms, although they shared the same language and beliefs and are named after their greatest city, Mycenae. Here evidence of their culture was first discovered.

The Mycenaeans built their great palaces on hill tops, surrounded by massive stone walls. This type of fortified city was called an *acropolis*, which means "high city" in Greek. These fortifications made their cities much easier to defend from attack. Mycenaean society was based around farming and trade, and they founded colonies on Rhodes and Cyprus. They also seem to have been brave and successful warriors. Many examples of armour and weapons have been found in the graves of Mycenaean kings and nobles.

***Minoan pottery** was very skilfully made. Minoan potters made huge clay jars, taller than a person, for storing oil, wine and grain. These jars were called* pithoi. *Many such jars were discovered during the excavation of the magnificent palace of Knossos.*

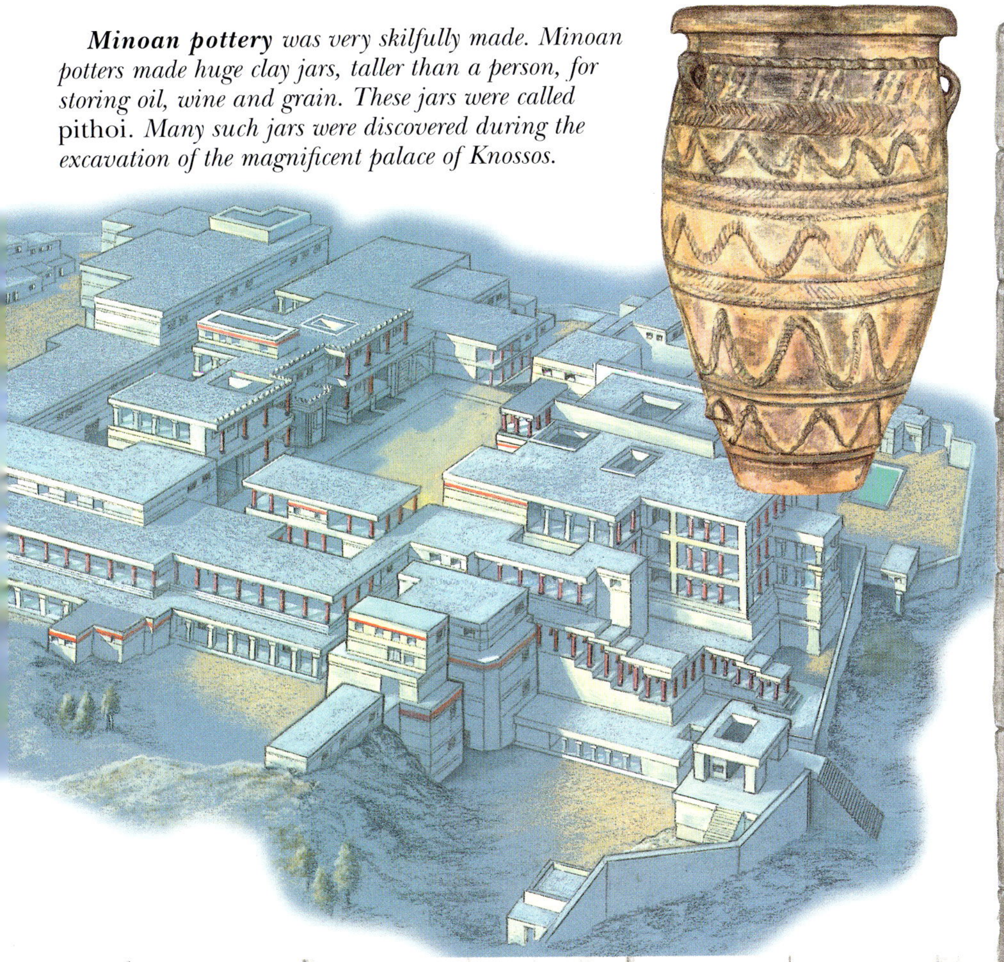

MINOANS

c. 6000 BC The first farmers settle in Crete.
c. 3000–1000 BC People on Crete and mainland Greece learn how to make bronze.
c. 2000 BC The first palaces are built on Crete.
c. 1700 BC The palaces are destroyed by earthquakes and are later rebuilt.
c. 1600 BC The first Myceneans reach Crete.
c. 1450 BC A volcanic eruption destroys all the palaces on Crete, Knossos included.
c. 1100 BC The end of Minoan civilization.

◁ ***Knossos** was the largest Minoan palace. Built around a central courtyard (used for religious ceremonies) it had 1300 rooms. The walls of the royal apartments were decorated with frescos, or wall paintings, which have provided valuable clues about Minoan life. The ruins of Knossos were found by Sir Arthur Evans in 1894.*

In 1876, the German archaeologist Heinrich Schliemann, began excavating a circle of stone slabs that lay just inside the city walls of Mycenae. Inside the circle, he made a startling discovery – a group of five shaft graves, sunk deep into the ground. The graves contained the bodies of 16 members of the Mycenaean royal family, five of whom had exquisite gold death masks covering their faces. Alongside lay a priceless hoard of golden treasure, including swords, goblets, crowns and necklaces, which had been buried with their owners.

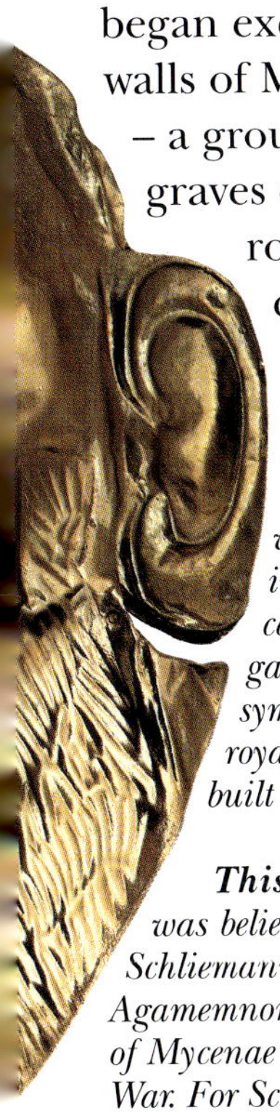

***The Lion Gate** was the main gateway into Mycenae. The two carved lions above the gate may have been symbols of the Mycenaean royal family. The gate was built in about 1250 BC.*

***This gold death mask** was believed by Heinrich Schliemann to cover the face of Agamemnon, the legendary king of Mycenae and hero of the Trojan War. For Schliemann, finding the mask was a dream come true. Modern scholars, however, disagree. They think that the graves date from about 300 years before Agamemnon's time.*

MYCENAEANS

c. 1600–1100 BC The Mycenaeans dominate mainland Greece.
c. 1450 BC The Mycenaeans become rulers of Crete.
c. 1250 BC The traditional date of the fall of Troy.
c. 1200 BC Mycenaean culture begins to decline, possibly due to crop failure and a weak economy. People begin to abandon the great cities.
c. 1100–800 BC The Dark Ages in Greece.

▽ ***The Trojan War** began when King Agamemnon led a Mycenaean army to bring back Helen, his sister-in-law, who had eloped with Paris, a Trojan prince. According to legend, the Mycenaeans took the city by smuggling soldiers into Troy inside a huge wooden horse.*

Ancient China

ANCIENT CHINA

***c.* 1766–1027 BC** The Shang dynasty rules China.
1027–256 BC The Zhou dynasty rules China.
***c.* 551 BC** Birth of the great teacher, Confucius.
481–221 BC The so-called Warring States Period when most of China is in civil war.
221 BC Shi Huangdi unites China and founds the Qin dynasty. He becomes China's first emperor.
212 BC The Burning of the Books by Shi Huangdi.
210 BC Death of Shi Huangdi.
202 BC Qin dynasty collapses and the Han dynasty rules China until AD 9.

The earliest civilizations in China grew up along the banks of three major rivers – the Chang Jiang (Yangtze), Xi Jiang (West River) and Huang He (Yellow River). Farmers used the river water to irrigate their crops but they also faced the frequent risk of floods that could devastate their harvests.

From about 2205 BC, China was ruled by a series of dynasties (families). The first for which experts have reasonable evidence is the Shang dynasty, which began in about 1766 BC. The Shang ruled China for more than 400 years. At the end of the 11th century BC, however, the Shang were conquered by the Zhou. Their rule lasted until 221 BC. During this time many wars were fought between the rival kingdoms that made up the Zhou lands, but it was also a period of economic growth and of trading success, with Chinese silk, precious jade and fine porcelain being traded abroad.

By 221 BC, the kingdoms of China had been at war for more than 250 years. Gradually, the Qin (or Ch'in), a war-like dynasty from the northwest united the country and established the empire that gives China its name. The first emperor of the united

▽ ***A terracotta soldier*** *from the enormous underground tomb of Shi Huangdi. He was buried in 210 BC with all that he needed to survive the afterlife. This included a vast army, 10,000 strong, of life-sized clay soldiers.*

▷ ***The Great Wall of China,*** *built between 214 and 204 BC, formed a huge barrier more than 2250 km long, 9 m high and wide enough for chariots to drive along it. Thousands of peasants were sent to work on the wall. If their work was below standard, they were put to death.*

2000 BC 1500 BC 1000 BC 500 BC AD 1 AD 500

▷ ***The earliest Chinese writing*** *is found on oracle bones used by the Shang to predict the future. By the time of the Zhou dynasty, several thousand characters were in use. At first, the characters were drawn as picture symbols. Gradually they became more abstract in form.*

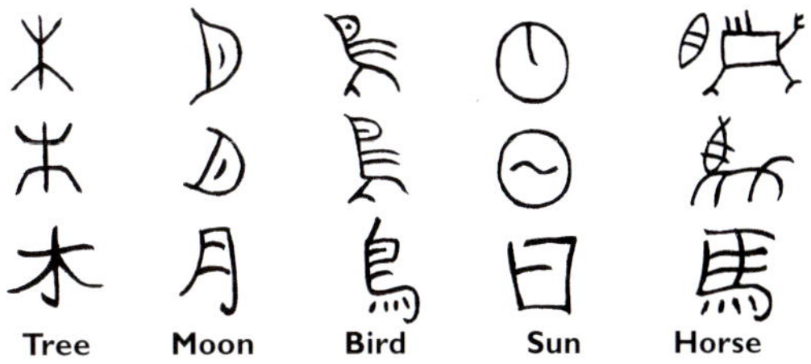

China, Shi Huangdi, reorganized government and standardized money, weights and measures. A road and canal network was also built to link up the various parts of the country and the Great Wall of China built across the northern border to keep the hostile Hsung Nu people (the Huns) out. Shi Huangdi was a brilliant but ruthless general and politician, burning books and putting scholars to death because their ideas did not match his own. Despite his achievements, however, the Qin dynasty was overthrown in 206 BC, four years after Shi Huangdi's death.

▽ ***Early copper coins****, some in the shape of knives, spades and other tools, were different in each Chinese state. Under Shi Huangdi, money was standardized. All coins were round with a hole in the middle so that they could be strung together for safe-keeping.*

CONFUCIUS

The prophet and philosopher Confucius was born in about 551 BC in northern China. This was a time of great conflict and warfare. Confucius gave up his government job and dedicated himself to teaching people how to live in peace with each other. His thoughts and teachings were so influential that they formed the basis of the Chinese civil service right up to the beginning of this century.

Phoenicians

The greatest traders and seafarers of the ancient world were the Phoenicians. They lived along the eastern coast of the Mediterranean (now part of Syria, Lebanon and Israel). Here, in about 1500 BC, they founded their greatest cities – Tyre, their main port, and Sidon. These became the flourishing centres of the vast Phoenician trading network.

The Phoenicians traded goods, such as glassware, timber, cedar oil, purple-dyed cloth and ivory throughout the Mediterranean, venturing as far west as Britain and down the African coast. In return they bought silver, copper and tin. Cedar wood and oil were among their most valuable exports. (The wood used to build King Solomon's temple in Jerusalem is said to have come from Tyre.) The Phoenicians themselves were named after their most famous and costliest export, a purple-red dye made in Tyre from a type of shellfish and known as *phoinos* in Greek.

◁ ***Phoenician glassware*** *was highly prized in the ancient world. The Phoenicians perfected the art of glass-making (first developed by the Egyptians) and also invented the technique of glass-blowing. Their glassware was considered a luxury and was much in demand.*

Some Phoenician merchants set up trading colonies, such as the great city of Carthage on the north coast of Africa (now Tunisia). Founded around 814 BC, Carthage was a great power in the western Mediterranean, long after Phoenicia itself was conquered.

ALPHABET

By about 1000 BC, the Phoenicians had developed a simple alphabet made up of 22 letters. Vowels were later added by the Greeks with whom the Phoenicians competed for trade. In time, the Greek version of the alphabet was adapted by the Romans for writing Latin, and this forms the basis of the alphabet we use to write English today.

◁ ***This terracotta head*** *dates from the 2nd century BC. Phoenician craft workers were famous for their skills. Potters, ivory carvers, metal workers and carpenters produced goods for everyday use and for export.*

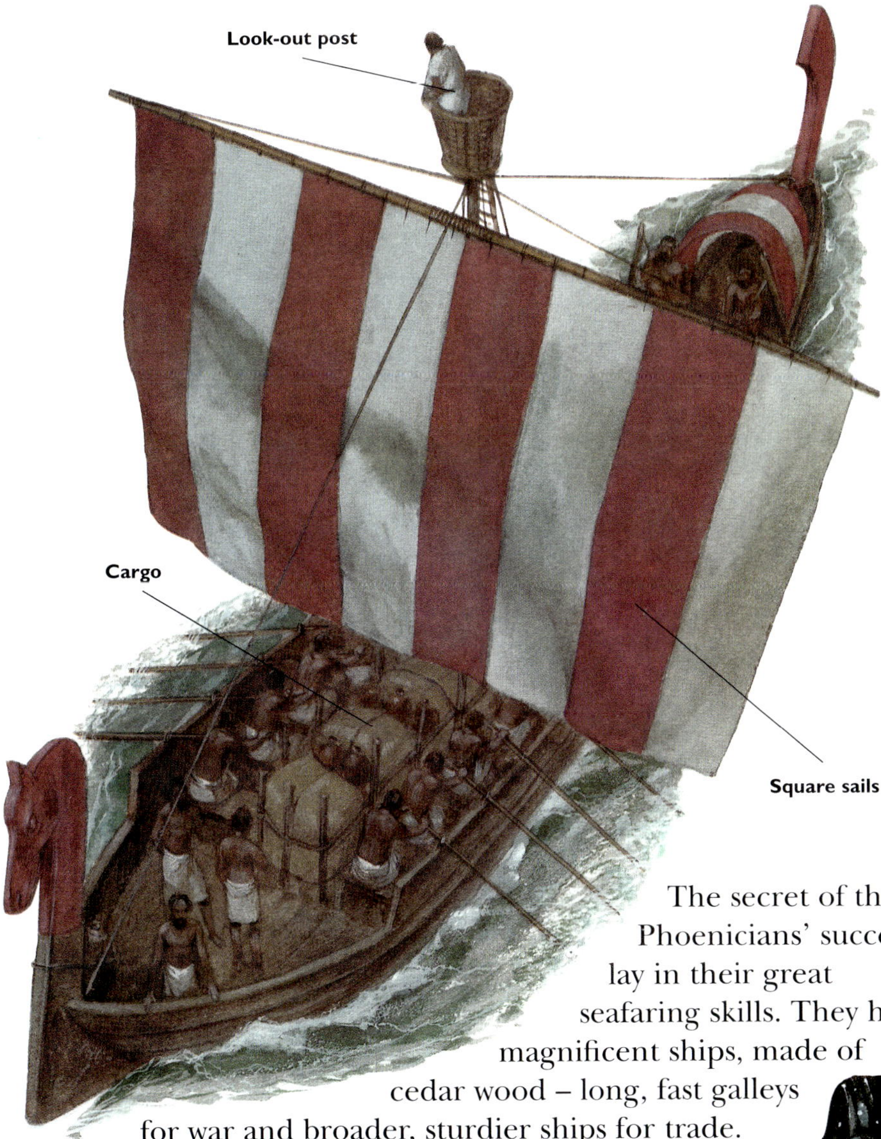

PHOENICIANS

c. **1200 BC** The beginning of Phoenician rise to power.
c. **1140 BC** The Phoenician colony of Utica is founded in North Africa.
c. **1000 BC** The Phoenician alphabet is well developed.
c. **814 BC** The city of Carthage is founded in North Africa.
729 BC The Assyrian king, Shalmaneser V, invades Phoenicia.
c. **727 BC** The Greeks adopt the Phoenician alphabet.
332 BC Alexander the Great conquers Phoenicia.
146 BC Rome defeats Carthage at the end of the Punic Wars.

◁ ***A Phoenician trading ship*** *harnessed the power of the wind with its large square sail, while rows of oarsmen allowed the ship to sail in any direction. A look-out kept watch for pirates who might attempt to steal the lucrative cargo. Trade was so important to the Phoenicians that Carthage had two harbours – one for merchant ships and one for the navy.*

The secret of the Phoenicians' success lay in their great seafaring skills. They had magnificent ships, made of cedar wood – long, fast galleys for war and broader, sturdier ships for trade. The cargo, stored in large clay pots, was lashed securely beneath the deck. The ships had heavy keels and used both sails and oars, which gave them greater manoeuvrability and speed. Even though they had no accurate maps or charts, the Phoenicians were expert navigators, relying on the winds and stars to find their way. Their fame spread far and wide. When the Egyptian pharaoh, Necho II, decided to send an expedition to attempt to sail around Africa in about 600 BC, he hired a crew of Phoenicians and a Carthaginian admiral to put his plan into action. The expedition is said to have taken three years to complete.

▽ ***Phoenician portraits*** *made from glass. The Phoenicians made clear glass from sand and quartz. They added pigments to give it colour.*

◁ ***This map shows*** *the main Phoenician trade routes and colonies. From about 1200 to 350 BC, the Phoenicians were the leading trading nation in the Mediterranean. Phoenicia itself was conquered many times, for example by the Assyrians and Babylonians.*

5000 BC 4500 BC 4000 BC 3500 BC 3000 BC 2500 BC

Ancient America

From about 1200 BC, two great civilizations grew up in ancient America – the Olmecs in western Mexico and the Chavin along the coast of northern Peru. Their ancestors had crossed the Bering Strait from Asia to America thousands of years before. At first they lived as nomadic hunter-gatherers. Later they settled in permanent villages and began to fish and farm.

The Olmec civilization, believed to be the first to develop in North America, began in about 1500 BC as a small group of villages around the Gulf of Mexico. Gradually, these villages grew and merged with one another to form larger towns. One of the main centres of Olmec culture was La Venta, situated on an island near the coast. The people of La Venta earned their living by fishing the rich waters and farming. The Olmecs were also skilled artists and craft workers. They built huge earth pyramids where religious ceremonies were held, and produced hundreds of sculptures and carvings from stone, jade and clay. Many figures and masks have been found that show a creature that is half-human and half-jaguar, suggesting the worship of a powerful god. The Olmecs also developed a system of writing that influenced many later cultures in the region.

▽ ***Huge stepped pyramids*** *made of earth were built by the Olmecs. Here they worshipped their gods and performed religious ceremonies. At La Venta, the pyramid was 34 m high. Around it lay several plazas, or squares, paved to look like jaguar masks. The people of La Venta lived in timber and thatch dwellings and ate corn, fish and turtles.*

The Chavin civilization began in Peru in about 1200 BC and lasted for about 1000 years. It is named after the site of Chavin de Huantar, which dates from about 850 BC. Chavin de Huantar was a great religious centre, with a huge stone temple surrounded by a maze of rooms and passageways. At the heart of the temple was a great statue of the Smiling God, with a human body and a snarling face. The Chavin also worshipped jaguar spirits, eagles and snakes. Their culture had a great influence throughout Peru.

◁ ***These jade and serpentine figures*** *were part of a group found at La Venta in 1955. The tiny figures were arranged as if they were taking part in a special ritual or ceremony. They had then been carefully buried with sand.*

ANCIENT AMERICA

This map shows the locations of the Olmec and Chavin civilizations in North and South America, and their major cities and centres. The Chavin was the most widespread of the early cultures in the Andean region. It was followed by the Nazca and the Moche. In North America, the Olmecs were one of the most influential cultures ever to emerge. Their homeland was the Gulf Coast of Mexico.

ANCIENT AMERICA

c. **1200–300 BC** The Olmec civilization flourishes on the coast of western Mexico.

c. **1200–200 BC** The Chavin civilization flourishes on the coast of northern Peru.

c. **1100 BC** Olmecs build a great ceremonial centre at San Lorenzo.

c. **1000 BC** Olmec city of La Venta becomes a major centre for fishing, farming and trade.

c. **850–200 BC** Chavin de Huantar in the Peruvian Andes is at the height of its power.

c. **700 BC** Olmecs abandon San Lorenzo.

c. **400–300 BC** La Venta is abandoned and destroyed.

◁ ***The Olmecs*** *carved massive stone heads. Some stood almost 3 m high. These may have shown the heads of rulers, gods or famous players of a sacred ball-game.*

▽ ***A Chavin stone bowl*** *carved into the shape of an animal and decorated with geometric patterns and swirls. Chavin craft workers produced large quantities of clay pots and sculptures, which they traded with their neighbours.*

Assyrians

The Assyrians originally lived in a small area of land around the river Tigris (now in northern Iraq). For many years, they were ruled over by their powerful neighbours in Sumer and Akkad. Then, in about 2000 BC, the Assyrians gained their independence. They established a line of warrior-kings, under whose leadership they conquered a mighty empire, which was at its greatest during the New Assyrian empire (around 1000–612 BC).

The Assyrians were tough, fearless soldiers. They ruled by force and showed no mercy. Their army was huge, well organized, well trained and well equipped. It was originally made up of farmers who fought when there was no work to do on their farms. Later, a permanent army was set up, made up of thousands of men, many of whom were prisoners of war. The Assyrian king demanded annual tributes of goods and crops from conquered people. If a city refused to pay its tribute, it was dealt with ruthlessly. The city was destroyed and its people tortured or marched off to become slaves. By 612 BC, however, the Assyrian empire had become too large and unwieldy, and it fell to the invading Medes and Babylonians.

The Assyrian kings believed that they

▷ ***This stone carving*** *from the palace at Nineveh dates from about 650 BC and shows the hunt leaving with dogs and cages. The Assyrians used some carvings as warnings. Palace visitors were shown into a room decorated with scenes of the king executing rebels!*

▽ ***The Assyrian army*** *used fearsome assault towers mounted on wheels to breach (break through) the city walls of their enemies. The towers' iron-tipped battering rams could be swung to the left or right to smash through walls and doors.*

THE HITTITES

The Hittites were a war-like people from Anatolia (in modern-day Turkey) much feared for their military skill. Among other achievements, they were the first to use chariots for warfare, which gave them a great advantage over their enemies. The Hittites conquered Babylon, Mesopotamia and parts of Syria before being crushed in about 1200 BC by the Sea Peoples, raiders who operated around the Mediterranean.

had been chosen to rule by the gods and so represented the gods on Earth. They were given grand, rather boastful titles such as "King of the Universe". The king was head of the government and army. He was also responsible for the temples and priests. To display their wealth and power, kings built magnificent cities and palaces. The earliest capital of Assyria was Ashur, named after the country's chief god. King Ashurnasirpal II (883–859 BC) preferred to build his fabulous palace in the city of Nimrud. The walls were decorated with carved stone reliefs, telling of the king's conquests as well as showing everyday life. The splendid throne room was guarded by huge stone monsters, with the bodies of bulls or lions, wings and bearded human faces. The last great ruler of Assyria, Ashurbanipal, made the city of Nineveh his capital.

ASSYRIANS

c. 2000–1450 BC The Old Assyrian empire.
1813–1781 BC Reign of King Shamshi-Adad, a great warrior and empire builder.
c. 1363–1000 BC The Middle Assyrian empire.
1298 BC King Adadnirari I takes the title King of the Universe.
c. 1000–612 BC The New Assyrian empire. A huge empire is conquered.
900–625 BC Assyria and Babylon are constantly at war with each other.
883–859 BC Reign of King Ashurnasirpal II who builds a fabulous palace at Nimrud.
745–727 BC Reign of King Tiglathpileser III who conquers Israel.
721–705 BC Reign of King Sargon II who builds a palace at Khorsabad.
668–627 BC Reign of King Ashurbanipal who makes Nineveh his capital. He sacks the great cities of Thebes, Babylon and Susa.
612 BC Assyria is invaded and conquered by the Medes and Babylonians.

▷ ***King Ashurbanipal*** *(668–627 BC) was the last great ruler of the Assyrian empire. He was a ruthless military leader, but also a great patron of the arts, building a splendid palace, library and gardens at Nineveh.*

△ ***Assyrian soldiers*** *used inflated animal skins to help them swim across fast-flowing rivers. This enabled the army to mount a surprise attack on their enemies. In battle, Assyrian soldiers wore armour of leather or chainmail and carried shields for protection.*

Babylonians

Babylon first grew powerful under the rule of King Hammurabi (*c.* 1792–1750 BC). Before this, Babylon had been one of several small kingdoms in Mesopotamia. Hammurabi conquered the other kingdoms and extended Babylon's frontiers to include Sumer and Akkad. The city of Babylon, with its magnificent temples and palaces, became the capital of the new empire.

Hammurabi was a just and diplomatic ruler. He is famous for his code of law, the oldest surviving in the world. The laws were recorded on clay tablets and stone pillars for all to see. After his death, Babylon declined in power and was invaded by the Hittites, Kassites, Chaldeans and Assyrians. The Assyrian king, Sennacherib, destroyed the city in 689 BC. In the 6th century BC, however, during the reign of King Nebuchadnezzar II, Babylon regained its former glory. The king conquered a huge empire and rebuilt the city on a very grand scale, surpassing any other city in the ancient world. Babylon was finally captured by the Persians in 539 BC and became part of the mighty Persian empire.

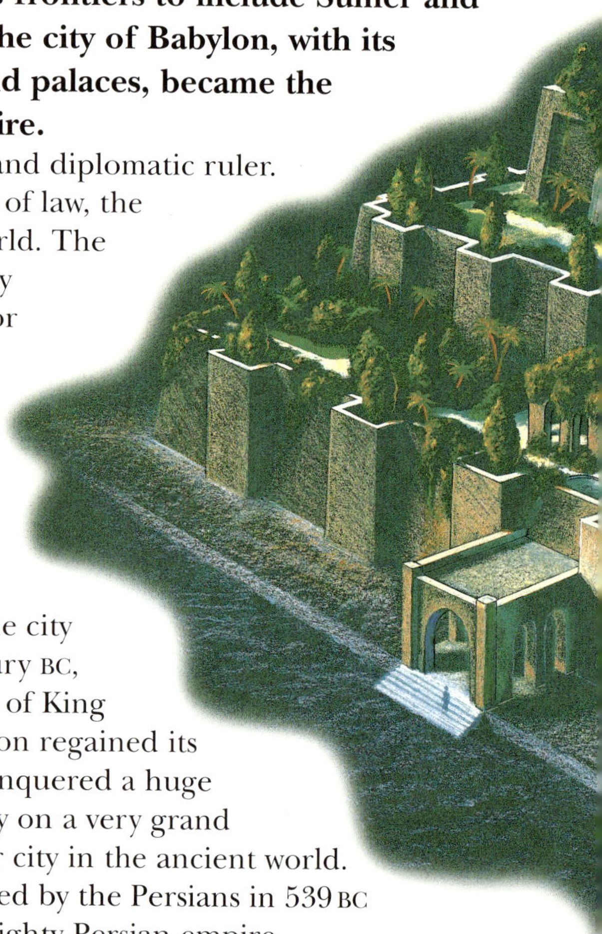

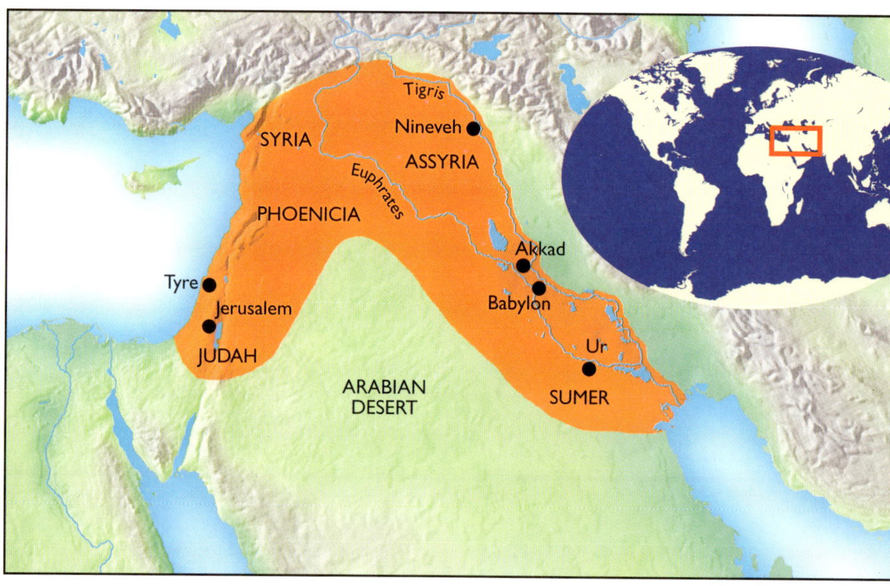

BABYLONIANS

c. 1894 BC The Amorite people establish the minor kingdom of Babylon in Mesopotamia.

c. 1792–1750 BC Reign of King Hammurabi. Babylon first rises to power.

c. 1595 BC Babylon is plundered by the Hittites, then falls to the Kassites.

c. 1595–1155 BC The Kassites rule Babylon.

c. 1126–1105 BC Reign of King Nebuchadnezzar I.

c. 731–626 BC The Assyrians and Chaldeans fight for control of Babylon.

c. 626–529 BC The Neo (New) Babylonian empire. Babylon re-emerges as a major power in the Near East.

c. 626–605 BC King Nabopolassar defeats the Assyrians and rules Babylon. Babylonian army, under Nebuchadnezzar defeats Egypt to win Syria.

△ ***King Nebuchadnezzar II** ruled Babylon from around 605 BC to 562 BC. Among many other military campaigns, he captured Syria and Palestine and conquered the city of Jerusalem, forcing many of its people to live in captivity in Babylon. His story is told in the Old Testament of the Bible, in the Book of Daniel.*

c. 605–562 BC Nabopolassar's son, Nebuchadnezzar II, rules Babylonia.

c. 597 BC Nebuchadnezzar conquers Judah (southern Palestine) and puts down three rebellions there.

586 BC Nebuchadnezzar destroys Jerusalem and exiles its people to Babylon.

c. 539 BC Babylon is conquered by the Persians.

▽ ***The Hanging Gardens of Babylon*** *were one of the Seven Wonders of the world. Legend says that Nebuchadnezzar's Persian wife, Amytis, missed the green hills of her homeland so much that she built a terraced hill of her own, close to the palace, and planted the gardens with exotic plants and trees.*

The awe-inspiring city of Babylon stood on the banks of the river Euphrates (near Baghdad in modern-day Iraq). The capital of the Babylonian empire, it was also a major trading centre and a flourishing religious complex, especially for the worship of the god Marduk, the patron of the city. In fact, the name Babylon means "Gate of the God". King Nebuchadnezzar II rebuilt the city in magnificent style, with enormous city walls, some 26 m thick, and eight massive bronze gates. The grandest gate, the Ishtar Gate, opened on to the Processional Way, which linked the great Temple of Marduk inside the walls to an important religious site outside the city. At the New Year's festival, statues of the gods were paraded along this route and through the gate, while stories were told of Marduk's famous triumph over chaos. Nebuchadnezzar also built a breathtaking palace between the Ishtar Gate and the river Euphrates. Built around five spacious courtyards, it was known as "the Marvel of Mankind".

BABYLONIAN SCIENCE

The Babylonians were excellent mathematicians and astronomers and made many important discoveries. Like the Sumerians, they used base 60 to calculate divisions of time and of circles. They understood fractions, squares and square roots, and could predict eclipses of the Sun and Moon. The Babylonians were the first to use a system of weights in about 2600 BC. The ancient metal weights shown above are in the shape of lions. The Babylonians also drew the oldest known map of the world. Inscribed on a clay tablet, it shows Babylon at the centre of the Earth.

◁ ***This map shows*** *the extent of the Babylonian empire under Nebuchadnezzar II. His army defeated the Egyptians to take Syria. In 586* BC *Nebuchadnezzar conquered Judah by destroying Jerusalem and transporting the survivors back to Babylon as slaves.*

▷ ***The Ishtar Gate*** *marked the northern entrance to the city and was named after the goddess of love and war. The gate's brilliant blue tiles were decorated with bulls and dragons, symbols of Marduk.*

Ancient Greece

BATTLE SHIPS
A turning point in the Persian Wars was the sea battle of Salamis in 480 BC. The Greeks lured the Persian fleet into a narrow channel of water, then the navy inflicted a heavy defeat. Greek warships had sails and several banks of oars on either side, which made them very fast and easy to manoeuvre. During the Persian Wars, Greek ships were used to ram enemy ships in order to sink or badly damage them. Greek archers then fired arrows at the stricken Persian crew.

By about 800 BC, Greece saw the rise of a new civilization that transformed the ancient world and whose influence has lasted to the present day. Ancient Greece was divided into small, independent city-states, each with its own government and laws. The two most important were mighty Athens and Sparta.

Most city-states were ruled by a group of wealthy nobles, known as an *oligarchy*. Resentment led to revolts and absolute rulers, called *tyrants*, were appointed to restore law and order. In about 508 BC, however, a new type of government was introduced in Athens. It was called *democracy*, meaning "rule by the people", and gave every male citizen a say in how the city should be run. Many modern countries now use this form of government as a basis for their governments today.

The Classical Period in Greece (the time in which Greek culture was at its most splendid) lasted from about 500 BC to 336 BC. During this time Greece was involved in two great wars – the series of Persian Wars (490–449 BC) and the Peloponnesian Wars (431–404 BC). When the Persians invaded Greece in 490 BC, the city-states joined forces against the invaders and succeeded in defeating them. One of the most famous battles of the war took place at Marathon in 490 BC. A messenger called Pheidippides, ran the 40 km back to Athens carrying news of the Greek victory. The marathon race was born! Greece's newly-won security did not last long. Relations between Athens and Sparta began to deteriorate and, in 431 BC, war broke out between them. The Peloponnesian Wars lasted for 27 years and tore the country apart.

▷ ***A hoplite**, or Greek foot soldier, was the most important part of the Greek army. Each soldier carried a heavy round shield, protecting his body from neck to knees. A long spear was used to stab an opponent and a split skirt-like tunic allowed easy movement.*

◁ ***Zeus** was the king of gods and ruler of the heavens. The ancient Greeks worshipped many gods and goddesses. The most important were the Olympians, who lived on Mount Olympus, the highest mountain in Greece.*

After laying seige to Athens, the Spartans starved the Athenians into submission. In 404 BC, Athens was forced to surrender. The city never recovered from its defeat.

Life in Sparta was very different from that in Athens. It revolved around training Spartan citizens to be fearless warriors, ready to defend the city-state from foreign invaders and to keep the population under control. Every male Spartan had to train for war. Boys as young as seven were sent away to army camp where the strict discipline and harsh conditions were designed to turn them into the toughest fighters in Greece. Girls too were allowed to take part in sports, to make them strong and healthy. Such activity was frowned on elsewhere in Greece.

△ ***The Parthenon*** *was built on top of the Acropolis (a high hill in Athens) in the 5th century BC. It was dedicated to Athena, goddess of wisdom, war and of Athens itself. Many beautiful Greek temples were built, where sacrifices and offerings were made to the gods.*

ANCIENT GREECE

c. **900 BC** State of Sparta founded by the Dorians.

c. **800–500 BC** The Archaic Period – Greece revives after a period called the Dark Ages, when it was in decline.

776 BC The first Olympic Games are held at Olympia.

c. **750–550 BC** Many Greeks leave the mainland and establish colonies around the Mediterranean.

c. **700 BC** The Greek poet, Homer, composes the *Iliad* and the *Odyssey*.

c. **508 BC** Democracy is introduced in Athens.

△ ***Pericles*** *was leader of Athens from 443 BC to 429 BC. He was the most famous and popular politician of the Golden Age (479–431 BC), a period that followed the Persian defeat at Salamis. Pericles ordered the rebuilding of Athens after its destruction by the Persians, and the building of the Parthenon.*

▽ ***In battle****, Greek hoplites formed a phalanx — a block of soldiers eight or more rows deep. Two opposing phalanxes would charge each other, until one gave way under the onslaught. Soldiers in the front line jabbed at their enemies' faces and necks.*

Greek Culture

Greek civilization came to an end more than 2000 years ago, when Greece became part of the Roman empire. Yet its influence on politics, philosophy, art and architecture, language and literature had a huge effect on Roman culture and can still be felt today. Much of the language we use and many of our ideas about science and art come from ancient Greece.

The ancient Greeks were great scholars, thinkers and teachers. At first, they answered questions about life and nature with stories about the gods. Later, they started to look for more practical, more scientific ways of making sense of the world about them. These scholars were called philosophers, which means "lovers of knowledge", and they looked at all aspects of life.

Drama and sport played a very important part in the lives of the ancient Greeks. Greek theatre grew from the performance of songs and dances at an annual festival dedicated to Dionysus, the god of wine. These performances were acted out by a group of men called a *chorus*. At first, plays were performed in the market place. Later, many great open-air theatres were built all over Greece.

△ ***Greek vases*** *were decorated with scenes from daily life as well as stories from mythology. Much of our knowledge about the ancient Greeks comes from vases and vessels. They show what the Greeks wore, what jobs they did, how they lived and so on.*

▽ ***Greek actors*** *were all men. They wore masks and costumes to show if their characters were happy, sad, male, female, old or young. The Greeks were the first to build theatres and the largest could hold an audience of 18,000 people.*

Sport was important not only as a means of entertainment, but also to keep men fit and healthy for fighting. There were many competitions, both local and national, for athletes to take part in. The oldest and most famous were the Olympic Games, held every four years at Olympia, in honour of Zeus. For the five days of the games, a truce was called between the city-states to allow the athletes safe passage to Olympia. Athletes trained hard for months before the games. Discipline was strict and breaking the rules harshly punished. But for the winners it was all worthwhile. Their prize was a simple olive crown, cut from the sacred tree, and a hero's welcome, fame and fortune, awaited them at home.

Corinthian column

Ionic column

Doric column

△ ***The styles of column*** *that the Greeks developed for their grand public buildings and temples are known as classical orders. The two main styles of column were Doric and Ionic. A third, more elaborate style, called Corinthian, was introduced in Roman times.*

◁ ***Socrates*** (c. *469–399* BC) *the son of an Athenian sculptor, was one of the most influential of all ancient Greek philosophers. He taught people to think about good and evil, in order to improve their own behaviour. Some people did not approve of his ideas and he was forced to commit suicide.*

c. 500–336 BC The Classical Period. Greek culture reaches its height.
490–449 BC The Persian Wars. The Greeks are victorious.
479–431 BC The Golden Age of Athens, a time of great prosperity and achievement for the city.
447–438 BC The Parthenon is built in Athens.
431–404 BC Athens and Sparta fight the Peloponnesian Wars. Sparta wins with Persian help.
430 BC Plague devastates Athens.
371 BC Sparta is defeated by the Greek city-state of Thebes.
362 BC The Thebans are defeated at the battle of Mantinea by the Spartans and the Athenians.
338 BC The Greeks are defeated by the Macedonians at the battle of Chaeronea. This spells the end of Greek independence.
336–30 BC The Hellenistic Period.
147–146 BC Greece becomes part of the Roman empire.

△ ***At the Olympic Games,*** *throwing the discus was one of five events in the pentathlon. The others were running, jumping, wrestling and throwing the javelin. The winner of this very demanding competition was declared the best all-round athlete at the games. The ancient Olympics ended in* AD *395. The games were revived in 1896 by Baron Pierre de Coubertin.*

Alexander the Great

Amid the squabbling and disunity that took hold of Greece in the aftermath of the Peloponnesian Wars, the new power of Macedonia, in the northwest, went largely unnoticed. The Macedonians took full advantage of the situation to take control of Greece.

When Philip II came to the throne in 359 BC, he united and extended the kingdom, reorganized the army and transformed Macedonia into the greatest military force of the day. In 338 BC, at the battle of Chaeronea, Philip's army gained control of Greece, uniting the Greeks and Macedonians against the mighty Persians. In 336 BC, however, Philip was assassinated and the throne passed to his 20-year-old son, Alexander. An even more brilliant leader and general than his father, it took Alexander just 13 years to conquer a vast empire that stretched from Greece in the west to India in the east. It was the largest empire in the ancient world and helped to spread Hellenistic (Greek) culture far and wide.

In 334 BC, Alexander led his army against the Persians, in order not only to conquer their lands, but to replenish his royal treasuries with their great wealth. In 333 BC, he defeated the Persian king Darius III, at the battle of Issus, and by 331 BC, had conquered the whole of Persia and

▷ ***Petra**, the "rose-red city" in Jordan, was partly redesigned and rebuilt in Greek style by Alexander's architects. During his travels, Alexander founded many cities, often called Alexandria. This helped to spread Hellenistic art and culture.*

◁ ***Alexander** on his favourite horse, Bucephalus.*

▷ ***The map shows** the extent of Alexander's empire and the routes he followed to conquer the east.*

◁ ***The battle of Issus*** *depicted on a huge mosaic, found at Pompeii, Italy, in 1831. At Issus in Syria, Alexander crushingly defeated the Persian army, under the leadership of King Darius III, in 333* BC.

▽ ***The city of Persepolis*** *was the magnificent capital of the Persian kings. Built by Darius I, the ruins of the city lie near Shiraz in modern-day Iran. When Alexander captured Persepolis in 331* BC, *he burned Darius' splendid palace to the ground.*

become its king. To strengthen the ties between the two peoples, Alexander tried to include Persians in his government. He also wore Persian clothes and married a Persian princess, Roxane. Alexander went on to invade India, defeating King Porus at the battle of the river Hydaspes. It was to be his final expedition. His exhausted army refused to go any farther and Alexander was forced to retreat to Babylon. He died there, of a fever, in 323 BC, at the age of 32. After his death, his empire was fought over by his leading generals and eventually divided among them.

DARIUS I AND THE PERSIANS

During the reign of Darius I (521–486 BC), the Persian empire was extended from Turkey in the west to northern India in the east. The empire was reorganized into provinces, called *satrapies*, and a great highway built, from Turkey to Iran, for carrying messages from the king to all parts of his empire. From 499 BC to 479 BC, Darius' troops were involved in the Persian Wars against Greece and were defeated at the battle of Salamis in 480 BC.

ALEXANDER THE GREAT

359 BC Philip II becomes King of Macedonia.
356 BC Alexander is born. He is educated by, among others, the philosopher Aristotle.
338 BC At Chaeronea, Philip wins control of the Greek city-states.
336 BC Philip is murdered. His son, Alexander, becomes king at the age of 20.
334 BC Alexander's army invades the Persian empire.
333 BC Alexander defeats a huge Persian army led by Darius III at the battle of Issus.
332 BC Alexander marches on and conquers Egypt.
331 BC Alexander again overwhelmingly defeats the Persians at the battle of Gaugamela. Darius is assassinated and Alexander becomes King of Persia.
327 BC Alexander reaches India.
324 BC Alexander's tired army mutinies. Alexander turns back towards the west.
323 BC Alexander dies in Babylon.
323–281 BC The wars of the Diadochi (generals). The empire is split into three – Persia, Egypt, Macedonia.
147–146 BC Macedonia becomes part of the Roman empire.

△ ***The Persian army*** *was very efficient. Its greatest strength lay in its archers and cavalry troops. There was also an elite force of 10,000 warriors, called the Immortals. Even so, it was no match for Alexander's battle tactics.*

The Celts

The Celts probably first lived in France and Austria from about 600 BC. Gradually, Celtic tribes spread farther afield, across southern and western Europe, conquering the lands and settling in hill-forts and farms. They were finally defeated by the Romans and much of their territory was brought under Roman rule.

Despite the Celts' reputation as fearless, ruthless warriors, they were highly skilled metal-smiths, making beautifully decorated weapons, jewellery and drinking cups. They were also gifted poets and musicians, passing down stories of their gods and history by word of mouth, as they had no written language.

THE CELTS

c. **600–500 BC** Celtic culture develops in Austria and France.

c. **400 BC** The Celts build farms and hill-forts in southern and western Europe.

390 BC The Gauls (French Celts) sack the city of Rome.

225 BC The Romans defeat the Gauls at the battle of Telamon in Italy.

58–50 BC Julius Caesar conquers all of Gaul (France).

52 BC Vercingetorix leads a revolt against the Romans in Gaul but is defeated by Caesar.

AD 61 Boudicca is defeated in a revolt she leads against the Romans in Britain.

▷ ***Safe within a hill-fort,*** *each family lived with their animals in circular wooden huts, with thatched roofs and walls covered in wattle and daub. A huge iron cooking cauldron hung over the fire in the centre of the hut.*

▽ ***Celtic craft workers*** *made beautiful objects out of metal, such as this horse harness made of silver. They decorated their work with distinctive geometric patterns of spirals and curves, animal figures, religious motifs and human faces.*

Roman writers recorded details of Celtic life and culture. They reported, among other things, that the Celts worshipped many different gods and goddesses and offered sacrifices in their honour. Religious rituals and ceremonies were performed by priests, called druids. In charge of each of the Celtic tribes was a leader, or chieftain. One of the most famous was Vercingetorix, a chieftain of the Arveni, a tribe in central Gaul (France). In 52 BC, he led a successful rebellion against the Romans but was later defeated by Julius Caesar's well trained army.

The Celts were great warriors, famed and feared for their bravery in battle. Individual warriors often fought on their own and not as part of an organized army. Wars frequently broke out between the rival Celtic tribes. This helped the Romans to defeat the Celts more easily than if they had been a unified and efficiently run military force. Many tribes built huge fortresses on the tops of hills, surrounded by massive, protective walls. Inside the people of the tribe could live, safe from attack. Victory in battle was celebrated in grand style, with lavish feasts, hard drinking and the recital of long poems, telling of the deeds of the Celtic heroes and gods. Their greatest god was Daghdha, the "Good God", who controlled the weather and the harvest and brought victory in battle. All the members of the tribe attended a banquet, which could last several days.

BOUDICCA

The Roman emperor Claudius invaded Britain in AD 43, but this did not mean an end to Celtic opposition to Roman rule. In AD 60, Boudicca (or Boadicea), the queen of the Iceni, a Celtic tribe from East Anglia, led a revolt against the Romans in Britain. At first, the queen and her army enjoyed great success, taking the towns of Colchester, London and St Albans (Verulanium) and killing some 70,000 Romans. But her army was eventually defeated in AD 61 and Boudicca killed herself by drinking poison.

▽ ***Maiden Castle*** *is a Celtic hill-fort in Dorset, England. Like other Iron Age hill-forts, it was built on high ground, giving it a clear view of the surrounding countryside and of any intruders. The concentric earthworks of the fort made it difficult to attack.*

The Romans

According to legend, the city of Rome was founded in 753 BC by twin brothers, called Romulus and Remus. Abandoned by their wicked uncle to die on the banks of the river Tiber in central Italy, the boys were rescued by a she-wolf. Then they were found and raised by a shepherd.

To repay the she-wolf for her kindness, Romulus and Remus vowed to build a city in her honour, on the Palatine Hill where she had found them. In a quarrel about the city boundaries, Remus was killed and Romulus became the first king of Rome and gave the city his name. From humble beginnings as a small group of villages, populated by criminals and runaway slaves, Rome grew to become the magnificent capital of the most powerful empire the western world had ever seen.

△ ***Romulus and Remus**, according to legend, were suckled by a she-wolf before being rescued by a shepherd. The legend goes on to tell how the twins founded Rome, with Romulus becoming its first king. This statue of the wolf dates from the 6th century BC, but the twins were added much later in AD 1510.*

▷ ***Gods and goddesses** surround the edge of this artefact. The Romans worshipped thousands of gods, including the state deities, such as Jupiter, king of the gods and Mars, god of war. Each Roman family also worshipped their own guardian spirits, called the Lares, Penates and Manes.*

▽ ***Octavian**, the first emperor of Rome, was known as Augustus or "revered one". He was a great politician, reforming every aspect of government and restoring peace and prosperity to Rome.*

▷ ***The forum**, or market place, in Rome as it looks today. Rome grew to become the largest city in the ancient world, with over a million inhabitants. It was a city of great constrasts, with magnificent public buildings, such as temples, law courts and triumphal arches in the forum, but also overcrowded tenement blocks where the poor lived.*

At first, Rome was ruled by kings, beginning traditionally with Romulus. Then, in about 509 BC, King Tarquin the Proud was expelled from Rome and for the next 500 years Rome became a republic. Power passed to the Senate, a law-making body made up of important nobles and headed by two senior officials, called consuls. They were elected every year to manage the affairs of the Senate and the Roman army. By about 50 BC, Rome had conquered most of the lands around the Mediterranean. But all was not well. Rivalry between army generals and tensions between rich and poor plunged Rome into a bloody civil war. The old republic crumbled. In 27 BC, Octavian, the adopted son of Julius Caesar, became the first Roman emperor, charged with restoring peace and stability to Rome. Under the rule of the emperors, Rome reached its greatest extent, ruling over much of Europe, North Africa and the Near East.

▷ ***This fresco,*** *or wall painting, comes from Pompeii, which was destroyed in AD 79 by a volcanic eruption. Many buildings, however, were superbly preserved under the ash and lava that smothered the town.*

HADRIAN'S WALL

Emperor Hadrian ruled Rome from AD 117 to 138. He halted the growth of the empire that had taken place under Trajan (AD 98–117) and concentrated instead on strengthening the defence of its borders. Fortified walls were built along the most vulnerable borders in Germany, Africa and Britain. The best preserved is Hadrian's Wall in Britain, built in AD 122 to defend the empire's northernmost frontier.

THE ROMANS

753 BC The traditional date for the founding of Rome.
c. **509 BC** The founding of the Roman Republic.
264–146 BC The Punic Wars between Rome and Carthage in North Africa. Carthage is destroyed and Rome rules the Mediterranean.
49 BC Julius Caesar becomes dictator of Rome.

△ ***Julius Caesar,*** *a brilliant Roman general, was elected consul in 59 BC. After his term in office, he led the armies in Spain and France and invaded Britain briefly in 55 BC. In 49 BC, he defeated his rivals in Rome to seize power as dictator. He was assassinated by a group of senators on 15 March, 44 BC.*

31 BC Octavian defeats Antony and Cleopatra at the battle of Actium and takes control of Egypt.
27 BC The end of the Republic and start of the Roman empire.
27 BC–AD 14 Octavian takes the title Augustus and rules as the first Roman emperor.
AD 14–37 Tiberius rules.
AD 37–41 Caligula rules.
AD 41–54 Claudius rules.
AD 54–68 Nero rules.
AD 64 Fire devastates Rome.
AD 69 The year of the four emperors.

Roman Society

AD 69–79 Vespasian rules the Roman empire.
AD 79–81 Titus rules.
c. AD 80 The Colosseum is completed in Rome.
AD 81–96 Domitian rules.
AD 96–98 Nerva rules.
AD 98–117 Trajan rules. The empire reaches its greatest extent.
AD 117–138 Hadrian rules.
AD 166–167 The empire is devastated by a plague.
AD 180 End of the Pax Romana, or Roman Peace, a time of stability in the empire.
AD 286 Emperor Diocletian divides the Roman empire into west and east, each with its own emperor.
AD 391 Christianity becomes the official religion of the Roman empire.
AD 410 Sack of Rome by Alaric the Goth.
AD 451 Attila the Hun invades Gaul.
AD 476 The last western emperor, Romulus Augustulus, is deposed. The eastern empire continues as the Byzantine empire.

The amazing expansion and success of the Roman empire was due largely to its army, the best trained and best equipped in the world.

At first, the army was formed to protect the city of Rome and was largely made up of volunteer soldiers. Under the leadership of the general, and consul, Marius (155–86 BC), the army was reorganized into a more disciplined and more efficient fighting force. Soldiers were paid wages and joined up for 20 to 25 years. For many young men from good families, the army provided a stepping stone to a glittering political career.

In the army itself, ordinary soldiers were grouped into units, called legions, each made up of about 5000 men. The legions, in turn, were made up of smaller units, called centuries, of 80 men commanded by soldiers called centurions.

△ ***A Roman woman's** life largely depended on how rich or poor she was. Wealthy women did not go out to work. They were expected to run the home and have children. Poorer women worked on farms, in shops and as needlewomen.*

△ ***The Colosseum** amphitheatre was built to stage gladiator fights, a hugely popular form of entertainment in ancient Rome. Gladiators were trained slaves or prisoners who fought each other or wild animals to the death. The Colosseum could hold up to 45,000 spectators seated by their social class.*

The sight of the well-trained legions of Rome marching into battle behind their standards topped by a silver eagle (the symbol of Jupiter, king of the gods) must have struck fear and trepidation into the hearts of Rome's staunchest enemies.

Roman society was divided into citizens and non-citizens. There were three classes of citizens – *patricians*, the richest and most influential aristocrats; *equites*, the wealthy merchants, and *plebians*, the ordinary citizens, or 'commoners'. All citizens were allowed to vote in elections and to serve in the army. They were also allowed to wear togas. Non-citizens included provincials, people who lived outside Rome itself but in territory under Roman rule, and slaves. Slaves had no rights or status. They were owned by wealthy citizens, or by the government, and did all the hardest, dirtiest jobs on which the Roman empire heavily relied. Many slaves were treated cruelly but some were well looked after, and even paid a wage, so that they could eventually buy their freedom. Most upper-class Romans followed careers in politics or in the army. Poorer citizens worked as farmers, shopkeepers or craft workers. Buildings, mining and all hard, manual labour was done by the vast workforce of slaves.

HANNIBAL

From 264 BC to 146 BC, Rome waged war against the Phoenician city of Carthage, on the North African coast, to gain control of the Mediterranean. These were called the Punic Wars. In 218 BC, at the start of the Second Punic War, the Carthaginian general, Hannibal, led a surprise attack on the Romans by marching over the Alps and into Italy with 35,000 men and 37 elephants. Carthage, however, was finally defeated at the end of the third Punic War.

◁ ***A centurion and aquilifer*** *(standard bearer). Experienced soldiers rose to become centurions, or officers. They wore crested helmets so that they could easily be seen in battle. The aquilifer was a veteran soldier who carried the aquila, or eagle, into battle.*

▷ ***Roman soldiers*** *wore chainmail tunics with plumed bronze or iron helmets to make them look taller. They carried two basic weapons – spears were thrown as they closed with the enemy, while short swords were more effective in close combat. When attacking a fortress, legionaries formed a 'tortoise', with their long shields held above their heads and on each side. This hard shell protected them from any missiles hurled at them by the enemy.*

5000 BC 4500 BC 4000 BC 3500 BC 3000 BC 2500 BC

Empires of Africa

The first great African civilization, apart from ancient Egypt, grew up in Nubia (now in northern Sudan) around 2000 BC. Called the kingdom of Kush, it was conquered by Egypt in 1500 BC. However, in about 728 BC, Kush defeated Egypt and ruled that country for the next one hundred years.

△ ***The Nok*** *were named after the village where many terracotta figures, like the one shown above, were found. These sculptures give us valuable information about what the Nok were like. Many later West African cultures borrowed ideas from the Nok artists.*

In the 3rd century BC, the capital of Kush moved to Meroe, on the banks of the Nile. The city became an important centre of iron-working in the region.

Another early centre of iron-working was in western Africa (now in northern Nigeria) and developed from a group of farming settlements in about 600 BC. These people were known as the Nok and their culture flourished until about AD 200. The Nok mined iron and smelted it in clay furnaces. They used the iron to make farming tools, such as hoes and axes, to clear the surrounding land

EMPIRES OF AFRICA

From 2000 BC The kingdom of Kush begins in Nubia.

c. **900 BC** Kush gains its independence from Egypt.

c. **600 BC** The Nok culture begins in northern Nigeria.

c. **AD 200** The Nok culture comes to an end, but has a lasting effect on the artistic styles of Africa.

2nd century AD The kingdom of Axum (now in Ethiopia) rises to power.

AD 320–350 King Ezana rules Axum and converts to Christianity.

c. **AD 350** Axum overruns the city of Meroe and brings the Kushite kingdom to an end.

6th century AD Axum rules part of western Arabia.

c. **AD 1000** The kingdom of Axum collapses as a result of Islamic expansion.

△ ***This map shows*** *where the kingdoms of Kush and Axum and the Nok culture were located in Africa. Iron-working quickly spread from North Africa to West Africa during the 1st millennium BC.*

▷ ***Life in a Nok village*** *centred around farming and iron-working. To smelt iron, the iron ore (a metal-bearing rock) was put into a cylindrical pit furnace made of clay. Air was pumped in with bellows to raise the temperature inside the furnace. This separated the metal from the rock. Potters also used furnaces, or kilns, to fire their fine terracotta heads.*

◁ ***A group of Nubians*** *shown in a wall painting from an ancient Egyptian tomb. The Nubians are bringing gifts for the Egyptian pharaoh. Trade with Nubia was extremely important for Egypt and expeditions were sent to bring back gold, copper, cattle and slaves. From the countries beyond Nubia came exotic animals, such as monkeys and giraffes, as well as ivory, incense and ebony.*

▷ ***The people of Axum*** *built huge stone towers, called obelisks, up to 30 m tall. The towers were carved from single stone slabs and decorated with religious scenes. They may have been symbols of Axum's power or burial monuments for the royal family. Many remain standing today.*

for their crops. The Nok also made iron arrowheads, spears and knives, as well as stone tools and many distinctive clay sculptures and figures.

The kingdom of Axum rose to power in about the 2nd century AD. Located at the southern end of the Red Sea in northeast Africa (now in northern Ethiopia), Axum lay on an important trade route. The kingdom grew rich from buying and selling spices, incense and ivory. Its major trading partners were Arabia, Egypt and Persia. People also worked as farmers, builders and craftsmen. The people of Axum originally worshipped their own local gods, but in about AD 320, their king, Ezana, was converted to Christianity. By the end of the 5th century AD, most of the people of Axum had also become Christians and Christianity gradually spread to other parts of Africa. In the 6th century AD, Axum had conquered part of western Arabia. By AD 1000, however, the kingdom had collapsed as a new Islamic empire from Arabia expanded its influence.

Empires of India

In about 321 BC, a young prince, Chandragupta Maurya, founded an empire that stretched right across northern India, from the Hindu Kush in the west to Bengal in the east. This was the first Indian empire.

Chandragupta's grandson, Ashoka, who came to the throne in 269 BC, extended the empire still farther, until most of India came under Mauryan rule. In 260 BC, Ashoka's army fought a particularly bloody battle against the people of Kalinga in eastern India. Sickened by the killing and bloodshed he saw, Ashoka was filled with remorse. He converted to Buddhism and, from now on, vowed to follow its teachings of peace and non-violence. Ashoka travelled far and wide throughout his empire, listening to

△ ***The gateway to the great stupa of Sanchi**, part of which is shown here, was built during Ashoka's reign. Stupas are dome-shaped, Buddhist shrines. The first stupas contained relics of the Buddha himself. Ashoka built further stupas throughout his empire, in places sacred to the Buddha.*

◁ ***Exquisite wall paintings** cover the Buddhist cave temples at Ajanta in western India. The paintings date from the time of the Gupta empire, although the caves were carved out over thousands of years. Some paintings show scenes of everyday life and of life at court. Others show scenes from the life of the Buddha. Art, architecture and literature thrived under the Guptas.*

people's views and complaints and trying to improve their lot – a most unusual step for an emperor of that time. He also carved edicts on pillars and sent out special officers to explain his own policy of religious tolerance, respect for other people and peace.

After the collapse of the Mauryan empire in about 185 BC, India was divided into a number of smaller, independent states and kingdoms. Then, in AD 320, Chandra Gupta I, the ruler of the kingdom of Magadha, in the Ganges valley, enlarged his kingdom and, to increase his status and power, he married a princess from a respected royal family. The Gupta empire ruled northern India for the next 200 years. Chandra Gupta's son and heir, Samudra Gupta, extended his father's empire and increased its trading links. He was succeeded by Chandra Gupta II, the greatest of the Gupta kings. During his reign, India enjoyed a Golden Age.

Under the patronage of the Guptas, arts and literature flourished, as did science, medicine and mathematics. The greatest poets and artists of the time were invited to visit the splendid royal court. Hinduism replaced Buddhism as the major religion of the empire, and many new temples and shrines were built. Sanskrit, the sacred, classical language of India, became the language of the court.

HINDUISM

The Hindu religion began more than 4000 years ago as ideas from the Indus Valley civilization mingled with those of subsequent invaders. Under Ashoka, Buddhism became the major religion of India. Hinduism enjoyed a revival under the Guptas although Buddhism remained very strong. Today, more than three-quarters of Indians are Hindu. The main symbol of Hinduism is the word 'Om', the name of God, which is shown below.

EMPIRES OF INDIA

c. **563 BC** Birth of the Buddha in Lumbini, Nepal.

c. **483 BC** Death of the Buddha in Kushinagara, India.

c. **321 BC** Chandragupta seizes power and founds the Mauryan dynasty.

269–232 BC Reign of Ashoka Maurya, Chandragupta's grandson and the greatest ruler of ancient India.

△ ***Emperor Ashoka Maurya,*** *one of India's greatest ever rulers, has had a lasting effect on modern India. In Sarnath, where the Buddha first taught, Ashoka erected a tall pillar, topped with four lions and four wheels, the symbols of Buddhism. Today, this is the national emblem of India.*

260 BC Ashoka converts to Buddhism after the battle of Kalinga.

c. **185 BC** The Shunga dynasty replaces the Mauryans.

c. **AD 320** The beginnings of Gupta power emerges in the Ganges valley.

c. **AD 350–550** The Gupta empire brings a Golden Age of Hinduism to India.

AD 380–415 The reign of Chandra Gupta II, the greatest of the Gupta kings.

c. **AD 550** Hun invasions weaken Gupta power. The empire splits into smaller kingdoms.

◁ ***In early Buddhist art,*** *the Buddha himself was not shown. Instead he was represented by a symbol, such as footprints, a stupa, wheel, lotus flower, bodhi (sacred fig) tree or an umbrella held over an empty throne.*

The Middle Ages

Kings and conflicts 500–1400

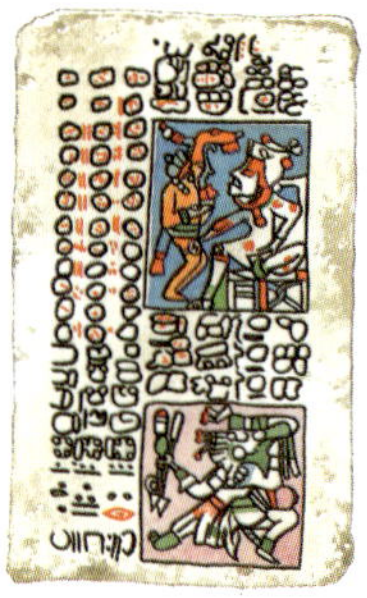

The period from about 500 to 1400 in Europe is known as the Middle Ages, or the medieval period. It began with the fall of the Roman empire and ended with the Renaissance, when a revival of art and learning swept through Europe.

The medieval period was an age of wars and conquests. Some wars were fought to gain more territory while others were wars of religion, fought between people of differing faiths in an age when religion dominated most people's lives. At this time China's civilization was far in advance of the rest of the world. Africa and America saw the emergence of strong, well-organized empires based on trade, while the spread of Islam from Arabia across the Middle East and into North Africa and Spain brought a new way of life to a vast area.

During the Middle Ages, ordinary people lived simply, as farmers in villages or as craftworkers in towns. Many built their own houses, made their own clothes and grew their own food. Poor people obeyed local landowners or lords, who in turn served a more powerful king or emperor. The rulers ordered castles and palaces, temples and cathedrals to be built. These huge stone buildings often took many years, even centuries, to construct.

Few people travelled far from their homes. Those who did venture into foreign lands included merchants, soldiers and a few bold explorers who wrote accounts of their travels. Few people could read or write, and learning was passed down by word of mouth. In Europe, the monasteries were centres of learning, while in Asia the Chinese and Arabs led the way in science and technology, medicine and astronomy.

THE MIDDLE AGES

500s Eastern Roman empire at its height.
529 First abbey in Europe: Monte Cassino (Italy).
600 Teotihuacan civilization in Mexico.
c. **610** Prophet Muhammad begins preaching in Arabia.
700 Mayan civilization at its height.
711 Moors invade Spain.
732 Battle of Poitiers checks Muslim advance in Europe.
750 Founding of Abbasid dynasty.
751 Founding of Carolingian dynasty.
787 Viking attacks on England begin.
800 Charlemagne crowned Holy Roman Emperor.
802 Founding of Khmer empire in Southeast Asia.
866 Vikings capture York in England.
900 Rise of Toltecs in Mexico; Ghana empire in Africa.
c. **1000** Vikings land in North America.
1066 William of Normandy defeats Harold to take English crown.
1096 First Crusade to the Holy Land.
1150 Temple of Angkor Wat (Cambodia) completed.
1206 Genghis Khan rules Mongols.
1215 Mongols invade China.
1249 First college of Oxford University founded.
1270 Eighth and last Crusade.
1271 Marco Polo travels to China from Venice.
1294 Death of Kublai Khan.
1300s Renaissance begins.
1325 Aztecs found Tenochtitlan.
1348–1349 Black Death ravages Europe.
1453 End of 100 Years War.
1453 Fall of Constantinople.
1454 Gutenberg's printing press.
1500 Inca empire at its peak.

Byzantium

For over 500 years, the Roman empire brought a unique way of life to a vast area of land. In 476, the western half of the empire collapsed, overrun by invading German tribes. In the east, however, Roman rule continued to flourish under what is called the Byzantine empire.

The old Greek city-port of Byzantium (modern-day Istanbul in Turkey) was the centre of the eastern Roman empire. The Romans renamed it Constantinople after the first Byzantine emperor, Constantine, and it became the seat of the Byzantine emperors and the centre of the eastern Christian church. Within the Byzantine empire, ancient Greek and Roman culture and learning was preserved. The Byzantines greatly appreciated music, poetry and art, and decorated their churches, such as Hagia Sophia in Constantinople, with highly complex and finely detailed frescoes (wall paintings) and mosaic pictures made from hundreds of tiny pieces of glass or stone fitted together.

The Byzantine empire reached its peak in the 500s, under the emperor Justinian. His general Belisarius won many battles and expanded the empire to include Italy,

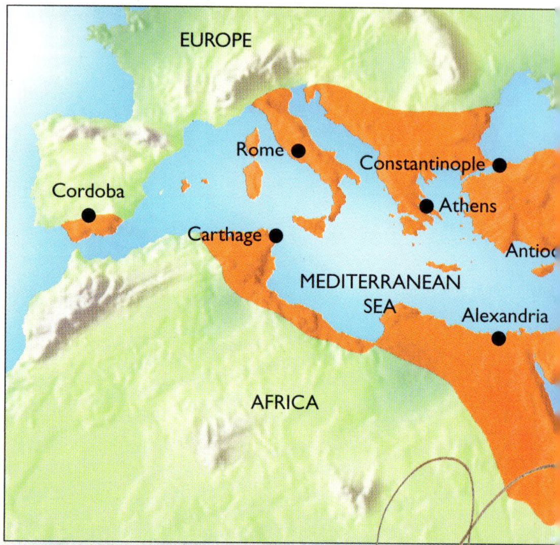

◁ ***Byzantine artists made exquisite mosaics,*** *pictures made from coloured stones and glass, and gold, to decorate walls of churches. This mosaic of the Magi, or wise men visiting Jesus, is in the Church of Sant' Apollinare Nuovo in Ravenna, Italy, and dates from the 6th century when the Byzantines occupied the city.*

▽ ***This map shows the Eastern Roman empire*** *at its height, in the 500s. From their capital at Byzantium, the Eastern Roman emperors controlled the eastern Mediterranean and an area that extended around the southern Mediterranean coast as far as North Africa and Spain.*

Greece, Turkey, parts of Spain, North Africa and Egypt. Justinian's wife, Theodora, helped him govern the empire and was almost as powerful as her husband. Justinian issued a code of laws which later formed the basis for the legal system in many European countries.

Most of the empire's people were farmers, living in small villages. Traders came to sell goods in the towns and Constantinople was a busy port and meeting place for peoples from as far away as Spain, China and Russia.

Warlike invaders from the east – Avars, Slavs, Bulgars – threatened this last Roman empire. Justinian's reign was a last flourish of imperial power. The invaders carved off chunks of territory and after Justinian's death in 565, Byzantium was never as strong again. The empire was weakened by frequent wars and eventually fell to the Turks in 1453.

△ ***The magnificent 6th-century church of Hagia Sophia*** *in Istanbul, later a mosque and now a museum. It took only six years to build and was completed in 537. The Muslim minarets were added later.*

◁ ***Chariot races were more than just thrilling entertainment.*** *Watched by the emperor, howling mobs in the Hippodrome cheered for Blues or Greens to show their support for one or other of the rival political factions in Byzantium. The Empress Theodora was an enthusiastic Green supporter.*

BYZANTIUM

330 Constantinople is founded.
408 Emperor Theodosius begins building a great wall to protect Constantinople.
445 Attila the Hun attacks, but is paid to go away.
476 Fall of the western empire.
***c.* 501** A long series of wars with Persia begins.
527–565 Reign of Justinian I.
678 An Arab siege of Constantinople is defeated.
900s Second golden age. The Balkans and Russia come under Byzantine influence.

△ ***Constantine the Great*** *(275–337) was the first Christian emperor of Rome. He moved the empire's capital from Rome to Byzantium and renamed it Constantinople.*

1054 Christian church in Constantinople breaks with church in Rome.
1081 Alexius I Comnenus seizes power and introduces government reforms.
1200 Empire begins to break up under attacks from Turks and Bulgarians.
1204 Constantinople is sacked by Crusaders.
1341–54 Civil war in the empire.
1453 The Turks capture Constantinople – end of the Byzantine empire.

The Franks

THE FRANKS

241 First mention of Franks, fighting the future Roman emperor Aurelian in Mainz.
350 Franks brought under Roman rule.
428 Salian Franks (living in the Netherlands and lower Rhineland) throw off Roman rule and invade Gaul, led by King Chlodio. His successor is Merovich.
451 Franks join with Romans to defeat Attila the Hun at the battle of Châlons.
***c.* 466** Clovis born and in 481 succeeds his father Childeric as king.
486 Franks defeat the last great Roman army in the West, at the battle of Soissons.
496 Clovis defeats the Alemanni near the river Seine.
506 Franks defeat the Visigoths.
511 Clovis dies.
540 Franks control most of Gaul and also lands farther east in what is now Germany.
600 Austrasians and Neustrians struggle for supremacy.
687 After the battle of Tertry against the Neustrians, the Austrasian Pepin of Herstal becomes the most powerful Frankish leader.
732 Charles Martel defeats the Muslim army at the battle of Poitiers.
751 Last of the Merovingian kings, Childeric III, is overthrown. Pepin the Short (Charlemagne's father) becomes king and founds the Carolingian dynasty.

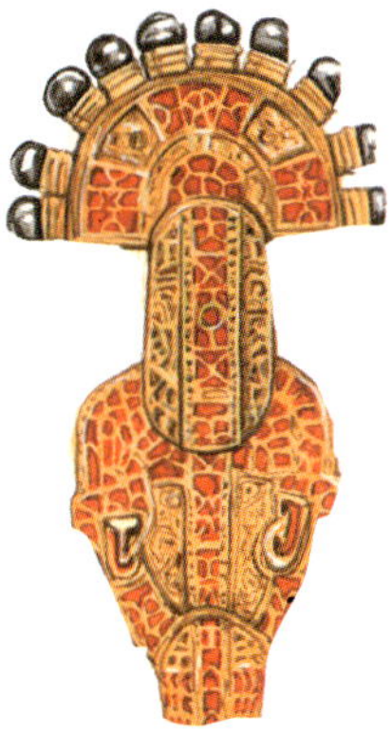

The Franks were the strongest of all the western European peoples who struggled for land and power after the end of the Roman empire in 476.

Under their first great leader, Clovis, the Franks spread out from their homeland around the river Rhine (in what is now Germany). They fought their neighbours, such as the Visigoths and Burgundians, until, by 540, they had conquered most of the old Roman province of Gaul (modern France, which is named after the Franks).

Clovis defeated rival chieftains to bring all the Frankish tribes under his control. His family became known as the Merovingian dynasty, after his grandfather Merovich. Clovis became a Christian and ruled from Paris, governing his lands through Church bishops and noblemen. These nobles or lords held estates known as manors, on which peasants ploughed the fields. In battle, the Franks used a curved throwing axe called a *francisca* and a two-handed broadsword called a *scramasax*. Frankish leaders were always ready to defend their estates and to conquer new lands.

This eagerness to ride into battle meant that the nobles and lords needed servants for military service. In return for this service, the servants were granted land – the beginnings of feudalism (see pages 86–87). Rival families jockeyed for the king's favour and in the 600s two rival clans, whose members held the important position of Mayor of the Royal Palace, fought for power.

▷ ***Two sides of a Frankish stone monument,*** *possibly a gravestone. The carving on one side (near right) shows a warrior with a long broadsword, a favourite weapon of the Franks.*

▽ ***The Franks were farmers.*** *They tilled their fields in strips, using wheeled ploughs pulled by oxen, which meant they could farm land not farmed before.*

The winners were the Austrasians, who ousted the Neustrians, and their chief Pepin of Herstal founded a new ruling family.

The Franks went on fighting. Pepin's son Charles Martel, known as the Hammer, won an historic battle at Poitiers against Muslim invaders in 732 (see pages 70–71). Although his title was Mayor of the Palace, Martel was effectively king, and expanded Frankish territory. His defeat of the Muslims checked the advance of Islam into central Europe. Martel's son Pepin the Short, established the new Carolingian dynasty. He was the first Frankish king to be anointed by the pope, in 754. The greatest of the Frankish rulers was Pepin's son, the emperor Charlemagne (see pages 76–77).

△ ***Franks riding to battle.*** *These tough warriors, with their shaven heads and topknots, are wearing light mail armour. They were formidable cavalry fighters, whose loyalty was rewarded with booty from conquests. Frankish armies defeated Romans, Gauls, Visigoths and others who tried to halt their expansion.*

△ ***An ivory carving shows Gregory the Great,*** *pope from 590 to 604. From the time of Clovis, the Franks were Christian, and the power of the Pope and his bishops as local rulers, alongside nobles, continued in Frankish lands.*

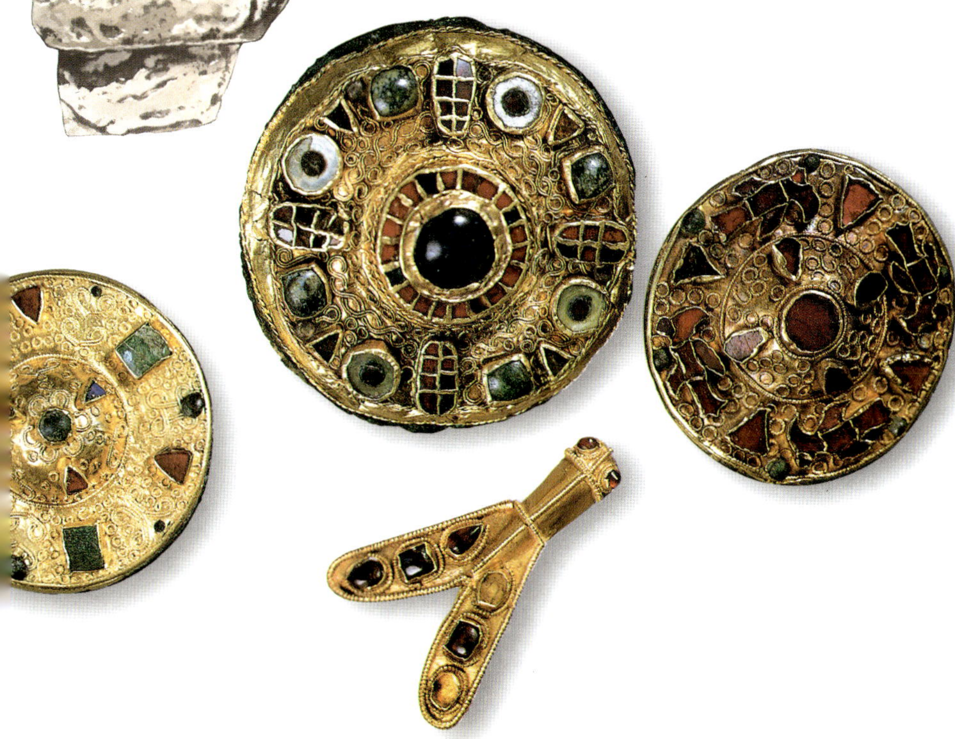

◁ ***Examples of fine metalwork from the Frankish period.*** *The Franks were skilled craftworkers as well as soldiers. These gold and enamel buckles, dating from the 6th–7th centuries, would have been worn by a rich Frankish noble or warrior chief.*

The Rise of Islam

The religion of Islam was directly influenced in the early 600s by the prophet Muhammad. The religion he preached changed the course of history, by uniting the peoples of Arabia to form a huge Arab empire that stretched almost from China to the border of France.

In the early 7th century, the Arab peoples were not united in any way. Some farmed the land while others were traders crossing the desert with camel-drawn caravans. At this time they all worshiped different gods. Then, in about 610, an Arab merchant named Muhammad preached a new religion, Islam, which means "submission to the will of God". According to Muslim belief, Muhammad was sent by God as a messenger. Muhammad was well respected in his home town of Mecca and his influence grew but many Meccans resented his new teaching and began to persecute him and his followers. In 622 he was driven out of Mecca and was invited to move to Yathrib (now Medina). His journey there is commemorated as the Hegira, which begins the Muslim calendar. Muhammad had several religious revelations and his teachings were written down in the Koran, the holy book of Islam. He set out religious laws that included five daily prayers and a month of fasting.

From 624 Muhammad and his followers had to fight their enemies. In 630 they captured Mecca, and smashed the pagan idols in the Kaaba, the holiest shrine in the city. Muhammad continued to preach and live simply.

TOLERATION OF JEWS

Muslims, Christians and Jews got on well in many parts of the Islamic world, for example in Spain where the three communities coexisted peacefully after the Muslim conquest in 711. Muslim rulers tolerated Jewish and Christian minority communities in their lands because in the teachings and beliefs of the three religions there is much that is shared and especially a faith in one true God.

◁ ***Muhammad's flight,*** *or emigration, from Mecca to Medina became a source of inspiration to his followers. Here he hides with only a spider for company. The episode, known as the Hegira, marks the start of the Islamic calendar (July 16, 622 in the Christian calendar).*

▽ ***Muslim pilgrims walking around the Kaaba,*** *the most holy shrine in Mecca. The Kaaba is believed to contain the Black Stone which was given to Ishmael by the angel Gabriel.*

When he died in 632, Muhammad left a daughter, Fatima, but no son and he did not name anyone to succeed him. His friend and father-in-law, Abu Bakr, was chosen as first caliph (successor), but an argument soon broke out between Muhammad's followers. Some, known as Shiites, thought only the descendants of Fatima and her husband, Ali, should succeed Muhammad. Others, who came to be known as Sunnis, believed that any follower of Islam could succeed Muhammad. The argument soon became political as well as religious and has not been settled to this day.

Muhammad is presented as reflecting an ideal: courageous, resolute, yet gentle. He preached a new way of worship and created a state from a collection of Arab tribes. The new Muslim state was soon to defeat much larger empires and create a new and powerful force in the world.

◁ ***The Dome of the Rock in Jerusalem stands over the rock*** *from which, Muslims believe, Muhammad ascended to heaven with the angel Gabriel to speak with God before returning to earth to spread the new religion of Islam. It was built as a shrine for pilgrims, between 685 and 691. It stands on Temple Mount, and is the oldest surviving monument.*

لا إله إلا الله محمد رسول الله

◁ ***The Koran*** *set out rules to reform society. For example, it told Muslim believers to protect the poor and respect women. It still forms the basis of many laws in Muslim countries today.*

THE RISE OF ISLAM

570 Probable date of Muhammad's birth.
595 Probable date of Muhammad's marriage to Khadijah.
610 Muhammad begins preaching in Mecca.
619 Khadijah dies.
622 Flight to Yathrib (Medina), known as the Hegira. This episode marks the start of the Islamic calendar.
624 Battle of Badr, when the Muslims defeated the Meccans.
625 Muhammad's teachings are written down in the Koran, the holy book of Islam.
627 Meccans besiege Medina but fail to capture the city.
628 Peace agreement made, then broken by Meccans.
630 Muhammad leads an army into Mecca capturing the city and smashing the pagan idols there.
632 Muhammad dies. Abu Bakr becomes the first caliph, but other Muslims choose Ali as their leader. Islam begins to spread beyond Arabia.
634 Before his death, Abu Bakr, the first caliph, completes conquest of Arabia. Abu Bakr is succeeded by Omar.

◁ ***Women in traditional dress*** *outside the great Ummayad Mosque in Damascus, one of the most important cities in the history of the Islamic world.*

The Spread of Islam

After Muhammad's death, his followers spread Islam by preaching and by conquest. By the 700s, Muslims controlled most of the Middle East and North Africa.

Islam spread quickly under the influence of the Muslim leader, Abu Bakr. Abu Bakr died in 634 but the next caliph, Omar, continued the spread of Islam. After Omar was murdered, the Ummayad family fought for power against the Shiites. The Shiite leader Ali was murdered in 661 and the Ummayads controlled the growing Islamic empire from their capital, Damascus, in Syria.

The Byzantine and Persian empires were much too weak to withstand the Muslim attacks. After Syria and Palestine, the Muslims then conquered Egypt and Persia.

△ ***A Muslim astronomer.*** *Muslim astronomers observed the stars. Scholars preserved the ideas of the Greek astronomer, Ptolemy, about the universe.*

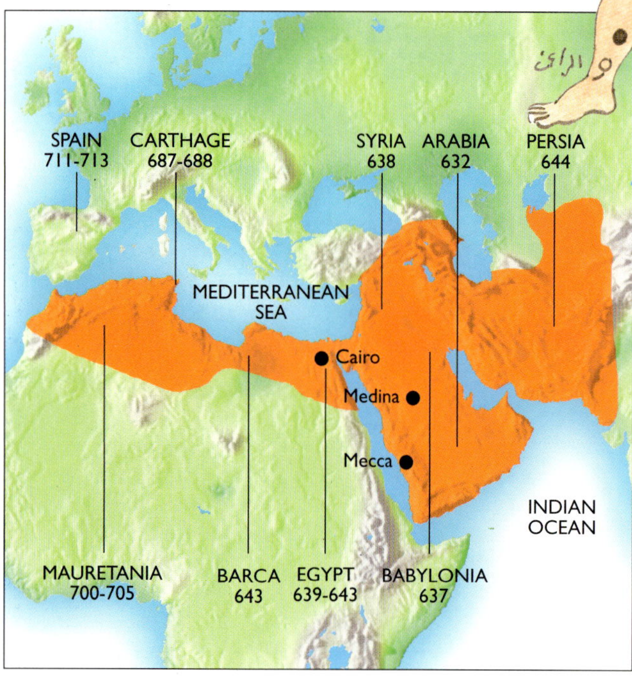

△ ***Islamic conquests beyond Arabia*** *began in 634. In 81 years the new religion had spread from Persia in the east to southern Spain in the west.*

▽ ***What we call Arabic numerals*** *were developed from the Hindu number-system, through Arab trade with India and Muslim study of Greek texts. Arab numerals made maths easier, and spread across Europe.*

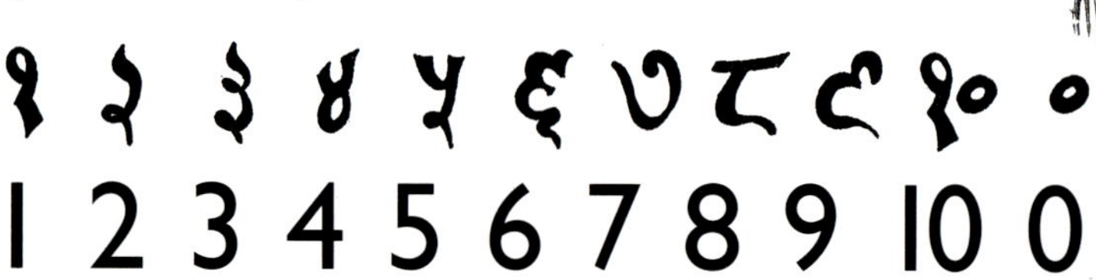

They moved east into Afghanistan and India. By 700 most of coastal North Africa was in Muslim hands and there was a Muslim fleet of warships in the Mediterranean Sea.

Muslims from Morocco invaded southern Spain, but any further advance into Europe was halted by the Frankish army of Charles Martel in 732.

Ummayad rule lasted until the mid 700s when Abu al-Abbas, a descendant of Muhammad, founded a new dynasty, the Abbasids, and moved the capital to Baghdad (in what is now Iraq). Baghdad became the centre of a rich new Islamic civilization, blending many cultures. Islam was remarkably successful. Arabic was spoken and written throughout the Islamic world, apart from Persia, so it was easy for people to trade and exchange ideas. By 786 the court of the caliph Harun al-Rashid (famous because of the stories about him in *The Thousand and One Nights)* at Baghdad was a centre for Arab science and learning, and there were Islamic mosques from Afghanistan to Spain.

◁ ***The Alhambra*** *in Granada, Spain, was built by Muslim and Christian builders between 1248 and 1354.*

△ ***Harun al-Rashid*** *(766–806) was caliph from 786. The power of the Abbasid dynasty of caliphs peaked during his reign.*

◁ ***A European view of life behind the palace doors*** *of a Muslim ruler. Islam permitted a man to have four wives but only if he guaranteed to treat them all equally. It also gave women rights to property, to custody of their children, and to maintenance after divorce.*

THE SPREAD OF ISLAM

638 Syria and Jerusalem are conquered by Muslim armies.

642 Egypt is conquered.

643 Muslims defeat the Persians.

644 Caliph Omar is murdered and is succeeded by Othman, leader of the Ummayad family.

655 Arabs defeat Byzantines in a sea battle off the coast of Egypt.

656 Othman is murdered and the Shiite leader Ali becomes caliph.

661 Ali is murdered. Ummayads now in full control.

661 Caliph Muawiya moves the Islamic capital from Mecca to Damascus.

685–705 Caliph Abdalmalik sets up a new government system for the empire.

698 Arabs capture Carthage in North Africa.

711 Moors (Arabs and Berbers from Morocco) end Visigoth rule in southern Spain.

732 Abd-al-Rahman, ruler of Spain, invades France but is defeated at Poitiers by Frankish army led by Charles Martel.

750 Abbasid dynasty is founded. Arab empire is at its greatest extent stretching from the borders of France to the river Talas in central Asia.

756 The last Ummayad ruler flees from Damascus and sets up a new caliphate at Cordoba in Spain.

762 Abbasids make Baghdad the capital of Islamic empire.

786 Harun al-Rashid, the fifth Abbasid caliph, brings a new political unity to the Islamic empire.

American Civilizations

▽ ***A massive stone figure at Tiahuanaco, in Bolivia.*** *This was the first planned city in the Andes. Many such figures have been found at the site.*

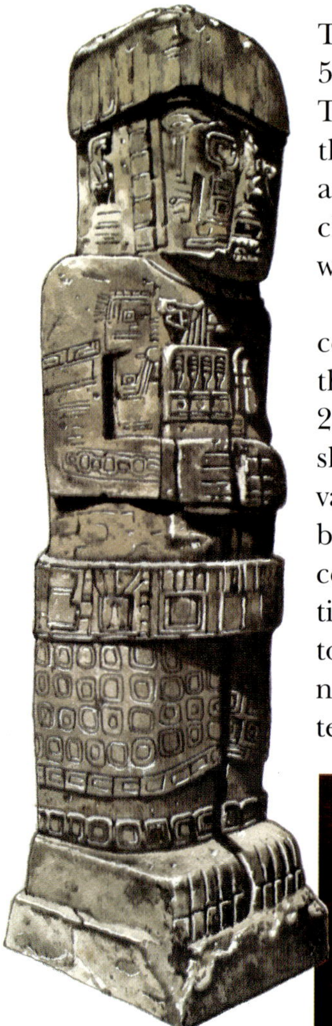

Many impressive civilizations flourished in North and South America. The people of these civilizations built cliff-top palaces, huge earth mounds and pyramid temples, although they had no wheeled vehicles. A few fragments of their civilizations' achievements still survive today.

The Anasazi people lived in what is now the southwestern United States. They grew corn and built amazing apartment blocks in which as many as 5,000 people shared cliff houses called pueblos with hundreds of rooms. Their descendants were known as the Pueblo. Also in the southwest lived the Hohokam people, who dug irrigation canals to water their crops and, like the Anasazi, wove cotton cloth and made decorated clay pottery. Farther east, the Mississippian people built well-planned towns of single-family houses.

Around AD 700 the largest city in America was in central Mexico. Teotihuacan was a city of more than 100,000 people containing 600 pyramids, 2,000 apartment blocks and thousands of craft shops. People had lived in the Teotihuacan valley since about 500 BC, growing crops and building pyramid temples from stone blocks cemented together with clay. Teotihuacan's time of greatest power was from about AD 350 to 750. After that it was overshadowed by a new power, the Toltecs who built their own temple-city at Tula.

▷ ***The Tlalocan mural is one*** *of the best known wall-paintings at the Mexican temple-city of Teotihuacan. It shows Tlaloc, the god of rain and harvests. Here he is shown as a source of fertility. Teotihuacan, "the city of the gods", was an important city for over 600 years.*

1000 1100 1200 1300 1400

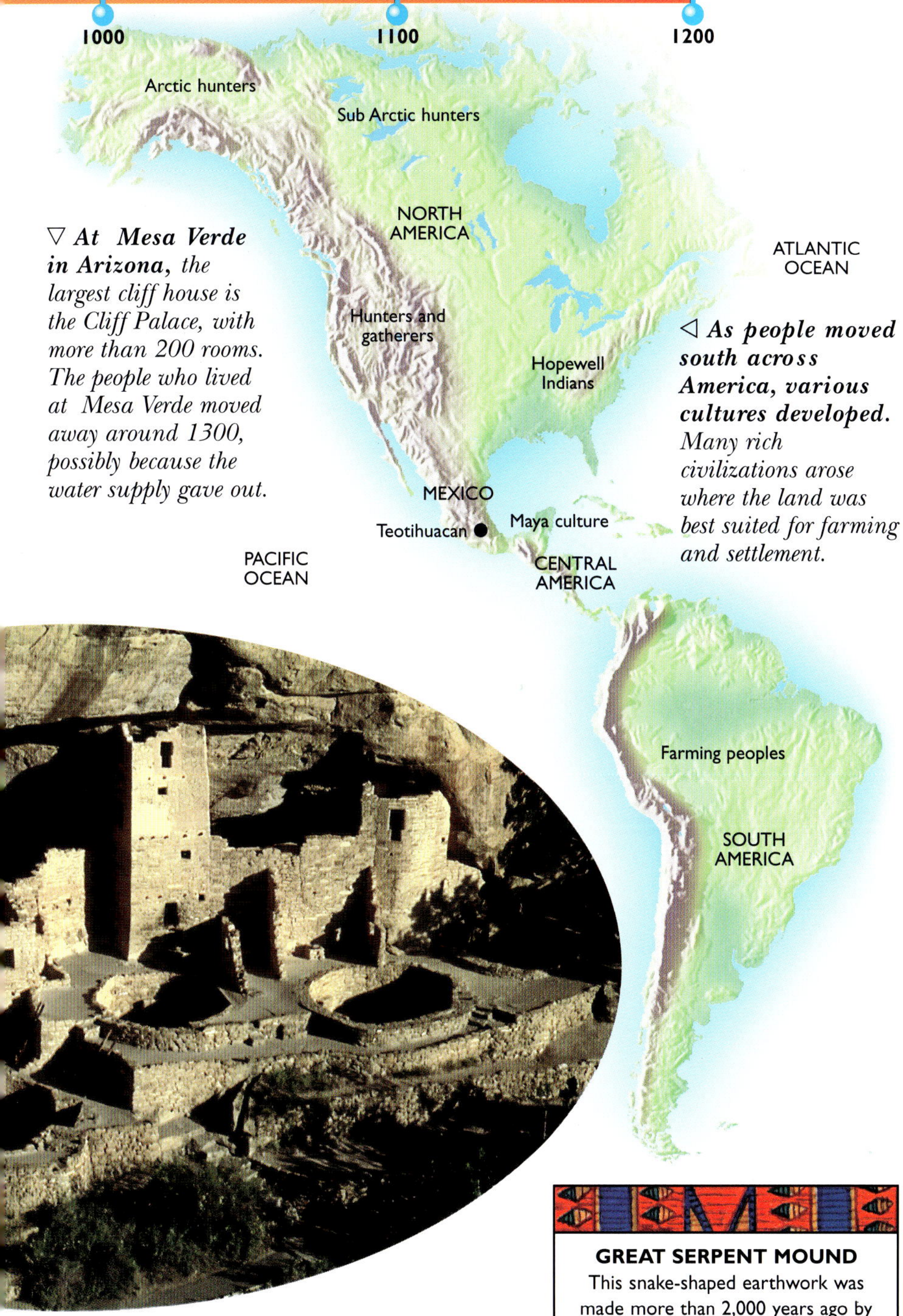

◁ ***As people moved south across America, various cultures developed.*** *Many rich civilizations arose where the land was best suited for farming and settlement.*

▽ ***At Mesa Verde in Arizona,*** *the largest cliff house is the Cliff Palace, with more than 200 rooms. The people who lived at Mesa Verde moved away around 1300, possibly because the water supply gave out.*

At 3,500 metres, high in the Andes, South America, was the city of Tiahuanaco, which flourished between 500 and 1000. Here people used llamas as pack animals and paddled reed boats on Lake Titicaca. Other city-states of the Andes, such as Huari in Peru, were greatly influenced by Tiahuanaco. Most South Americans, like the Mochica of Peru, built houses and temples of mud brick (adobe). The Nazca of Peru marked out giant pictures in the desert with furrows and stones – amazing animal designs that are best seen from the air!

GREAT SERPENT MOUND

This snake-shaped earthwork was made more than 2,000 years ago by the Adena people of Ohio, in the United States. It is about 400 metres long and a little over 1 metre above ground level. The mound was a sacred burial place, and the snake grew bigger as more burials were added to it. Similar mounds were built by later people, including the Hopewell (about 300 BC to AD 200).

AMERICAN CIVILIZATIONS

600 Teotihuacan (Mexico) is at its most powerful. The Huari state begins its rise in the Peruvian Andes. Tiahuanaco (Bolivia) is at its strongest.

700 Early Anasazi culture develops in southwestern USA. The Anasazi begin to build multi-storey houses.

750 Teotihuacan is destroyed. About this time, Tiahuanaco also declines.

800 Nazcas of Peru lose their independence after the Huari move into their lands.

900 Rise of Toltecs in Mexico.

968 Toltecs set up their capital at Tula.

1000 Mississippian culture at its height; its main city is Cahokia in what is now Illinois, USA.

1100 Rise of the Chimu kingdom in Peru.

Late 1100s End of the Toltec state; Tula is destroyed.

1200s The Cliff Palace is built at Mesa Verde in Colorado, USA.

△ ***The peoples of the Andes used llamas*** *to carry loads. These sure-footed, hardy animals also provided wool and meat.*

The Maya

The Maya lived in Central America. Their civilization lasted more than 700 years and they built huge cities with magnificent stone temples that can still be seen today.

The Maya were at their most powerful from about 200 to 900, although their culture lasted until the Spanish conquest of Central America in the early 1500s. The Maya lived in well organized city-states, each with its own ruler who controlled trade in obsidian, cacao, cotton and other goods and fought wars with neighbouring city-states. Bird-catchers traded colourful feathers, which were used to make headdresses. In the countryside, farmers cleared forest land and terraced the hillsides to grow beans, corn and squash. They raised turkeys and kept bees, but the Maya had no domestic animals other than dogs and no vehicles other than toy carts.

The largest Mayan city was Tikal, in what is now Guatemala, with a population of 60,000. Crowds filled the large squares around the pyramid-temples to watch ceremonies conducted by priests, who studied the heavens to predict eclipses of the Moon and Sun. Religion was important to the Mayas and, to win favours from their many gods, they made sacrifices. Mostly they sacrificed animals but they also threw human victims into sacred wells.

The Maya played a sacred ball-game, in which players hit a rubber ball through a stone ring with their hips.

THE MAYA

3372 BC First date in Mayan calendar.

400 BC By this time the Maya had already built several large pyramid-temples, like those at Tikal in Guatemala.

AD 250 Start of the great or classic period of Mayan civilization. The Maya borrow some of their ideas from the people of Teotihuacan.

***c.* 700** Mayan cities reach greatest prosperity.

***c.* 900** Mayan civilization declines, possibly caused by disease or crop failures. Some major Mayan towns are abandoned. People move from the lowlands to the highlands of Mexico and Guatemala and build new cities there.

900 Chichén Itzá becomes the most important Mayan city. Unlike earlier cities, it is governed by a council, not by a single ruler.

990 Toltec people take over Chichén Itzá.

***c.* 1250** Maya culture revives: Chichén Itzá is replaced by Mayapan as the chief Mayan city.

1440 Rebellion against Mayapan rulers by some other cities. Maya unity weakened as states fight one another.

1517 Start of Spanish conquest of Maya lands. By the mid 1500s all the Maya are ruled by Spain.

△ ***A Mayan calendar.*** *The Mayan number system was based on 20, and their farmers' calendar had 18 months of 20 days each.*

▽ ***A Mayan ruler enters his city on a litter.*** *Each city ruler was a god-king. Everyone had to worship him and offer tribute in the form of goods, food (such as corn), or work (such as temple building). Sculptures and wall-paintings celebrated royal triumphs, listed family trees, and linked kings with the mighty gods.*

1000 1100 1200 1300 1400

△ ***The Maya settled in a region*** *of what is now Mexico from the Yucatan peninsula in the north to the Pacific coast in the south. There were some 50 states, each with its own ruler and sacred city, such as Chichén Itzá, Tikal and Copán.*

▽ ***A jadeite mask made by a Mayan artist.*** *Jadeite is a hard, green gemstone, highly valued by pre-Columbian Americans. The Maya were skilful sculptors and painters. Much of their art was religious and this mask may have been used by a priest during a ceremony.*

They invented the first writing in America, and wrote codexes (folding books)with pages of tree bark, three of which survive. They also set up tall carved stones to commemorate dates and important events. Their number system was based on 20 (not 10, like ours) and they had two calendars, one with 360 days and another (associated with the Mayan gods) that had 260 days. Many people in Mexico still speak Mayan languages today.

Charlemagne

CHARLEMAGNE

742 Probable date of birth of Charlemagne.
752 Anointed king with brother Carloman by the Pope.
768 Charlemagne's father, Pepin the Short, dies.
771 Charlemagne becomes sole ruler of the Franks.
772 Charlemagne starts war with Saxons and converts them to Christianity.
774 Makes Lombardy (Italy) part of his empire.
778 Charlemagne invades Spain to fight Muslims but on its return, the Frankish army is attacked by the Basques at the battle of Roncesvalles in the Pyrenees.
782 Alcuin, an English monk, comes to the palace school at Charlemagne's court.
788 Wars with Lombards, Bavarians, Avars, Bretons and other peoples.
800 Charlemagne is crowned Emperor of the West by Pope Leo III on Christmas Day. Frankish rule widens the development of the feudal system as a means to defend Charlemagne's lands.
804 Last of Charlemagne's 18 campaigns against the Saxons.
808 Charlemagne fights the Danes.
814 Charlemagne dies. His son, Louis the Pious, succeeds, but is not as strong a ruler.
817 The empire is split between Louis's sons Lothair, Pepin and Louis the German. Later a fourth son, Charles the Bald, receives a share.

▷ ***Charlemagne's empire*** *grew from the lands of Austrasia (France and Germany) he inherited from his father Pepin in 768 and his brother in 771 (in orange on the map). The Frankish empire was at its biggest extent soon after (orange and red).*

Charles I, King of the Franks was known as Charlemagne (Charles the Great). He founded the Holy Roman empire and was regarded by many people as the ideal ruler and is still well known today.

Charlemagne was born in 742. His father was King Pepin, son of the famous soldier, Charles Martel, and founder of the new Frankish ruling family (later called the Carolingian dynasty, after Charlemagne). In 768 Pepin died, leaving his kingdom to his sons Carloman and Charlemagne. When Carloman died, Charlemagne was left in sole control.

A very tall man, convinced of his own destiny, Charlemagne had learned much from his ruthless warrior father. He led his armies out of the Frankish homeland of France into what are now the Netherlands, Germany and Italy. He was a Christian and wherever he conquered non-believers, such as the Saxons of Germany and the Avars of Hungary, he forced them to become Christians and to take part in mass baptisms.

There was more to Charlemagne than simply waging wars of conquest. Although uneducated, he had great respect for scholarship.

His capital at Aachen was the glittering centre of his empire, with a splendid palace and heated swimming pool, but the emperor himself dressed and lived simply. He spoke Latin and Greek, had books read aloud to him and invited famous scholars like Alcuin of York to his court to train teachers and to transcribe ancient Roman writings.

Charlemagne's position as Europe's strongest leader was recognized in 800 when the Pope crowned him Holy Roman emperor. After he died in 814, his empire was weakened by attacks and civil wars, and was soon split between his three grandsons. However, his fame made him a legend and the Holy Roman empire that he founded lasted in one form or another until 1806.

Charlemagne's life story was written by a scholar named Einhard, at the request of the emperor's son, Louis the Pious. After Charlemagne's death, many stories were written about him, for example a skirmish during his retreat from a campaign in Spain in 778 became the subject of the medieval epic poem *The Song of Roland.*

▽ ***Charlemagne's tomb*** *at the imperial capital, Aachen, dates from 1215 and is decorated in gold and precious stones. Artists working 400 years after Charlemagne's death had written descriptions of his appearance, but no likeness of him to copy.*

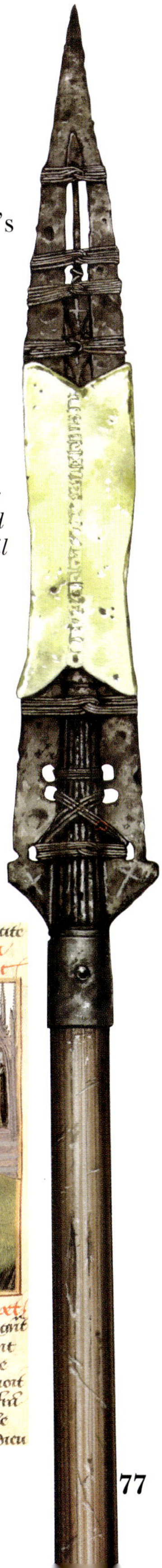

▷ ***The iron lance of the Holy Roman emperors*** *was a holy relic as well as a symbol of power. Around the spearpoint is a gold sheath stretched over a nail reputedly from Jesus's cross, as recorded by the inscription that runs along it.*

▽ ***A French book illustration*** *of the 15th century shows Hugh Capet, king of France from 987 to 996, receiving the keys of the town of Laon. Hugh Capet founded the new Capetian dynasty on the death of the last Carolingian ruler, Louis V. The Carolingians traced their ancestry back to Charlemagne.*

The Khmer Empire

Between the 9th and the 15th centuries, the Khmer empire of Cambodia dominated Southeast Asia. The Khmers were highly skilled builders and engineers, constructing cities with massive temple complexes, palaces, lakes and canals.

Before the Khmer empire was established in 802, two earlier Khmer states had ruled the region – the first was called Funan, which, from 600, was followed by Chenla. The Khmer empire was the creation of a strong king named Jayavarman I, who united people living in what are now parts of Cambodia, Thailand, Laos and Vietnam. He and his successors were worshipped as gods and as such were responsible for the well-being of their people.

The ancient books of the Khmers have long since been destroyed, so what we know about them comes mostly from Chinese writings. The Chinese bought spices and rhinoceros horns from the Khmers. There are also many stone carvings in the ruins of the Khmers' greatest buildings, in the temple of Angkor Wat and in the city of Angkor Thom. These carvings show people going about their everyday activities, as well as recording sacred stories and victories in battle.

△ ***Trumpeting elephants** with archers on their backs caused panic among their enemies as the Khmer armies went to war. Bells and gongs added to the tumult as the Khmers attacked. The Khmers held on to their conquests until they in turn were conquered, by invaders from Thailand. Costly building schemes contributed to their downfall.*

▷***The Temple of Angkor Wat** (about 1113 to 1150) is the largest of the temples built in the Khmer lands. It measures 1,555 metres by 1,372 metres, and its central towers rise to 65 metres high. The temple was dedicated to the Hindu god, Vishnu, but became a Buddhist shrine in the 1500s.*

▷ ***At the height of their power, the Khmer rulers*** *controlled much of what are now Laos, Thailand and Vietnam, with the fertile farmlands around the Mekong River and Lake Tonle Sap.*

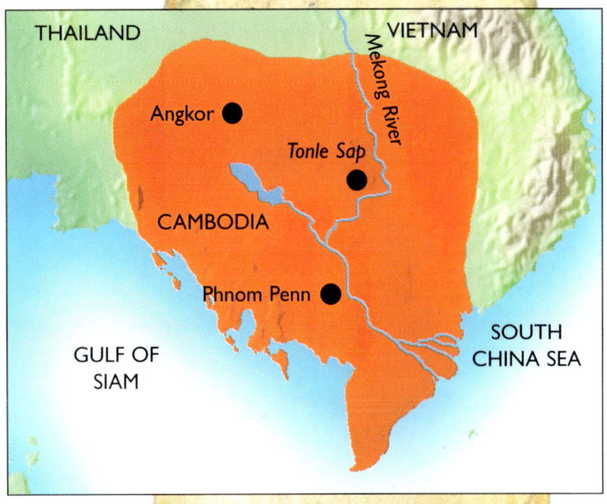

The Khmers built their wealth on rice growing. They dug irrigation ditches to water their rice fields and were able to grow three crops a year. Never far from water, they built houses on stilts along riverbanks and around the shores of the lake called Tonle Sap.

The Khmer empire reached its height in the reign of Jayavarman VII (1181–1220) – a time of energetic construction of roads, hospitals and temples. Like all Khmer kings, he was a Hindu, although most of the people in the empire were Buddhists. The Khmers were fierce warriors, who used trained war elephants to terrify their enemies. This worked well until the 1400s when they, in turn, were overrun by the Thais. The great city and temple at Angkor were abandoned to the jungle.

The ruler who built Angkor Wat was Surayavarman II, leader of the Khmers from 1113 to about 1150. He was a successful war leader who fought in Thailand and Vietnam. When new, his great temple, with its gilded towers and water-filled moats, must have been a spectacular sight.

THE KHMER EMPIRE

802 King Jayavarman I founds the Khmer empire.
900 Early stages of building the city of Angkor Thom (then called Yasodharapura).
1113–1150 Construction of the temple of Angkor Wat.
1181 Start of reign of King Jayavarman VII (to 1220).
1300s Khmer empire is weakened by extravagant building schemes, quarrels within the royal family and wars with the Thais.
1431 Thai army captures Angkor. End of the Khmer empire. A smaller Khmer kingdom lasts until 1863, when the French take control of Cambodia and Angkor Wat is rediscovered.

▽ ***Traditional houses in Cambodia,*** *on stilts, as protection from flooding. Around Lake Tonle Sap, the largest freshwater lake in Southeast Asia, people still live by fishing and trading by boat.*

The Vikings

THE VIKINGS

Late 700s The trading town of Hedeby in Denmark is founded.

841 Vikings found Dublin on east coast of Ireland.

850 Probable date of the Oseberg ship burial in Oslo Fiord, Norway; it is the richest Viking ship-burial so far found.

***c.* 860** Vikings begin to settle in the Baltic region. Vikings rule Novgorod in Russia.

***c.* 861** Ingolf is the first Viking to reach Iceland.

862 Vikings led by Rurik are invited by the Slavic and Finnish peoples of north Russia to rule them.

874 First Viking settlers reach Iceland.

900s Viking traders visit Constantinople, which they call Miklagaard.

960 King Harald Bluetooth of Denmark becomes a Christian.

982 Erik the Red reaches Greenland and founds settlement.

***c.* 1000** Erik's son, Leif Eriksson, lands in North America and calls the new land Vinland. But the Vikings never succeed in making a permanent settlement there.

1000 Jorvik is a prosperous town of about 10,000 people, the biggest Viking settlement in England.

1030 At the end of the reign of King Olaf the Holy, Norway is Christian.

1100s Swedish Vikings are the last to give up their old gods and convert to Christianity.

The Vikings set sail from their homelands in Scandinavia (Norway, Sweden and Denmark) to raid the coasts and rivers of Europe, reaching to the Mediterranean and the Black seas. But not all the Vikings were raiders – many were peaceful farmers and traders who chose to settle in the new lands.

The Vikings' homelands in Scandinavia had mountains and forests, but little good farmland. Most Vikings lived close to the sea, tending small fields where they grew rye, barley, wheat and oats, and vegetables such as turnips and carrots. They kept cattle and sheep, and caught fish in the rivers and fiords. Traders travelled on horseback or by boat to market towns like Kaupang in Norway or Hedeby in Denmark, to sell furs, reindeer antlers and walrus ivory in exchange for weapons, jewels and pottery.

Viking families lived in houses made of wood, stone or turf. Smoke from the cooking fire found its way out through a hole in the roof, and in the smoky darkness people sat at wooden benches and tables to eat. Around the fire they played dice games and told stories. The Vikings loved telling stories, especially about their heroes and gods. The most important god was Odin the wise and one-eyed, but the most popular was Thor, the thunder god, whose symbol was a hammer.

▷ ***Many Vikings lived on small farms,*** *often near to rivers or the sea. They planted cereals and vegetables, and kept pigs, cows, goats and sheep.*

Everyone worked hard. A Viking farmer often had thralls (slaves) to help with the work, but most men were karls (freemen). The leader of each community was the richest landowner or jarl, who was expected to share his wealth with his followers, by feasting and entertaining them in his great hall. The most powerful jarls in each country became King Viking leaders and tried to prevent quarrels becoming bitter blood-feuds between families. They also led bands of warriors on voyages.

The Vikings grew rich through trade and agriculture and as the population increased, farmland became increasingly scarce. From the late 700s, the Vikings began to venture from their homelands in search of better farmland and more riches.

Vikings were tough. They were used to hardship. They enjoyed huge meals, stirring tales of heroes, and physical sports such as wrestling, horse fights and ice skating.

THE THING

The Viking law court was called the Thing. It was a meeting of local people held every year, and normally lasted for several days. Any freeman who had a complaint or an argument to settle could speak at the Thing. His neighbours would listen to his complaint or to both sides of a disagreement, and then give a judgement. A person refusing to obey the Thing's verdict became an outlaw – anyone could kill them.

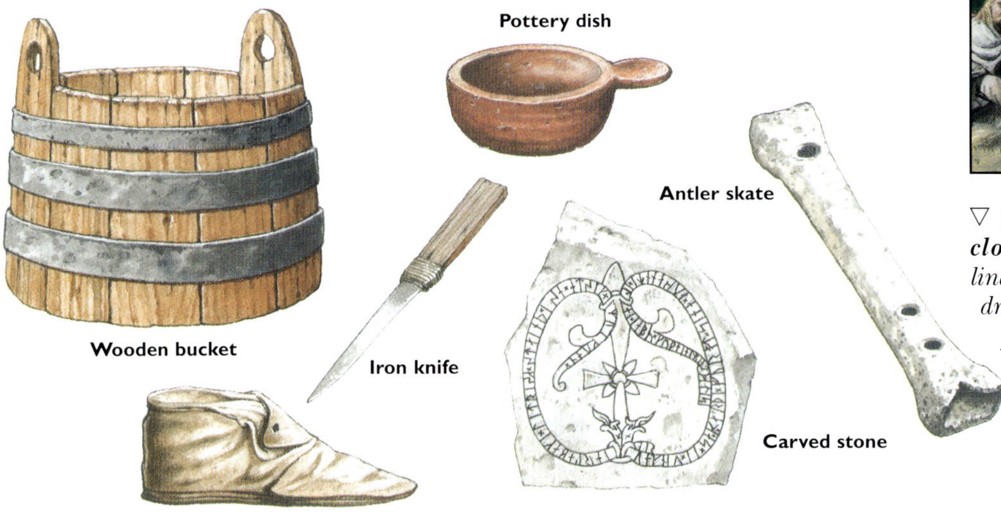

▽ ***Vikings wore hard-wearing clothes*** *made from woollen or linen cloth. Women wore a linen dress with a wool tunic on top, fastened by brooches. Keys or combs hung from a chain, since the clothes had no pockets.*

△ ***Viking farmers made the most of their household items,*** *including tools, clothes and furniture. They also made things to sell at market. Wood, ivory, deer antler, leather, pottery, bone and iron were common materials.*

The Vikings Abroad

When the Vikings sailed overseas in their longships, they were ready to kill and plunder. They went in search of trade and new lands in which to make their homes.

Viking longships were fast and strong enough to cross oceans. From the late 700s bands of Vikings set sail from Scandinavia to land on the coasts of western Europe. The sight of a Viking sail soon caused panic, for people knew the Vikings were fierce fighters with their favourite weapons – iron swords and axes. They raided monasteries and towns, carrying off slaves and booty.

The Vikings were also looking to seize land. Viking attacks on England began in 787, and from 865 Vikings from Denmark had begun to settle in eastern England. Vikings also settled in the Orkney and Shetland islands off the coast of Scotland, and the Isle of Man and Ireland. They attacked what is now France, but were bought off with the gift of Normandy in 911.

Sailing west into the Atlantic Ocean, Norwegian Vikings settled in Iceland (874) and Greenland (982), and landed in North America (c. 1000).

WEIGHING COINS

Vikings valued coins by weight, so many traders carried balance scales to check that a customer's money was good and to show another merchant that he wasn't being cheated. Small lead weights such as those below were used to check coins. Small scales for weighing silver have been found at Jorvik and other Viking settlements.

Scales

Lead weights

Silver penny

◁ ***Viking warriors wore chain-mail tunics or leather jerkins,*** *though leather jerkins were more common. At close quarters, the axe made a fearsome weapon. A Viking sword was heavy and was swung in a wide arc.*

▽ ***Raiders rush from their longships*** *during an attack on the English coast. The oared ships could be rowed up rivers and land on beaches, so Vikings often took their enemies by surprise.*

Swedish Vikings travelled as far east as the Black Sea, trading with Greeks and Arabs who called them the Rus – from which comes the name Russia. Vikings wandered in the markets of Baghdad and Constantinople, and goods from such exotic places found their way back to Viking towns such as Jorvik (York) in England and Dublin in Ireland.

Where Vikings settled, they often mingled with the local people. In England, King Alfred of Wessex led the fight against the invaders, but Viking settlements in eastern England (the Danelaw) left a permanent legacy in customs, laws, place names and language. Viking words, for example, include knife and calf.

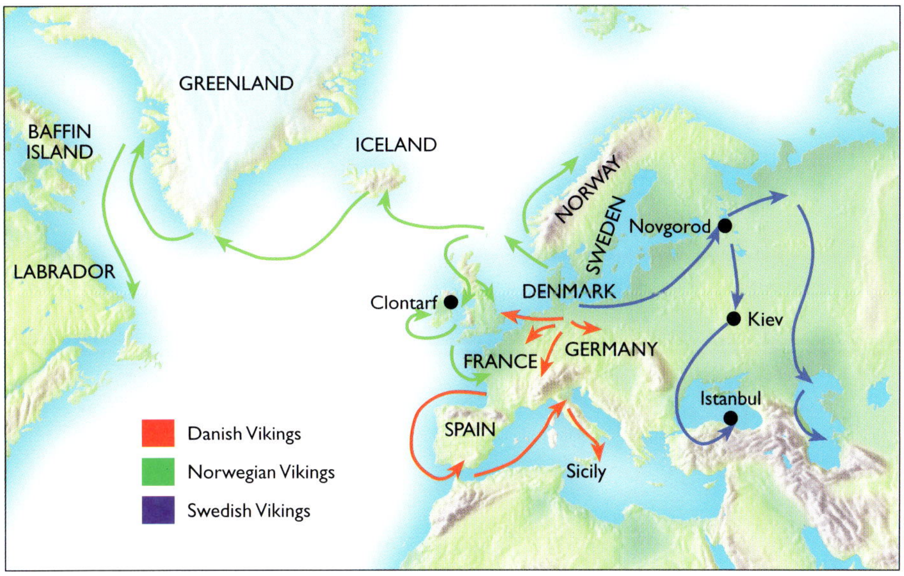

△ ***Viking trade routes took*** *them by sea and overland from Scandinavian market towns such as Hedeby (Denmark) to Jorvik (York), Dublin, Iceland and the Baltic. Vikings travelled as far east as Novgorod (Russia), Baghdad and Istanbul.*

THE VIKINGS ABROAD

787 First reported Viking raids on English coast.

795 Vikings begin attacks on Ireland.

834 Vikings raid Dorestad (in what is now the Netherlands).

865 Great army of Vikings lands in England.

866 The Vikings capture the city of York (Jorvik) in England.

878 English and Vikings agree to divide England between them after Vikings are defeated by King Alfred.

886 Viking siege of Paris is lifted after they are paid a huge treasure by King Charles II of France.

911 Vikings under Rollo are given Normandy to prevent further attacks on France.

1014 Irish victory at the battle of Clontarf means that the Viking dominance of Ireland is at an end.

1016–1035 Reign of Canute, Viking king of England, Denmark and Norway.

1066 Last big Viking attack on England, by Harold Hardrada of Norway. His army is defeated by King Harold at the battle of Stamford Bridge.

1066 William, Duke of Normandy, defeats King Harold at the battle of Hastings, England.

1072–1091 Norman armies conquer Sicily.

Life in a Monastery

In medieval Europe thousands of men and women devoted their lives to the Church, working, praying and studying in monasteries and nunneries. Across Europe, monasteries became centres of western art and learning.

Men and women who became monks or nuns obeyed the rule, or way of life, originally set down in the 500s by, amongst others, St Benedict of Nursia. He taught that a monk or nun should be poor, unmarried and obedient. Monks wore simple robes, shaved their heads and lived together in communities known as monasteries. The head of the monastery was the abbot, who often managed large estates and sometimes even commanded his own knights. The head of a nunnery, or a religious house for women, was called an abbess.

Monks and nuns followed a daily programme of prayer and worship, attending eight services every day. Monks ate together in the refectory, and worked in the fields or in workshops. At first they made most of what they needed, including their own bread, butter, cheese and ale, though later lay brethren did the hard work. They cared for the sick, gave food and shelter to travellers, and carefully copied out books, painting the pages with brilliantly coloured letters and pictures, called illuminations. Precious books were stored in monastery libraries during the Middle Ages for study by priests and friars.

△ ***Founded in 909, Cluny Abbey in France is one of many abbeys in Europe*** *built during the Middle Ages. An abbey was a religious community of monks or nuns, headed by an abbot or abbess. Some large abbeys were like walled towns, where the monks lived in seclusion from the outside world.*

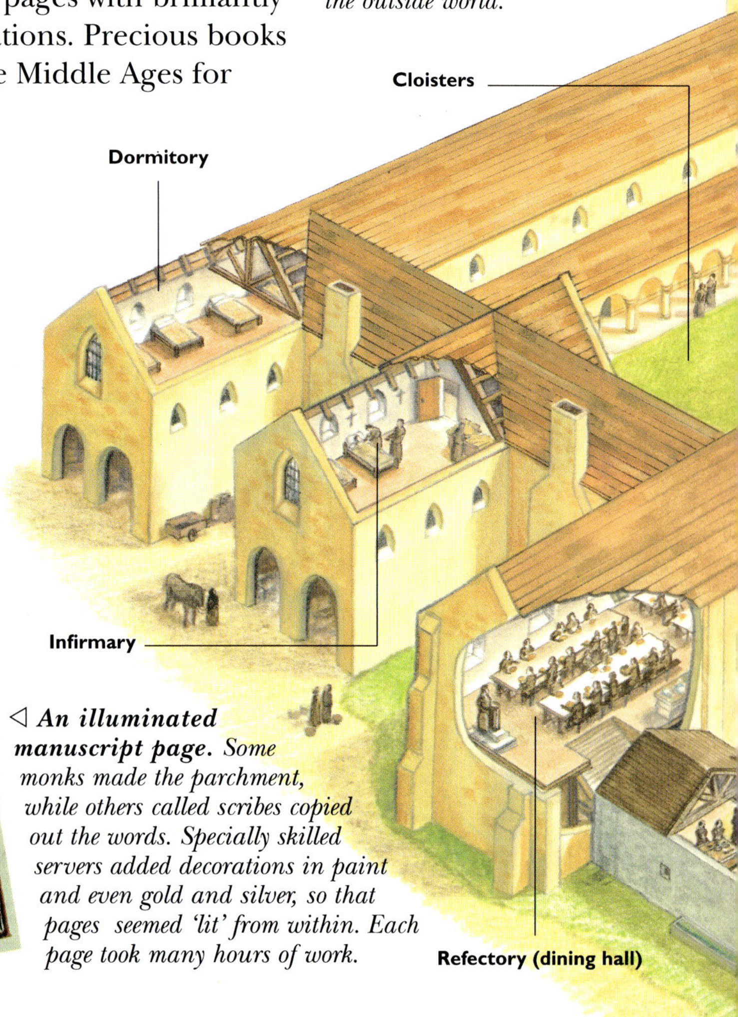

◁ ***An illuminated manuscript page.*** *Some monks made the parchment, while others called scribes copied out the words. Specially skilled servers added decorations in paint and even gold and silver, so that pages seemed 'lit' from within. Each page took many hours of work.*

CHRISTIAN PILGRIMS
Pilgrims in the Middle Ages made journeys to visit holy places or shrines (the relic of a saint, for example). People journeyed as far as Jerusalem, or to the catacombs (underground tombs) in Rome where early Christians had worshipped. In England, the most famous shrine was that of St Thomas à Becket at Canterbury. It was just such pilgrims that Chaucer wrote about in his *Canterbury Tales*.

These books were often the basis of the first universities.

There were several organizations, or orders, of monks. These included the Benedictines, Carthusians and Cistercians. In the 1200s new orders of travelling preachers, known as friars, were formed.

Friars such as the Dominicans and the Franciscans (founded by St Francis of Assisi) did not live behind monastery walls, but wandered the countryside, asking for food and shelter and preaching Christianity to the people.

◁ ***A monastic community*** *followed a daily routine of work and worship. At its heart was the chapel. There were herb gardens and cloisters, an infirmary for the sick, workshops and farm buildings.*

LIFE IN A MONASTERY

Late 400s Simple monasteries are founded in Ireland, for hermits living in groups, each in his own hut or cell.
***c.* 480–550** Life of St Benedict of Nursia, who founds the first order of monks in 529.
500s St Columba founds a monastery on the Island of Iona.
529 First European abbey at Monte Cassino in Italy is founded. Benedictine rule is formulated here.
597 St Augustine founds the first English Benedictine monastery at Canterbury.
820 Plans for the ideal abbey are circulated around Europe, influencing the design of monastery buildings.
910 Cluniac order is founded.
966 Mont St Michel in France is built by the Benedictines.
1042 Edward the Confessor founds the first Westminster Abbey, England.
1084 Order of Carthusians is founded.
1098 Cistercian order is founded.
1100 First hospital (monastery) founded by the Knights of St John (known as the Hospitallers) to shelter pilgrims journeying to the Holy Land.
1119 Order of Knights Templar founded.
1170–1221 Life of Domingo de Guzman, founder of the Dominican friars.
1181–1226 Life of St Francis of Assisi, founder of the Franciscan friars.
Late 1100s University of Paris is founded.
1189 Teutonic Knights founded in Jerusalem.
1225–1274 Life of St Thomas Aquinas, one of the great monk-scholars of the Middle Ages.
1249 First college of Oxford University is founded.

The Feudal System

In western Europe, feudalism was a form of contract in the European upper classes whereby power was wielded across different castle-dominated districts.

In the Middle Ages, land was owned by a powerful lord (a king or a nobleman) or by the Church. The lord gave land to those who followed him and fought for him, who were called vassals. In return, a vassal promised to serve his lord by fighting for him and collecting taxes from the people who lived on his land. This was the key idea behind feudalism.

Feudalism developed among the Franks in the 700s (see pages 66–67). There had been many years of fighting and confusion following the collapse of the Roman empire in the late 400s. The Franks thought that a warrior-chief should look after his followers and reward them in return for their loyalty. Chiefs, or lords, held the land on which poor people (peasants) lived. Instead of owning or renting their own land, peasant-farmers were bound to serve their lord. In return, the lord protected them. This was not a bad system in troubled times.

▷ ***"March", from a 15th-century manuscript*** Les Tres Riches Heures de duc de Berry, *by the Limbourg brothers. It shows shepherds, peasants and springtime farm tasks.*

DOMESDAY BOOK

The Domesday (Doomsday) Book was a survey of England made on the orders of William the Conqueror in 1085. Commissioners took details of who owned what land, and how many people lived in each village, collecting figures for 1085 and 1066. There are records for most old English villages and towns, but not for London.

▷ ***In feudal society,*** *the king held land and power. Next came the barons and bishops, and the mounted knights. In the middle were merchants and town craftworkers. Servants, foot-soldiers and peasants came at the bottom.*

▷ ***William, Duke of Normandy*** *and first Norman king of England, was crowned in Westminster Abbey on Christmas Day, 1066. He put down rebellions ruthlessly, and left a firmly-governed kingdom to his sons. William kept about a quarter of English land for himself, granting the rest to his followers in return for military service. Every landholder had to swear allegiance to the king, and pay taxes on the land they held.*

Feudalism grew as kings granted more land to knights, the brave warriors on whose loyalty and fighting skills kings depended. It spread from France to England and Spain and was taken by the Crusaders to the East. Each lord governed his own lands, where his word was law. If there was war, he had to supply soldiers to the king's army. He acted as judge in disputes between his vassals, whether they were lesser nobles or humble peasants.

The feudal system began to fall apart in the 1200s. One reason was economic: people began to use money more, and preferred to pay rent for land rather than be bound by feudal service.

In the 1300s, new weapons such as crossbows, gunpowder and cannon changed the way wars were fought. Cannons could smash castle walls and crossbows could pierce armour. Feudal lords and knights became less powerful.

THE FEUDAL SYSTEM

Late 400s Fall of the Roman empire leads to a breakdown in law and order across western Europe.

700s Feudal system starts among the Franks, based on arrangements for land-holding and defence. Threat of attack by Muslims from Spain encourages its spread.

700s Vassals have to supply soldiers to serve the lord on a certain number of days, usually 40 in every year.

1066 Normans bring the feudal system to England and strengthen it.

1100 It is now usual for a lord's oldest son to inherit his land holding or fief. (The word feudal comes from a Latin name for fief.)

1200s Feudalism becomes more complex, with layers of vassal-lord relationships from the king downwards.

1215 King John signs the Magna Carta, limiting the powers of the King of England.

1265 Simon de Montfort, a baron, calls ordinary citizens to a meeting with barons and churchmen – the first real Parliament in England. This rebellion against King Henry III fails, but royal power in England is never the same again.

1300s Knights become less effective against bowmen and cannon. This speeds the end of feudalism.

Knight Merchant Archer Peasant Beggar

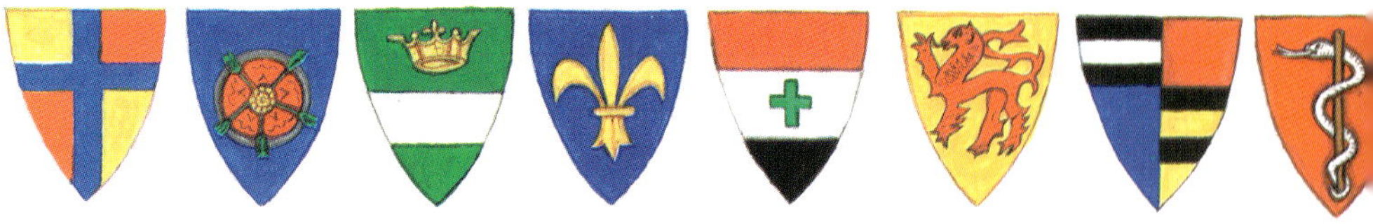

Life in a Castle

LIFE IN A CASTLE

500 Byzantines build strong stone castles and walled cities.
800s Arabs build castles in the Middle East and North Africa.
950 Earliest known French castle built at Doue-la-Fontaine, Anjou.
1000s Normans develop the motte (mound) and bailey (enclosure) castle. Normans wear chain mail armour.
1078 William I begins building the Tower of London, England.
1100s Stone keeps become the main castle stronghold.
1142 Crusaders take over Krak des Chevaliers in Syria.
1150–1250 Thousands of castles are built across what is now Germany.
1180s Castles with square-walled towers are built.
1200s The concentric or ring-wall castle is developed. Soldiers returning from the Crusades bring this improved design to Europe.
1205 Krak des Chevaliers is rebuilt by Knights.

▷ ***Feasting in the great hall.*** *The lord and lady sit on a raised dais, and knights and other members of the household at lower tables. Servants carry food from the kitchen outside, while dogs scavenge for scraps.*

Castles formed a mighty chain, linking together a conqueror's lands. Mighty stone fortresses dotted the landscape of Europe and the Middle East throughout the Middle Ages.

The earliest medieval castles were earth-mounds with a wooden stockade on top. Castles like these were built by the Norman invaders of England, often on the site of earlier Saxon and Roman forts. They were soon enlarged and strengthened, with water-filled ditches or moats, stone walls protected by towers, and a massive central stronghold called a keep. Castles were often built on hilltops, or to guard harbours, rivers and vital roads.

Medieval castles were private fortresses for the king or lord who owned them. Safe inside, he ruled his lands and planned to make war on his enemies. A castle was also a family home, although early castles were cold and draughty, with no glass in the windows and only rushes on the stone floor. In the great hall, the lord and his followers feasted on food carried by servants from the kitchen. At night, everyone slept on the floor around the central fire, while the lord and his lady retired to their small private room, known as the solar. Before around 1300, there were no bathrooms and lavatories emptied into the surrounding moat. For amusement, the lord and his friends hunted deer and boar in the forest or watched trained falcons bring down their prey.

The castle was patrolled and defended by foot-soldiers with spears and bows and by armoured knights on horseback. Knights practised with sword, lance and axe, with their squires – young men training to be knights. When a castle was attacked, the defenders needed enough food and water to withstand a siege

◁ ***Knights carried shields to ward off blows*** *and to identify themselves to friends. In the later Middle Ages, a shield displayed its owner's coat of arms (family badge).*

lasting weeks or even months. The castle walls had to be thick enough to stand firm against catapults, tunnels and battering rams. The occupants often suffered from starvation or disease, and were forced to surrender. In due course, cannon and barrels of gunpowder placed in tunnels were far more effective at knocking down walls. This new technology eventually brought the age of castles to an end by the 1500s.

△ ***Jousting was combat on horseback*** *between two knights with blunt-tipped lances. It took place in a field, and was a social occasion with a large audience. A tournament was a bigger, rougher affair, in which groups of knights fought mock battles, sometimes with fatal mishaps. Safety measures, including blunt swords and padded armour, were only introduced in the 1300s.*

The Crusades

For European Christians, the Crusades were holy wars, with the promise of plunder in the service of the Church. For more than 200 years, Christian and Muslim armies fought for control of the Holy Land, the territory around Jerusalem in the Middle East.

Many Christian pilgrims visited Jerusalem, which was a holy city to Jews and Muslims, as well as to Christians. But Jerusalem was held by Muslim Turks and, in 1095, they banned Christian pilgrims from the city. This angered both the western Christian church based in Rome and the eastern Christian church based in Constantinople. From Rome, Pope Urban II called on Christians to free Jerusalem and so launched the First Crusade, or war of the cross. In 1096 a European force joined with a Byzantine army from Constantinople. Their leaders were inspired by religious faith and by a less spiritual desire to increase territory and wealth.

▽ ***Krak des Chevaliers**, now in Syria, has sheer rock walls on three sides and a moat. The Muslims captured it by sending in a fake letter. Believing the message was a surrender order from their own leaders, the Crusaders inside opened the gates.*

▽ ***Once Crusaders had conquered lands,** they built strong castles to defend them. To capture a castle, soldiers had to break down massive gates, while arrows, boiling oil and rocks were thrown on their heads. Castle defenders under siege faced starvation and bombardment by giant catapults which lobbed balls of flaming tar, the heads of prisoners or diseased corpses over the walls.*

1000 1100 1200 1300 1400

KEY
First Crusade
Second Crusade
Third Crusade

▷ ***Crusaders*** *found the weather in the lands around Jerusalem incredibly hot. They soon learned from the Muslim soldiers and wore airy, loose robes over their armour and protected their heads from the Sun. They wore a red cross on their surcoat.*

◁ ***The journey to the Holy Land*** *was long and mostly done on foot. Crusaders had to be tough to endure sickness, hunger, thirst and attack as they dragged their armour and supplies over rough, often desert, terrain.*

A Crusader knight

A Muslim warrior

In three years they captured Jerusalem and went on to set up Christian kingdoms in Palestine. But none of the seven later crusades matched this success.

The Crusades inspired many stories. There was bravery and honour on both sides. But the Crusades also had a less noble side. Before the First Crusade even set out, a People's Crusade wandered across Europe. This peasant army burned villages and was eventually massacred by the Turks. Then the Fourth Crusade of 1202 turned aside to loot the Christian city of Constantinople.

In the end, the Crusaders failed to win back the Holy Land. Europeans learned more about Eastern art and science, foods and medicine. Contacts and trade between Europe and Asia grew during the Crusades.

△ ***Transport ships*** *were loaded with soldiers and equipment bound for the Crusades. Special groups of knights were founded to protect Christians on their journey. These included the Knights Hospitallers and the Knights Templars who became rich and powerful.*

THE CHILDREN'S CRUSADE OF 1212

was inspired by two boy preachers. Fifty thousand children in two groups, one from France and one from Germany, set off for the Holy Land. Some children died on the journey across Europe. Many more were taken to North Africa and sold as slaves. The Pied Piper legend may be based on the tragedy of these lost children.

THE CRUSADES

1096 First Crusade is called by Pope Urban II. Peter the Hermit leads a peasant army across Europe.
1097 The main crusader army wins battle of Niceae (Turkey).
1099 The crusaders defeat the Turks and capture Jerusalem.
1147 Second Crusade sets out after Muslims capture the crusader kingdom of Edessa in 1144. German and French armies fail to cooperate and are beaten.

▷ ***Saladin (1138–1193)*** *was the greatest of the Muslim leaders who fought the Crusaders. He took Jerusalem, but in 1192 made peace with Richard I, allowing Christian pilgrims to enter the Holy City.*

1187 Saladin captures Jerusalem.
1189 Third Crusade is led by Frederick I Barbarossa of the Holy Roman empire, King Philip II of France and King Richard I of England.
1191 Crusaders capture the port of Acre in Palestine.
1202 Fourth Crusade attacks Egypt instead of Palestine.
1204 Crusaders capture and bury Constantinople.
1212 Children's Crusade: few of 50,000 children return.
1221 Fifth Crusade: Crusaders fight the Sultan of Egypt.
1228 The Sixth Crusade ends when the Muslim sultan hands over Jerusalem.
1244 Muslims retake Jerusalem.
1249 Seventh Crusade is led by King Louis IX of France.
1270 Eighth Crusade also led by Louis. He and many of his men die of plague in Tunis.
1291 Acre, last crusader stronghold, is captured.

A Medieval Town

In the Middle Ages, towns in Europe were noisy and crowded by day, but quiet and dark at night, the silence broken only by cat and dog fights, late-night revellers and watchmen calling out the hours. Churches, guilds, fairs and markets all drew people into the towns.

If you walked through a medieval town, you took care where you stepped, because most people threw out their rubbish into the muddy streets. Open drains ran alongside and smelled awful. To fetch water, people went to the town well or bought it from the water-seller, hoping it was clean. Pigs and chickens wandered in and out of small yards. Houses were built close together, with the top floors often jutting out over the street. Since most houses were made chiefly of wood, they caught fire easily. At night, the curfew bell warned people to cover or put out their kitchen fires.

Many houses were also shops and workplaces. Traders and craftworkers formed groups called guilds to organize their businesses and to set standards of work. Guilds also staged pageants, dramas and religious processions, and set up training schools. Some towns were famous for their fairs and attracted foreign merchants from all over Europe, as well as entertainers such as jugglers, clowns, acrobats, minstrels, performing monkeys

MONEY MAKES MONEY

European merchants usually carried silver coins, but Arabs preferred gold. As international trade increased, Italian merchants set up the first banks, using written bills of exchange to pay for goods instead of having to carry bags of heavy metal coins.

▽ ***Market day in a medieval town.*** *People brought in farm produce to sell, visited stalls and shops to spend their money, gossiped with their friends and drank at the ale house. Strolling musicians, acrobats, or a dancing bear amused the crowds. Beggars and pickpockets did well too.*

and dancing bears. Fairs also attracted quack doctors and pickpockets ready to cheat innocent visitors from the countryside.

In towns, work was to be found building magnificent cathedrals and churches, as well as castles and defensive walls. Large trading cities in Europe, such as Hamburg, Antwerp and London, grew rich from buying and selling wool and other goods carried across the sea in small wooden sailing ships. About 90 cities in northern Europe formed the Hanseatic League to fight pirates, win more trade and keep out rivals.

▷ ***This medieval painting shows French tradesmen at work in their town shops.*** *Tailors are stitching richly coloured cloth (left), while a grocer sets out his wares (right). In the background a barber shaves a customer and a furrier lays out animal pelts.*

A MEDIEVAL TOWN

1136 Fire destroys many old, straw-thatched buildings in London.

1162 Work begins on the cathedral of Notre Dame in Paris, which by 1210 is a unified city with paved streets, walls and 24 gates.

1200s Many new towns are founded in Europe; city-states in Italy and Germany develop.

1209 New London Bridge built.

1260 The Hanseatic League is formed, first by the German towns of Lubeck and Hamburg.

1285 English merchants are banned from selling their goods in churchyards.

1300 The wool trade is at its peak in England; large churches are built in prosperous wool towns.

1344 First known use of the name Hanseatic League.

1348–1349 People flee towns during the Black Death.

1377 London by now has at least 50 guilds and a population of more than 35,000.

1400s Morality plays, in which actors stage tales of good against evil, are performed in churches or on open carts in the street.

1400s–1500s Renaissance architects begin to rebuild cities such as Florence in Italy.

△ ***Stained-glass windows told stories in pictures.*** *In church, people who could not read looked at the colourful illustrations of Bible stories in the church windows to learn more about the Christian faith.*

The Mongol Empire

"Inhuman and beastly, rather monsters than men..." is how the English historian Matthew Paris described the Mongols in the 1200s. Mongol armies sent a shockwave of fear around Asia and Europe, conquering a vast area of land that formed the largest empire in history.

The Mongols lived on the plains of central Asia, from the Ural mountains to the Gobi Desert. They were nomads, wandering with their herds and living in portable tent-homes called yurts. Their leaders were chiefs called khans. In 1206, Chief Temujin brought all the tribes under his rule and was proclaimed Genghis Khan, meaning lord of all. In a lifetime of conquest, he seized an empire that stretched from the Pacific Ocean to the River Danube.

The Mongols quickly conquered the Persian empire. They continued their attacks after Genghis Khan died and, in 1237, a Mongol army led by Batu Khan, one of Genghis' sons, invaded Russia. In the end western Europe was saved only when the Mongols turned homeward on the death of Genghis' son Ogadai Khan in 1241. News of the Mongols' advance created panic in Europe – some Church leaders claimed that the Mongols were sent by God to punish Christians for their sins.

MARE'S MILK

Mongols lived with and from horses. They drank mares' milk, and fermented the milk in a skin bag hung from a wooden frame to make an intoxicating drink called kumiss. They drank to celebrate victories and sang to tunes played on fiddles with horsehair strings.

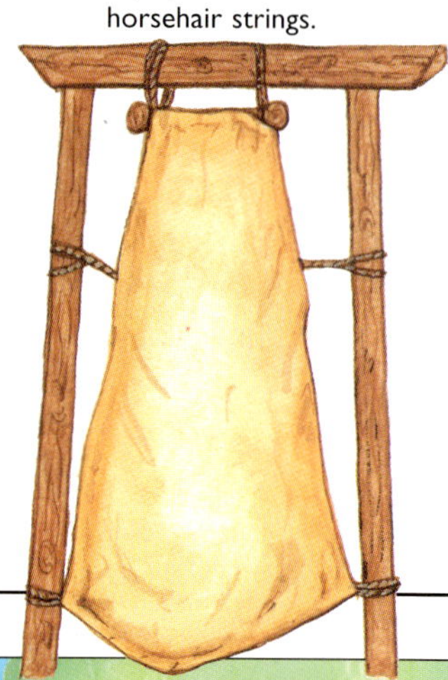

▽ ***Mongols preferred to fight on horseback.*** *Warriors controlled their horses with their feet, leaving their hands free to shoot bows and hurl spears. Mongol cavalry charges usually overwhelmed their enemies.*

△ ***The nomadic Mongols*** *roamed, seeking fresh grassland for their sheep, horses and goats, carrying their felt houses (yurts) with them on ox carts.*

▽ ***Genghis Khan's empire*** *stretched from the River Danube in the west to the Pacific shores of Asia in the east. Later, Tamerlane carved out his own huge empire.*

Enemies feared the Mongols' speed and ferocity in battle. Mongol soldiers travelled with five horses each and were expert with bow and lance. They also learned how to use catapult artillery against cities. In victory, the Mongols were usually merciless, slaughtering cities full of people and carting away treasure. Yet they ruled their empire fairly if sternly. They demanded taxes but encouraged trade and tolerated all religions.

MONGOL EMPIRE

1206 Temujin is chosen to be khan of all the Mongols and takes the new name Genghis Khan.

1211 The Mongol army attacks China.

1215 Beijing, capital of China, is taken by the Mongols.

1217 All China and Korea are controlled by the Mongols who make their new capital on the steppes at Karakorum.

1219 The Mongols sweep west to attack the empire of Khwarezm (Persia and Turkey).

1224 Mongol armies invade Russia, and then Poland and Hungary.

1227 Genghis Khan dies. His son Ogodai is chosen as the new khan in 1229.

1237 Mongol generals Batu and Subotai invade northern Russia. Their army is known as the Golden Horde.

1241 Ogodai dies and his armies pull back from Europe.

◁ ***Though ruthless in battle, Genghis Khan kept the peace in his empire. He wiped out whole cities, yet trade flourished.***

Kublai Khan and China

Genghis Khan's grandson was called Kublai Khan. When he became leader of the Mongols he moved from the windswept steppes of central Asia to rule the most splendid court in the world in China. At this time, China was the most sophisticated, technologically advanced country in the world.

Kublai Khan's armies overthrew the ruling Song dynasty in China. By 1279 he controlled most of this vast country, although his grip was less secure on the western parts of the empire. The new Mongol emperor moved his capital to Beijing, taking care to maintain many aspects of Chinese culture. China at this time had the world's biggest cities, including Kaifeng and Hangzhou (each with more than one million people). Chinese silks, porcelain and other luxuries astonished travellers from Europe and Africa.

One famous visitor to Kublai Khan's court was Marco Polo, an Italian explorer. He later wrote in praise of Chinese cities, with their restaurants and baths, of China's fine postal system and its paper money – as yet unknown in Europe. The Chinese had discovered many technologies such as paper-making. Other inventions included the magnetic compass, printing with movable type and, most amazing of all to startled foreigners, exploding gunpowder rockets.

MARCO POLO

In 1271 Marco Polo (1256–1323) travelled to China from Venice in Italy with his father and uncle, first by sea to Palestine and then by camel along the fabled Silk Road. This overland trade route linking China with the West had been made safe for travellers by Mongol rule. It was 24 years before the Polos returned to Italy. Marco Polo toured China in the service of Kublai Khan, calling him "the most powerful man since Adam".

▷ ***The Chinese began making paper about 105,*** *when the imperial workshops announced the new technology. Paper-makers used hemp or mulberry tree bark for fibre. Later, they mashed rags or old rope into pulp. Pulp was spread on mesh trays to dry into sheets. Early paper was used for wrapping and clothes, not for writing on.*

◁ ***Merchants travelled in caravans for protection*** *against bandits. From China, strings of laden camels followed the Silk Road across mountains and deserts to the markets of the Middle East. They rested at caravanserai, or rest-stations. The Silk Road provided the only regular contact between Europe and China.*

1000 1100 1200 1300 1400

△ ***Spices for flavouring food*** *(and to disguise the taste of bad meat) were traded from the East Indies and India to China and the West.*

Kublai Khan was a fair ruler as well as a brilliant general, and strengthened his empire by building long roads to connect far-flung territories. He organized charity for the sick and food supplies in case of famine. He also wanted to extend Mongol power and twice tried to invade Japan, but without success.

After the death of Kublai in 1294 the mighty Mongol empire began to decline and by the mid 1300s it had largely broken up. Then in 1369, Timur "Leng" (the lame), known as Tamerlane, made himself ruler of Samarkand in central Asia. He claimed descent from Genghis Khan and set out to re-create the Mongol empire. He conquered Persia, Iraq, Syria, Afghanistan and part of Russia. In 1397 he invaded India and then died on the way to China in 1405.

△ ***The Chinese developed a writing system*** *unlike any other. There were more than 40,000 characters, originally picture-signs, written with a fine brush. Calligraphy, the art of handwriting, is still admired today.*

KUBLAI KHAN

1216 Kublai Khan is born.
1260 Kublai is elected Great Khan of the Mongols.
1271 Marco Polo sets out from Venice for China.
1274 Kublai Khan sends an army to invade Japan, but it is driven back by a storm.
1276 Mongols defeat the Song fleet near Guangzhou.
1279 Kublai Khan rules all China.
1281 A second Mongol attack on Japan is foiled by a typhoon, which the Japanese call kamikaze, the divine wind.
1294 Kublai Khan dies.
1325 Ibn Battuta begins a 24-year journey from his homeland Morocco through Persia, India, Indonesia and on to China.

△ ***The Muslim traveller Ibn Battuta (1304–1369)*** *covered more than 120,000 kilometres on his wanderings and became a celebrity. He visited China in the 1340s, as an ambassador from the sultan of Sumatra.*

1368 Mongols are driven from China by Ming forces.
1395 Tamerlane, a descendant of Genghis Khan, invades large parts of southern Russia.
1398 Tamerlane takes Delhi.
1402 Tamerlane defeats Ottoman Turks at Ankyra.
1405 Death of Tamerlane.

The Black Death

The Black Death was the most horrific natural disaster of the Middle Ages. It was a devastating plague that killed many millions of people in Europe and Asia. One Italian historian wrote, "This is the end of the world".

The plague came to Europe from Asia in 1347. Disease ravaged a Mongol army fighting in the Crimea (southern Russia). The desperate Mongols catapulted diseased corpses over the walls of a fortress defended by Italians. When the Italians sailed home to Genoa, they carried the disease with them.

The disease was bubonic plague, passed to humans from infected rats through flea bites. The name "Black Death" came from the black spots that appeared on victims, who also developed swellings in their armpits and groin, or coughed up blood. Many people died the same day they fell ill. No medieval doctor knew why the Black Death struck or how to cure it. People killed cats and dogs believing they carried the disease, but not rats. To many Christians, the Black Death seemed a punishment from God, and religious fanatics took to the streets, whipping themselves as a penance for the sins of humanity.

The Black Death raged from China to Scandinavia. Sudden death struck daily and, as the epidemic spread, panic-stricken people fled from the towns.

THE BLACK DEATH

1344 Bubonic plague breaks out in China and India.
1347 The plague reaches Genoa in Italy and spreads west across Europe.
1348 By the summer, the disease is killing people in southern England. By the winter, Londoners are dying.
1349 Black Death spreads to Ireland, Wales and Scotland. Other regions affected include France, Spain, Germany and Russia.
1350 The epidemic reaches Scandinavia.
1353 Black Death epidemic eases. As many as 20 million people in Europe are dead.
1358 Peasants' uprising in northern France. Rebellion is savagely put down.
1381 Peasants' Revolt in England, with rioting in Essex and Kent.
1400 Further outbreaks of the Black Death continue until this date.

▽ ***Neither town governments nor local doctors could do much to fight the plague.*** *Many people fled, leaving the sick to die, but some brave people stayed to care for the victims. Houses were marked with crosses to show where the disease had struck. The dead were carried away in carts for burial.*

They took the plague with them. So many died (perhaps a third of the people in Europe) that it is possible that villages were left deserted and fields overgrown with weeds. The Church lost many priests, the only educated men of the time.

The repeated plague attacks throughout the 14th and 15th centuries left Europe short of labour and pushed up wages. Unrest over wages and taxes led to an uprising in France in 1358 and to the Peasants' Revolt in England, led by Wat Tyler in 1381.

The monasteries were particularly badly affected, as half England's monks and nuns died. In some monasteries, only a few monks survived. Three archbishops of Canterbury died in one year. It was a huge blow to the Church. People who lived through the Black Death gave money to the Church for new buildings. Yet some church leaders also complained of the money-grubbing and loose-living of those lucky enough to still be alive.

BLACK DEATH

The black rat carried the fleas that transmitted the disease. The rats travelled on ships from port to port, and as they moved the Black Death spread at terrifying speed. There were rats and fleas in every medieval town and in most houses. Rubbish in the streets and poor sanitation made towns an ideal breeding ground for disease. Many towns lost half their populations. Some villages were abandoned, leaving only the graves of the dead.

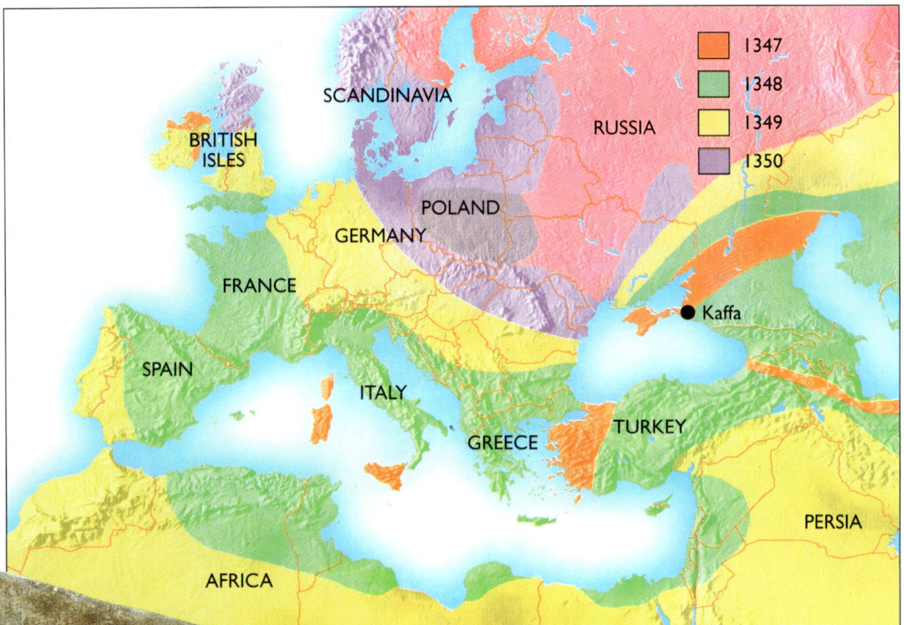

◁ ***This map shows how the Black Death spread.*** *As early as 1346 Europeans heard reports of a plague of terrible fury raging in China and India. The Black Death was about to hit them, like "the end of the world".*

▽ ***Estimates of how many people died vary.*** *This chart shows that the Black Death killed many more millions of people than World War I (1914–1918) – at least 25 million in Europe alone.*

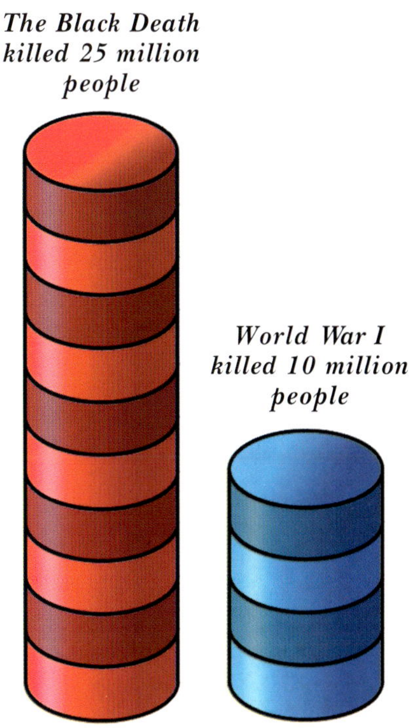

African Kingdoms

AFRICAN KINGDOMS

750 By this date most of North Africa has been overrun by Arab armies. Muslim faith spreads rapidly westwards.
770 In West Africa, Soninke people begin to build the kingdom of Ghana, led by King Maghan Sisse.
800 Ife kingdom in Nigeria and Kanem-Bornu (north of Lake Chad) become prominent.
800s Arabs and Persians set up trading posts at Malindi, Mombasa, Kilwa and Mogadishu in East Africa.
900s Ghana controls gold and salt trade and also buys cloth from Europe.
969 Fatimid dynasty conquers Egypt. They build a new capital at Cairo and found one of the first universities.
999 Baganda is first king of Kano in western Nigeria.
1043 Mandingo empire of Jenne founded in West Africa.
1054 Abdallah ben Yassim begins Muslim conquest of West Africa.
1062 Muslim Berbers called Almoravids build their capital of Marrakech.
1070 Ghana is conquered by the Almoravids.
1100 All Muslim Spain now part of Almoravid empire.
1163 Almohads overthrow Almoravids and rule northeast Africa and Spain.
1173 Saladin declares himself sultan of Egypt.
1190 Lalibela is emperor of Ethiopia (to 1225).
1200s Founding of Benin kingdom under the first oba, Eweka.
1240 Ghana becomes part of the new Mali empire when it is conquered by King Sundiata Keita.
1250 Mamelukes rule in Egypt.
1307 Mali empire at its height under Mansa Musa, with its capital at Timbuktu.
1332 Probable year of Mansa Musa's death.
1440–1480 Reign of the most famous oba of Benin, Ewuare the Great.

In this period, the riches of the mightiest kingdoms in Africa impressed Muslim and European visitors who came to their courts. Much of this wealth came from trade in gold, salt and slaves.

Many northern African kingdoms were Muslim and, from there, preachers took Islam to West Africa. In the kingdom of Ghana (modern-day Gambia, Guinea, Mali and Senegal), Muslim traders marvelled at warriors with gold-mounted swords and shields guarding the king in his capital of Koumbi Saleh. Even the guard dogs around the royal pavilion wore gold collars. Ghana reached the peak of its power in the 10th century when it controlled both the gold and salt trade.

In the 1300s, Muslim camel caravans crossed the Sahara Desert to the city of Timbuktu. They carried cloth and luxury items to exchange for slaves, leather goods and kola nuts (used as a drug). Timbuktu was the capital of Mali, an Islamic kingdom which replaced Ghana as the most powerful empire in West Africa. Mali's most famous ruler, Mansa Musa, made a pilgrimage to Mecca in 1324, with an entourage of 60,000 followers, giving away vast quantities of gold as he went. His fame spread as far as Europe, where his kingdom was shown on maps as a land glittering with gold. Spanish craftsmen decorated his palace. The emperor

◁ ***Mansa Musa on his pilgrimage to Mecca*** *riding at the head of a large army, with camels, horses, and foot-soldiers. His fame spread as far as Europe.*

▷ ***The empires of medieval Africa** included Ghana and later Mali and, in the west, the kingdoms of Kenam-Bornu, Ife and Benin. Timbuktu in the Sahara was a city famed for its wealth, when Mali was at the height of its power in the 14th century. It was later overshadowed by Jenne.*

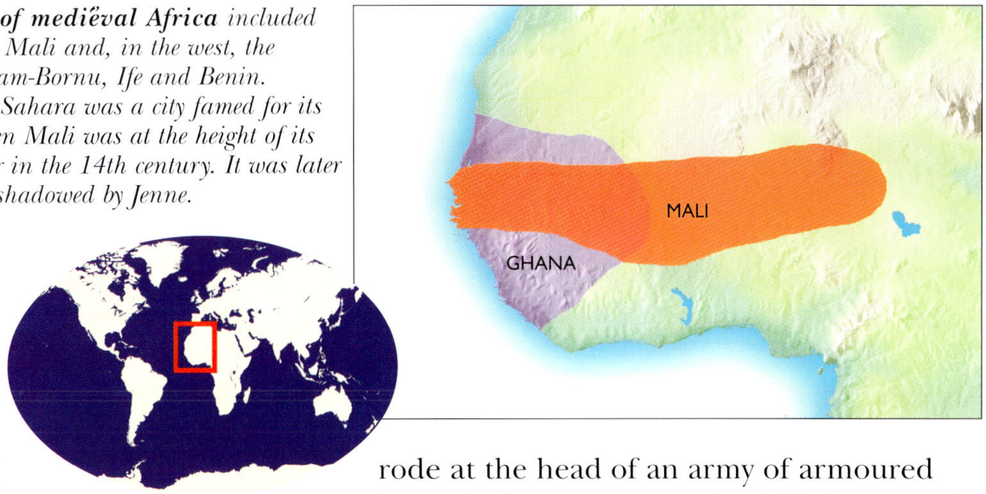

rode at the head of an army of armoured cavalry and a baggage-train of gold-laden camels.

Farther south were kingdoms just as splendid, such as Ife and Benin, where trade made powerful rulers rich. The craftworkers of Benin made cast bronze figures, the finest metal sculptures in Africa. Benin's ruler, the oba, lived in a walled city where he relaxed with his 100 or so wives. The people of Benin traded with the Portuguese, when their ships began sailing along the West African coast in the1400s.

In eastern Africa, people living in what are now Somalia, Kenya and Tanzania practised farming and herding, and also made iron tools. They traded in ivory, animal skins, and slaves with cities on the coast, which were visited by ships from Arabia and India. These trading cities, such as Kilwa in Tanzania, even sent ambassadors to China, and their rulers decorated their palaces with carpets from Persia and Chinese ceramics. The people of the east coast became Muslims in the 1100s, but people inland maintained traditional beliefs. The east-coast prosperity lasted until almost 1500, when the Portuguese took control of trade in the region and the trading cities were destroyed.

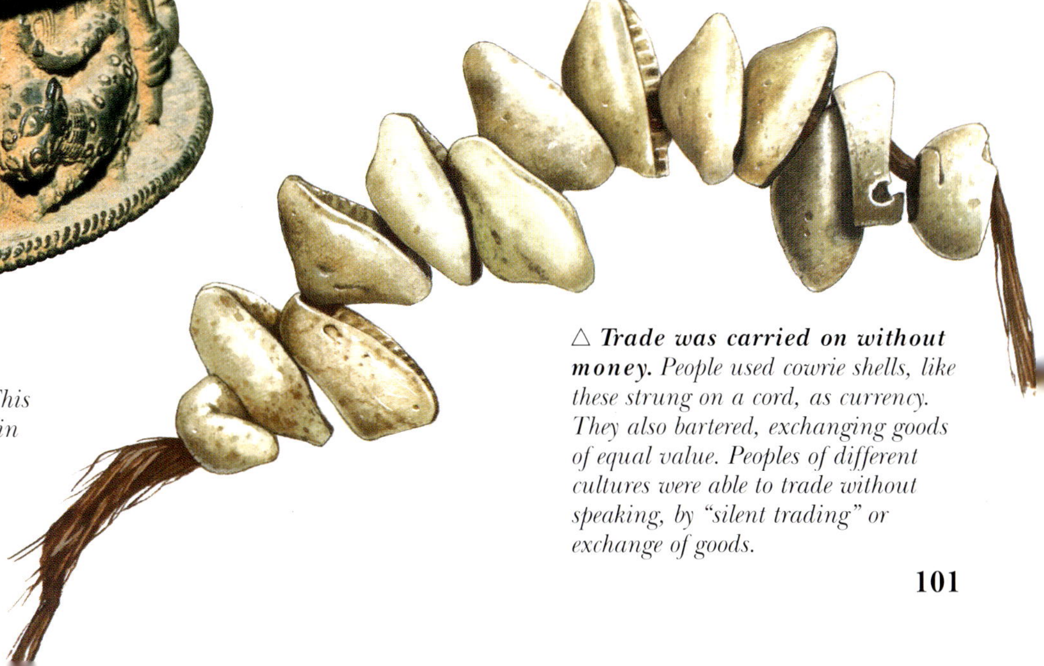

△ ***The craftsmen of Africa** were skilled in metalworking. This bronze hand altar shows a Benin king with his wives, servants and soldiers. The lost-wax process was used to make bronzes of superb quality.*

△ ***Trade was carried on without money.** People used cowrie shells, like these strung on a cord, as currency. They also bartered, exchanging goods of equal value. Peoples of different cultures were able to trade without speaking, by "silent trading" or exchange of goods.*

Japan's Warlords

Medieval Japan was a land without strong emperors. Power instead lay with warlords and they maintained control using their armies of fearsome samurai warriors.

The emperors of Japan were dominated by powerful military families. From these soldier clans came the shoguns, or overlords, who really ruled the country, such as the powerful Minamoto Yoritomo (1147–1199).

The shoguns drove off attacks from Mongol China with their fiercely loyal samurai warriors. A samurai held land, like a knight in Europe, but left farming to the peasants while he hunted or trained with sword and bow. The samurai eventually came to form an elite warrior class that practised Zen Buddhism, a philosophy which had been brought to Japan from China in 582.

From the 1300s, Japan was torn by violent civil wars between lords known as daimyos who built castles to guard their lands. The daimyos led armies of samurai warriors. In 1338 a samurai named Ashikaga Tokauji became the emperor's shogun.

THE DIVINE WIND

The Japanese felt the gods protected them from invasion. In 1274 and 1281, Kublai Khan sent Chinese fleets to conquer Japan. The first fleet withdrew, in the face of a storm. The second invasion fleet was scattered and sunk by a typhoon, which the Japanese called kamikaze, "the divine wind", and it was the subject of paintings like this one.

The Hundred Years War

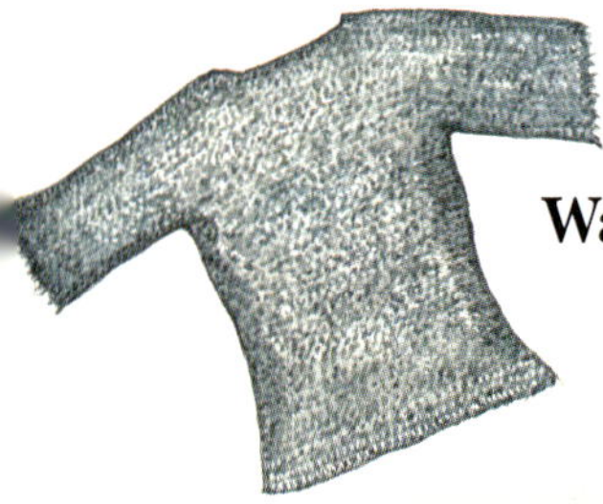

Edward III became king of England in 1327. He believed he also had a claim to the French throne so, in 1337, he declared war on France. War between England and France lasted on and off until 1453.

His forces won a sea battle at Sluys and two great land victories at Crécy and Poitiers, but were driven back by the French king Charles V and his commander Bertrand du Guesclin. In 1360 Edward gave up his claim to the French throne in return for land.

Years of truce followed until the English king Henry V renewed his claim to the throne in 1414. He led his troops to France where, in 1415, they defeated a much larger French army at Agincourt. To make peace Henry then married the French king's daughter, but he died in 1422 before his baby

◁ ***The death of Joan of Arc.*** *The English hoped her death would end French resistance, but in fact it was they who lost ground. The French were inspired to victory. By 1453 only Calais was left in English hands, and Joan's dreams for France had come true.*

His family thus became the governing family.

The most powerful daimyo was Hideyoshi Toyotomi (1537–1598), a peasant who rose to become a samurai warlord. He seized control of all Japan and tried but failed to conquer Korea. Hideyoshi controlled Japan from 1585 until his death. One of Hideyoshi's lieutenants, Ieyasu, became shogun in 1603, and founded the Tokugawa dynasty.

◁ ***A Samurai warrior wore a steel horned helmet*** *and body armour made in pieces from leather or lacquered iron strips, so it was fully flexible. He fought with bow, sword and lance. Modern martial arts have their origins in samurai training.*

son could become king of France. The fighting continued as the French were inspired by a peasant girl named Joan of Arc (1412–1431) who claimed to hear voices from God. She fought until the English caught her and burned her at the stake as a witch. Under the weak rule of Henry VI, the divided English lost ground. But English fortunes changed decisively when the Duke of Burgundy changed sides, and the English lost first Paris, then Rouen. By 1453, they had lost all French territory except Calais.

▽ ***Soldiers fought with halberd*** *(far left), longbow, primitive cannon, and crossbow. Only knights, such as England's Black Prince, wore full armour. If knocked from his horse, a knight hoped to be ransomed.*

JAPAN'S WARLORDS

582 Buddhism reaches Japan.
939 Start of civil wars in Japan.
995 Literary and artistic achievements under rule of Fujiwara Michinaga (to 1028).
1192 Minamoto Yoritomo sets up military government or shogunate.
1219 Hojo clan rules Japan (to 1333).
1274 Mongols try to invade Japan, and again in 1281, but are driven back by storms and the "divine wind".
1333 Emperor Daigo II overthrows the Hojo shoguns and rules to 1336.
1336 Revolution followed by exile of Daigo II. Ashikaga family rule as shoguns until 1573.
1400s Long period of civil wars.

100 YEARS WAR

1337 Edward III goes to war with France, claiming the throne.
1340 Sea battle of Sluys (off Belgium) won by the English.
1356 Poitiers is a victory for the English led by Edward III's son, the Black Prince.
1380 Death of Charles V of France who was succeeded by the mad Charles VI.
1415 Victory at Agincourt gives Henry V control of France.
1420 Henry V marries Catherine, daughter of Charles VI.
1422 Henry V dies.
1431 Joan of Arc is burned to death.
1453 End of the Hundred Years War.

The Age of Discovery

Explorers and empires 1400–1700

The 1400s mark the end of the Middle Ages. In Europe, the new ideas of the Renaissance and Reformation transformed the way people thought about themselves and the world, and the way they lived. Three events are often picked out as marking the end of the medieval period and the start of the modern age. They are the fall of Constantinople in 1453, which ended the last traces of the old Roman empire; the development of printing in the 1450s, which made books available to anyone who could read; and the first voyage of Christopher Columbus to the Americas in 1492.

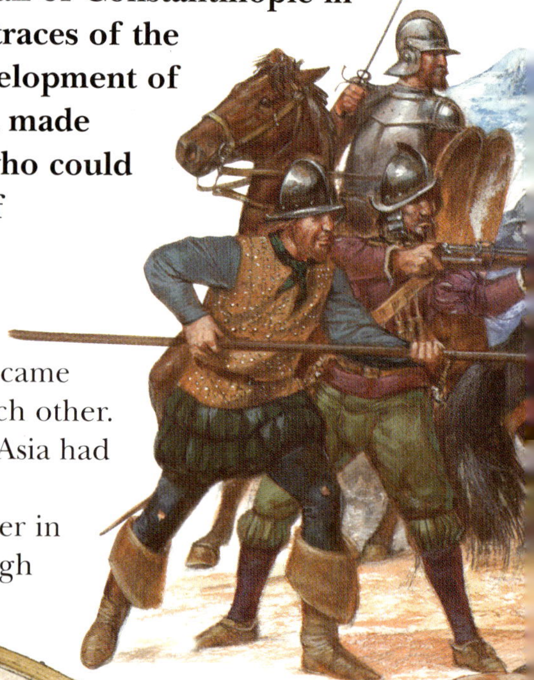

This period marks a time when the peoples of the world came into increasing contact with each other. People in America, Africa and Asia had greater contact with Europe. Europeans increased their power in the world through trade, through

the use of new technology such as cannons and muskets, and through a restless search for new lands and wealth that sent explorers and adventurers across the oceans. By the 1600s, several European countries had established permanent colonies overseas.

This period also saw many new ideas and challenges to old beliefs. Religious quarrels led to bitter wars. There were power struggles between kings and parliaments, as democratic government slowly developed. From the 1500s, there were startling advances in science, with inventions such as the telescope and microscope revealing new wonders, and prompting new questions. Great scientists such as Copernicus, Galileo and Newton challenged the old ideas, and a new freedom of thought began to shake the foundations of society.

THE AGE OF DISCOVERY

1464 Rise of Songhai empire in Africa.
1488 Portuguese explorers reach the southern tip of Africa.
1492 Columbus sails from Spain to America.
1497 Portuguese explorers sail across the Indian Ocean to India.
1500 Renaissance at its height in Italy.
1501 Start of Safavid dynasty in Persia.
1517 Martin Luther begins the Reformation in Europe.
1520 Suleiman rules the Ottoman empire.
1522 First round-the-world voyage by Magellan's expedition.
1526 Babur founds the Mughal empire in India.
1535 Spain completes conquest of the Aztec and Inca empires.
1543 Copernicus puts forward the revolutionary idea that the Sun, not the Earth, is the centre of the Solar System.
1568 War of liberation in the Spanish Netherlands begins.
1571 Battle of Lepanto is a victory for European Christians against the Muslim Ottoman Turks.
1588 Spanish Armada fails to invade England.
1590 Japan is united by Hideyoshi.
1606 First known European landing in Australia.
1609 Galileo uses a telescope to study the stars and planets.
1618 30 Years War begins.
1620 Mayflower pilgrims from England land in America.
1642 English Civil War begins.
1643 Louis XIV becomes king of France.
1665 Isaac Newton demonstrates the nature of light.

The Renaissance

The Renaissance was a rebirth of interest in the art and learning of ancient Greece and Rome and many historians say that it marked the end of the Middle Ages and the beginning of our modern world. It began in northern Italy in the 14th century and spread throughout Europe, changing the way Europeans saw themselves and how they thought about the world.

The Renaissance began in the universities and monasteries of Italy, where people rediscovered old manuscripts in Latin and Greek on science, art and literature. Some of these manuscripts were brought to Italy by Greek scholars fleeing Constantinople after that city's fall to the Ottoman Turks in 1453. Scholars tried to understand Greek and Roman beliefs, which placed more emphasis on the significance of human life on Earth rather than on an afterlife. In literature, great Italian poets such as Petrarch began to explore human emotion. By the early 1500s, three painters of genius – Leonardo da Vinci, Michelangelo and Raphael – were at the height of their powers, bringing a new energy and realism to art while architects designed new and elegant buildings that echoed the classical styles of ancient Greece and Rome.

The Renaissance was fuelled by new technology. Printing with movable type, developed by Johannes Gutenberg in Germany, made books cheaper and more plentiful, so new ideas could be read by more people.

▷ ***The great dome of Florence Cathedral in Italy,*** *designed by Filippo Brunelleschi, the first major architect of the Italian Renaissance. Work on the dome, inspired by his study of Rome's ancient buildings, began in 1420. It took 14 years to complete.*

▷ ***The new universe,*** *as conceived by the Polish astronomer Copernicus in his revolutionary new theory of 1543. He put the Sun, not the Earth, at the centre of the universe. This challenged the established theory of the 2nd-century Greek astronomer Ptolemy.*

▽ ***A flying machine*** *drawn, but never built, by the Italian Leonardo da Vinci. This sketch shows a kind of ornithopter, a machine that would flap its wings, like a bird. As well as being an artistic genius, Leonardo was a visionary, devising several futuristic machines.*

Some new ideas were astounding, such as the revolutionary suggestion by a Polish scientist, Nicolas Copernicus, that the Sun and not the Earth was the centre of the Solar System.

The Renaissance changed the Western world forever.

▷ ***Dante Alighieri whose poem* The Divine Comedy** *explores love, death and faith. Dante wrote in his own language, Italian, and not Latin, the language of scholars.*

▽ ***A print workshop in Denmark, about 1600.*** *The technology of printing with a screw press and metal type spread throughout Europe. Books were printed cheaply in many languages, and read by more people, eager for information.*

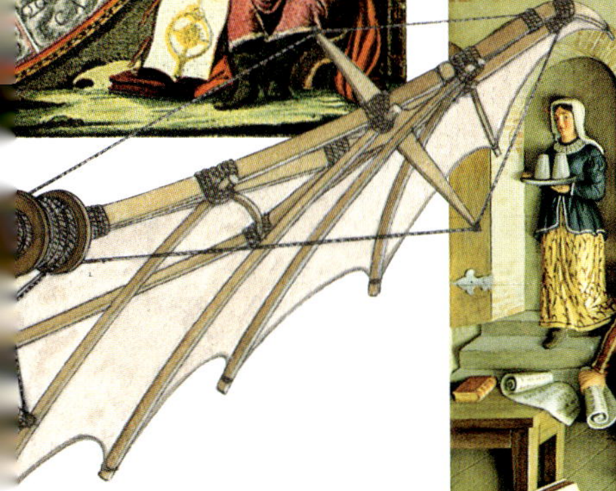

THE RENAISSANCE

1306 Italian artist Giotto di Bondone paints frescoes (wall-paintings) which are more life-like than typical medieval paintings.

1308 Dante Alighieri begins writing *The Divine Comedy*, in his native Italian not Latin.

1387 Geoffrey Chaucer begins *The Canterbury Tales*, written in English. Florence University appoints its first professor of Greek.

1416 Italian sculptor, Donatello, breaks new ground with free-standing figures, including his nude David.

1453 Constantinople is captured by the Turks; many of its scholars flee to Italy.

1454 Johannes Gutenberg perfects printing with movable type. By 1476 William Caxton is printing in London.

1466–1536 Life of Desiderius Erasmus, a Dutch scholar, philosopher and writer. He published studies of the Old and New Testaments.

1478 Lorenzo de Medici makes Florence a centre of art and learning. Sandro Botticelli finishes his painting *Primavera* (spring).

1503 The rebuilding of St Peter's in Rome begins. Leonardo da Vinci paints the *Mona Lisa*.

1508 Michelangelo paints the ceiling of the Sistine Chapel in the Vatican, Rome.

1513 Niccolo Machiavelli, an Italian political writer, writes *The Prince* on the theory of government.

1516 Sir Thomas More publishes *Utopia*.

1532 Hans Holbein, Flemish artist, is at work in England.

1543 Nicolas Copernicus puts forward his ideas about the Solar System.

1590 William Shakespeare is writing plays in England.

The Aztecs

The Aztecs were fierce warriors who conquered a huge empire that eventually reached all the way across Mexico and was at its height in the early 1500s. But in 1521, Aztec rule came to a sudden end when they lost their empire to a small band of Spanish treasure-seekers.

The Aztecs came to dominate other Native Americans in Central America by fighting constant wars with their neighbours. Their capital, Tenochtitlan, was founded in 1325 on an island in the middle of Lake Texcoco, which is now the site of modern-day Mexico City. Tenochtitlan was a walled city of 100,000 people. It had stone temples and a network of canals along which people paddled canoes. Roads on top of raised causeways linked the island to the mainland and Aztec farmers

▷ ***The heart of the Aztec empire was the Valley of Mexico,*** *but it extended far east into what is now Guatemala. Most major cities were built in the fertile central Valley of Mexico. Each was a busy market centre.*

THE AZTECS

***c.* 1200** Aztecs settle in the Valley of Mexico.
1325 The traditional date for the founding of Tenochtitlan.
1400s Aztecs control the surrounding region, in alliance with the neighbouring city-states of Texcoco and Tlacopan.
1440–1469 Reign of Montezuma I. The empire is extended.
1500 The empire is at its height. The Aztecs rule more than 10 million people, most of whom belong to other tribes.
1502 Montezuma II becomes emperor.
1519 Spaniards led by Hernando Cortés march on Tenochtitlan. They are aided by tribes hostile to the Aztecs, and are welcomed by Montezuma who believes Cortés is the god Quetzalcoatl.
1520 The Aztecs rise up against the Spanish invaders. Montezuma is wounded and dies.
1521 Cortés and his men attack and capture Tenochtitlan. End of the Aztec empire.

▷ ***Like the Maya, the Aztecs built pyramid-temples.*** *This Mayan pyramid at Uxmal gives some idea of what the Aztec Great Temple at Tenochtitlan may have looked like before the Spanish reduced it to rubble.*

GODS AND SACRIFICE

Religious ceremonies played a large part in Aztec peoples' lives. They went to war partly to capture prisoners for sacrifice to their gods. To win the gods' favour, and to ensure bountiful harvests and good fortune, priests cut open the bodies of their victims on top of stepped temples, using a sacrificial knife with an obsidian blade like the knife illustrated below. The Aztecs believed that the hearts and blood of the victims nourished the gods. The religious ceremonies that included sacrifices had to be performed on the right day, according to the sacred 260-day calendar used by the Aztecs.

sacrificial knife

◁ ***The great Calendar Stone*** *bears in its centre the face of the Sun-god Tonatiuh. The stone measures 3.7 metres across and weighs about 25 tonnes. It was unearthed in Mexico City in 1790.*

▽ ***Aztec warrior chiefs wore feather headdresses.*** *Throughout their empire, there was a profitable trade in bird feathers and other animal products, such as jaguar skins. Poor people wore simple clothes made from plant-fibre. They grew corn and vegetables to feed the rulers in the city.*

grew vegetables on artificial islands built in the lake.

The Aztecs were very skilled in sculpture, poetry, music and engineering. They worshiped the Sun as the giver of all life, and each year priests sacrificed thousands of victims to the Sun-god, cutting out their hearts as offerings. Other sacrificial victims were drowned or beheaded. These deaths, the Aztecs believed, were needed to bring good harvests and prosperity.

Aztec farmers grew corn, beans and tomatoes, and Aztec merchants traded throughout the empire. The ruling class were warriors, wearing jaguar skins and headdresses made from the tail feathers of the quetzal, a sacred bird. All warriors had to capture at least one enemy for sacrifice, and conquered peoples were forced to pay taxes to the Aztec emperor.

In 1519 Spanish treasure-seekers led by Hernando Cortés attacked the Aztecs. The Aztecs believed Cortés was a god, and their emperor Montezuma II was taken prisoner. Aztec spears and clubs were no match for Spanish guns and by 1521 the Aztec empire was finished.

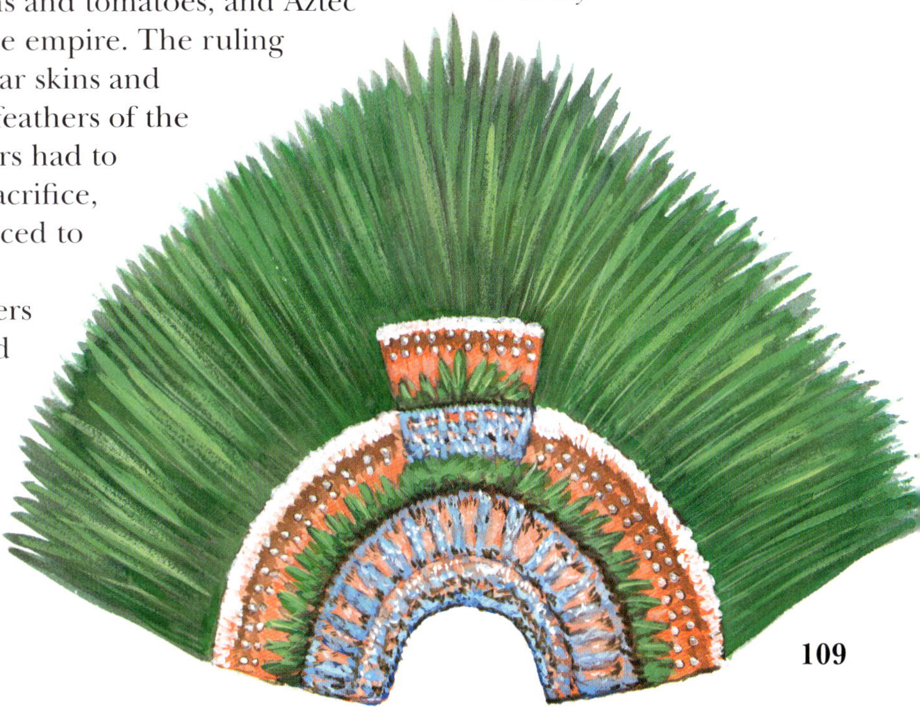

The Incas

THE INCAS

1200 Incas begin to conquer neighbouring peoples in the Andes region.

1438 Inca empire starts, under Pachacuti, the ninth Inca (king) who fights off an invasion from a neighbouring state, the Chanca. He rebuilds Cuzco as the empire's capital.

1450–1500 Under Topa Inca and his son, Huayna Capac, the empire is extended from Peru into modern-day Bolivia, Chile, Ecuador and Colombia.

1525 About this time, the first potatoes are taken to Europe from South America.

1527 Death of the emperor Huayna Capac; civil war starts between his sons Atahualpa and Huascar.

1532 Atahualpa defeats Huascar, who is imprisoned and later killed. Francisco Pizarro, with 167 soldiers, attacks Atahualpa's forces and captures Cuzco.

From the mountains of Peru, the god-emperor of the Incas ruled a highly-organized empire. Civil war, and Spanish invasion finally caused the empire to fall.

The Incas took over from the Chimu as rulers of the Andes mountains of South America. Their civilization reached its peak in the 1400s under the ruler Pachacuti who defeated an invading army from a neighbouring state. Pachacuti went on to reform the government of the Inca kingdom, appointing officials to run the country and a central administration to control the building of towns and the efficient working of farms and workshops. From the capital city Cuzco, Pachacuti and his successors greatly increased the Inca empire to include parts of Chile, Bolivia and Ecuador. The Incas built stone cities and fine roads for trade – by barter since they used no money. Farmers terraced the mountain slopes to grow corn, cotton and potatoes. In 1525 the Inca empire was at its greatest extent. In 1527 Huayna Capac died and the empire was split between his two sons.

In the 1530s a Spanish expedition led by Francisco Pizarro arrived to seek gold in South America. The Europeans were impressed by the

▽ ***The Spanish were vastly outnumbered in their battles with the Incas.*** *But they had horses, armour and guns. Many Incas fought gallantly, but with their king murdered, they were quickly defeated.*

△ ***A gold raft depicting El Dorado,*** *a legendary ruler whose body was said to be dusted with gold every year. Such tales aroused the greed of European invaders.*

▽ ***A mosaic mask made from mussel shells.*** *Masks of gods' faces were worn by Inca priests for ceremonies, and were often richly decorated.*

Inca capital city of Cuzco – its palaces and temples, sanitation and water supply, and the fortress of Sacsahuaman with huge stones which fitted together perfectly without using mortar. Although they had neither writing nor wheeled vehicles, the Incas' many skills included music, bridge-building and medicine. Some scientists believe that all Incas shared the same blood group and that it is possible that they were able to practise blood transfusion.

Though few in number, the Spaniards had horses and guns, both new to the Incas. The Incas were weakened by seven years of civil war. In 1532, Pizarro captured the Inca ruler Atahualpa and demanded for his ransom a room full of gold and two rooms full of silver. It was paid but Atahualpa was killed by the Spaniards anyway. The leaderless Inca armies were swiftly defeated, although resistance to Spanish rule continued from scattered mountain forts, such as Machu Picchu, until 1572.

△ ***The Incas had a swift communication system,*** *using fast runners carrying messages in the form of quipus (knotted cords). A message could be sent more than 200 kilometres in a day along a system of paved roads.*

1400 1433 1466 1500 1533

Voyages of Discovery

In the late 1400s and 1500s, Europeans set out to explore the oceans. Building stronger ships capable of longer voyages, they went in search of trade, new lands and treasure.

When the Byzantine empire fell to the Ottoman Turks in 1453, the old trade links by land between Europe and Asia were cut. How would Europeans get the spices from Asia that were essential to flavour their food? To find new routes to the spice-producing islands and out of curiosity and the spirit of adventure, Europeans set sail.

The Portuguese were the first to go exploring. The Portuguese prince, Henry the Navigator, took a keen interest in shipbuilding and navigation. He directed Portuguese sailors west into the Atlantic and south to explore the west coast of Africa, where they set up forts and traded in gold and ivory. Spanish, French, Dutch and English sailors followed. Instead of sailing east, some sailed west hoping to find a route to India. One famous voyage was made by Christopher Columbus, the first 15th century explorer to cross the Atlantic and return. Portugal and Spain began to settle and plunder the Americas, dividing it between them by treaty. By 1517 the Portuguese had reached China and nearly 30 years later they arrived in Japan.

△ ***Philip II became king of Spain in 1556 and ruled until 1598.*** *A devout Catholic, he encouraged his sailors and soldiers to explore and plunder, and convert to Christianity the "heathen" peoples they conquered. During his reign, overseas trade and conquests brought fabulous wealth to Spain. He worked incredibly hard, alone in an office in his huge palace El Escorial (built 1563–1584).*

▽ ***Navigators used the cross-staff and astrolabe to fix their ships' position by the sun and stars.*** *The magnetic compass pointed North, but was not always reliable.*

The ships used by the explorers were small, but more seaworthy than the clumsy vessels of the Middle Ages. They used a mixture of square and lateen (triangular) sails for easier steering and greater manoeuvrability. Sailors had only crude maps and simple instruments to guide them on voyages lasting many months. In 1519 a Portuguese captain, Ferdinand Magellan, set out from Spain with five ships. They sailed around South America, across the Pacific Ocean to the Philippines (where Magellan was killed in a fight with local people) and across the Indian Ocean to Africa. Only one ship found its way home to Spain, becoming the first ship to sail completely around the world.

NEW WORLD FOODS

As well as gold and silver treasures, European explorers brought back new foods from the Americas. Potatoes, tomatoes and peppers, plants native to America, were all unknown in Europe before 1500. Potatoes were at first a luxury, served only to rich people at banquets. Chocolate, from the cacao tree, was first brought to Spain from Mexico in 1520. Also from the New World came tobacco, turkeys and maize.

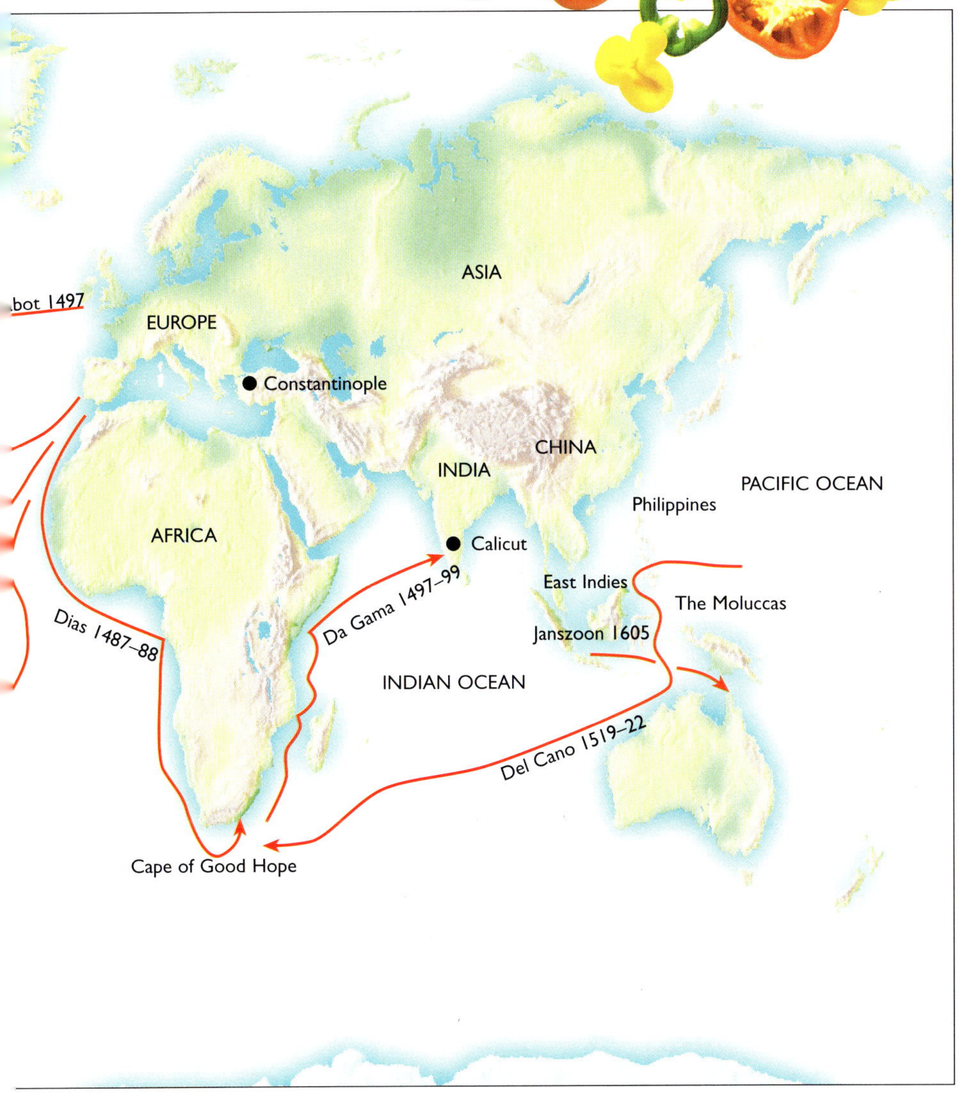

VOYAGES OF DISCOVERY

1419 Portuguese sail to the Madeira Islands.

1431 Portuguese reach the Azores.

1488 Bartolomeu Dias of Portugal explores west coast of Africa as far south as Cape of Good Hope.

1492 Christopher Columbus, an Italian sailing for Spain, makes his first voyage to America with three ships.

1494 Spain and Portugal divide the Americas between them by the Treaty of Tordesillas.

1497 John Cabot, an Italian in the service of England, sails to Canada. The Portuguese explorer Vasco Da Gama sails round Africa to India.

1500 Pedro Alvares Cabral from Portugal sails to Brazil in South America.

1501 Italian Amerigo Vespucci sails to South America. A map published in 1507 names the continent America after him.

1509 Spain begins settlement of the Americas.

1513 Spanish explorer Vasco Nuñez de Balboa is the first European to see the Pacific.

1517 Portuguese traders reach China.

1522 First round-the-world voyage is completed by Ferdinand Magellan's Spanish crew.

1524 Italian Giovanni da Verrazano searches for a northwest passage from Europe to Asia.

◁ ***The voyages of Magellan, Columbus and Da Gama*** *revealed to Europeans that the world was larger than ancient geographers had believed. They sailed across oceans and landed on continents unknown to earlier Europeans.*

Spain and Portugal

Spain became the superpower of Europe in the 1500s. Spanish and Portuguese explorers led the way in the European voyages of discovery, to the Americas and to Asia.

Medieval Spain was divided between Christian and Muslim kingdoms. After wars of reconquest, the two Christian monarchs who ended Muslim rule in Spain were Ferdinand of Aragon and Isabella of Castile. In 1469 Ferdinand and Isabella were married, uniting Spain's two strongest Christian kingdoms. By 1492 their forces had captured Granada, the last Muslim outpost in Spain. The new rulers were intolerant of other religions and set up the Spanish Inquisition to search out heretics – both Christians who held different beliefs from the established Church and people of other faiths, such as Jews.

In the 16th century, Spain became Europe's strongest nation. Its power was based on a strong army, which fought wars in Europe (against the Dutch, for example) and on a large navy,

▽ ***In the 1400s, Spain was not yet one kingdom.*** *Aragon and Castile were the strongest Christian kingdoms, while Granada was ruled by Muslim emirs, who had once held southern Spain.*

▷ ***Columbus leaves the court of Spain,*** *having won the support of King Ferdinand and Queen Isabella for his westward voyage. Columbus set sail on August 3, 1492. He was convinced that the Atlantic was a narrow ocean.*

HENRY THE NAVIGATOR

Prince Henry of Portugal (1394–1460) dreamed of exploration overseas, and brought together seamen, shipbuilders and mapmakers to plan voyages. With Henry's encouragement he Portuguese built new, stronger ships called caravels. They sailed west to reach the Canary Islands and the Azores, and south to explore the coast of Africa. Each voyage took the explorers further into the unknown.

which controlled the profitable trade in gold and silver from Spain's newly conquered empire in the Americas. Spanish power reached its peak during the reign of Charles I (1516–1556) who also became Holy Roman emperor in 1519 and so controlled lands in Germany, Austria and the Netherlands, as well as parts of France and Italy. On his death, his lands were divided between his son Philip II (who ruled Spain, the Netherlands and Spanish colonies in the Americas) and his brother Ferdinand (who became Holy Roman emperor).

By 1580, the Spanish empire included Portugal. With its long Atlantic coastline and shipbuilding skills, Portugal had led the way in European exploration of the oceans. Its sailors had opened up new trade routes to Asia. The Portuguese already controlled an overseas empire that included large stretches of coastline in East and West Africa, Brazil and India, as well as trading posts such as Goa in India, Macao in China and many islands in Southeast Asia.

▷ ***Arabic script on Spanish stonework.*** *Muslim craftworkers left a brilliant legacy in southern Spain, especially in the architecture of cities such as Granada and Cordoba.*

▽ ***Catherine of Aragon (1485–1536) was the daughter of King Ferdinand and Queen Isabella of Spain.*** *In 1509 she became the first of the six wives of King Henry VIII of England. Henry divorced Catherine because she did not produce the son he wanted.*

SPAIN AND PORTUGAL

711 Muslims invade southern Spain (which includes what later becomes Portugal).

Early 1000s Muslim central rule of Spain collapses in civil war. Many small Moorish states and cities are set up. Christian states begin the reconquest of Spain.

1043–1099 El Cid (Rodrigo Diaz de Vivar), warrior hero of medieval Spain, fights for Christian Castile.

1143 Portugal gains independence from Castile.

Late 1200s Granada is the only Moorish kingdom in Spain.

1385 John I of Portugal fights Spain and makes an alliance with England. His son, Henry the Navigator, begins Portugal's rise as a sea power.

1479 Aragon and Castile become one kingdom.

1492 Moors are forced out of Granada. Jews are expelled from Spain. Columbus sails to America.

1512 Ferdinand seizes Navarre to complete unification of Spain.

1521 Spain conquers Aztec empire in Mexico.

1535 Spain conquers Inca empire of Peru.

1556 Philip II becomes king of Spain: Spanish empire is at its height.

1565 Spain colonizes the Philippines.

1568 War in the Spanish Netherlands begins.

1571 Battle of Lepanto: warships of Spain and Austria defeat a Turkish fleet in the Mediterranean.

1580 Spain conquers Portugal and holds it until 1640.

1588 Spanish Armada sails to invade England, but fails.

African Empires

AFRICAN EMPIRES

1300s European rulers try to contact the legendary Prester John. Great Zimbabwe is the heart of a powerful Bantu kingdom, one of a chain from the Indian Ocean coast north to the Congo River.

1335 The Songhai ruling dynasty is founded.

1341 Suleiman is king of Mali to 1360.

1430s Portuguese begin exploring the west coast of Africa.

1460s Portuguese explorers reach Sierra Leone and buy ivory, pepper, palm oil and slaves from the kingdom of Benin.

1464 Songhai breaks away from Mali's control.

1468 Sonni Ali captures Timbuktu.

1481 Portuguese traders set up a fortress at Elmina in the Gulf of Guinea. The Portuguese use such forts as bases to trade with African rulers.

1488 Portuguese explorer Bartolomeu Dias rounds the Cape of Good Hope.

1493 Askia Muhammad I heads new ruling dynasty in Songhai, now at its peak, and takes over Mandingo empire.

1506 The African kingdom of Kongo has its first Christian king, Afonso I.

1511 A Portuguese explorer reaches Great Zimbabwe, by now in decline.

1520 A Portuguese mission travels to Ethiopia (lasts until 1526).

***c.* 1530** The transatlantic slave trade from Africa to the Americas begins.

1571–1603 Idris Alawma rules the empire of Kanem-Bornu in the Sudan region.

1591 Songhai empire is defeated by Moroccans, aided by Spanish and Portuguese soldiers.

Africa in 1500 was a continent with many kingdoms and empires. The richest African rulers commanded trade in gold, ivory and slaves – goods that attracted European traders.

Portuguese traders sailing the coasts of West Africa heard tales of wondrous kingdoms in the heart of the continent. The strongest was Songhai, a Muslim kingdom that controlled trade across the Sahara Desert. In 1464 King Sonni Ali freed Songhai from the control of the Mali empire and went on to overrun the empire, expanding Songhai and its capital, Gao. A new dynasty was founded in 1493 by Askia Muhammad I, who gained great wealth from the trading cities of Jenne and Timbuktu. He commanded a large army and ruled from a splendid court through a sophisticated system of government departments. Songhai rule lasted until 1591, when it was overthrown by Moroccans armed with guns.

Another Muslim empire stretched through parts of modern-day Chad, Cameroon, Nigeria, Niger and Libya. This was Kanem-Bornu, an empire that thrived on trade between northern and southern Africa and reached its peak under Idris Alawma from

▷ ***Traders gather to do business in Timbuktu.*** *The city at the southern edge of the Sahara Desert was the centre of the gold and salt trade. Its Muslim scholars acted as counsellors to the ruler of the Songhai empire, Askia Muhammad I. Merchants came from as far as Morocco to sell cloth and horses there.*

▽ ***Ethiopia was a mostly Christian kingdom.*** *Ethiopian Christians built churches like this one, cut from solid rock. Fifteen rock churches survive at Lalibela (then called Roha), the capital in the 1200s. The cross-shaped church is actually hollowed out of the rock.*

PRESTER JOHN

Travellers told tales of Prester ("priest") John, a fabulously rich ruler. He was first said to be a Christian king in Asia, and later to be the ruler of Ethiopia in Africa. One story claimed he had a magic mirror in which he saw everything going on throughout his empire. Another story tells that, in one of Prester John's kingdoms, great ants dug up gold for his treasury.

about 1570. In northeast Africa was Ethiopia, a Christian empire in the heart of Muslim Africa. Europeans heard tantalising tales of its legendary Christian ruler, Prester John. Here, and to the south, Africans lived by farming and cattle-herding.

By 1450 a settlement at Great Zimbabwe in central Africa was at its greatest extent. Built over a period of about 400 years, Great Zimbabwe was probably a royal residence surrounded by massive walls and a high tower. Used by rulers as their stronghold and administrative centre, the site was a major religious, political and trading centre. The people of this prosperous African kingdom used copper and iron, and traded in gold with Sofala on the east coast (present-day Mozambique). By 1500 the civilization that built Zimbabwe was in decline.

▷ ***The ruins of Great Zimbabwe.*** *The walled citadel was once surrounded by village houses, fields and grazing cattle. The stone walls were built for defence and to show the power of the ruler.*

▽ ***This map shows the most important kingdoms of Africa at this time*** *– Songhai in the western sub-Sahara region, Kanem-Bornu further east, Ethiopia in the mountainous northwest, and Great Zimbabwe in central-southern Africa.*

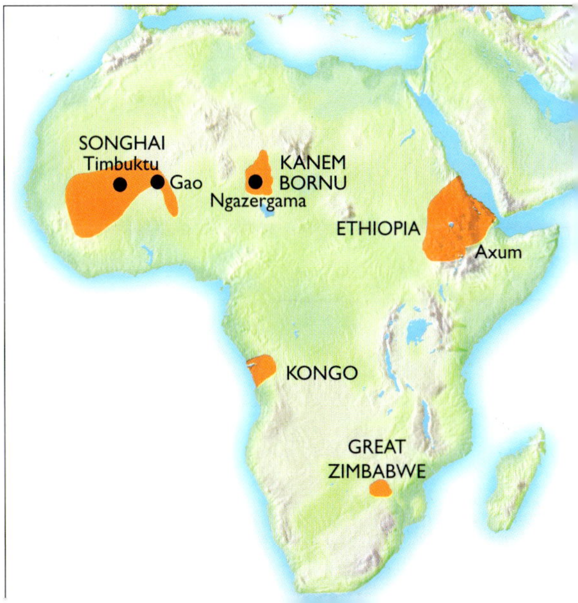

The Reformation

The Renaissance aimed to restore church practice closer to the Old and New Testaments. These changes in thinking led to the Reformation – a challenge to the established Christian church in western Europe.

The Renaissance led to writers from the time before Christ (mainly those of ancient Greece and Rome) being read again, and their ideas inspired a new philosophy known as humanism – the belief that humans were in control of their own destinies.

Humanism arose at a time of growing discontent in the western Christian church over the way the church was run. In 1517 Martin Luther, a German monk, protested publicly at what he saw as the church's theological corruption and called for reform. His campaign began what is known as the Reformation and led to the formation of the Protestant church as his ideas

◁ ***John Calvin, religious reformer, was born in France.*** *He believed that only people chosen by God would be saved from damnation. His reforms became known as "Calvinism".*

THE REFORMATION

1498 Savonarola, an Italian friar who preached church reform, is burned at the stake in Florence.
1517 Start of the Reformation. Martin Luther nails 95 theses against the sale of indulgences (pardons for sins) on a church door in Wittenberg, Germany.
1519 Ulrich Zwingli starts the Reformation in Switzerland.
1521 The Diet (assembly) of Worms is convened. Luther is excommunicated.
1529 Henry VIII breaks with Rome so that he can divorce Catherine of Aragon. In 1534 he is made head of the Church of England.
1532 John Calvin starts Protestant movement in France.
1534 Ignatius Loyola founds the Society of Jesus, or Jesuits.
1536 Dissolution of the monasteries in England.
1541 John Knox takes the Reformation to Scotland.
1549 A new prayer book, the Book of Common Prayer, is introduced in England.
1555 England returns to Catholicism under Mary I. Archbishop Cranmer is burned at the stake.
1558–1603 Elizabeth I, a Protestant, rules England.
1562 Religious wars in France between Catholics and Huguenots (Protestants).
1568 Protestant Dutch revolt against Spanish rule starts.
1572 St Bartholomew's Day Massacre: many Huguenots in France are killed.
1581 Protestant Netherlands declare independence from Spain (not recognized by Spain until 1648).
1588 Defeat of the Spanish Armada.
1598 Edict of Nantes gives Protestants and Catholics in France equal rights.

were taken up and spread by rebels in other countries such as Ulrich Zwingli in Switzerland and John Calvin in France.

The new technology of printing spread these new ideas. The Bible, which previously had been available only in Latin, the language of scholars, was translated into local languages for all to read. Some rulers used discontent with the church to further their own affairs. Henry VIII of England, for example, wanted his marriage to Catherine of Aragon dissolved. He asked the Pope for a divorce, but when the Pope refused, Henry broke with the church in Rome as a means to get his own way.

From 1545 the Catholic church fought back with a movement known as the Counter Reformation, sending out Jesuit priests to campaign against the spread of Protestantism and convert the peoples of the Spanish empire. The split between Christians in western Europe led to wars as countries struggled with new religious alliances. Catholics and Protestants persecuted one another, often in the cruellest ways. As religious disputes in Europe continued into the 1600s, some people left Europe and sought religious freedom in the new world of America.

◁ ***Martin Luther believed that people were saved by faith alone,*** *that the Bible was central to that faith, and that church services should be in everyday languages, not in Latin.*

▽ ***The Spanish sent the Armada against England in 1588 to restore Catholic rule.*** *An English fireship attack off Calais helped fight off the planned invasion, and the great fleet was eventually wrecked and scattered by storms around the coasts of northern Britain.*

◁ ***King Henry VIII made himself head of the Church of England*** *to gain a divorce. He was not, in fact, a supporter of Protestant beliefs.*

Ottomans and Safavids

The Ottoman capture of Constantinople in 1453 marked the beginning of a Turkish golden age. They controlled the eastern Mediterranean and the Near East, and their armies moved west to threaten Europe. They fought many wars against their Muslim rivals in Persia, the Safavids.

After the fall of Constantinople, the Ottoman Turks renamed the city Istanbul and it became the centre of a Muslim empire that, at its peak, stretched from Algeria to Arabia and from Egypt to Hungary. Most of these conquests were made during the rule of Suleiman I (1520–1566), who was known as the Law-Giver to his own subjects and as the Magnificent to Europeans. The Turks invaded Persia (modern-day Iran), captured Baghdad, took control of the island of Rhodes and crossed the river Danube into

▽ ***A map showing the Ottoman and Safavid empires.*** *Lawyers, poets, architects and scholars came to the royal courts of their rulers from all over the Islamic world.*

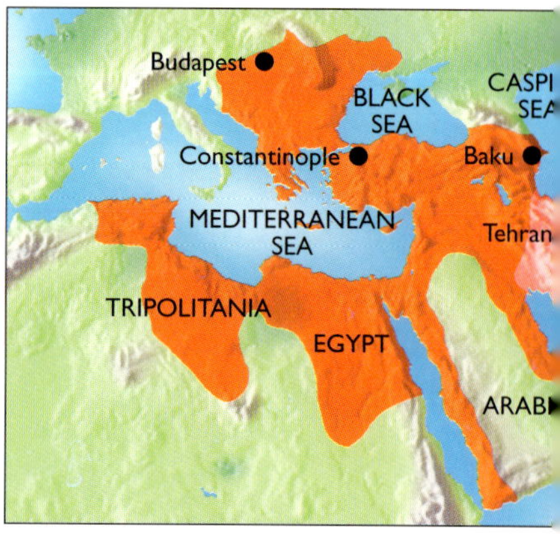

▽ ***The Ottoman sultan Suleiman I*** *made the Ottoman empire a power to be respected and feared, not just in the Middle East but in Europe as well. He was called Suleiman the Magnificant.*

Hungary, where they won the battle of Mohacs in 1526.

By 1529 the Turkish army was outside the city walls of Vienna and looked likely to burst into western Europe. However, the siege of Vienna was lifted and Europe relaxed. Ottoman fleets of galleys (oared warships) controlled the Mediterranean Sea and Turkish pirates, such as the fearsome Barbarossa (Khayr ad-Din Pasha), raided ports, captured merchant ships and carried off Christians to be slaves. Ottoman sea power, too, was checked, when in 1571 a combined Christian fleet defeated the Turkish fleet at the naval battle of Lepanto in the Gulf of Corinth in Greece. This battle ended Turkish threats to Europe by sea.

Suleiman also tried three times to conquer Persia, which from 1501 was under the rule of the Safavid dynasty founded by Shah Ismail I. Here the people were Shiites, not Sunni Muslims as in the Ottoman empire. Safavid rivalry with the Ottomans continued under Shah Abbas I (1557–1628). From his capital of Isfahan with its beautiful tiled mosques, Shah Abbas I ruled not only Persia but also most of Mesopotamia (modern-day Iraq). Wars between the two empires continued throughout the 16th century and helped to stop the Ottoman empire advancing into Europe.

△ ***The Battle of Lepanto in 1571*** *was fought in the Gulf of Corinth between a Turkish fleet of about 273 galleys and a Christian fleet of 200 galleys and heavier galleasses. The Turks were defeated. They lost at least 20,000 men, the Christians about 8,000. This was the last great sea battle between fleets of galleys.*

◁ ***The Ottoman sultans lived in the walled Topkapi Palace,*** *which was surrounded by beautiful gardens. Begun in 1562, the Palace is now a museum of Ottoman treasures, including a library of 40,000 documents.*

▽ ***A Persian carpet of the 1500s.*** *Spinners and weavers made these famous carpets of knotted wool and silk. Traditional designs included flowers, leaves and various geometric shapes. They featured soft colours and elegant patterns.*

OTTOMANS AND SAFAVIDS

1288 Osman becomes ruler of the Ottoman Turks. Defeats Byzantine army in 1301.
1402 Tamerlane rules most of Ottoman empire (until he dies in 1405).
1453 Ottomans capture the city of Constantinople which is renamed Istanbul.
1463 Ottoman Turks conquer Bosnia, having already captured Serbia (1459).
1501 Foundation of the Safavid dynasty in Persia, by Shah Ismail I.
1516 Ottoman Turks conquer Egypt, defeating Mamelukes.
1520 Suleiman I becomes sultan of the Ottoman empire.
1522 Turks capture Rhodes.
1526 Battle of Mohacs in Hungary is won by the Turks.
1529 At the siege of Vienna, capital of Austria, the Turks fail to capture the city.
1534 Turks capture Tunis, Baghdad and Mesopotamia.
1565 Turks attack Malta, but are fought off by the Knights of St John.
1571 Battle of Lepanto. Don John of Austria destroys the Ottoman fleet led by Ali Pasha.
1587 Shah Abbas I comes to the throne of Persia.
1590 Turks and Persians make peace.
c. **1600** The Ottoman empire begins to decline.

The Mughal Empire

The Mughal dynasty ruled a mighty empire in India for nearly three hundred years. Its founder, Babur, was followed by an even greater ruler, Akbar, under whose reign there was a great flowering of Mughal art and learning.

Babur was a Muslim chieftain from Afghanistan who made his name by capturing Samarkand, once the capital city of his ancestor Tamerlane. But Babur's eyes were on a greater prize. With his army, and the cannon that his gunners used with great skill, he moved into northern India. In 1526 Babur defeated the sultan of Delhi's army at the battle of Panipat, thus founding the Mughal dynasty. Babur was a shrewd and able ruler, but he died four years after his triumph. His son Humayun succeeded him, but he faced dangerous rebellions and, after a reign of ten years, was driven out of India and remained in Persia for fifteen years.

The golden age of Mughal India began in 1556 under the rule of Akbar. Then only 13, he was Babur's grandson and inherited Babur's talents. Akbar defeated several Hindu kingdoms, but did not antagonize them. A great military leader, he widened the empire still further by war and skilful diplomacy and his capture of Bengal, with its riches of rice and silk, was the high point of his career. A conqueror who crushed rebellions, Akbar was also famed as a wise and just ruler. He tolerated all religions, even

△ ***The Taj Mahal*** *was built between1631 and 1648 for the favourite wife of India's Mughal emperor, Shah Jahan. 20,000 workers and artists helped create this most beautiful building. It is made of white marble.*

▷ ***A Sikh today.***
The Sikh religion was founded in the Punjab region of northern India in the early 1500s by Guru Nanak. The Sikhs fought for freedom from Mughal rule, inspired by their gurus (teachers).

permitting Hindus and Portuguese Christians to discuss their faiths at his court. He introduced new styles in art and architecture, making his royal court of Fatehpur Sikri a centre of learning for the Mughal empire that he ruled until his death in 1605.

Akbar was succeeded by his son, Jahangir who preferred the company of painters and poets to ruling a large empire. In 1627 his son, Shah Jahan, succeeded him and set about enlarging the empire. He, too, was a great patron of the arts and paid for many splendid buildings, such as the Taj Mahal near Agra. But Shah Jahan had a tragic end, when in 1657 he fell ill and an argument broke out among his sons over who should rule. His third son, Aurangzeb, won the struggle and killed his other brothers, imprisoning his father and seizing the throne. Shah Jahan died in captivity and was buried next to his wife in the Taj Mahal.

Aurangzeb was the last great Mughal ruler, expanding the empire to its greatest extent. Unlike his predecessors, however, Aurangzeb was a strict Muslim and extracted taxes from non-Muslim subjects. He also destroyed many Hindu shrines. After Aurangzeb's death in 1707 the Mughal empire began to break up. He was hailed as the greatest of all the Mughal emperors.

△ ***Akbar leads his troops in battle.*** *This 1568 painting shows Mughal soldiers, equipped with firearms, storming an enemy fortress. War elephants were used like tanks by armies in India during Akbar's brilliant wars of conquest.*

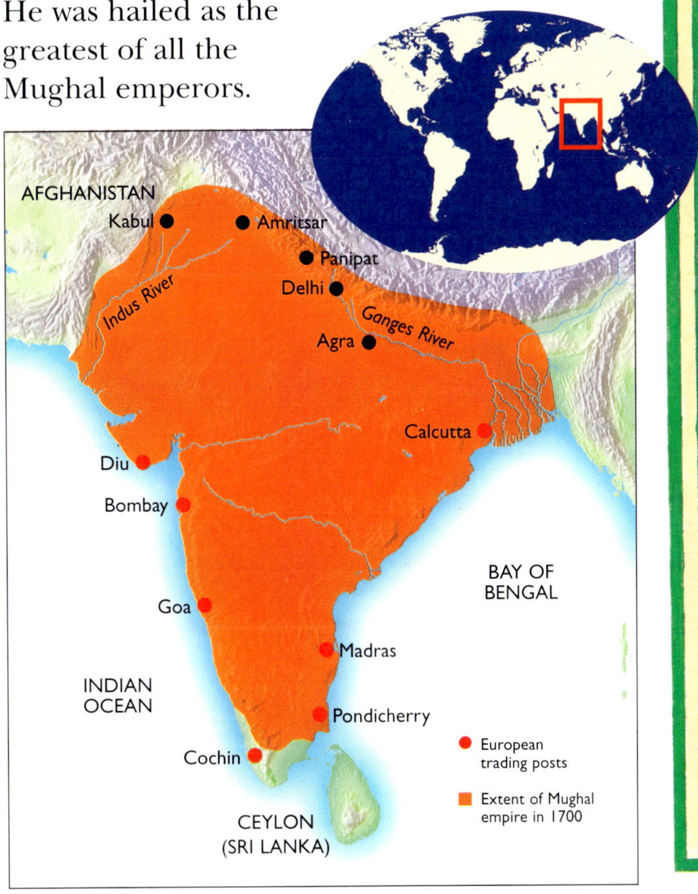

MUGHAL EMPIRE

1526 Foundation of the Mughal dynasty. Victory at Panipat against the sultan of Delhi, Ibrahim Lodi, gives Babur control of northern India.

1529 Akbar defeats the Afghans.

1530 Humayun becomes emperor.

1540 After Humayun is defeated by Sher Shah, a ruler of eastern India, he is exiled to Persia (until 1555).

1542 Akbar, grandson of Babur, is born.

1556 Start of Akbar's reign; he wins a second battle of Panipat against the Hindus.

1565 Akbar extends his rule to southern India. A great fort is built at Agra.

1567 Akbar subdues the Rajput princes, storming the fortress of Chitor with mines and artillery.

1569 Fatehpur Sikri is founded.

1575 Akbar conquers Bengal.

1600 British East India Company is formed.

1605 Akbar is succeeded by Jahangir, a weak emperor.

1627–1657 Rule of Shah Jahan.

1658–1707 Rule of Aurangzeb.

1664 Hindu Marathas overrun western India.

1720s Mughal empire collapses.

◁ ***A map of the Mughal empire.*** *Akbar ruled from Agra and Fatehpur Sikri. He defeated the Delhi sultan at Panipat. Akbar organized an efficient land tax system to govern his vast empire.*

Ming China

In the 1300s the Mongol grip on China grew weak. A revolt drove out the last Yuan (Mongol) emperor, and in 1368 a Buddhist monk took his place and called himself Ming Hong Wu founding a new dynasty. The Ming dynasty ruled China for almost 300 years.

Under Hong Wu, Chinese self-confidence and national pride reasserted itself. Initially an able and efficient ruler, though despotic later, the first Ming emperor established good government that ensured a long period of peace and prosperity for China. Hong Wu made Chinese society more equal by abolishing slavery, confiscating large estates and redistributing them among the poor, and demanding higher taxes from the rich. China began to reassert its power over its neighbours and a strong army was maintained to withstand foreign attacks.

Hong Wu was succeeded by emperors who continued the good works he had begun. They sponsored the arts, so making the Ming period one of great creativity, especially in porcelain. In the early 1400s, Chinese ships (then the largest in the world) made voyages as far as Africa and Arabia in fleets under the command of admiral Zheng He. The Ming emperors were also great builders and from 1421, they lived within the walls of the Forbidden City in

△ ***Chinese soldiers fight against invading Japanese samurai.*** *In the 1590s the Japanese tried to invade Korea, which the Chinese regarded as their allies.*

▽ ***The Forbidden City in Beijing.*** *Yung Lo, third Ming emperor, made Beijing his capital in 1421. The emperor lived in seclusion inside the Forbidden City. No foreigner and no Chinese outside the imperial household was allowed to enter the Forbidden City.*

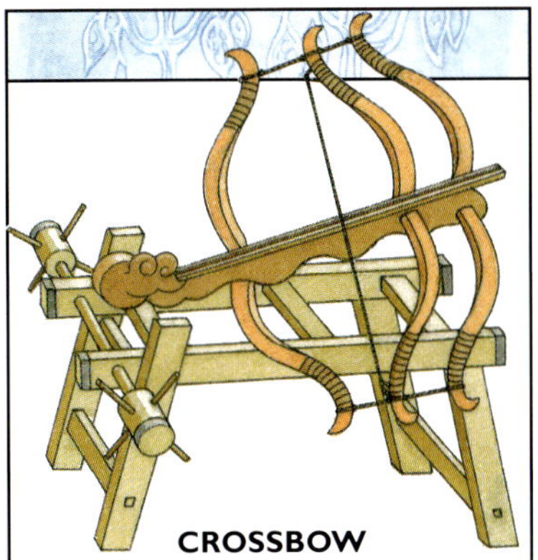

CROSSBOW
A Chinese artillery crossbow. A powerful bow like this could fire an arrow up to 200 metres, and pierce a wooden shield. The Chinese developed a number of other ingenious weapons, including gunpowder rockets and bombs, which they first used about AD 1000.

Beijing, a huge complex of palaces, temples and parks into which no foreigner was admitted. Few Chinese ever saw inside the Forbidden City, apart from the emperor's family and the officials and servants of the royal household.

China's first contacts with European traders began in the 1500s, when Portuguese ships arrived. By 1557 the Portuguese had a trading settlement in Macao, and Matteo Ricci, a Jesuit missionary, came to China in 1583. Western traders were eager to buy Chinese porcelain and silk and a new drink, tea, which first reached Europe in 1610.

The Chinese had seldom looked far beyond their borders and after the mid-1500s the government banned voyages overseas. As the most powerful empire in the world, Ming rulers regarded China as the centre of the world. They defended their territory and weaker subject-peoples against foreigners such as Hideyoshi of Japan, whose armies tried to invade Korea in the 1590s but later withdrew.

MING CHINA

1368 Foundation of the Ming dynasty in China.

1398 Death of the first Ming emperor, Hong Wu, who has extended his rule to all China and to Mongolia and Manchuria.

1405–1433 Zheng He leads seven voyages westwards to explore India and East Africa. The Chinese demand tribute from the countries their ships visit, regarding them as inferior.

1421 The capital is moved from Nanjing to Beijing.

1449 The Ming emperor is captured by the western Mongols, a rare setback for the Ming armies. He resumes the throne in 1457.

1505–1560 A period of poor government by two cruel and pleasure-loving emperors.

1514 Portuguese traders arrive in China, followed by the Dutch in 1522.

1551 Chinese government bans voyages beyond Chinese waters.

1557 The Portuguese set up a trading base at Macao.

1560 Ming forces drive off Mongols and pirate raids, until peace and prosperity are restored. China's population approaches 150 million.

1575 Spanish begin trade with China.

1592–1598 Ming armies help Koreans fight off Japanese invaders.

1644 The last Ming emperor, Ssu Tsung, commits suicide.

△ ***Italian missionary Matteo Ricci*** *learned the language and customs of China. He visited Beijing in 1607, presenting two clocks to the emperor.*

Oceania

The people of Oceania – Australia, New Zealand and the Pacific islands – lived by hunting and food gathering, fishing and farming. They had come from southern or eastern Asia thousands of years before, travelling between the islands by canoe.

▽ ***Flightless birds, called moas,*** *lived in New Zealand. There were a number of different species, the tallest being 3 metres tall and weighing over 250 kg. The last moas died out in the 1700s.*

The first aboriginal peoples of Australia probably arrived there from the islands of Southeast Asia about 40,000 years ago. They lived by hunting and gathering and were isolated from the rest of the world. They developed a sophisticated way to exploit the wide variety of environments found in Australia, using boomerangs for hunting and gathering seeds, grubs, roots, tubers and fruit. They developed a rich cultural life that included the myths of the Dream Time and beautifully ornate rock paintings often on sacred sites.

The Polynesians are the most widely spread people in the world. Their ancestors first lived in eastern Asia and, about 3,500 years ago, set sail in open canoes to find new lands to live in. They set out into the unknown in canoes loaded with the essentials of their life – coconuts, taro, yams, bananas, breadfruit, pigs and chickens – and used their skills and luck to colonize the vast Pacific Ocean. Their canoes reached as far as Easter Island in the western Pacific and the Hawaiian Islands in the north.

◁ ***One of the mysterious stone heads on Easter Island.*** *The island in the Pacific was settled from about AD 400, probably by Polynesians. The tallest figure is 11 metres high. More than 600 stone statues are scattered around the island.*

△ ***The Maoris of New Zealand*** *built wooden stockades, called pas. Warriors fought from platforms on the walls, and to capture an enemy's fort was a great triumph. The victors took the food stored inside.*

One of the last places they colonized was New Zealand.

Polynesian Maoris first came to New Zealand probably in about AD 750. As their culture developed, there were frequent blood-feuds and wars between Maori groups. The Maoris built hill-forts with stockades and platforms from which warriors hurled weapons (and insults) at their enemies outside. They decorated their faces and bodies with tattoos to show their standing in the community – the more tattoos, the higher the position.

Australia was settled by Aborigines in prehistoric times and later visited by Indonesian traders, but was otherwise isolated. A Portuguese ship may have strayed far enough south for its crew to sight New Zealand or Australia in the 1500s. A mysterious large island is shown on European maps made in the 1540s. The first known landing in Australia by Europeans was made in 1606 and European explorers only reached New Zealand in 1642.

OCEANIA

- *c.* **400** First settlers land on Easter Island.
- *c.* **750** Maoris start to settle New Zealand by this time.
- **1300** By this date all New Zealand is settled. Huge stone statues are erected on Easter Island.
- **1500s** Portuguese navigators begin to explore the Pacific.
- **1519–1521** Ferdinand Magellan's ships cross the Pacific Ocean during the first-ever circumnavigation of the globe.
- **1526** Portuguese land on Papua New Guinea.
- **1567** Spanish explorer Mendana de Neyra visits the Solomon Islands.
- **1577–1580** English explorer Sir Francis Drake explores the Pacific during his round-the-world voyage.
- **1606** Dutch sailor Willem Jansz lands on the west coast of Australia.
- **1615** Luis Vaez de Torres of Spain explores coasts of New Guinea and northern Australia.
- **1642** Dutch sailor Abel Tasman explores the coast of Tasmania and New Zealand's South Island.

▷ ***A tattooed Maori warrior chief,*** *painted in the 19th century. Maori weapons included clubs, stabbing spears and long staves. Both men and women were tattooed, to show their rank. Fighting was part of Maori culture, and tribal feuds were common.*

▽ ***A Maori war canoe sets out on a raid.*** *Like other Pacific islanders, the Maoris built canoes for sea travel. People moved from island to island across the Pacific Ocean in wooden canoes, often twin-hulled like modern catamarans. Some settlements were the result of accidental voyages but others, of planned migrations in fleets of large canoes.*

The Thirty Years War

The religious conflicts that started after the Reformation continued into the 17th century. The most serious was the Thirty Years War. It began in 1618 as a protest by the Protestant noblemen of Bohemia (now part of the Czech Republic) against their Catholic rulers, the Habsburg Holy Roman emperors.

The noblemen chose a Protestant to become King Frederick of Bohemia, but in 1619 Ferdinand II became the new Holy Roman emperor. Rebellion against Ferdinand's rule soon spread to Germany and, determined to turn his whole empire back to Catholicism, Ferdinand sent his army to attack Bohemia.

The Bohemians were hoping for help from other Protestant countries in Europe, but at first this did not arrive. In 1620 Ferdinand's army defeated Frederick's so completely that Frederick and his family were forced to flee to the Netherlands. Soon Catholicism was the only religion allowed in Bohemia. A year later Spain, also ruled by the Habsburgs, joined the war on the side of the Holy Roman empire and sent an army to fight the Protestant Dutch. By 1625 Spain seemed likely to win and so the Dutch asked Denmark and England for help. Many English soldiers, however, died of plague before they could fight and by 1629 Habsburg armies had also defeated the Danes.

▽ ***King Gustavus II Adolphus*** *of Sweden leading his troops into battle. A brave and inspiring leader, he always fought at the head of his men. He went to war against the Habsburgs because he believed the Protestant religion was in danger of being destroyed. He also thought that the Swedish economy, which depended heavily on trade, was being threatened by a Spanish plan to extend their power to the Baltic Sea, which Sweden itself wanted to control.*

CARDINAL RICHELIEU
The French statesman Richelieu (1585–1642) started his rise to power as adviser to Marie de'Medici, the mother of French king Louis XIII. In 1629 he became Louis's chief minister and began building up the power of the French crown. He ruthlessly suppressed Protestantism in France, but supported the Protestant states in the Thirty Years War in order to defeat Spain and make France the most powerful country in Europe.

△ ***In 1618, a group of Bohemian nobles*** *threw two Catholic governors out of a window in Prague Castle. This act, called the Defenestration of Prague, sparked off the Thirty Years War.*

▷ ***This map shows*** *how Europe looked after the Treaty of Westphalia was signed in 1648. France was the dominant power, while Switzerland, many states in Germany and part of the Netherlands became independent.*

Believing the Protestant religion to be in danger, the Swedish king Gustavus II Adolphus led his army to war against Spain and the Holy Roman empire in 1630. He defeated them at Breitenfeld in 1631 and his army was victorious again at Lutzen in 1632. But Gustavus was killed just after the battle of Lutzen, and two years later Sweden also withdrew from the war.

Finally France, although Catholic, entered the war in order to curtail Habsburg power. At first Spain was victorious, but from 1637 the French and their Protestant allies were able to defeat them. The war ended in 1648 with the Treaty of Westphalia, which gave religious freedom and independence to Protestant states. The long war devastated many states in Germany. Some lost over half their population through disease, famine and fighting.

THIRTY YEARS WAR

1618 War starts with the Defenestration of Prague.
1619 Ferdinand II is crowned Holy Roman emperor.
1620 Ferdinand's army enters Bohemia and defeats Protestant king Frederick.
1621 Fighting breaks out between Dutch and Spanish in the Rhineland.
1625 Denmark and England join in the war on the side of the Dutch. The Danes do most of the fighting.
1629 Denmark and England withdraw from the war.
1630 King Gustavus II Adolphus of Sweden joins the war on the side of the Protestants.
1631 Swedish victory at the battle of Breitenfeld.
1632 Gustavus is killed after the battle of Lutzen. His chancellor, Oxenstierna, takes command, but is not as successful.
1634 Sweden withdraws following defeat at Nordlingen.
1635 Richelieu takes France into the war against Habsburgs.
1637 French and allies start to defeat Spain.
1643 Following French victory at Rocroi, Olivares (Spain's prime minister) falls from power.
1648 The Treaty of Westphalia brings an end to the Thirty Years War.
1659 Spain and France cease fighting; France becomes the most powerful country in Europe.

TOKUGAWA JAPAN

1543 Birth of Tokugawa Ieyasu.
1550 Ieyasu is sent as a hostage to the Imagawa family.
1560 Ieyasu returns to his own lands and allies himself with the warlord, Nobunaga.
1582 Nobunaga commits suicide. He is succeeded by Hideyoshi.
1584 After several small battles, Ieyasu allies himself with Hideyoshi.
1598 Hideyoshi's death starts a new struggle for power among Japan's warlords. Ieyasu is one of the leaders.
1600 Ieyasu defeats his rivals at the battle of Sekigahara.
1603 The emperor appoints Ieyasu shogun and the Tokugawa period begins.
1605 Ieyasu abdicates as shogun but continues to advise his successors on how to run the country.
1613 The population of Edo is estimated to be 150,000, including 80,000 samurai.
1616 Death of Ieyasu.
1635 All the daimyos are forced to have a house in Edo and spend several months of each year there to make sure that they are not secretly plotting against the shogun.
1637 Christianity is banned in Japan and all foreigners, apart from the Dutch, are forced to leave.
1680 The production of silk, cotton, paper and porcelain flourishes at this time.
1700s Merchants and tradesmen prosper for much of this century, but the daimyos and samurai become less wealthy than they had been.
1830s Peasants and samurai rebel against the Tokugawas.
1867 The last Tokugawa shogun is overthrown.

Tokugawa Japan

The Tokugawa, or Edo, period in Japan marked the end of a series of civil wars and brought a long period of stability and unity. In 1603, Tokugawa Ieyasu became the first of the Tokugawa shoguns (powerful military leaders and effective rulers of Japan). He and his descendants held office until 1867.

Tokugawa Ieyasu was born in 1543, a time when the Japanese warlords were fighting among themselves for control of the country. When Ieyasu was seven, he was sent as a hostage to the Imagawa family at Sumpu. There he learned the skills of fighting and government. When the head of the Imagawa family was killed in battle, Ieyasu returned to his own lands and began a long and well-planned struggle for power. By 1598 he had the biggest army in Japan. He also had the best organized and most productive estates in the country, centred on the fishing village of Edo. In 1603, after defeating his enemies, the emperor appointed Ieyasu to the position of shogun, giving him power to run the country on the emperor's behalf.

△ ***Kabuki drama*** *developed as a popular art form in 17th century Japan. Plays were performed to music, and costumes and make-up were very elaborate, especially for the female roles, which were always in fact played by men.*

The emperor lived in Kyoto, but Ieyasu set up his government at Edo. He turned the village into a huge, fortified town, which later became known as Tokyo. He reorganized the country into regions called domains, each of which was led by a daimyo. The daimyo had to control the local groups of warriors, known as samurai, and also promise to support Ieyasu as shogun. This helped to bring peace to Japan. Ieyasu abdicated in 1605, but continued to hold real power until his death in 1616.

At first, Japan was open to foreigners and often visited by Portuguese, English and Dutch traders. Missionaries converted many Japanese to Christianity. Ieyasu thought the new religion might undermine his rule and from 1612 missionaries were discouraged. In 1637 they were banned altogether and all Japanese Christians had to give up their religion or be put to death. At the same time, the shogun also decided that it would be easier to keep law and order in Japan if there was no foreign influence at all, so he banned all traders, apart from the Dutch who were allowed to send one trading ship each year to the port of Nagasaki.

△ ***Tokugawa Ieyasu*** *(1543–1616) as shogun encouraged agriculture and Confucianism in Japan. He firmly controlled the nobles and their families.*

Despite Japan's isolation from the rest of the world the country flourished. The population and food production increased, but taxes were heavy and many small crimes were punishable by death. Eventually rebellions started and in 1867 the Tokugawa dynasty was overthrown.

JAPANESE SOCIETY

Under the Tokugawas society was rigidly controlled – people were expected to commit suicide if they were disgraced in any way. Wealthy women were treated as ornaments. They had to wear very high shoes and long flowing gowns, which made it almost impossible for them to walk, while complicated hairstyles made it difficult for them to move their heads.

◁ ***Samurai warriors*** *were trained to fight from childhood. Their main weapons were bows and arrows, single-edged swords and daggers. They fought on foot or on horseback and wore armour and masks to make them look more frightening as well as for protection.*

△ ***Himeji castle*** *was built by the warlord Hideyoshi, who ruled Japan as dictator from 1582 until his death in 1598. The castle was his stronghold in the civil wars that tore Japan apart. Under the Tokugawas, the power of the warlords was greatly reduced.*

The Dutch Empire

Until 1581, the Netherlands, or Low Countries, was made up of 17 provinces, which included Belgium, Luxembourg and the Netherlands. From 1482 they were part of the Holy Roman empire, ruled by Philip of Burgundy. When he died in 1506 they passed to his son, Charles. Charles became king of Spain in 1516, so they became a Spanish possession. The majority of the people in the northern provinces followed the Protestant religion and Charles' son, Philip II, persecuted them for this.

When they refused to give up Protestantism, he used terror tactics to try and persuade them. This led to a series of revolts from 1568 to 1581, led by William of Orange. Then the seven northern provinces declared their independence from Spain, calling themselves the Republic of the United Netherlands.

Sea-faring, trade, finance and fishing were the main ways of making a living in the Netherlands and following the declaration of independence in 1581, these all increased in importance. Amsterdam became the chief city and was home to many wealthy merchants and bankers.

△ ***Traders from the Dutch East India Company*** *buying goods from the locals at the Cape of Good Hope at the tip of southern Africa. They needed these supplies to continue their journey to the East Indies.*

◁ ***A flowering in Dutch art*** *was sparked off by wealth from trade and an end to Spanish rule. This painting is by Jan Vermeer (1635–1675) who lived in the town of Delft. Most of his paintings were of everyday subjects, such as this woman writing a letter, but they show the costumes and furnishings in great detail and rich colours.*

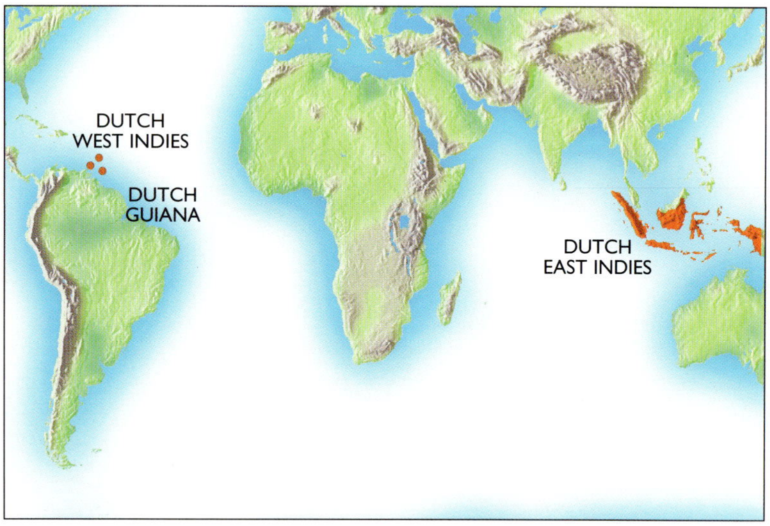

△ ***This map shows*** *the Dutch trading empire. The Dutch East Indies (now Indonesia) were rich in spices. Sugar, rice and slaves were traded in Guiana (now Surinam).*

▷ ***Coffee, tea, cinnamon and cloves*** *were some of the most valuable goods traded by the Dutch East India Company.*

△ ***William of Orange*** *(1533–1584) led the Dutch in several revolts against Spanish rule. He was elected the first ruler of the Republic of the United Netherlands and was killed by a Spanish agent.*

Although Spain did not yet recognize their independence, the Dutch started to build up a trading empire. In 1599 they began to take control of the Moluccas, or Spice Islands, from the Portuguese and in 1602 the Dutch East India Company was set up to encourage more trade with the islands of the East Indies. In 1619 the Company set up its headquarters in Batavia (now Djakarta) on the island of Java. Then, helped by its own army and ships, the Company drove the Portuguese and English merchants out of the area. The Dutch East India Company went on to take control of Ceylon (now Sri Lanka) and several ports in India. In 1652 it set up a colony at Cape Town on the southernmost tip of Africa to supply its ships sailing between the Netherlands and the East Indies.

Other Dutch merchants sailed westwards and, in 1621, they set up the Dutch West India Company. This took control of several islands in the Caribbean, as well as Guiana on South America's mainland, some islands off the coast of Venezuela and parts of Brazil. The company traded in slaves, tobacco and sugar.

This trading empire helped to make the Dutch very wealthy people. Their trade was jealously guarded, however, and this led to wars with England in the second half of the 17th century.

THE DUTCH EMPIRE

1568 Dutch led by William of Orange begin revolt against Spanish rule.
1576 Spanish troops destroy Antwerp. Many inhabitants move to Amsterdam.
1577 The Netherlands makes a pact with England to fight against the Spanish.
1579 Seven northern provinces of the Netherlands form the Union of Utrecht.
1581 The Republic of the United Netherlands declares independence. William of Orange is elected ruler.
1599 Dutch take control of the Moluccas from Portugal.
1602 Dutch East India Company is founded.
1621 Dutch West India Company is founded.
1648 Spain recognizes Dutch independence at the end of the Thirty Years War.
1651–1674 Three Anglo-Dutch wars between the Netherlands and England are fought over trade.
1689 William III of Orange and his wife Mary, daughter of James II of England are offered English throne. The Netherlands starts to decline as England becomes more powerful.

△ ***The cultivation of tulips*** *started in the Netherlands in 1562 when a cargo of bulbs arrived from Turkey. In the 1630s the flowers became so popular people invested large sums to develop new varieties.*

Colonizing North America

The Spanish and French were the first Europeans to explore North America. French traders and missonaries explored the north, which they named Canada, while to the south, the Spanish founded what is now New Mexico, exploring California and Texas.

In the late 16th century, small groups of Europeans began to settle in North America. The first serious attempts at colonization were made by Sir Walter Raleigh, an English explorer, in the 1580s in an area he called Virginia. These early colonies all failed, but in 1607 Raleigh set up a more successful colony named Jamestown. Although the colonists had to struggle against hunger, disease and battles with the Native Americans, whose land they were occupying, the colony managed to survive, encouraging other people to join them.

Probably the most famous early settlers are the Pilgrim Fathers, who left Plymouth in England in 1620. A group of religious dissenters, they were looking for a place to practise their religion in peace. Landing near Cape Cod in Massachusetts, they founded a small settlement and called it Plymouth Plantation.

▷ ***Many Native Americans*** *helped early settlers to survive. They taught them which crops were best suited to the land and climate and how to raise them. They also traded goods with the settlers.*

◁ ***Sir Walter Raleigh*** *(1552–1618), a favourite of Elizabeth I, named Virginia in honour of her. He introduced tobacco and potatoes to Britain. In 1615 he led a failed expedition to South America and was executed by James I on his return.*

△ ***The* Mayflower**, *the ship the Pilgrim Fathers and their families sailed on from England to America in 1620. They planned to land in Virginia, but were blown off course by storms and landed much farther north, near Cape Cod. It was the middle of winter when they landed and only 54 of the original 102 passengers survived until spring.*

Like many of the first settlers, they relied heavily on help from and trade with the Native Americans to survive. Four years later, the Dutch West India Company founded the colony of New Netherlands on the Hudson River and in 1625 they built a trading post on Manhattan Island, calling it New Amsterdam.

Meanwhile the French were starting to colonize Canada. Samuel de Champlain founded Quebec in 1608 and from there he explored beyond the St Lawrence River as far as Lake Huron, claiming all the land for France. Later, other French explorers in the south travelled along the Mississippi River and claimed the whole river valley for France, calling it Louisiana after the French king Louis XIV.

Many of the colonists earned their living by farming, producing food for themselves and crops for export to Europe, such as tobacco, indigo and rice. There were also many traders and trappers who either exchanged European goods, such as guns and alcohol, with the Native Americans for animal furs, or hunted and trapped the animals for themselves.

△ ***The first settlements*** *were built near a good water supply. The settlers cut down trees to build simple log cabins to live in and barns for their animals. The cleared land was fenced in and used for growing crops such as maize and squash. Turkeys were kept for food and tobacco was grown for export.*

EUROPEANS FIGHT FOR NORTH AMERICA

The English, French and Spanish claimed large areas of North America for themselves, even though there was already a large population of Native Americans there. Some tried to convert the Native Americans to Christianity while others came to trade, especially in furs, or to farm. As colonization increased, bitter battles were fought with the Native Americans and between colonists over who owned the land.

COLONIZING NORTH AMERICA

1513 Juan Ponce de Leon claims Florida for Spain.
1535–1542 Francisco de Coronado claims New Mexico, California, Arizona and Texas for Spain.
1536 Jacques Cartier explores the St Lawrence River in Canada, and claims it for France.
1584 Sir Walter Raleigh begins colonization of Virginia.
1608 French explorer Samuel de Champlain founds Quebec.
1609 The Spaniard Juan de Onate establishes Santa Fé as the capital of New Mexico.
1610 Henry Hudson discovers Hudson Bay in Canada.
1612 Settlers in Virginia start to plant tobacco.
1614 John Rolfe, a Virginia colonist, marries Pocohontas, a Native American princess.
1619 The first slaves from Africa arrive in Virginia to work on tobacco plantations.
1621 The Pilgrim Fathers hold the first Thanksgiving Day celebration following their first successful harvest.
1630 By this date there are around 16,000 English settlers in Massachusetts.
1636 Harvard College is founded in Cambridge, Massachusetts.
1641 The French start trading for furs in Michigan.
1664 The English capture New Amsterdam from the Dutch and rename it New York.
1670 The Hudson Bay Company is set up to encourage trade, especially in furs, between Canada and England.
1673 Two Frenchmen, Jacques Marquette and Louis Joliet, explore the Mississippi River from its source to Arkansas.
1679 Fur traders from France become the first Europeans to see the Niagara Falls.
1682 The explorer La Salle claims the whole Mississippi river valley for France.
1683 The first German settlers arrive in Pennsylvania.
1689 The first of three wars breaks out between British and French colonists in North America. It lasts until 1697, with each side wanting to control all the lands occupied by Europeans.

The English Civil War

The English Civil War broke out during the reign of Charles I, who came to the throne in 1625. Charles believed in Divine Right – God had given him the right to rule and so he was not answerable to parliament or to the people. He soon came into conflict with parliament over such issues as raising taxes, religion and his right to imprison opponents.

Determined to have his own way, Charles dissolved parliament in 1629 and ruled without it for the next 11 years. With the help of three ministers, he found ways of raising money without taxation.

In 1639, however, rebellion broke out in Scotland. Charles did not have enough money to fight a war. He could only raise taxes through parliament, so in April 1640 he recalled its members. But parliament would not give Charles the money he needed unless he let them elect the chief officers of the state. Charles refused and tried to arrest his five leading opponents in the House of Commons.

△ ***Royalist soldiers*** *were also called Cavaliers. They wore their hair long and dressed flamboyantly, wearing wide-brimmed hats with feathers and shirts of fine linen trimmed with lace and bright coloured jackets. Most Royalists were Catholics or members of the aristocracy.*

△ ***Oliver Cromwell*** *(1599–1658) was a country gentleman and Member of Parliament before the Civil War. He helped recruit, train and command the New Model Army. As Lord Protector he tried to impose parliamentary rule in Scotland and Ireland by force.*

▽ ***The execution of Charles I*** *took place on a scaffold outside the banqueting hall of Whitehall Palace. A large crowd gathered to watch the event on January 31, 1649.*

PURITANS

People of the Puritan faith were Protestants who wanted to purify the Church of England of its pomp and ritual. They dressed in simple, modest clothes without jewellery or make-up and disapproved of entertainment such as dancing and the theatre. They spent much of their time at prayer. The Pilgrim Fathers who sailed to America were Puritans and many more followed them to escape religious persecution.

◁ ***This map shows*** *the main battles of the war. The pink areas are lands held by the king after the battle of Marston Moor (1644) in which he lost control of the north. Parliament controlled the rest of the country.*

▽ ***Parliament's soldiers*** *were known as Roundheads because of their short hair cuts. They wore plain woollen jackets over linen shirts. Iron breastplates and helmets protected them from serious injury.*

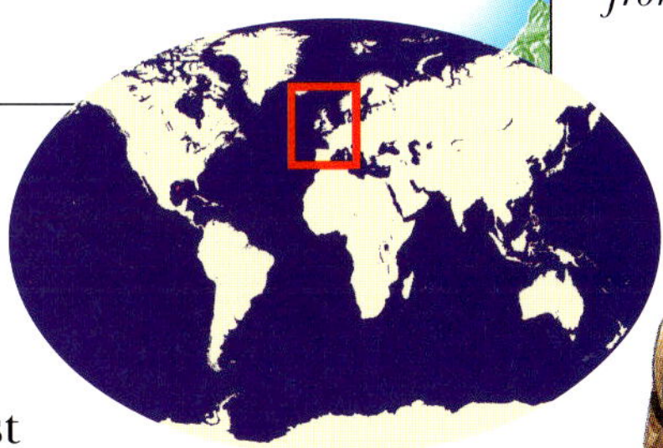

This action made civil war unavoidable.

Both sides raised large armies of volunteers and the first major battle took place on August 22, 1642 at Edgehill in the English Midlands. That battle ended with no clear victory for either side and, over the next four years, fighting took place in almost every part of the country. As well as the major battles, there were many skirmishes and sieges in which both civilians and soldiers suffered. Towns and even families were divided in their support, with rich and poor people equally likely to support either side. At first the king's forces, or Royalists, were the more successful. Parliament's supporters, or Roundheads, were led by able generals such as Oliver Cromwell who commanded a professional army, called the New Model Army. The Roundheads eventually defeated Charles' forces in 1645. Charles surrendered to the Scots, who handed him over to parliament, but he managed to escape and plotted with the Scots to start a second civil war, which broke out in 1648. It was quickly crushed and Charles was tried for treason. He was found guilty and executed in January 1649.

England became a commonwealth (republic), which at first was ruled by parliament. But its members quarrelled, so from 1653 Oliver Cromwell ruled as Lord Protector. When he died in 1658 he was succeeded by his son Richard, who was weak and soon removed from office. The people wanted a king once more and so in 1660 Charles I's son was invited back from exile to reign as Charles II.

ENGLISH CIVIL WAR

1625 Charles I succeeds James I and marries Henrietta Maria, a Spanish princess.

1629 Parliament tries to curb Charles' power and is dismissed.

1637 Charles forces the English Prayer Book on Scotland.

1639 Rebellion breaks out in Scotland.

1640 Charles calls a new parliament in April, but dismisses it after three weeks. He recalls parliament again in November.

1641 Charles makes peace with the Scots, but rebellion breaks out in Ireland.

1642 In January, Charles tries to arrest five MPs in the House of Commons, sparking off civil war. The first major battle takes place at Edgehill, Warwickshire.

1645 The New Model Army, led by Sir Thomas Fairfax and Oliver Cromwell, decisively defeat Royalists at Naseby, Leicestershire.

1646 Charles surrenders to the Scots.

1647 Charles is handed over to parliament. He is seized by the army and escapes to the Isle of Wight.

1648 Charles, aided by the Scots, starts a second civil war, but is quickly defeated.

1649 Charles goes on trial for treason on January 20 and is executed on January 31.

1651 Charles' son goes into exile in France.

1653–1658 Oliver Cromwell rules as Lord Protector.

1660 Restoration of the monarchy; Charles II comes to the throne.

The Slave Trade

Africa had a long history of slavery, but until the early 16th century this was only on a relatively small scale. Before this, most people who were enslaved were taken as prisoners of war or as a punishment for crime. Some were sold to Arab traders who sold them on as servants for a profit. The situation began to change when Europeans started to visit the coasts of Africa.

Elsewhere, European explorers were busy colonizing America and the islands of the Caribbean, setting up huge plantations of crops such as sugar cane. In many places, they enslaved the native population to do the work for them. But bad conditions and European diseases began to wipe out the native people, so the colonists started to look for workers to replace them. Some convicts were brought from Europe, but they were few in number and soon fell ill and died. The colonists then looked to Africa for slaves and the slave trade began on a much larger scale.

Soon huge numbers of people were being captured in the interior of Africa. Chained together so they could not escape, they were forced to march to the coast. There they were sold to European slave traders, put on to ships and taken across the Atlantic. Conditions on board ship were terrible with not enough light, air, food or water.

THE SLAVE TRADE

1441 The first Portuguese ship brings gold and slaves back from West Africa to Europe.
1448 Portuguese set up the first trading post in Africa. Slaves are taken there to be sold.
1493 Christopher Columbus introduces sugar cane from Europe to the Caribbean.
1502 Spanish take the first slaves from Africa to America to work on plantations.
1570s The Portuguese take slaves from Africa to Brazil to work on sugar plantations and in processing plants.

△ ***Harriet Beecher Stowe*** *(1811–1896) wrote* Uncle Tom's Cabin *in 1852 to raise support against slavery in the southern United States.*

1619 The first African slaves arrive in Virginia to work on tobacco plantations.
c. 1680 The average plantation in Barbados has 60 slaves.
1681 By now there are about 2,000 slaves in Virginia.
1683 Almost all the native peoples of the Caribbean, have been wiped out.
1700s The slave trade is at its peak. Cities such as Bristol, Liverpool and Nantes grow rich on the profits.
1730 By now, about 90 per cent of Jamaica's population are of African origin.
1780s People start to campaign against slavery.

▽ ***On a sugar plantation*** *some slaves worked in the fields and others worked in the processing factories. For all slaves, the work was heavy, conditions were bad, and hours were long. Even those who worked in the plantation owner's house were often badly treated, underfed and beaten.*

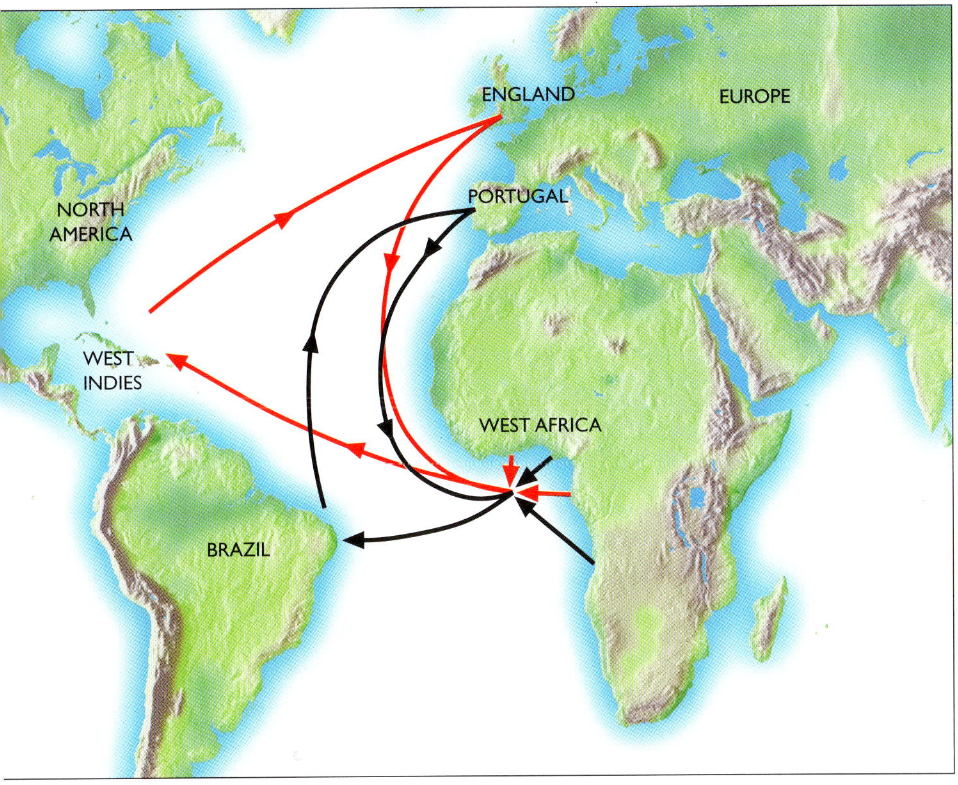

△ ***This map shows*** *the triangular trade route taken by slave ships. Ships sailed from Europe to Africa with guns and cloth to buy slaves. The slaves were carried on the 'Middle Passage' to the Americas where they were sold. They returned home with sugar, rum and cotton.*

A SLAVE AUCTION

When African slaves arrived in the Caribbean, South America or the colonies of North America they were sold at auction to the highest bidder. Africans from different cultures, who spoke different languages, were thrust together. Because they could not understand each other, this prevented them making plans to escape.

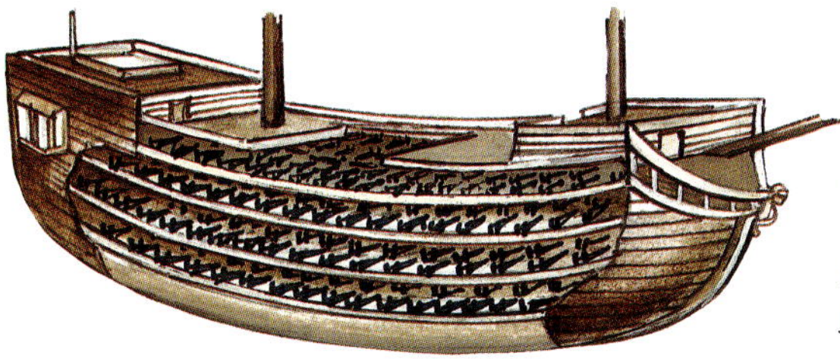

◁ ***Slave ships*** *were designed to carry more than 400 people, packed in as tightly as possible, on the two month voyage from West Africa to the Americas.*

The slaves were still chained together and packed into so small a space that they could not move about. As many as a third died on each eight-week journey. The ones who did survive were often separated from their families and sold to different slave owners.

Slaves faced a hard life on the plantations where the work was heavy and the hours were long. Their accommodation was poor and they were often badly fed. Many were also whipped or beaten for the smallest mistake and many died soon after arriving on the plantations. Even the strongest rarely survived for more than ten years and very few ever saw their homeland again.

The slave trade reached its peak in the 18th century, when between six and seven million people were shipped from Africa to America. The impact on traditional African societies was devastating, destroying entire kingdoms while others grew rich and rose to power on the trade. From the 1780s onwards, however, some Europeans began to realize how cruel slavery was and started to campaign against it.

▽ ***Slaves were often brutally ill-treated.*** *This slave is wearing a heavy iron collar to prevent him lying down to make sure that he could not rest while he was working. Many slaves were worked to death.*

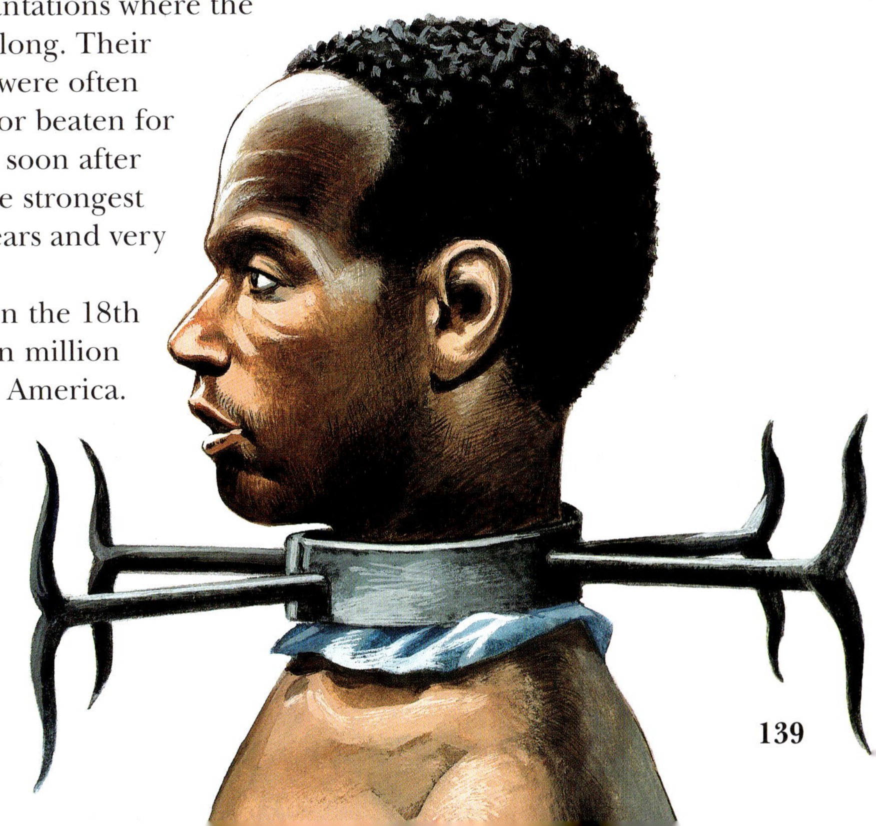

Louis XIV

Louis XIV of France was the most powerful of all European monarchs in the 17th century. An absolute ruler, he made decisions without regard to the common people or even to the nobility. Louis XIV came to the throne in 1643 when he was just five years old. His mother ruled on his behalf as regent until 1651. During this period, there were constant arguments between her and the council of nobles who wanted a share of the power. There was also a rebellion against the crown in 1648 when the people revolted against the heavy taxes they had to pay. When this revolt spread to the nobles, Louis fled from Paris and did not return until 1653. He was determined that a similar rebellion should never happen again.

In 1661, when he was old enough to rule alone, Louis dismissed the council of nobles and took the government of France into his own hands. He chose his own advisers and met with them each morning to discuss what had to be done. His chief adviser was Jean Colbert, controller-general of finance. France was already the most powerful country in Europe and, by reorganizing taxes and reforming the legal system, Colbert made it the most efficient, too. To increase its wealth, Colbert set up new industries and improved communications with with a network of new roads, bridges and canals.

LOUIS XIV

1638 Birth of Louis, son of Louis XIII of France and his wife Anne of Austria.
1643 Louis succeeds to the throne as Louis XIV.
1648 At the end of the Thirty Years War, France is the most powerful nation in Europe.
1653 Prime minister Jules Mazarin finally puts down the five-year uprising known as the Fronde and Louis returns to Paris.
1660 Louis marries Marie-Therese of Austria, daughter of the king of Spain.
1661 Mazarin dies and Louis takes control of France.
1662 Work starts on rebuilding Versailles. In some years Louis spends a quarter of the country's income on the palace.
1667 Start of war with Spain over the Netherlands. Louis gains control of Flanders, but has to retreat in 1668.
1672 Start of six-year Dutch war, which ends in victory for France.
1678 Louis moves his court to Versailles.
1685 Persecution of the Huguenots forces many of them to leave France.
1689–1697 War of the Grand Alliance, led by Britain against France, ends in French defeat.
1701–1713 War of the Spanish Succession in which Louis fights for control of the Spanish empire. Louis ensures the Spanish throne for his grandson, but brings France close to collapse.
1715 Death of Louis XIV at the age of 77.

▽ ***The palace of Versailles,*** *18km southwest of Paris, was built on the site of a royal hunting lodge between 1662 and 1710. The centre of government, the nobility were encouraged to live there, too, under the king's watchful eye.*

THE PLAYS OF MOLIERE

Louis XIV was a great patron of the arts and literature. One of his favourite dramatists was Jean Baptiste Molière (1622–1673), often called the father of modern French comedy. From 1659 to 1673 Molière wrote and directed many plays at Versailles. He also acted in his plays and died shortly after collapsing on stage during a performance.

To protect France's position as Europe's dominant power, Colbert increased the size of the navy from 20 to 270 ships. He also enlarged France's merchant fleet to encourage trade.

These policies should have made France very rich, but Louis spent vast sums of money on building a magnificent new palace at Versailles near Paris. He also spent much of the money on wars. Louis wanted to expand French territory to reach the Alps, the Pyrenees and the Rhine River, which he thought of as France's natural frontiers. To help him do this he greatly expanded the army and engaged in three major wars between 1667 and 1697.

The peasants and workers were heavily taxed to pay for Louis's extravagance, while the nobles and clergy paid nothing. Two bad harvests in a row left thousands starving, but any protests were quickly and severely crushed. After years of religious tolerance, the Huguenots, or French Protestants, were again persecuted by their Catholic rulers and from 1685 they were threatened with imprisonment or death if they did not give up their faith. As a result, around 300,000 fled abroad. As many of them were skilled craft workers, the French economy suffered from their loss.

When Louis died in 1715, his five-year-old great-grandson succeeded him. The boundaries of France were firmly established, but the country was financially weak after all the years of warfare.

△ ***The Hall of Mirrors****, the most magnificent room at Versailles. The palace's ornate gilded statues, glass, tapestries and paintings all stressed the king's magnificence and its style was copied throughout Europe.*

▷ ***Louis XIV*** *(1638–1715) was glorified by artists and writers as the Sun King. He was jealous of his personal reputation, or glory, which he considered to be inseparable from that of France, the country he ruled for 72 years.*

Revolution & Industry

The world in turmoil 1700–1900

The two centuries between 1700 and 1900 were a time of conflict, revolution and change in many parts of the world. Some of these changes were political, while others were economic or social. Empires were won and lost, kings and governments toppled, and agriculture, industry and transport developed rapidly.

The countries of northwest Europe grew more powerful, while Spain and Portugal declined. The 13 American colonies declared their independence from Britain in 1776 to become the United States of America. They were helped by the French, who in 1789 had their own revolution, overthrowing their king and becoming first a republic and then an empire. By 1793 this action had led to wars between France and several other European countries, including Austria, Britain, the Netherlands, Portugal, Prussia, Russia and Spain. The wars lasted until 1815 when the French emperor Napoleon was finally defeated. The Spanish and Portuguese colonies in South America took advantage of the wars in Europe to gain their independence, and by 1830 they were all free of foreign rule. Later conflicts in Europe united the separate states of Germany and of Italy into two countries, while conflict over slavery in the United States of America led to a four-year civil war.

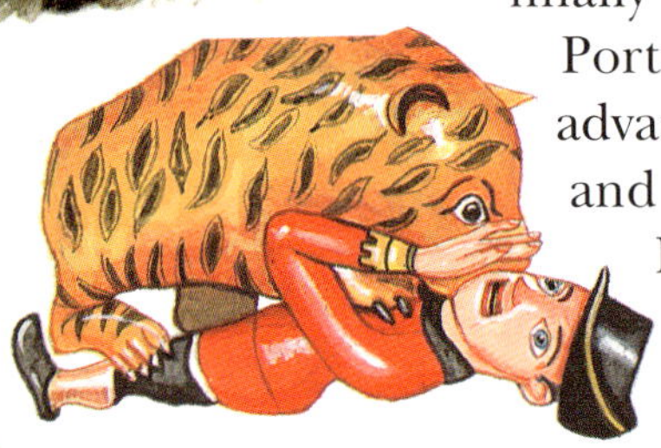

Revolutions in agriculture, industry and transport affected the lives of even more people, especially in Europe and America. Canals and railways made travel overland easier, while steam-powered ships were

faster and more reliable than sailing ships had been. New methods of farming made it possible to feed more people, and large numbers left the countryside to make a living in the rapidly expanding towns. Factories in towns used machines to produce vast quantities of goods once made by hand. To provide raw materials and a ready market for these factory goods, many European countries began to build up new empires overseas. Britain tightened its control on India throughout this period and laid claim to Australia and New Zealand and many islands in the Pacific. In the Scramble for Africa, between 1880 and 1900, the European powers divided up the whole continent of Africa among themselves. China, Japan and Russia stayed largely isolated from the rest of the world and gradually stagnated. Millions of Europeans settled in the United States of America and forced the Native Americans to leave the lands they had lived in for thousands of years.

REVOLUTION & INDUSTRY

1644 Manchus overthrow the Ming dynasty of China.
1682–1725 Peter the Great rules Russia.
1730 Four-crop rotation begins in England.
1740 Frederick the Great becomes king of Prussia, which then dominates Europe.
1756–1763 Seven Years War: France, Austria and Russia clash with Britain and Prussia.
1768 James Cooke sets out on the first of three voyages to the Pacific.
1776 On July 4, the Continental Congress in America adopts the Declaration of Independence.
1789 On July 14, a mob seizes the Bastille in Paris and the French Revolution starts.
1791 Thomas Paine's *The Rights of Man* published.
1804 Napoleon declares himself emperor of France.
1808 Independence struggles begin in South America.
1821 Napoleon dies in exile.
1837–1901 Queen Victoria's reign, during which the British empire includes a quarter of the world's people.
1848 Year of Revolutions affects most of Europe.
1856 Indian Mutiny.
1869 Union Pacific Railroad links east and west coasts of America.
1861 The American Civil War begins.

The Russian Empire

Peter the Great transformed Russia from an isolated, backward nation into a major European power. Nearly 40 years after his death, another great ruler, Catherine the Great, carried on his ambition.

Peter the Great, or Peter I, became tsar of Russia in 1682 when he was just ten years old. At first he ruled with his half-brother Ivan V. When Ivan died in 1696, Peter ruled on his own until 1725. Russia had been expanding rapidly since 1639, but it was still a very backward country compared with the rest of Europe. Peter was determined to change this and for 18 months he toured western Europe, studying what was happening there. He met kings, scientists and craft workers, as well as people who knew about industry, farming and ship-building. In the Netherlands he even disguised himself as an ordinary workman and took employment in a shipyard for a while.

When Peter returned to Russia, he put the knowledge he had gained to use. He built up the Russian navy and established a modern iron industry. He encouraged other industries and farming, improved and expanded the army and built new roads and canals to help trade.

Peter also realized Russia needed a seaport that was not ice-bound in winter, but this meant it had to be on either the Baltic or Black seas, neither of which was in Russian territory. In 1721 Peter won a war against Sweden and gained Estonia and Livonia, both of which were on the Baltic. To reflect Russia's growing wealth and his own power, Peter also moved the capital north from Moscow to St Petersburg.

△ ***Catherine the Great*** *ruled Russia from 1762 to 1796. She was ruthless and ambitious, and many European leaders feared her power. She was a follower of the Enlightenment and made plans to improve the education system and reform the law, but they all came to nothing.*

◁ ***Peter the Great*** *ruled Russia from 1682 to 1725. An immensely tall (over 2m) and strong man, his physical presence matched his character. Energetic and strong-willed he could be brutal, even imprisoning and torturing his own son.*

BOYARS

The boyars were a group of privileged and wealthy landowners who had advised the Russian rulers on affairs of state since the 10th century. They held important posts in the government and wore long beards as a sign of their great status. After his visit to Europe, however, Peter the Great abolished the boyars' powers. He cut off their beards (as he had his own) as a visible sign of the great changes that were sweeping Russia.

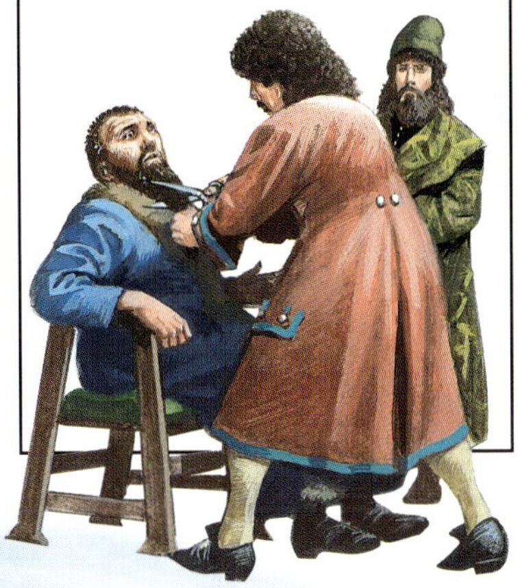

In the countryside, however, the serfs (peasants) were worse off as Peter increased the amount of tax they had to pay. In spite of this, Russia was more secure and advanced at Peter's death in 1725 than it had been when he came to power.

In 1762, another powerful ruler came to the throne. Catherine II (the Great) was Prussian by birth, but married the heir to the Russian throne in 1745. He was murdered six months after becoming tsar and Catherine declared herself empress, even though the crown should have gone to her son. Like Peter I, she encouraged western ideas and used warfare to gain territory for Russia, fighting the Ottoman empire in 1774 and 1792, and Sweden in 1790. She also claimed much of Poland when it was partitioned (divided up). Conditions did not improve for the serfs, however. They were still heavily taxed and often faced starvation in order to pay the government. Those who complained were severely punished. A revolt in 1773 was harshly put down to discourage rebellions.

RUSSIAN EMPIRE

1638 Peter the Great is born.
1696 Peter becomes sole ruler of Russia.
1700–1721 Great Northern War against Sweden.
1703 St Petersburg is founded. Peter calls it his "window on Europe".
1712 St Petersburg becomes the capital. It replaces Archangel on the Barents Sea as the main seaport.
1722–1723 War with Persia gives Russia access to the shores of the Caspian Sea.
1725 Peter the Great dies.
1729 Catherine is born Sophie Freederike Auguste von Anhalt-Zerbst in Prussia.
1742–1762 Elizabeth, daughter of Peter the Great, rules Russia.
1745 Catherine marries her cousin, Peter III, heir to the Russian throne.
1762 Catherine becomes empress of Russia after her husband's death.
1773 A revolt by the serfs is brutally crushed.
1787 On a tour of Russia, Catherine meets healthy, well-fed, well-dressed actors while the real serfs are hidden from sight.
1796 Catherine dies and is succeeded by her son.

△ ***St Petersburg*** *was designed and built by European architects. It had many palaces, churches and government buildings. Its broad, tree-lined main streets were crossed by waterways and bridges.*

◁ ***A carriage with runners****, like a sleigh, gliding through the snow. Russian winters were so cold and snowy that carriage wheels had to be removed and replaced by runners.*

▽ ***Russian peasant houses*** *made of wood gave little protection from the worst of the weather. Life was a constant struggle for the serfs. They paid heavy taxes and, if the harvest was bad, they often went hungry.*

Manchu China

The Ming dynasty had ruled China since 1368, but in the early 17th century, rebellions against high taxes and an unpopular government began. At the same time, tribes in Manchuria, northeast of China, were uniting.

By 1618 the Manchu were strong enough to take control of and hold on to the Ming province of Liaotung. When a rebellion in China led to the capture of Beijing, the capital, in 1644, Ming officials asked the Manchus to help them defeat the rebels. Instead, the Manchus seized power and set up a new dynasty, known as the Qing, which ruled China for more than 250 years.

The Manchus considered themselves superior to the Chinese and lived apart from them. They made Chinese men wear their hair in pigtails and marriages between the Chinese and the Manchus were forbidden. From the start, however, they adopted the Chinese way of government and employed former Ming officials. Gradually they also

△ ***The only port Westerners were permitted to use*** *in the early 19th century was Canton. The Chinese, however, imposed many controls. For example, traders were only allowed to live and store their goods in a very small area around the port.*

◁ ***This map shows*** *the extent of the Qing dynasty's empire in orange It is much larger than China today whose boundary is shown in blue.*

MANCHU CHINA

1618 United Manchu tribes take control of the Chinese province of Liaotung.
1630s The Chinese people start to rebel against the high taxes imposed on them by the Ming dynasty.
1644 The Manchus take control of Beijing and overthrow the Ming dynasty.
1661 Kangxi becomes the second Qing emperor. He conquers Taiwan, Outer Mongolia, parts of Siberia in Russia and Tibet. He is fond of learning and opens up the country to foreign trade and ideas.
1692 Kangxi gives Jesuit missionaries permission to spread Christianity to the Chinese. They are tolerant of Chinese traditions, but later missionaries are not.
1704 All missionaries, except the Jesuits, are expelled for not tolerating Chinese traditions.
1722 Death of Kangxi.
1736 Qianlong, grandson of Kangxi, becomes emperor of China and rules for 60 years. The first two-thirds of his reign mark the height of Manchu power.
1770 After about this date, Qianlong's rule begins to decline. He closes all but one port to foreign traders and tries to keep China isolated from the rest of the world.
1792 Lord Macartney becomes the first British ambassador to China. He takes scientific instruments, clocks and air-guns as gifts for the emperor, but does not get permission to increase trade.
1796 Qianlong abdicates, but still dominates government even in retirement.
1799 Qianlong dies.
1840 From this date the Qing dynasty starts to decline as a result of rebellions in China and successful attacks on the country by foreigners.

adopted the Chinese way of life, which made their rule more acceptable to the Chinese people.

Under the Qing dynasty, China flourished once more. Its empire grew to three times the size it had been under the Ming, and the population trebled from 150 million to 450 million people. Production of silk, porcelain, lacquerware and cotton expanded, and trade, especially with Europe, increased greatly. The Chinese still considered their products to be better than anything else in the world and accepted only gold and silver in exchange for them. China's wealth came from farming, as it could produce almost all the food its people needed, and it grew tea for export. It could also provide all the tools and other equipment the farmers used to grow their crops.

During the 18th century, however, it became increasingly difficult for China to ignore European imports. Europeans, and especially the British, urgently wanted to find markets for their new products. Although the emperor Qianlong tried to restrict Europeans traders to just one port, they wanted to sell their goods to all parts of China. In 1792, Britain sent its first ambassador to the Chinese court with a request to be allowed to trade more widely. But the emperor would not give his permission, as he wanted China to remain isolated from the influence of other countries. This policy gradually changed China from a rich and successful country into a poor and backward one.

▽ ***Only the emperor*** *was allowed to wear a silk gown embroidered with a five-clawed dragon. On taking control of China the Manchu made the Chinese adopt their tradition of wearing their hair in a pigtail as a sign of loyalty. The Manchu wore superior clothes to the Chinese.*

▷ ***Beautifully shaped vases*** *made from fine porcelain and decorated with patterns of leaves, flowers and animals were exported to the West. Porcelain, lacquerware and silk were in great demand in Europe and America during the Qing dynasty.*

◁ ***Beijing*** *expanded greatly under the Ming who added many palaces and temples, building a new wall and moat around the city. The Qing left the inner city unaltered, but new palaces and temples were added outside the city wall, to the west of the capital.*

The Enlightenment

THE ENLIGHTENMENT

1632–1704 Life of English philosopher John Locke. He believed that all men were equal and free and that the authority of government comes only from the consent of the governed.

1687 Sir Isaac Newton publishes his *Philosophiae Naturalis Principia Mathematica* in which he sets out his theories about light and the visible spectrum, the three laws of motion and the existence of gravity.

1724–1804 Life of German philosopher Immanuel Kant. He spends his life trying to discover the laws which govern the way people live.

1743 Benjamin Franklin sets up the American Philosophical Society in Philadelphia. Its members are interested in science as well as philosophy.

1743–1794 Life of French chemist Antoine Lavoisier, the first to establish that combustion (burning) is a form of chemical action.

1751 The first volume of the *Encyclopédie* is published.

1751 Carl Linnaeus publishes his *Philosophia Botanica.*

1755 Samuel Johnson's *Complete Dictionary of the English Language* is published. It contains over 43,000 words.

1768 The *Encyclopaedia Britannica* is first published.

1788 *The Times* newspaper is first published in London.

1791 Thomas Paine's *The Rights of Man* is published. This work greatly influences America in its fight for independence from Britain.

1792 Mary Wollstonecraft's *A Vindication of the Rights of Women* is published. It argues for equal opportunities in education for everyone.

The Enlightenment was a period from the late 17th century into the 18th century, when new ideas about government, personal freedom and religious beliefs began to develop in Europe.

The Enlightenment was influenced by the growth in scientific knowledge that began in the mid-17th century. People looked for reasons why things happened as they did. Modern chemistry and biology grew out of this questioning and our knowledge of physics and astronomy increased greatly. Medicine also improved as people began to study the human body and how it worked.

During the 18th century people began to look at the whole world and the role of people within it. The French philosopher and writer François Marie Voltaire

▷ ***A botanical drawing of sunflowers*** *from* Philosophia Botanica *by Carl Linnaeus, published in 1751. Linnaeus was a Swedish botanist who was the first to classify the plant and animal kingdoms, defining and grouping living things into species. Linnaeus wrote many books on the subject.*

▽ ***The* Encyclopédie**, *compiled by French writer and critic Denis Diderot, was written by experts in many different subjects and aimed to further all branches of knowledge. The first volume was published in 1751. The work was completed in 1772 and comprised 17 volumes of text and 11 volumes of pictures.*

△ ***A reconstruction of* Endeavour**, *the ship that British captain James Cook set out in to explore the South Pacific in 1768. Scientists and skilled artists on board recorded the plants, animals and people they met on the voyage.*

INFLUENTIAL WOMEN

The scene below shows a lecture being given in the salon, or drawing room, of Madame Geoffrin in Paris, in 1725. Noblewomen like Madame Geoffrin were great patrons of learning and the arts. By persuading well-known scholars, writers and philosophers to give private lectures to them and their friends in their homes, they encouraged the discussion of new ideas. Women such as Marie Anne Lavoisier also helped advance science. She assisted her husband, Antoine Lavoisier, in his experiments on gas and later edited his work.

attacked the Church and governments of the day. Another Frenchman, Jean-Jacques Rousseau, criticized civilization itself, saying people should not try to obtain more possessions or power than they needed. Both challenged the idea of absolute monarchy and the tradition that the nobility and clergy were entitled to special privileges. Other great thinkers of the Enlightenment included the economist Adam Smith, the historian David Hume, the philosopher Immanuel Kant, and the writers Mary Wollstonecraft and Samuel Johnson.

These new ideas, together with those of other scholars and philosophers of the time, spread rapidly. Many had their thoughts published in books or pamphlets. Others wrote letters to the newspapers or gave lectures. The wealthy and well educated in France often met in the drawing-rooms of noblewomen to discuss the latest books, plays and issues of the day.

People began to question the way they were governed. A belief that everyone had the right to knowledge, freedom and happiness inspired the American War of Independence and the French Revolution and eventually led to an end to slavery and the break up of Spain's empire in South America.

▽ ***François Marie Voltaire*** *(1694–1778), novelist, playwright, scientist and philosopher. He famously said, "I may disagree with what you say, but I will defend to the death your right to say it."*

▷ ***Ballet*** *in the 18th century was performed in public for the first time. Ballerinas began to wear clothes that were less constricting and easier to dance in.*

The Agricultural Revolution

Until the end of the 17th century, farming methods in Europe remained unchanged from the Middle Ages. Most people still lived in the country and were able to grow just enough food to feed themselves with a little spare to sell at the local market.

The land people farmed was in small strips, scattered over three or four large open fields that surrounded each village. To keep the land fertile, one field had to remain unplanted, or fallow, each year and so produced nothing. This system worked quite well while the population was small in number and most people could grow at least some of their own food. As the population began to increase, however, more people moved to live in the newly expanding towns where there was no land on which to grow crops. This meant that, if everyone was going to be fed, better ways of growing crops and organizing farms had to be found.

Some of the earliest experiments in agriculture were carried out in the Netherlands, in order to create more land that was suitable for farming. The Dutch drained water from

▽ ***Miles of stone walls*** *were built across many parts of Britain as more fields were enclosed. Some stone was dug out of the fields, but the rest had to be cut from quarries. Elsewhere, hedges and brick walls were erected.*

▽ ***New, larger breeds*** *of farm animals were bred during the 18th century. Artists often painted portraits of the best of them, together with their proud owners, as in this picture called* Mr Healey's Sheep.

CROP ROTATION

Crop rotation increased the fertility of the soil without having to leave any fields lying fallow with grass for a year. Using four fields, a farmer planted wheat in the first, turnips in the second, barley in the third and clover in the fourth. Each year the crops were rotated, so in the following year wheat was grown in the second field, turnips in the third, barley in the fourth and clover in the first. The clover put goodness back into the soil, while the turnips broke it up at a deeper level, so improving it for wheat and barley.

▷ ***A seed drill*** *made a series of even holes into which seeds fell. A worker then raked over the holes. Before this, seeds were scattered on the ground by hand. They fell unevenly and often failed to germinate, or were eaten by hungry birds.*

lakes and reclaimed land from the sea, using pumps powered by windmills to keep the water out. This cost a great deal of money, so Dutch farmers could not afford to leave any of their fields unplanted. Instead, they experimented with crop rotation, in which four different crops were planted in the same field over a four-year period. This idea was copied in Belgium and Britain who also reclaimed large amounts of low-lying land near the sea. Other experiments involved farm machinery. The plough was improved and the horse-drawn seed drill and hoe were invented. These allowed several rows of seeds to be sown and later weeded all at the same time.

In many areas, the land itself was reorganized. The large, open fields were divided up into smaller ones, separated by fences, hedges or walls. Laws were passed in Britain giving landowners the right to enclose common land, which had previously been used for grazing by everyone in the village. Sometimes whole villages were demolished and the people forced to move away to make more space for the new system of enclosed fields.

Farmers also began to experiment with breeding bigger and more profitable cattle, sheep and pigs. They grew crops such as turnips which would feed the animals over the winter when the grass stopped growing. This made sure that there would be plenty of animals to breed from again in the following spring.

The population of Europe continued to rise and more people left the countryside to live in towns and cities. By the end of the 18th century, however, the revolution in agriculture made sure that there was enough food to feed them all.

THE AGRICULTURAL REVOLUTION

1701 British inventor Jethro Tull invents the seed drill.

1715 By this date the Dutch have reclaimed over 147,500 hectares of land.

1730 Introduction in England of four-crop rotation to make better use of land.

1759–1801 Enclosure Acts passed by British parliament enclose over 3,000,000 hectares of common land.

1790 A professorship of agriculture and rural economy is set up at Edinburgh University.

1796 A school for farmers is set up at Keszthely in Hungary. There students learn from the experiences of others.

1800 By this date the weight of the average cow in Britain has more than doubled from 100 years earlier as a result of careful breeding.

1840 German farmer Justus von Liebig publishes the first book on using chemicals in farming.

△ ***The fantail windmill*** *was invented in 1745. Before this, a windmill's main sails needed moving whenever the wind changed so that they faced into the wind and worked efficiently. The fantail was attached to the main sails and moved them when the wind shifted.*

1700 1725 1750 1775

Austria and Prussia

Europe in the 18th century was dominated by absolute monarchs. Rulers of all they surveyed, they built lavish palaces and attracted artists and intellectuals to their "enlightened" courts. Two of the richest and most powerful European states at that time were Austria and Prussia.

Austria was ruled by the Habsburgs, a family that had dominated Europe since the 13th century. Through a series of wars, inheritances and marriages, the Habsburgs came to rule a vast area of land that by the 16th century had become too large for one person to rule alone. The Habsburg emperor, Charles V (and I of Spain) divided his lands so that one half was governed from Madrid in Spain while the other was governed from Vienna in Austria. In 1700 the Spanish Habsburgs died out, but the Austrian Habsburgs continued to assert their power.

In 1740 Maria Theresa came to the Austrian throne. She pulled Austria back from virtual bankruptcy, restoring its power and under her rule Austria became the artistic centre of Europe. Artists from all over Europe came to work on its grand building projects.

△ ***Maria Theresa*** *(1717–1780) inherited the throne of Austria in 1740. Three other rulers claimed the throne and war broke out among her rivals. Her position was secured in 1748 when the war was ended.*

▽ ***Wolfgang Amadeus Mozart*** *(1756–1791) playing at the court of Maria Theresa. Mozart first played at court when he was only six years old. Born in Salzburg, he later settled in Vienna where he became a friend of the composer Franz Joseph Haydn (1732–1809).*

△ ***The Schonbrunn Palace*** *in Vienna was built between 1696 and 1711. Then on the edge of the city, it was the Habsburgs' summer palace. Originally planned to rival Versailles, it had 1,440 rooms and was set in formal gardens, surrounded by a park.*

Maria Theresa was succeeded in 1780 by her son Joseph II, who was a follower of the Enlightenment. He was concerned with the living conditions of his poorer subjects and began reforms such as freeing the serfs and abolishing privileges.

Frederick II (the Great) became king of Prussia in 1740. He inherited a well-organized state with an efficient and powerful army, which he used to increase Prussia's power. Frederick was an outstanding general, his greatest victory being at Rossbach (1757) when he routed a combined French and Austrian army twice the size of his own. Under his leadership, Prussia emerged from struggles to dominate Europe as a major power. He introduced economic reforms, religious freedom, and abolished torture in the belief that only a ruler with absolute power could improve society.

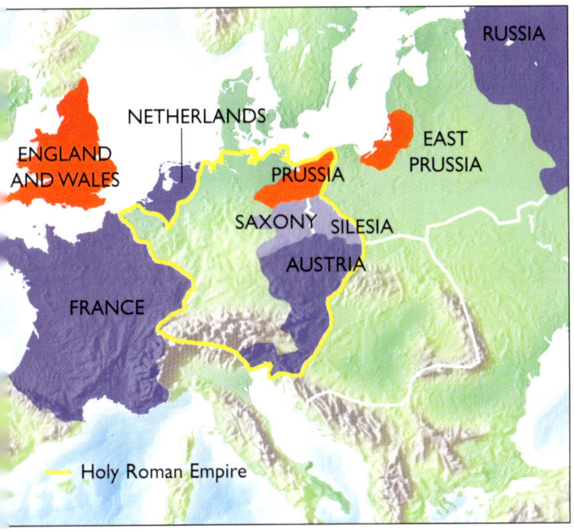

◁ ***The Seven Years War*** *(1756–1763) was a clash of interests between European powers. France, Austria and Russia opposed Prussia and Britain. At the end of the war Prussia gained Silesia seized from Austria and Britain took control of France's colonies in India and America.*

▽ ***Frederick the Great*** *(1712–1786) of Prussia was a cultured man, but also a stern administrator and very ambitious. He encouraged the study of science and agriculture and also improved education for middle class boys.*

AUSTRIA AND PRUSSIA

1700 By this date Austria has reconquered Hungary from the Ottomans. The last Spanish Habsburg monarch dies and Spain is ruled by the Bourbons of France.
1701 Frederick III Elector of Brandenburg is crowned Frederick I, King of Prussia.
1711 Charles VI, Archduke of Austria, becomes Holy Roman emperor.
1713 Frederick William succeeds as king of Prussia. He centralizes government and creates a powerful regular army.
1740 Charles VI dies and his daughter Maria Theresa inherits the Austrian throne. War breaks out as rivals challenge her right to rule. Frederick II (the Great) becomes king of Prussia and seizes Silesia from Austria.
1756–1763 Seven Years War. France, Austria and Russia clash with Britain and Prussia.
1757 Battle of Rossbach. Prussia defeats a much larger Austrian and French army.
1758 Frederick defeats Russians at Zorndorf.
1765 Maria Theresa rules Holy Roman empire with her son Joseph.
1772 First partition of Poland by Austria, Prussia and Russia.
1780 Maria Theresa is succeeded by Joseph.
1781 Joseph introduces major reforms and frees the serfs.
1786 Frederick the Great dies.
1795 Final partition of Poland between Austria, Prussia and Russia. Poland ceases to exist until 1919.

Birth of the USA

Before 1750, fighting frequently broke out between British and French colonists in North America over trade and wars in Europe. This fighting was brought to an end when British control of all Canada was agreed by the signing of the Treaty of Paris at the end of the Seven Years War (1756–1763).

With the threat from the French removed, British colonists in America no longer relied on Britain for defence. But Britain needed American taxes to pay for governing their new French territories. By this time there were about two million people living in Britain's 13 colonies in America. They produced most of the food and goods they needed, but taxes were imposed on imported goods, such as tea, and legal documents.

By 1770 the colonists were becoming increasingly unhappy with the British government. Even though they had to pay British taxes they had no say in how government was run. The colonists declared that "taxation without representation is tyranny". Britain reacted by sending more soldiers and, in April 1775, an armed confrontation between colonists and British troops took place at Lexington in Massachusetts.

BIRTH OF THE USA

1763 End of the Seven Years War between France and Britain. Britain gains control of France's territory in Canada and India.
1765 Protests start against British taxes in the American colonies.
1770 At the Boston Massacre, British troops fire on a crowd of colonists and kill five of them.
1773 At the Boston Tea Party, colonists board three ships in Boston harbour and throw their cargoes overboard as a protest against the tax on tea.
1775 The American War of Independence starts.
1776 On July 4 the Continental Congress adopts the Declaration of Independence. British forces capture and burn New York.
1777 British army is defeated at Saratoga, New York. France joins war on America's side.

△ ***Thomas Jefferson** (1743–1826) was a lawyer and politician who helped to draft the Declaration of Independence. In the war he was an ambassador in Europe. From 1801 to 1809 he was president of the United States.*

1777 British capture Philadelphia, Pennsylvania.
1778 The British capture Savannah, Georgia.
1779 Spain joins the war on America's side.
1780 The Dutch join war on America's side. British victory at Charleston, South Carolina.
1781 After a siege at Yorktown, Virginia, the British army surrenders.

PAUL REVERE

Paul Revere is one of the heroes of the War of Independence. He is shown here on his brave ride from Boston to Lexington to warn of the approach of British soldiers. Although he was captured, his mission was successful. He has been famously immortalized by American poet Longfellow who wrote: "Listen my children and you shall hear Of the midnight ride of Paul Revere."

▽ ***George Washington** became commander of the American forces in 1775. On Christmas night 1776, he led his troops across the ice-strewn Delaware River and went on to defeat the British at the battle of Trenton, one of the first major American victories in the War of Independence. In 1789, he was elected the first president of the United States, serving two terms.*

The colonists formed an army of their own, commanded by George Washington and on June 17 the two armies clashed at Bunker Hill, near Boston. The British were successful, but the War of Independence had begun.

Fighting continued and on July 4 1776 the colonial leaders passed the Declaration of Independence from Britain. The British government refused to accept this. Under Washington's continuing command, the colonists' army increased in size, becoming better equipped and better trained, and began defeating the British. France, Spain and the Netherlands all joined in on the colonists' side, making it difficult for Britain to keep its army supplied. The six-year war ended in 1781 when the British surrendered at Yorktown. Two years later, Britain recognized an independent United States of America.

△ ***British troops**, trained for fighting in European wars, found fighting in America very different. Standing in close-packed ranks, firing volleys of shot, they presented good targets for the American sharpshooters. The British won the battle of Bunker Hill (1775), but at a terrible cost of 1,000 casualties against 400 American casualties. British infantrymen (left) wore red long-tailed coats and so were known as "redcoats".*

▽ ***The Declaration of Independence** was signed on July 4 1776, by delegates from the 13 colonies. It separated them from Great Britain and created the United States. It is recognized as one of the great documents of history.*

The French Revolution

△ ***Maximilien Robespierre*** *(1758–1794) was a lawyer who was elected to the Estates General in 1789. In 1793, he started the Reign of Terror and during the following nine months thousands of opponents of the Revolution were put to death, until he himself was denounced and guillotined.*

In the 18th century, society in France was divided into three classes, known as estates. The first estate was the nobility, the second was the clergy and the third was everyone else. Only people in the third estate paid taxes, however, and discontent grew as taxes kept increasing.

In 1788, a bad harvest made food scarce and pushed up prices leaving many poorer people facing starvation. The government was also short of money, as a result of extravagant kings and costly wars. Many well-educated members of the third estate knew about the ideas of the Enlightenment and some had helped America in its war of independence from Britain. This made them realize how unfair the system was in France. When the French king, Louis XVI, called a meeting of the Estates General (the nearest France had to a parliament) in 1789 to try and raise more money, the third estate started to rebel. They said that if they had to pay taxes, they should have a say in the way the country was run. Louis XVI refused this request and locked them out of the room at Versailles in which the Estates General was meeting.

The third estate decided to hold its own meeting on a tennis court at Versailles. Calling themselves the National Assembly, its members refused to move until the king listened to their demands. Unrest was growing elsewhere – in Paris a mob attacked the Bastille, a royal prison, and soon riots broke out all over France.

▷ ***The Place de la Concorde*** *today is an important site in the heart of Paris, but in 1793 it was where the guillotine stood. Another important revoutionary site, the Bastille, was demolished soon after its capture on July 14 1789.*

The National Assembly then made its Declaration of the Rights of Man. These included liberty, equality and the right to resist oppression. Louis XVI refused to agree to this and so he and his family were arrested and brought back to Paris, where they were held in the Tuileries until 1793. Finally, as the king still refused to give more power to the people, he was put on trial and executed.

This was the start of the Reign of Terror, led by Maximilien Robespierre, which lasted until 1794. During that time thousands of people were arrested and put to death. Austria, Britain, the Netherlands, Prussia and Spain all declared war on France. Frightened by this turn of events, Robespierre's colleagues ordered his execution. A new government, the Directoire, was set up. The threat of civil war in 1795 lead to the rise to power of an ambitious French general – Napoleon Bonaparte.

MARIE ANTOINETTE

Marie Antoinette (1755–1793) was the daughter of Marie Theresa of Austria and married Louis XVI in 1770 when he was heir to the French throne. Young and pretty, she was popular at the start of Louis's reign in 1774. But Marie was extravagant and soon the people turned against her. On hearing that Parisians were rioting over bread shortages, she is quoted as callously saying "let them eat cake".

◁ ***During the Reign of Terror*** *around 500,000 people were arrested and 17,000 of them were put to death by public execution on the guillotine. Many of the victims were aristocrats, whose deaths attracted large crowds. Their bodies were buried in unmarked graves.*

THE FRENCH REVOLUTION

1789 On May 15 the Estates General meets for the first time since 1614. The third estate breaks away and forms the National Assembly. On July 14, the French Revolution starts when a mob seizes the Bastille. On August 26 the Declaration of the Rights of Man is made. On October 5 a mob marches from Paris to Versailles and returns with the king and his family as prisoners.

1791 The royal family try to escape but are brought back to Paris.

1792 In April, France declares war on Austria and Prussia. In September France is declared a republic.

1793 Louis XVI is executed in January, Marie Antoinette in October. The Reign of Terror starts. Austria, Britain, Netherlands, Prussia and Spain are now at war with France.

1794 Robespierre's execution in July ends the Reign of Terror. France is governed by the Directoire, a committee of five men.

1795 Napoleon Bonaparte's rise to power starts when he defends Paris against rebels.

Oceania

The first European to see the continent of Australia was the Dutch explorer Willem Janzoon, who landed on its northeast tip in about 1605. Over the next 20 years, other Dutch explorers also landed briefly on the north and west coasts of Australia, but, like Janzoon, none of them ventured inland.

Another Dutchman, Abel Tasman, was sent from Batavia (Indonesia) in 1642 to find out more about the extent of the great southern continent. On this voyage, Tasman sailed to Tasmania, New Zealand, Tonga and Fiji. Two years later he sailed south again, travelling along the north coast of Australia. But he thought the land looked too poor and did not think that any Europeans would want to live there.

In the 18th century, the British navigator, James Cook, made three famous voyages to the Pacific. His first voyage left in 1768 and with him went scientists and skilled artists to record the plants, animals and people they met. It took him around New Zealand, then to the eastern and northern coasts of Australia. Cook landed at Botany Bay on the southeast coast and claimed the territory for Britain, even though it was already inhabited by Aboriginal Australians. On his second journey he explored many of the Pacific Islands and in 1776, on his third voyage, he went to New Zealand once more, then explored the Pacific coast of South America before going to Hawaii.

In 1788 the British government started transporting convicts to the penal colony of Port Jackson, which had been set up in Australia. Some convicts stayed on when their

OCEANIA

1605 The Dutch explorer Willem Janzoon lands briefly on the northeast coast of Australia but does not venture inland.

1642 Anthony van Diemen, the Dutch governor-general of Batavia, sends Abel Tasman to explore the South Pacific. Tasman sees Tasmania, which he names Van Diemen's Land.

1644 Tasman's second journey, during which he sails along the north coast of Australia.

1686 The English explorer William Dampier reaches Australia.

1699 The British Admiralty sends Dampier on a second voyage to Australia; he returns in 1701.

1768 Captain James Cook's first voyage to the South Pacific; it lasts until 1771.

1772 Captain Cook's second voyage to the South Pacific. This voyage also lasts for three years.

1776 Captain Cook's third and last voyage to the South Pacific. It ends in tragedy in 1779 when he is killed in a quarrel with the Hawaiians.

1788 The first penal colony is set up in Australia and convicts are transported there from Britain.

1793 The first free settlers from Britain arrive in Australia. They settle in the area of Botany Bay.

1803 Settlers from Britain start going to Tasmania for the first time.

1813 By this date merino sheep have been introduced into Australia and the settlers have spread farther north and west, beyond the Blue Mountains.

1840 Maori leaders sign the Treaty of Waitangi with the British. It offers them land rights and full British citizenship. The treaty is not honoured and war breaks out (1843–1848).

1851 The discovery of gold in Victoria results in the Gold Rush and brings many more settlers to Australia.

▽ ***Captain James Cook*** *and the crew of the* Endeavour *meeting Maoris in New Zealand for first time. Between 1769 and 1770, Cook spent six months charting the coast of New Zealand, also attempting to establish good relations with the people he visited.*

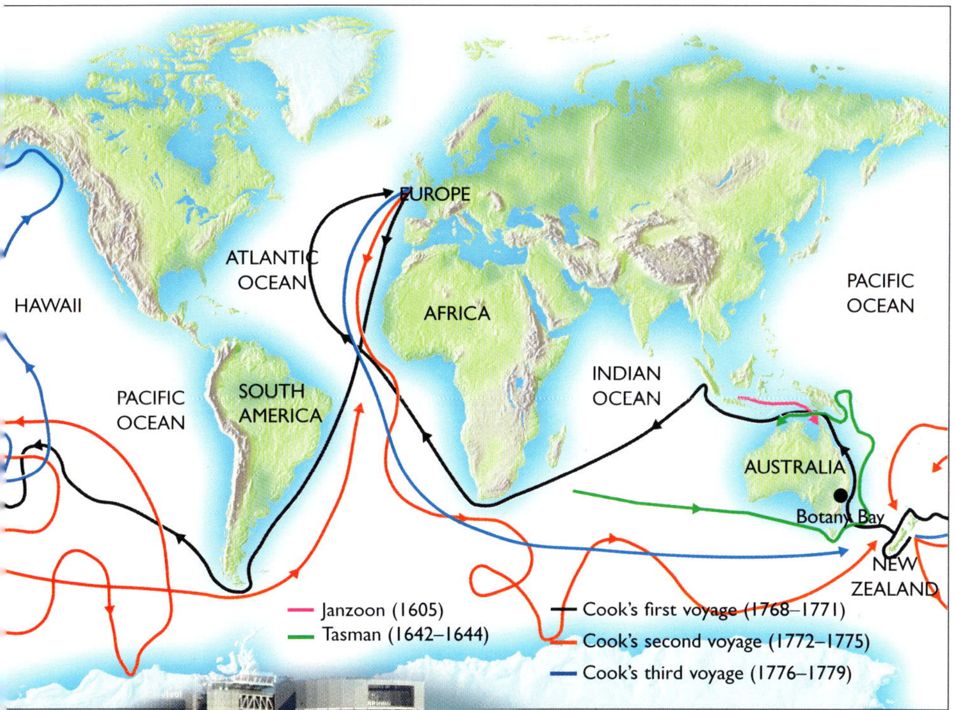

◁ ***This map shows*** *the routes followed by Willem Janzoon and Abel Tasman, as well as the three voyages made by James Cook. These three men did more than any other Europeans to map the coasts of the Pacific Ocean.*

THE MAORIS

When James Cook arrived in New Zealand, there were around 100,000 Maoris living there. They were skilled sailors and woodworkers who had migrated to New Zealand from the Pacific Islands of Polynesia about 800 years earlier. At first they lived by hunting, but by the 18th century most were self-sufficient farmers, living in villages and growing sweet potatoes and other crops. They used stone and wood for their tools and weapons, and this put them at a disadvantage when European settlers started to arrive. In 1840 the first British colonists founded Wellington on land bought from the Maoris. Britain claimed New Zealand and sent a governor to sign an agreement with the Maoris, called the Treaty of Waitangi, granting them land rights and offering British citizenship. Their rights were not protected, however, and war broke out. It ended in defeat for the Maoris in 1848.

◁ ***Sydney*** *is the oldest and largest city in Australia; both Botany Bay and Port Jackson are in Sydney. With its fine natural harbour, it developed from a penal colony into a thriving town, which by 1850 had a population of 60,000. Schools, hospitals, churches and court houses were built and several parks laid out.*

sentences were completed and from 1793 they were joined by free settlers in ever increasing numbers. These settlers had little respect for the Aboriginal Australians whose homelands they were stealing. They did not understand Aboriginal beliefs that the people belonged to the land and not the other way around and they had no respect for Aboriginal sacred places. Instead, missionaries were sent to try and convert the Aboriginals to Christianity. Settlers in New Zealand treated the Maori population in the same way and soon the native peoples began to die in large numbers. Many were shot by the settlers or killed by the diseases they brought. Others simply lost the will to live as they lost a way of life they had followed for thousands of years.

▷ ***Aboriginal paintings*** *on rocks and tree bark often depicted animals and people, in highly stylized forms. They were painted in pigments made from coloured earths and were drawn in order to keep the spirits of the creator ancestors alive.*

Napoleon

△ ***This map shows** the French empire under Napoleon I and the dependent states that were virtually part of it. The main battles of the Napoleonic Wars are also shown.*

Napoleon Bonaparte was born on the island of Corsica in 1769. The son of an Italian nobleman, he made his name in the French army, rising to become the emperor of France. The start of the 19th century was dominated by war as he set out to achieve his aim of ruling Europe.

At the age of 15 Napoleon went to military school in Paris, becoming an officer in 1785. A supporter of the French Revolution, he gained his first victory in 1793 when he siezed the port of Toulon from French rebels being aided by British and Spanish troops. Following this, Napoleon fell from favour with the French leadership until 1795, when he was recalled to Paris to defend the city against rebels who threatened to cause a civil war. In 1796 he was given command of the army in Italy and by 1797 he had conquered Milan and Mantua.

▷ ***Josephine de Beauharnais** (1763–1814) married Napoleon in 1796. The widow of a French general executed in 1794, she had important political connections. Their marriage was annulled in 1809, because she failed to produce a son.*

NAPOLEON'S ACHIEVEMENTS

Apart from the Code Napoleon (which forms the basis of many countries' legal systems today) Napoleon also changed how wars were fought with new tactics and formations. Much of his success was based on his popularity and in 1802 he introduced the Legion of Honour to reward oustanding service to the state.

Other Italian states, including Sardinia and Naples, surrendered and Napoleon was put in command of the invasion of Egypt.

The French hoped that invading Egypt would disrupt the British trade route to India and so cause massive unemployment and unrest in Britain. In 1798 the French army defeated the Egyptians at the battle of the Pyramids and the Ottomans at the battle of Aboukir Bay, before the British navy under Nelson defeated the French navy at the battle of the Nile.

Napoleon returned to France, determined to overthrow the Directoire, or committee, that ruled the country. France needed a strong leadership after the instability following the Revolution and many welcomed his return. In November 1799, the Directoire was overthrown and in 1802 Napoleon became First Consul. Two years later, he proclaimed himself Emperor of France. He was determined to reorganize France, and in 1804 he introduced the Code Napoleon, which enshrined in law some of the principles of the French Revolution. The code protected property rights, established the equality of all people before the law and allowed people to practise their religion freely.

△ ***At the Battle of Austerlitz*** *in December 1805, a French army of 73,000, under the command of Napoleon and his generals Soult and Bernadotte, defeated an army of 87,000 Austrians and Russians. The enemy was lured into a valley where many were killed.*

NAPOLEON

1769 Birth of Napoleon at Ajaccio, Corsica.

1785 Napoleon becomes an officer in the French army.

1795 Napoleon defends Paris against rebels and prevents civil war breaking out.

1797 A French army led by Napoleon drives Austrians from much of north Italy and negotiates a peace.

1798 Nelson defeats the French fleet at the battle of the Nile, in Egypt.

1799 Napoleon returns to France and seizes power. Austria, Britain, Russia and Turkey join forces to fight the French.

1801 By this date, only Britain is still at war with France.

1802 Napoleon plans to invade Britain, even though the two countries have signed a peace agreement this year.

1803 Britain declares war on France once more.

1804 Napoleon declares himself emperor of France.

1805 Nelson defeats French fleet at battle of Trafalgar. Napoleon's army defeats the Austrians and Russians at the battle of Austerlitz.

1806 Napoleon's army defeats the Prussians at Jena.

1807 Napoleon's army defeats the Russians at Friedland. France controls Portugal.

1808 The Peninsular War starts when Napoleon places his brother Joseph on the throne of Spain. British forces arrive in Portugal.

1809 Napoleon wins a decisive victory over the Austrians at Wagram. Napoleon marries the Austrian emperor's daughter, Marie Louise.

1811 Birth of Napoleon's son, Napoleon II, in March.

1812 Napoleon's army invades Russia but is defeated by the harsh climate. In Spain the French army is defeated at Salamanca.

△ ***A cartoon of the Duke of Wellington*** *who was given a dukedom in 1814 after defeating Napoleon's armies in Spain. In 1815, Wellington defeated Napoleon again, at Waterloo.*

Napoleonic Wars

As well as ruling France, Napoleon continued leading its army. He was a brilliant general and had thousands of conscripted men at his command.

Between 1803 and 1805 France was at war with Britain. Napoleon knew that the only way to win was to land his army in Britain and to do so he needed control of the seas. He persuaded the Spanish to help, but in October 1805 the combined fleet of France and Spain was defeated at Trafalgar by the British fleet, under the command of Lord Nelson. Napoleon then decided to blockade the transport of British goods across Europe. When Portugal refused to agree to this, Napoleon marched his army through Spain to invade Portugal in 1807. The following year he removed the king of Spain from the throne and gave it to his brother, Joseph Bonaparte.

Britain sent troops to Portugal under the command of Arthur Wellesley (later Lord Wellington). At first Napoleon seemed undefeatable and by 1812 he had control of a vast area of Europe. In the same year, however, he attempted a disastrous invasion of

South American Independence

By 1800 Spain and Portugal still ruled vast colonies in North and South America. Most colonists hated being ruled by foreigners and paying taxes to distant governments. Some colonies had tried to break free, but none had succeeded. As the Napoleonic Wars in Europe brought chaos to Spain and Portugal, the colonies decided to try again to fight for independence.

The main fight against Spanish rule was led by Simón Bolívar from Venezuela and José de San Martin from Argentina. San Martin gained freedom for his country in 1816, but Simón Bolívar's fight was longer and more difficult. He had joined a rebel army that captured Caracas, capital of Venezuela, in 1810, but was then defeated by the Spanish. Bolívar became the army's leader in 1811 and spent three years fighting the Spanish. When he was defeated a second time, he went into exile in Jamaica. There he realized he could not defeat the Spanish

△ ***At the battle of Ayachucho*** *in 1824, Simón Bolívar's army defeated the Spanish, finally securing independence for Peru.*

▷ ***José de San Martin*** *freed Argentina from Spanish rule, then led his army over the Andes mountains to help the people of Chile gain their independence, too.*

Russia and his army in Spain and Portugal suffered its first setbacks. By 1813 Napoleon's empire was collapsing and in 1814 he was forced to abdicate. He managed to escape from his exile on the island of Elba, landing back in France in 1815. Given a hero's welcome, he raised a new army and marched into Belgium to defeat the Prussians at the battle of Ligny. But he was then defeated at the battle of Waterloo and exiled to St Helena.

△ ***Napoleon**, as well as being commander of the French army, was also admiral of the French navy, in whose uniform he is shown here. In 1806, he tried to disrupt British trade by using his ships to blockade all ports under French control, but this was not successful.*

army in an open battle, so, in 1819, he led his army over the Andes from Venezuela to Colombia where he defeated the Spanish in a surprise attack at the battle of Boyoca. Two years later, he freed Venezuela and in 1822 he freed Ecuador and Panama from Spanish rule. He then made them all part of a new state, called the Republic of Gran Colombia, with himself as president. Finally Peru was liberated and part of it was renamed Bolivia after Bolívar.

NAPOLEONIC WARS

1813 Napoleon's army is forced out of Spain after its defeat at Vitoria in June. In October his forces are heavily defeated at the battle of Leipzig.

1814 In April Napoleon is forced to abdicate and is exiled to the island of Elba, off the coast of Italy.

1815 In March Napoleon escapes from Elba and returns to France to raise a new army. He is defeated at the battle of Waterloo on June 18th.

1821 Death of Napoleon in exile on the island of St Helena in the South Atlantic.

◁ ***Napoleon's tomb** in the Hotel des Invalides, Paris. When Napoleon died, he was buried in a simple grave on St Helena, but in 1840, his remains were dug up and reburied in the chapel of St Louis, in the Invalides. Inside the red stone sarcophagus, lie six coffins, one inside the other.*

SOUTH AMERICAN INDEPENDENCE

1808 Independence struggles begin in South America.

1816 José de San Martin leads Argentina to independence from Spain.

1817 At the battle of Chacabuco in Chile, San Martin and Bernado O'Higgins are victorious over the Spanish.

1818 Chile becomes independent from Spain.

1819 Colombia wins independence from Spain.

1821 Simón Bolívar's victory over the Spanish at Carabobo ensures independence for Venezuela.

1822 Brazil wins independence from Portugal.

1824 Bolívar wins independence for Peru.

1825 New republic of Bolivia is named after Bolívar.

1828 Uruguay wins independence from Spain.

◁ ***Bolivians today** wear dress that combines ancient patterns with Spanish influences. After independence, conditions for most people changed very little.*

The Industrial Revolution

The Industrial Revolution began in Britain in the mid-18th century, transforming society as people moved from the countryside to the town in order to work in factories.

Two events in the early 18th century helped make the Industrial Revolution possible. The first was Abraham Darby's discovery that coke instead of charcoal was a better fuel for smelting iron. The second was Thomas Newcomen's improved steam engine, used to pump water out of coal mines. These two inventions meant that more coal and better quality iron could be produced for industry.

Until the 1760s most goods were hand-made by people working at home or in small workshops. Many were spinners and weavers, producing woollen or linen cloth. Others made small metal items, such as nails, pins and knives. From the start of the century, however, there had been a rising demand for cotton cloth for clothes that were more comfortable to wear and easier to wash than either wool or linen. At first cotton was imported from India as rolls of ready-made cloth, but then raw cotton was imported and British spinners and weavers started manufacturing the cloth themselves.

In 1733 the invention of a flying shuttle speeded up the weaving process so much that ordinary spinning wheels could not produce

SPINNING JENNY

James Hargreaves, inventor of the spinning jenny, was a poor spinner and weaver. He named his new machine after his daughter, Jenny. Other hand-spinners feared the machine would put them out of work, and so they broke into Hargreaves' house and destroyed the machines he had there, forcing him to move to another town.

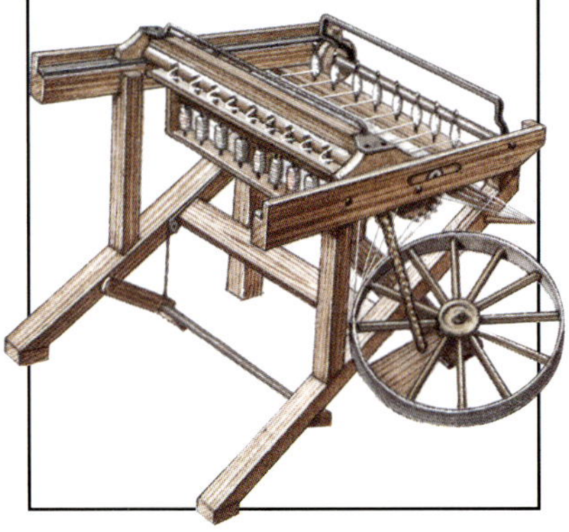

▽ ***A pithead** at Liverpool in England, painted in 1792. In the centre is a steam pump used to drain water from the mine. Steam engines were used to power all kinds of machinery in factories and mines.*

enough yarn to keep the weavers supplied. Then, in 1764, James Hargreaves invented the spinning jenny, which allowed one person to spin eight threads at once. Five years later, Richard Arkwright invented the spinning frame. This could spin more threads but needed water power to run it as it was too heavy to turn by hand. Factories were built near fast-flowing streams to house these new machines and soon the cotton industry began to develop on a very large scale. By 1790, James Watt's improvements to the steam engine meant that steam power could be used to drive machinery. This also increased the demand for coal to heat the water to make steam and for iron to make the engines and other machinery. Coal mines became bigger and deeper and iron works and foundries expanded, while canals (and later railways) were built to bring raw materials to the factories and take the finished goods away.

Towns boomed as people moved in to be near their place of work. Both housing and working conditions were often poor and many people, including children, suffered from malnutrition, disease, or accidents at work.

▽ ***The first public railway****, from Stockton to Darlington in England, opened in 1825. From 1830, steam locomotives were used to draw covered passenger carriages.*

△ ***Children worked in coal mines*** *from the age of five. Older children pulled heavy loads from the coal face to the bottom of the shaft, while younger children sat all day in total darkness, opening and closing doors to let the air circulate.*

INDUSTRIAL REVOLUTION

1698 Thomas Savery develops a steam engine to pump water out of mines.
1709 Abraham Darby discovers smelting iron with coke.
1712 Thomas Newcomen improves Savery's engine.
1733 John Kay invents the flying shuttle, greatly speeding up weaving.
1742 First cotton factories set up in Birmingham and Northampton.
1759 Bridgewater Canal built to take coal from the mines right to the centre of Manchester is begun.
1764 James Hargreaves invents the spinning jenny.
1769 James Watt designs more efficient condensing steam engine. Richard Arkwright invents spinning frame powered by water. Josiah Wedgwood builds a pottery in Staffordshire.
1779 Samuel Crompton invents the spinning mule, a cross between the spinning jenny and the spinning frame. First iron bridge is built.
1799 Steam engines are now being used to drive machinery in paper, flour and textile mills.
1808 Richard Trevithick demonstrates his steam locomotive in London.
1811 Start of "Luddite" protests against new machinery.
1815 Humphrey Davy invents the safety lamp – it warns miners of explosive gas.
1825 The first passenger railway from Stockton to Darlington opens.
1842 Act bans all women and children under the age of ten working underground in coal mines.

Europe in Turmoil

EUROPE IN TURMOIL

1830 Riots break out as ordinary people demand a say in government.

1831 Belgium declares independence from the Netherlands.

1832 Greece becomes independent from the Ottoman empire.

1838 In Britain, the People's Charter is published to demand political reforms. Its supporters become known as Chartists.

1844 Friedrich Engels makes a study of the lives of workers in Manchester, England.

1848 The Year of Revolutions affects most of Europe.

1852 In France, the Second Republic is replaced by the Second Empire.

At the end of the Napoleonic Wars, many parts of Europe were in a state of chaos. Many people were living in poverty, partly as a result of the wars, but mostly because the population of Europe had almost doubled in number in just a century.

There was not enough land for everyone to make a living in the countryside, while in the towns there were more people than there were jobs. Even those who did have work were often badly paid, poorly housed and inadequately fed, while the people they worked for were wealthy and lived in luxury.

Although the French Revolution was long since over, many people remembered its promises of liberty and equality. Very few poor people had the right to vote and so the only way they could bring about change in their countries was by revolution. Revolt broke out in France in 1830 and quickly spread to other countries as a growing number of people were able to read about events in newspapers. These revolts were soon crushed, but the desire for change did not go away. Ordinary people still wanted a say in government and a share in the wealth enjoyed by the rich.

In 1848 so many revolutions and protests broke out again throughout Europe that it was known as the Year of Revolutions. But this time they were not all for the same reasons. In Britain the Chartists demonstrated for political reforms and votes for all men.

▽ ***Riots broke out*** *in Berlin in 1848. Women and children were brutally attacked by Prussian soldiers as demands for reform and a united Germany were crushed.*

◁ ***The revolutions of 1848*** *were sparked off by a small, local revolt in Palermo on the island of Sicily on January 20. This inspired a revolt in France on February 24. Soon the spirit of protest had spread across Europe. Only Spain, Russia and Scandinavia remained calm.*

▽ ***This map shows*** *the main centres of unrest during 1848, "the Year of Revolutions". By the end of 1849 all the revolts had been quashed but governments had been forced to listen to their people's complaints and realize the importance of nationalism.*

In Ireland some people agitated for their country to become an independent republic, free from Britain. In France some rioters in Paris, who were demanding votes for all men and a new republic, were shot and killed by soldiers, but in Belgium, Denmark and the Netherlands reforms were made peacefully.

The revolutions in Germany and Italy had a different cause, however, as both nations were made up of a number of separate states, each with its own government. Many German people wanted all the German states to be united into one country, while many Italians wanted their country to be united, too. In contrast, there were many other groups of people in the vast Austrian empire who were not Austrian. They had their own languages and their own ways of life and they wanted the empire to be broken up into a number of separate and independent states to reflect this.

Despite the numbers of people and countries involved, all the revolutions in 1848 were squashed by the end of the following year. Only the French achieved one of their aims – their king, Louis Philippe, abdicated and the monarchy was briefly replaced by the Second Republic. The ideas that drove these revolutions and unrest did not go away, however. Many governments realized that they would have to make some reforms, while scholars, philosophers and economists began to look for different ways of governing countries and distributing wealth more fairly. The most famous political thinkers of this time were the German socialists Karl Marx and Friedrich Engels who, in 1848, published their ideas as *The Communist Manifesto*.

FEARGUS O'CONNOR

Feargus O'Connor (1794–1855) was elected to the British parliament in 1832 as member for County Cork in Ireland. When he lost his seat in 1835, he began agitating for votes for all men. He led the Chartists from 1841 until 1848 and was renowned for his brilliant speeches.

Exploring Africa

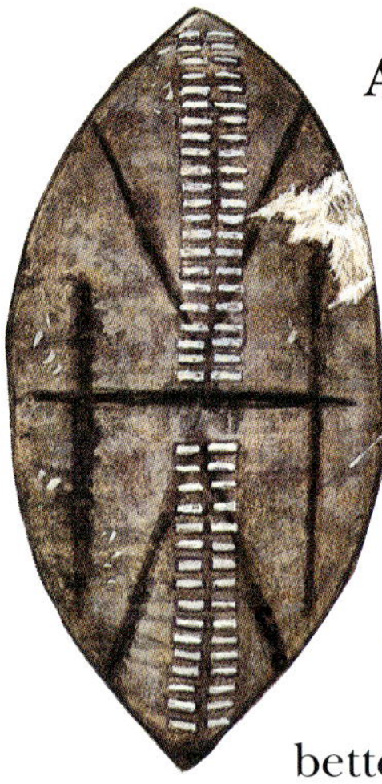

Although Europeans had been trading with Africa since the 16th century, they knew very little about the interior of the continent. They hardly ever ventured beyond the trading posts on the coast, partly because travelling was difficult in many places and partly because they were afraid of catching deadly diseases or being attacked by wild animals.

As the views of the Enlightenment became better known, the situation began to change. In Britain especially, people became more curious about the interior of Africa and in 1788 an association was formed in London to encourage exploration and trade in Africa. At the same time, many Europeans started to campaign for slavery to be abolished. They also thought that Africans should become Christians and so, from around 1800, increasing numbers of missionaries were sent out. Many went to Cape Colony (now part of South Africa), which the British took from the Dutch in 1806. This was the largest European settlement in Africa with a population of around 21,000 people.

EXPLORING AFRICA

1788 The Association for Promoting the Discovery of the Interior Parts of Africa (the African Association) is set up in London.
1795 The African Association sends Mungo Park to explore the river Niger.
1805 Mungo Park drowns while leading a second expedition along the Niger.
1806 Britain takes control of Cape Colony from Dutch.
1807 The British slave trade is abolished.
1822 Liberia in West Africa is founded as a country for escaped slaves.
1828 Frenchman Rene August Caillie is the first European to journey to Timbuktu, Mali, and return alive.
1830 The French invade Algeria.
1835 Start of the Great Trek; the Boers leave Cape Colony and British rule to head north.
1841 Arrival of David Livingstone in South Africa to work as a missionary.
1845 The British Bible Society sends James Richardson across the Sahara Desert from Tripoli to Ghudamis and Ghat.
1848 Livingstone sets out on his first expedition.
1852 Livingstone starts on a four-year journey across Africa, following the Zambezi River.
1858 On their second expedition to find the source of the Nile, Richard Burton and John Speke become the first Europeans to see Lake Tanganyika.
1865 Slavery is abolished in the United States.
1866 Livingstone sets out on an expedition to find source of the Nile. Three years later, the journalist Henry Stanley is sent to look for him.
1873 Death of Livingstone.
1878 The Zulu War with Britain breaks out in southern Africa. After six months, the British are victorious.
1879 Stanley is hired by the king of Belgium to help him set up an empire in Africa.

AN END TO SLAVERY

The trade in transporting Africans to the plantations of the Americas generated huge profits, but at great human cost. During the 18th century, many people in Europe and North America, spurred on by new beliefs in human rights, began to condemn slavery. Campaigns against the trade finally succeeded when the British slave trade was abolished in 1807, with slavery finally ending throughout the British Empire in 1833. In 1822 Liberia was founded in West Africa as a home for freed American slaves, but it was not until the end of the American Civil War of 1865, however, that slavery ceased to exist in the USA, while in Brazil it lingered on until 1889.

△ ***Henry Stanley found David Livingstone*** *encamped at Ujiji on the shores of Lake Tanganyika in 1871. They spent several months exploring together, before Stanley returned to England.*

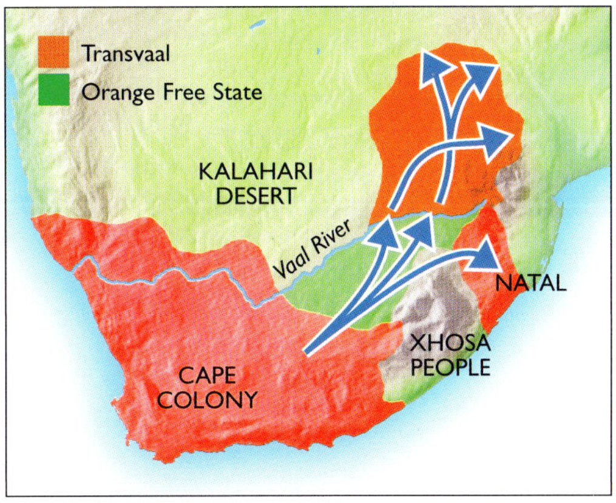

◁ ***This map shows*** *the route of the Great Trek, when the Boers went in search of new lands north of the Vaal River (Transvaal). Some Boers tried to settle the Zulu lands of Natal, but were defeated. Later, the British took over Natal.*

△ ***The Victoria Falls,*** *also called Mosi-oa-tunya (the Smoke that Thunders), on the Zambezi River. The first European to the see the falls was David Livingstone in 1855, who named them after the British queen Victoria.*

◁ ***Zulu warriors*** *attacking British soldiers. Warfare was an important part of Zulu life and from the 1820s they were the most powerful state in southern Africa. Armed with spears and round-headed clubs called knobkerries, their fighting tactics enabled them to kill many Boers and British soldiers, before eventually being defeated themselves in 1879.*

Most of the colonists were Dutch farmers, known as Boers. By 1835 many of them were unhappy with living under British rule and decided to set off on the Great Trek into the interior. After much hardship the trekkers formed two new republics, the Transvaal and the Orange Free State. But the trekkers came into conflict with the Zulus, whose homelands they had moved into. The Zulus attacked the Boers and the Boers retaliated. Eventually the Zulus were defeated by the British in 1879.

Many British expeditions explored Africa's interior along its great rivers between 1768 and 1875. From 1768 to 1773, James Bruce explored Ethiopia, and in two expeditions from 1795 to 1806 Mungo Park explored the Niger River. From 1852 to 1856 David Livingstone crossed the continent following the Zambezi River, and Richard Burton, John Speke and James Grant set out to look for the source of the Nile. Livingstone also set out to look for the source of the Nile in 1866, but lost contact with Britain for almost three years. Another expedition, sent out to look for him and led by journalist Henry Stanley, found him on the shores of Lake Tanganyika. After Livingstone's death, Stanley decided to continue exploring. His expedition of 1879 along the Congo River was paid for by the king of Belgium, who wanted to establish an overseas empire for himself. This was the start of the Scramble for Africa, in which Europe took control of almost the entire continent.

European Colonization of Asia

Europe had started trading directly with parts of Asia from the late 15th century. By the 17th century, this trade was so important that the British, Dutch and French each set up East India Companies to control and protect it.

The Dutch concentrated on the islands of Indonesia, while the British and the French fought over India until 1763, when the British East India Company took control.

In the 1830s, however, the Dutch decided they wanted to control more than just trade with Indonesia, and so they started to oversee agriculture on the islands. Where the local people had grown the crops they needed to feed their families, with a little spare to sell at market, the Dutch set up plantations on which crops were grown for cash. These crops included coffee and indigo (a plant from which a blue dye is made). By doing this, enormous profits were made by Indonesian princes and Dutch colonists. For the

HONG KONG

For nearly 70 years, China had restricted trade with the rest of the world. To force the country to open up its ports, Britain went to war against China from 1839 to 1842. Britain won and five ports were opened and Hong Kong Island became a British colony. Kowloon was added to the colony in 1860 and, in 1898, China gave the New Territories to Britain on a 99-year lease. With its fine harbour, Hong Kong became a centre of finance and trade, exporting textiles and clothing.

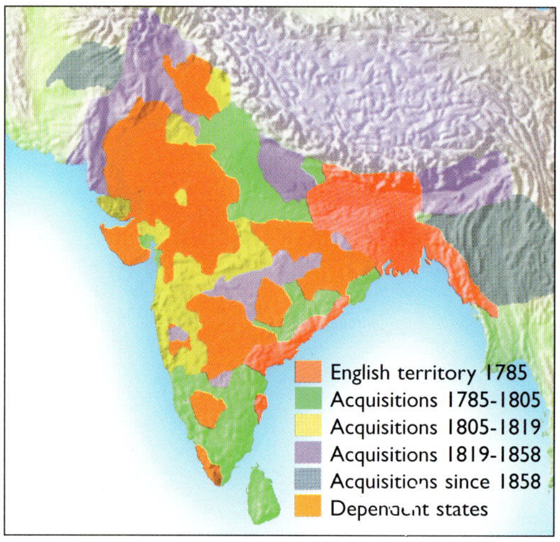

▷ ***This map shows** British control of India, which began in 1757. The dependent states were ruled by Indian princes under British protection. Until 1947, India also included the countries of Pakistan and Bangladesh.*

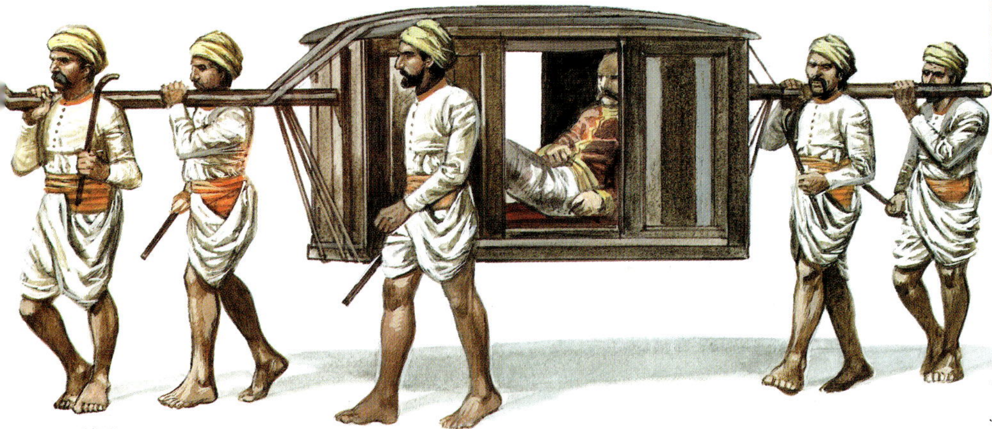

▽ ***Officials of the East India Company** were usually very wealthy and enjoyed a luxurious lifestyle. They had many servants to help them at work and in their homes, and were often carried from place to place in enclosed litters, called palanquins, like royalty.*

△ ***Many Europeans, when they went to India,** tried to live exactly as they would have done at home. Here Lady Impey, wife of the British Chief Justice of Bengal, is shown supervizing Indian tailors in 1782. Although in India, the decor and furnishings are typically British.*

ordinary people, however, there was hardship as they no longer had the time or the land to grow the crops they needed.

As well as controlling India (which then included Pakistan and Bangladesh) through the East India Company, Britain also began to build up colonies in Southeast Asia during the 18th and 19th centuries. One of the earliest was Singapore on the tip of the Malay peninsula, which came under British control in 1819. By 1867 Malacca and Penang had also become British colonies and in 1896 the remaining Malay states formed a federation under British advisors. Ruling through the local sultans, the British were able to control Malaya with few problems. Like the Dutch, however, they exploited the country's natural resources by setting up rubber plantations and mining the vast deposits of tin found in Malaya. Between 1824 and 1885 Britain also tried to take control of Burma (Myanmar) in order to protect India, part of which had been invaded by the Burmese in 1824. The Burmese resisted British colonization in a series of three wars, but they were finally defeated in 1885 and Britain took control of much of their country.

France, too, became involved in Asia again in the late 1850s when it began to take control of Indochina (now Cambodia and Vietnam). Many local people tried to resist French rule and colonization, but by 1888 they had all been defeated.

▷ ***Britain invaded Burma*** *not only to protect India, but also to gain access to Burma's valuable natural resources of teak, oil and rubies. In spite of having a larger and better-equipped army, however, the British had to fight three wars before they finally took control.*

COLONIES IN ASIA

1786 The British take control of Penang in Malaysia.

1789 The French East India Company ceases to exist.

1819 Foundation of the British colony of Singapore.

1824 Start of the Anglo-Burmese wars.

1841 Sultan of Brunei gives Sarawak to James Brooke.

1842 China cedes Hong Kong to Britain at the end of the First Opium War.

△ ***Chintz*** *was made in India for export to Europe. The beautifully printed cotton was made into dresses and furnishing.*

1856 Indian Mutiny leads to British government taking control of India from the East India Company.

1884 French victory at the battle of Bac-Ninh in Indochina.

1885 Burma becomes part of India at end of the third Anglo-Burmese War.

1887 French form Indochina, from Cambodia and Cochinchina, Tonkin and Annam (Vietnam).

1893 Laos is added to Indochina.

The British Empire

Queen Victoria succeeded to the British throne in 1837 and reigned for almost 64 years. At the time of her accession, trade and industry had already helped to make Britain one of the richest and most powerful countries in the world. Britain was also a land of great contrasts, with landowners and industrialists living in luxury, while the poor led very hard lives both in the towns and in the countryside.

Much of Britain's wealth came from her colonies, which were eventually known as the British empire. The earliest colonies had been established in the 17th and 18th centuries in places as far apart as Canada, India, Australia and the Caribbean. More were added by the Treaty of Vienna at the end of the Napoleonic Wars. During Victoria's reign, still more colonies were added, including New Zealand, many islands in the Pacific and Atlantic oceans, parts of the Far East and large areas of Africa, until, at its greatest extent, the empire contained a quarter of the world's land and a quarter of its people.

The colonies mainly provided raw materials for British factories and a ready market for their goods. At first, colonies were often run by trading companies, such as the East India Company in India and the Hudson's Bay Company in Canada, but gradually they all came under direct rule from Britain. India was the most prized and Britain went to great lengths to protect its trade routes with India.

△ ***Queen Victoria*** *(1819–1901) was just 18 years old when she inherited the British throne from her uncle, William IV. After her husband's death in 1861 she went into deep mourning and was not seen in public for many years.*

▽ ***Victoria's family tree.*** *Queen Victoria married Prince Albert in 1840. Several of their nine children made dynastic marriages with the royal families of Europe.*

Queen Victoria
(married Prince Albert of Saxe-Coburg-Gotha)

- ***Victoria*** *(married Frederick III of Germany)*
- ***Albert Edward, Edward VII*** *(married Princess Alexandra of Denmark)*
- ***Alice*** *(married the Duke of Hesse)*
  - ***Alice*** *(Alix) (married Nicholas II of Russia)*
- ***Alfred, Duke of Edinburgh and Saxe-Coburg-Gotha***
- ***Helena*** *(married Prince Kristian of Scheswig-Holstein)*
- ***Louise*** *(married Marquis of Lorne)*
- ***Arthur, Duke of Connaught***
- ***Leopold, Duke of Albany***
- ***Beatrice*** *(married Prince Henry of Battenburg)*

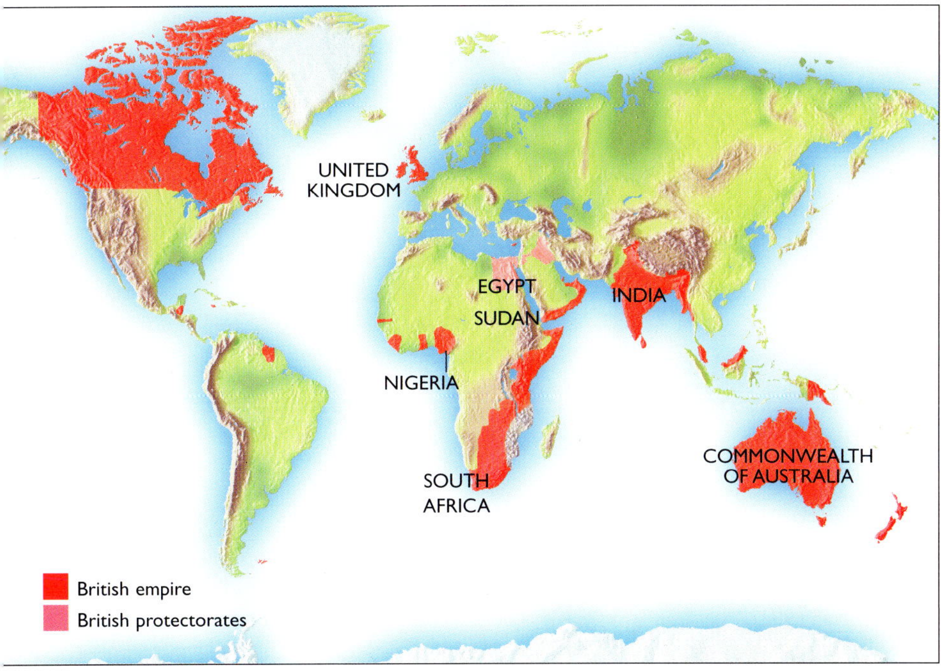

△ ***This map shows*** *the British empire in 1821. It was called "the empire on which the Sun never sets", because it was the largest empire the world had ever seen and spread right across the globe.*

▷ ***The potato famine*** *of 1845 to 1846 was caused by blight ruining the Irish potato crop. About one million died of hunger and many more lost their homes and emigrated to the United States.*

THE CRIMEAN WAR

The Crimean War (1853–1856) was fought between Russia on one side and Turkey, France and Britain on the other to limit Russia's domination of the Black Sea. Bad administration led to hundreds of thousands of lives being wasted. More men died in hospital than in battle until Florence Nightingale and 30 volunteers arrived to work in the military hospitals. On her return to England, she set up the first training school for nurses.

This was especially true after the opening of the Suez Canal in 1869, which cut 6,436 km off the journey from Britain to India. As British rule became firmly established, the economies of many of the colonies were also changed as plantations were set up to produce tea, sugar, coffee and spices for the British market. Other plantations produced rubber or cotton. Many people also migrated from Britain to Canada, Australia and New Zealand, where they set up farms producing wheat, cattle and sheep to export to Britain.

Towards the end of Victoria's reign, however, Britain began to lose its place as the world's leading industrial nation. Colonies, such as Canada and Australia became self-governing, but remained part of the empire until 1947 when it ended.

THE BRITISH EMPIRE

1763 Britain takes control of Canada

1788 First British settlement established in Australia.

1808 Sierra Leone becomes a British colony.

1815 Treaty of Vienna gives Cape Colony (South Africa), Ceylon (Sri Lanka), Mauritius, Malta and French islands in the Caribbean to Britain.

1829 Britain claims the whole of Australia.

1830 Britain starts to control the Gold Coast (Ghana).

1839–1842 Britain fights Opium Wars to open China to trade.

1840 By the Treaty of Waitangi Britain takes New Zealand.

1843 In West Africa, the Gambia becomes a British colony.

1845 English landowners do little to help their Irish tenant farmers as the Great Potato Famine strikes Ireland.

1851 The Great Exhibition is held in London. Exhibits from all parts of the empire are intended to show off Britain's success as an industrial and trading nation.

1853–1856 The Crimean War.

1857–1858 The Indian Mutiny leads to India being ruled directly from Britain.

1860 Lagos (Nigeria) is added to the empire.

1867 Canada becomes a British Dominion.

1875 Britain buys shares in the Suez Canal Company to control trade route to India.

1876 Victoria is crowned Empress of India.

1878 Britain takes Cyprus.

1882 Britain controls Egypt.

1886 Britain takes Burma.

1899 Britain controls Sudan.

1901 Death of Queen Victoria.

The American West

Since the United States had declared its independence from Britain in 1776, many settlers had arrived from Europe. At first most made their homes in the eastern states, but a few travelled farther west towards what are now Ohio, Michigan, Indiana and Illinois.

Many more people moved into the area around the Great Lakes after 1825 when the opening of the Erie Canal made the transport of people, farm products and manufactured goods much easier. Until 1803, however, the area to the west of the Mississippi River, known as Louisiana, was controlled by the French, who sold it to the US in that year. Soon explorers and traders began to venture farther west, setting up routes, or trails, which would later be followed by settlers.

In 1848, at the end of the Mexican-American War, people started travelling to the newly acquired land in the west.

◁ ***Railroads** helped open up the west by making rapid settlement possible. In 1869 the Union Pacific Railroad first opened, linking the east and west coasts. Other lines spread out across the Great Plains making it easy to transport goods and food, as well as passengers.*

GOLD RUSH

Gold was discovered in California in 1848, when it was still a province of Mexico. As the news spread, thousands of would-be miners rushed to the site in 1849. They used large pans to wash the river gravel, hoping to find gold among the pebbles. Some made fortunes, but many did not. With the influx of people from all over the world, cities such as San Francisco rapidly expanded, taking on a cosmopolitan air.

Known as pioneers, they made the journey in long trains of covered wagons. They took with them food and clothing, tools and furniture, not just for the journey but also to help them set up their new homes. When they reached their destination, each family chose a place to settle and started clearing the land ready for farming. The trees they chopped down were cut into timber and used to build homes. Tree stumps were pulled up and the land ploughed and seeds were sown. If the crops did not grow, then the family would have to go hungry or gather food from the wild as there were no towns or shops where they could buy supplies.

In spite of these hardships, the number of people heading west increased. The discovery of gold in California in 1848, and in Nevada and Colorado in 1859, brought thousands of prospectors from all around the world. Then, in 1862, the government passed the Homestead Act. In exchange for a small fee, this act gave 65 hectares of land to each family who would settle and farm for at least five years. Many thousands took up the offer, especially just after the Civil War. Soon towns and cities sprang up all over the Great Plains and west. But the land the government sold so cheaply was taken from the Native Americans who had lived there for thousands of years.

◁ ***Bison*** *(also called buffalo) lived on the Great Plains and were hunted by Native Americans who depended on them for food, shelter and clothing. The white settlers killed them in vast numbers.*

THE AMERICAN WEST

1803 The Louisiana Purchase. US buys the vast area west of the Mississippi from France.
1821 Opening of the Santa Fe Trail from Missouri to New Mexico.
1825 Opening of the Erie Canal.
1835 Texas claims independence from Mexico.
1836 Mexicans defeat the Texans at the Alamo, then are defeated themselves by Texan forces at San Jacinto.
1842 Border dispute between Canada and the US is settled.
1845 Texas becomes the 28th state of the US.
1845 Many Europeans emigrate to the US, especially from Ireland and Germany.
1846 War breaks out between the US and Mexico over land boundaries.
1848 Signing of the Guadalupe-Hidalgo Treaty ends the Mexican-American War. US, gains California, Nevada, Utah and Arizona, plus parts of New Mexico and Texas.
1849 Height of the Gold Rush.
1858 John Butterfield opens a stage route to the west.
1859 Many new mines open up in Nevada and Colorado.
1862 The Homestead Act encourages farmers to move to the Great Plains.
1867 US buys Alaska from Russia.
1869 The Union Pacific Railroad is completed.
1882 Huge copper deposits are discovered at Butte, Montana.
1893 The Great Northern Railroad reaches Seattle.

◁ ***Long trains of covered wagons*** *took pioneers westward. Made of wood, they had massive wheels and strong axles and were pulled by teams of oxen or mules. Inside was food, clothing, tools and furniture. Water was stored in a barrel slung on the side. Wagons were always in danger of attack by Native Americans whose land was being taken.*

The American Civil War

GENERAL ROBERT E LEE

Robert Edward Lee (1807–1870) was born in Virginia. The most talented military strategist of his day, towards the end of the Civil War he became commander in chief of the southern Confederate forces. Before the war, Lincoln offered him command of the Union army of the North, but he turned it down when Virginia withdrew from the Union. Although his side lost, he was an outstanding leader and probably the most able general of the war.

In the United States, by the early 19th century, the northern and southern states had slowly drifted apart for economic and social reasons. In the North, industry and trade had developed and towns and cities had increased. In the South, however, there was little industry and vast plantations relied on slave labour to grow cotton for export.

In the North, slavery had been banned since 1820, but the plantations of the South needed a huge labour force and relied on slaves who were still being brought from Africa. When Abraham Lincoln was elected president in 1861, his party was opposed to slavery and wanted it banned. Many people in the South saw this as a threat to their way of life and, in 1861, 11 southern states announced that they were breaking away from the Union to form their own Confederacy. When the United States government told them they had no right to do this, civil war broke out.

The other 23 states remained in the Union, so the North had more soldiers and more money, as well as the industry to provide the weapons and supplies they needed for war.

▽ ***At the battle of Bull Run,*** *Virginia, 1861, Confederate forces (right) under generals "Stonewall" Jackson and Beauregard defeated the Union army (left). It was the first major battle of the Civil War.*

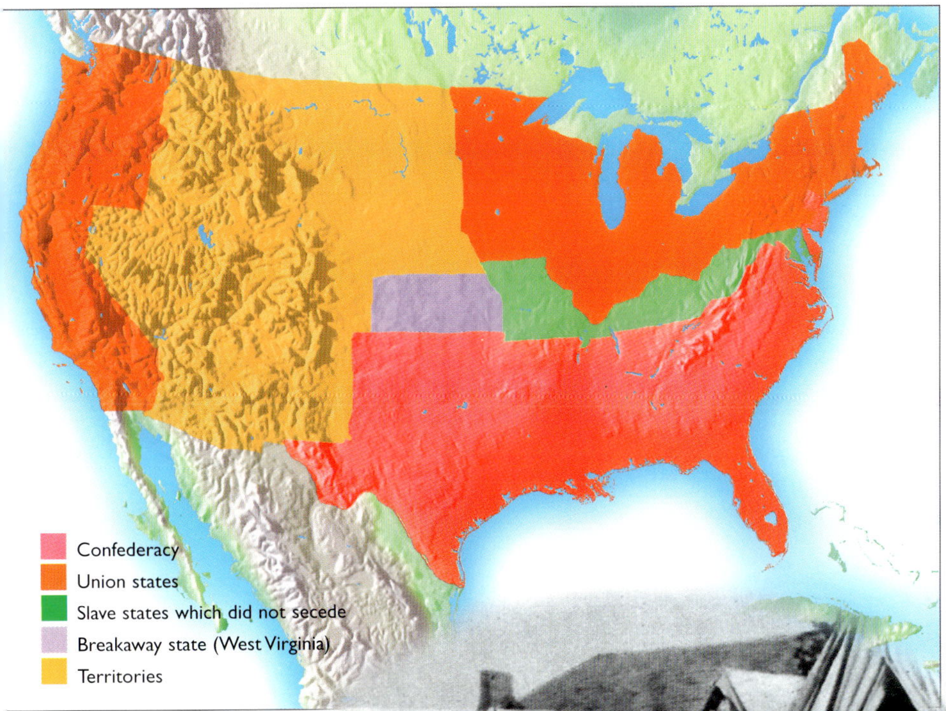

△ ***This map shows*** *the 11 Confederate states that broke from the Union. The Union then comprised the north-eastern and west-coast states and five northerly slave states, including West Virginia, which split from Virginia.*

△ ***Abraham Lincoln*** *(1809–1865) visiting the cemetery after the battle of Gettysburg, where he gave his famous Gettysburg Address in November 1863. Born in Kentucky, he is remembered as one of the great US presidents.*

The North also controlled the navy and so was able to blockade southern ports and prevent the South getting help or supplies from abroad. It also prevented the South from exporting cotton, so cutting off its wealth.

In spite of this, the early battles of the war were won by the South, which had brilliant generals and great enthusiasm for the fight. In July 1863, however, the war turned in favour of the North when Unionist troops defeated Confederate forces at the battle of Gettysburg, Pennsylvania, and another Unionist army captured the Confederate town of Vicksburg, Mississippi. In this same year Lincoln announced the abolition of slavery throughout the United States, which was later approved by Congress in 1865.

The war continued until April 1865 when the Confederate general Robert E Lee surrendered at Appomattox, Virginia. By this time, much of the South was in ruins. On both sides thousands of people had died, many in battle, but many more from disease and hunger. Five days after the surrender, Lincoln was shot by an assassin. Though the war was over, much bitterness remained in the South. Many southerners moved west and, even though the slaves were set free, with few resources their conditions hardly improved.

AMERICAN CIVIL WAR

1861 Civil War starts when Confederate troops attack the Union garrison at Fort Sumter, South Carolina. Confederates win the battle of Bull Run, Virginia.

1862 Confederate general Lee prevents Union army taking Richmond, Virginia and defeats another Union army at Fredericksburg, Virginia.

1863 Emancipation Proclamation is signed. Lee is defeated at Gettysburg, Pennsylvania. Grant's Union army captures Vicksburg, Mississippi.

△ ***Ulysses S Grant*** *(1822–1885) was the commander of the Union armies and led them to victory by his determination to win. He served as president of the US from 1869 to 1877.*

1864 Grant's Union forces besiege Lee's forces at Petersburg, Virginia. Union General Sherman captures Atlanta and Savannah, Georgia.

1865 Grant's forces capture Richmond, Virginia. On April 9, Lee surrenders to Grant at Appomattox, Virginia, bringing the war to an end. On April 15, Lincoln is shot in a theatre by actor and Confederate sympathizer John Wilkes Booth.

Native Americans

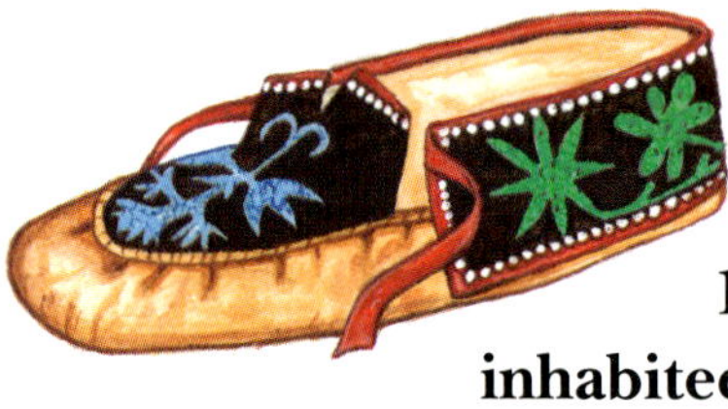

When the Europeans first reached North America in the 16th century, they found the land inhabited by many different tribes of Native Americans. Each had its own language and way of life, but they all lived in harmony with their environment, never taking more from it than they needed to survive.

They did not have horses or wheeled vehicles and, although they had some knowledge of using metal, most of their tools and weapons were made from wood or stone. On the west coast, where trees and fish were plentiful, Native Americans built wooden canoes and went fishing for their main food supply, while on the east coast they grew maize and tobacco in small plots around their villages and trapped animals in the surrounding woods. On the Great Plains they hunted buffalo (bison), while in the deserts of the southwest they built small dams to irrigate the land for growing maize, beans and squash.

The arrival of the Europeans soon had a disastrous effect on Native Americans. They had no resistance to diseases, such as measles and smallpox, that Europeans brought with them. Many were also killed in disputes over land. But the worst problems started in the 19th century when a huge influx of Europeans began to arrive in the United States.

In 1830 the American government passed the Indian Removal Act. This forced all Native Americans in the eastern states to leave their homelands to go and live on reservations far from the land that they knew, while their lands were taken over by European settlers. One of the first to suffer were the Cherokees, many of whom died on what became known as the Trail of Tears.

NATIVE AMERICANS

1830 The Indian Removal Act forces all Native Americans to move to reservations.

1837 Plains tribes are devastated by diseases brought by settlers from Europe.

1838 Cherokees march on the "Trail of Tears" to the west. Thousands die on the way and soon afterwards.

1860 At this date there are around 15 million buffalo living on the Great Plains.

1861–1890 Frequent wars break out between settlers and Native Americans.

1862 The Homestead Act allows settlers to buy land on the Great Plains very cheaply.

1864 The Navajos are forced to go on what is known as "The Long Walk" to Bosque Redondo. Many Cheyenne are massacred at Sand Creek, Colorado.

1865 Many more settlers start heading west after the end of the Civil War.

1868 General George Custer and the US cavalry brutally attack unarmed women and children in a Sioux village.

1876 The American government forces the Chiricahua Apaches to move from their homelands to a reservation in eastern Arizona. In June General Custer's forces are trapped and killed by Sioux and Cheyenne warriors at the battle of the Little Bighorn.

1885 By this date only about 2,000 bison are left.

1890 The US cavalry massacres over 200 Sioux at Wounded Knee Creek.

1952 The reservations are abolished and Native Americans are free to live where they want to.

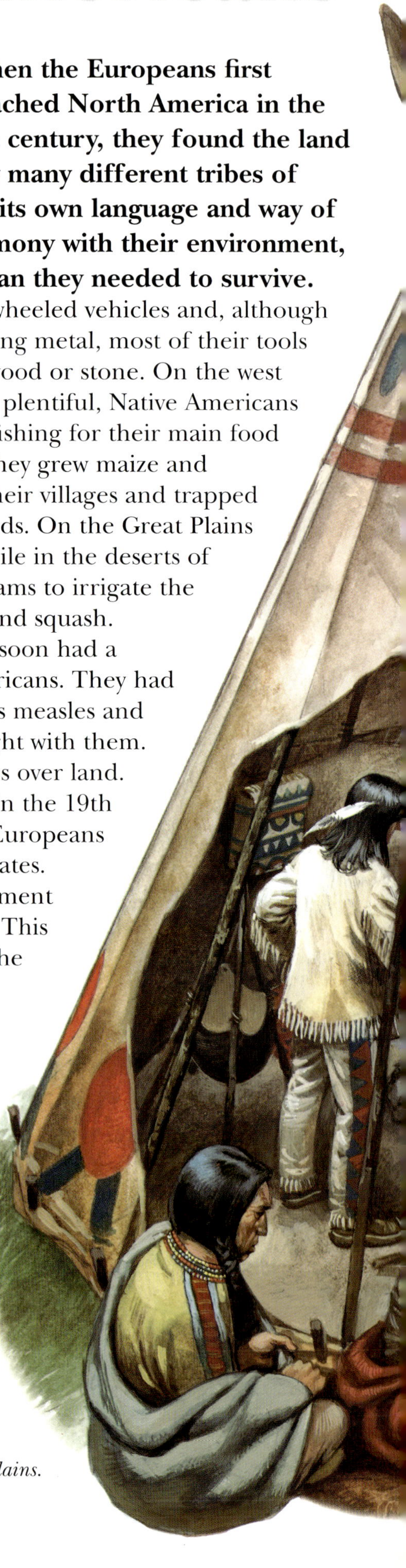

▷ ***The Sioux*** *were the largest nation of the Great Plains. They lived in tepees made of wooden poles covered in buffalo hide. Tepees could be quickly put up or taken down and were easy to transport, making them ideal for hunters following the herds of buffalo across the plains.*

△ ***Native Americans fought*** *a series of wars from 1861 to keep their land and stave off starvation. Experts in mounted marksmanship since the Spanish introduced guns and horses in the 17th century, their battle tactics often struck terror into the hearts of their enemies.*

GERONIMO

Apache chief Geronimo's (1829–1909) first name was Goyanthlay, which means "One Who Yawns". When Mexican troops killed his family, he became a fierce warrior, feared by both Mexican and American soldiers. He eventually surrendered and in 1905 took part in President Roosevelt's victory parade.

▽ ***Native Americans today*** *are proud of their heritage and try to keep their rituals, customs and languages alive. They have also staged protests to regain lost land.*

The situation grew worse throughout the century as more European settlers arrived and began to claim still more land to the west. On the Great Plains they did not share the Native Americans' respect for their environment. Instead settlers hunted buffalo for sport and between 1860 and 1885 they hunted the animals almost to extinction. Native American resistance was put down harshly by the US Army, although the Sioux managed to defeat 250 cavalrymen at the battle of the Little Bighorn in 1876. The final defeat of the Native Americans came in 1890 when over 200 unarmed Sioux men, women and children were killed at Wounded Knee Creek.

Unification of Italy

▽ ***Garibaldi handing** the Kingdom of the Two Sicilies to Victor Emmanuel in 1860. Victor Emmanuel was proclaimed the first king of a united Italy in 1861.*

GIUSEPPE GARIBALDI

Giuseppe Garibaldi (1807–1882) took part in a revolt in Italy in 1834 and had to spend the next ten years in exile in South America. He returned to Italy in time for the revolutions of 1848, but went back into exile when they did not succeed. On his return, Garibaldi gave his support to Victor Emmanuel and in 1860 he set out from Genoa with 1,000 volunteers to free Sicily and Naples

At the start of the 19th century, Italy was united under the control of Napoleon. After his defeat in 1815, its separate states were given back to their former rulers with only Piedmont–Sardinia remaining independent.

The states were ruled by foreigners, with Austria having the most power. During the 1820s and 30s opposition to foreign rule grew and the Risorgimento movement encouraged people to campaign for an independent and united Italy. Revolutions broke out in many states in 1848, but they were soon crushed. In 1858, Piedmont–Sardinia allied itself with France and defeated Austria. This was followed in 1860 by a successful revolt led by Guiseppe Garibaldi and his army of Redshirts.

Unification of Germany

Like Italy, Germany was also made up of many different states in the early 19th century. Following Napoleon's defeat in 1815, however, they joined together to form the German Confederation. This was made up of 38 states, of which Austria and Prussia were the most powerful.

From the start, Austria and Prussia competed against each other for leadership of the Confederation and in 1866 Prussia declared war on Austria. Their two armies met at Sadowa on the Elbe River on July 3 and the Prussians were victorious. The war ended on July 26 and the German Confederation was divided when Otto von Bismarck, the chief Prussian minister, set up a separate North German Confederation dominated by Prussia.

The French felt threatened by the growing power of Prussia, and on July 19, 1870 their emperor, Napoleon III, declared war on Prussia. On September 1 Napoleon III's army of 100,000 men was heavily defeated at the battle of Sedan on the French border and Napoleon III was taken prisoner. Three days later the people of Paris rose up against him and the French Second Empire was overthrown. The Prussian army then besieged Paris.

OTTO VON BISMARCK

Bismarck (1815–1898) started his rise to power in Prussia after the collapse of the Revolution of 1848. Becoming Prussian foreign minister in 1862, he determined to unite the north German states and make Prussia the ruler of a united Germany. To achieve this, he went to war with Austria and France. Germany was finally united in 1871 and Bismarck became its first chancellor.

▷ ***The unification of Italy*** *took only ten years. The last region to join was that around Rome, known as the Patrimony.*

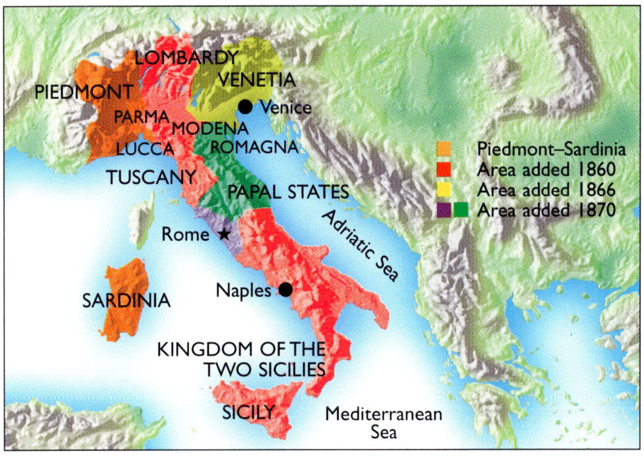

He conquered the island of Sicily first and then went on to conquer Naples. Meanwhile, the northern states had joined up with Piedmont–Sardinia and accepted Victor Emmanuel II as their king. Garibaldi handed Naples and Sicily to him in November 1860 and in 1861 Italy was declared a kingdom. Only Venice and Rome remained under foreign control and they became part of Italy in 1866 and 1871 respectively.

UNIFICATION OF ITALY

1815 After being briefly united under the control of Napoleon I, the Italian states are divided once more and given back to their former rulers.

From 1820s In the Risorgimento, secret societies are formed to oppose foreign rule.

1848 Unsuccessful revolutions break out in many states to try and bring about unification.

1849 Victor Emmanuel II becomes king of Piedmont–Sardinia.

1852 In Piedmont–Sardinia, Count Camillo Cavour forms his first government under Victor Emmanuel II. It is his hard work that unifies northern Italy.

1860 Garibaldi and his Redshirts set out to conquer the Kingdom of the Two Sicilies.

1861 Victor Emmanuel II becomes king of a unified Italy.

1866 Venice becomes part of Italy.

1871 Rome becomes part of Italy.

UNIFICATION OF GERMANY

1815 Thirty-eight German states form the German Confederation.

1848 Unsuccessful revolutions break out in many states to bring about unification.

1862 Bismarck becomes Prussia's foreign minister and determines to make Prussia the most powerful state in the German Confederation.

1864 Austria and Prussia declare war on Denmark over control of Schleswig-Holstein. The Danes are defeated and Schleswig-Holstein becomes part of the German Confederation.

1866 Prussia wins the Seven Weeks War against Austria. The North German Confederation is set up. Venice is taken from Austria and given to Italy.

1870–1871 Franco-Prussian War is won by Prussia.

1871 Creation of the German Second Empire, ruled by William II, the former king of Prussia.

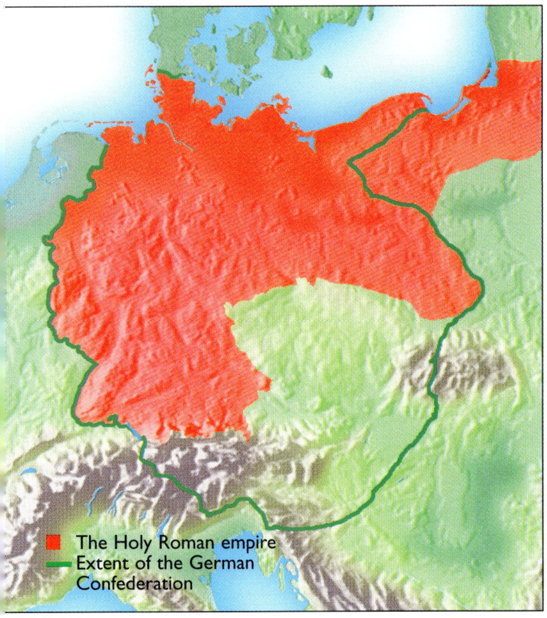

◁ ***This map shows*** *the mass of independent German states before unification. For many centuries, these states had formed the core of the Holy Roman empire, which was conquered by Napoleon I in 1806.*

▽ ***Napoleon III*** *(1808–1873) was the nephew of Napoleon I (Bonaparte) and came to power in France in 1848. In 1851 he declared himself emperor and set about transforming Paris and encouraging industry. After the Franco-Prussian War, his empire collapsed and he went into exile.*

When the Franco-Prussian War finally ended on May 10, 1871, Germany had taken control of Alsace and Lorraine from the French and the German Second Empire had been declared, with William II, King of Prussia, as its emperor and Otto von Bismarck as its chancellor.

Scramble for Africa

SCRAMBLE FOR AFRICA

1880 Leopold II, King of Belgium, claims the Congo as his own personal territory.

1882 Britain takes control of Egypt to secure access to the Suez Canal.

1884 The Conference of Berlin divides Africa up among seven European countries.

1889 The British conquer the Matabele and take their land, calling it Rhodesia.

1890 The Italians take control of Eritrea from where they try, but fail, to conquer Abyssinia (now Ethiopia).

1891 Tanganyika (now Tanzania) becomes a German protectorate. The French make northern Algeria part of France.

1893 The French take control of Mali.

1894 Uganda becomes a British protectorate.

1895 Kenya comes under British control and is known as the East African Protectorate.

1899 Start of the Boer Wars between Britain and the Boer people for control of southern Africa.

1910 The Union of South Africa is formed.

1911 The British colony of Rhodesia is divided into Northern Rhodesia (now Zambia) and Southern Rhodesia (now Zimbabwe).

1912 Morocco is divided into Spanish and French protectorates.

Most European nations had been content to have trading colonies around the coast of Africa. Only the British and the Boers in South Africa had moved inland and set up new settlements. In 1880 less than five percent of the continent was ruled by European powers. But within 20 years the situation had changed completely in what is known as the Scramble for Africa.

Seven European nations took control of the whole of Africa, apart from Liberia and Ethiopia. They were helped to do this by the opening of the Suez Canal, which linked the Mediterranean to the Red Sea and cut many kilometres off the journey to the east coast of Africa and India. They were also helped by improvements in transport (steamships were more reliable than the old sailing ships) and medicine that made it possible for Europeans to survive some of the diseases they met in Africa.

By 1884 Belgium, Britain, France, Portugal and Spain had already started to claim new colonies in Africa or expand their old ones. The newly-unified countries of Germany and Italy also wanted their share of the continent. To try and prevent any serious conflict, the European powers attended an international conference on Africa held in Berlin that same year.

▽ ***At Isandhlwana**, southern Africa, the Zulus resisted the British, wiping out 1,700 British soldiers at the start of the Zulu War in 1879. Later they were themselves defeated at the battle of Rorke's Drift.*

◁ ***This map shows*** *Africa in 1914, when the European powers had finished establishing colonies there. Only two countries on the continent remained independent: Ethiopia and Liberia.*

CECIL RHODES

Cecil Rhodes (1853–1902) was born in Britain and went to Natal in southern Africa when he was 17. He became a member of the Cape Colony parliament in 1881, becoming prime minister in 1890. He owned a large diamond mining company and helped to bring more territory under British control, but he failed in his ambition to give Britain an empire in Africa that stretched from the Cape to Egypt.

◁ ***The Suez Canal*** *was opened in 1869. This, together with the later construction of railways, made it much easier to travel to the east coast and the interior of Africa.*

The conference allowed the European powers to divide Africa among themselves, with no regard for the African peoples, their cultures or any natural boundaries. Any resistance to this by the Africans was crushed by large and well-equipped armies that were sent out from Europe and many thousands died in the fighting. Others suffered hardship and hunger as their traditional ways of life were destroyed and they were forced to work as cheap labour in mines and on plantations, growing crops such as cotton, tea, coffee and cocoa for export to Europe. Large areas of rain forest were cut down for their timber and many species of wild animals were hunted almost to extinction by white settlers who hunted for sport to pass the time.

In the British and German colonies, schools and medical centres were set up for the local people. Some were run by the government, others were run by missionaries who then expected the Africans to become Christians. In other colonies, however, the Africans were treated little better than slaves and nowhere did they have the right to vote or say how their country should be run.

◁ ***Patriotic posters*** *encouraging men to join the army appeared in Britain during the Boer Wars (1899–1902). A bitterly fought battle, around 20,000 Boer women and children died in British concentration camps in South Africa.*

▷ ***On the Great Trek*** *during the 1830s many Boers left Cape Colony and headed north in search of new farmland away from British rule. The African peoples, caught in the struggle between these two groups of warring whites, suffered greatly.*

The Modern World

Towards the Millennium 1900–1990s

At the start of the 20th century, large areas of the world were controlled by European powers. Britain, France, Belgium, the Netherlands, Portugal and Spain had built up great empires, while newly-united Germany wanted to expand the territory it controlled and this caused the outbreak of World War I in 1914.

Poor social and economic conditions led to rebellion in Ireland in 1916 and revolution in Russia in 1917. World War I ended in 1918 with defeat for Germany and its allies, but the peace that followed was an uneasy one. Growing unemployment in the 1920s was made worse by the Wall Street Crash in 1929 and the Great Depression that followed. A civil war in Spain from 1936 to 1939 brought the Fascists to power there, while in Germany and Italy Fascist parties were elected to government by promising people full-time employment, an escape from poverty and a renewed sense of national pride.

In 1939 World War II broke out, initially between Britain and France on one side and Germany on the other. Soon most of the countries in Europe, the British Commonwealth, the Soviet Union, the United States and Japan were also involved. The conflict lasted until 1945 and the peace that followed saw great changes in the world and the way it was ruled. The US and the Soviet Union emerged as superpowers, while Europe was divided between the capitalist West, supported

by the US, and the communist East, supported by the Soviets. Communists also came to power in China, and the European empires broke up as their colonies were granted independence. What became known as the Cold War broke out between the two superpowers and, although neither fought the other directly, both were involved in an arms race and a space race. They both also tried to expand their spheres of influence to Asia, Africa and South America, before the Cold War abruptly ended with the fall of communism and the collapse of the Soviet Union in 1991.

As the century draws to a close, and the information revolution gets under way, our world is both smaller and changing faster than ever before.

THE MODERN WORLD

1914 Austria declares war on Serbia and Germany on Russia and World War I begins.

1917 The Russian Revolution starts when the Bolsheviks led by Lenin seize power. They gain control of all of Russia only in 1921, after a bloody civil war.

1918 World War I ends with the loss of more than 8.5 million soldiers.

1921 Anglo-Irish Treaty gives Ireland independence, leaving Northern Ireland under British rule.

1929 Wall Street Crash sparks the Great Depression.

1933 Nazis led by Adolf Hitler come to power in Germany.

1936–1939 Spanish Civil War ends with victory for the Nationalists under Francisco Franco.

1939 Germany overruns Czechoslovakia, and then Poland, and World War II begins.

1941 The US enters the war following the Japanese attack on their naval base at Pearl Harbor.

1945 Germany surrenders. Japan surrenders after atomic bombs are dropped on Hiroshima and Nagasaki. United Nations formed. Europe is divided and the Cold War begins.

1947 Pakistan and India gain independence from Britain.

1948 The state of Israel is founded and the Arab League declares war.

1949 Communists led by Mao Zedong gain control of China.

1960s Most countries in Africa gain independence.

1965–1973 The Vietnam War.

1969 US astronaut Neil Armstrong is first to land on the moon.

1990 Germany is reunited.

1991 Soviet Union collapses and Cold War ends.

1994 Free elections in South Africa.

Votes for Women

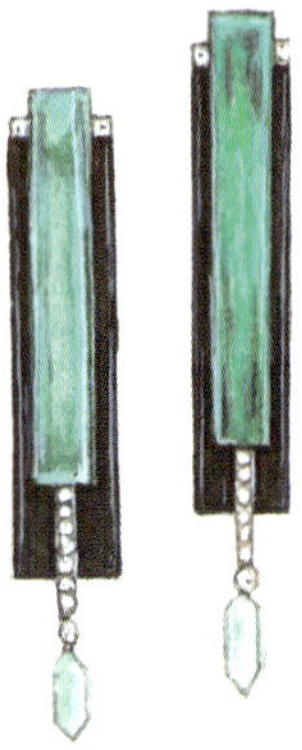

Women's right to vote was first suggested by British author Mary Wollstonecraft in her book *A Vindication of the Rights of Women*, published in 1792. At that time, most people had no say in the way they were governed. Groups, such as the Chartists in Britain, began campaigning for political reform in the 1830s, but they were only concerned with obtaining the vote for all men. Women were not included.

In the middle of the 19th century, however, a movement began in the United States with the aim of winning voting rights for women across the world. Its first meeting was held at Seneca Falls in New York state in 1848, when a convention on women's rights was led by Lucretia Mott and Elizabeth Cady Stanton. Many other public meetings followed, even though they were often fiercely opposed by those who did not want women to have the right to vote. The speakers included women such as Sojourner Truth and Harriet Tubman, both of whom had been born slaves.

The movement gained in strength throughout the rest of the 19th century and in 1890 Wyoming became the first state in the US to allow women to vote in local elections. Three years later New Zealand became the first country in the world to allow women to vote in national elections. (The electoral bill was passed by only two votes.) In Britain, this triumph encouraged various women's suffrage (right to vote) societies to unite in 1897.

△ ***Suffragettes campaigning*** *in the British general election of 1910. Not all those who supported women's right to vote were women, a few were men, including some politicians. Suffragettes campaigned on behalf of the politicians they knew would support their cause.*

▽ ***Many women campaigned peacefully*** *for the right to vote. Known as suffragists (to distinguish them from the more militant and derogatory term suffragettes), they marched through the streets, holding rallies to gain support for their cause.*

At first their campaigns were peaceful, but in 1903 one of their members, Emmeline Pankhurst, set up a new society called the Women's Social and Political Union (WSPU). It believed in actions rather than words and the WSPU held public demonstrations and attacked property in protest against women's lack of rights. Many of its members were arrested and sent to prison, where they often went on hunger strike to bring attention to their cause. In 1913 one member of the WSPU, Emily Davison, was killed when she threw herself under the King's horse at the Derby.

With the outbreak of World War I in 1914, the WSPU gave up its active protests and its members involved themselves in the war effort. Many women took on jobs traditionally done by men, proving that they were just as capable. In 1918 the vote was given to all British women over the age of 30, even though the age for men was only 21. Women in the US were given the right to vote in 1920 and in 1928 the voting age for British women was lowered to 21.

△ ***Emmeline Pankhurst****, founder of the WSPU, was arrested and imprisoned several times for destroying property. Other tactics included non-payment of taxes, disrupting political meetings and public demonstrations.*

▷ ***Suffragettes in prison*** *who went on hunger strike were forcibly fed by doctors and prison officers. Those who became too ill to endure prison life any longer were released, but they were re-arrested as soon as their health improved.*

VOTES FOR WOMEN

1848 First women's rights convention held at Seneca Falls, New York state.

1890 Wyoming allows women to vote in local elections.

1893 New Zealand gives women the vote in national elections.

1897 The National Union of Women's Suffrage Societies is formed in Britain.

1902 Australia gives women the right to vote.

1903 Emmeline Pankhurst forms the Women's Social and Political Union.

1905 The first two suffragettes are sent to prison in Britain.

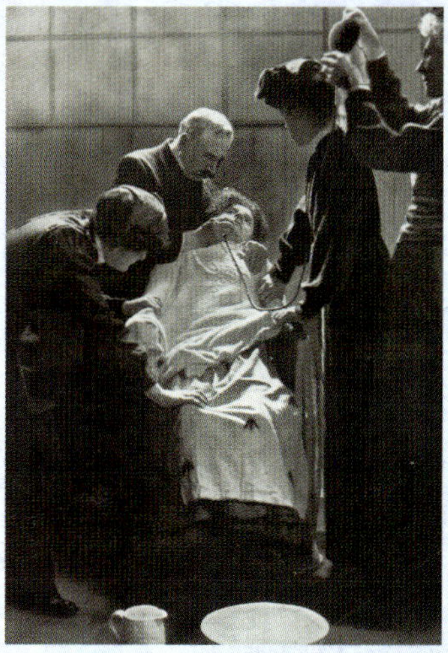

1906 Finland gives women the vote. The following year, the first women MPs are elected to the Finnish parliament.

1913 Suffragette Emily Davison is killed when she throws herself under the King's horse at the Derby. Norway gives women the vote.

1917 Russia gives women the right to vote.

1918 British women over the age of 30 are given the vote. Canadian women are given equal voting rights with men.

1919 Germany, Austria, Poland and Czechoslovakia all give women the right to vote.

1920 Women in the US are given the vote.

1944 France gives women the right to vote.

World War I

Towards the end of the 19th century, there was growing rivalry among the nations of Europe. Germany was quickly becoming a major industrial and military power and many countries, especially France and Britain, felt threatened by this.

At the same time, Turkey's Ottoman empire was breaking up. Newly-independent Serbia was gaining power and land and the empire of Austria-Hungary saw this as a threat. As a result, Germany formed the Triple Alliance with Austria-Hungary and Italy and pledged to defend each other in case of attack, while Britain, France and Russia formed the Triple Entente for the same purpose.

In the early 1900s both Britain and Germany added bigger and better battleships to their navies and all of Europe gradually expanded their armies. By 1914 it only needed one incident to spark off a war. This came when Archduke Franz Ferdinand was assassinated in Sarajevo, Bosnia. Franz Ferdinand was heir to the

WORLD WAR I

1878 Serbia gains independence from the Ottoman empire.
1882 Germany, Austria-Hungary and Italy form the Triple Alliance to defend each other in the event of war.
1891 France and Russia agree that, if either one is attacked, the other will give it full military support.
1904 Britain forms the Entente Cordiale with France.
1907 Russia joins with Britain and France to form the Triple Entente.
1908 Austria-Hungary occupies Bosnia-Hercegovina to stop Serbia taking control.
1912–1913 Balkan Wars between the Balkan League (Serbia, Bulgaria, Greece and Montenegro) and the Ottoman empire. Serbia's side is victorious.
1914 June 28 Gavrilo Princip assassinates Archduke Franz Ferdinand in Sarajevo.
July 28 Austria declares war on Serbia. Russia prepares to defend Serbia from Austria.
August 1 Germany declares war on Russia to defend Austria.
August 3 Germany declares war on France, Russia's ally.
August 4 German armies march through Belgium to France. Britain declares war on Germany. World War I begins.
August 26 Germany defeats Russian forces at the battle of Tannenberg.
September At the battle of the Marne the Allies halt German advance on Paris. German victory at the Masurian Lakes leads Russia to retreat from East Prussia.
November At the end of the battle of Ypres German forces are prevented from reaching the Channel.

▷ ***This map shows*** *the major battlefronts of World War I. There were dozens of bloody battles on the Western Front, where opposing armies dug in with defensive trenches. There were over a million casualties at the Somme in 1916.*

▽ ***Tanks*** *were a British invention that made their first appearance in battle at the Somme in 1916. Their tracks allowed them to travel over barbed wire and across rough ground. From 1917, they helped to break the stalemate of trench warfare.*

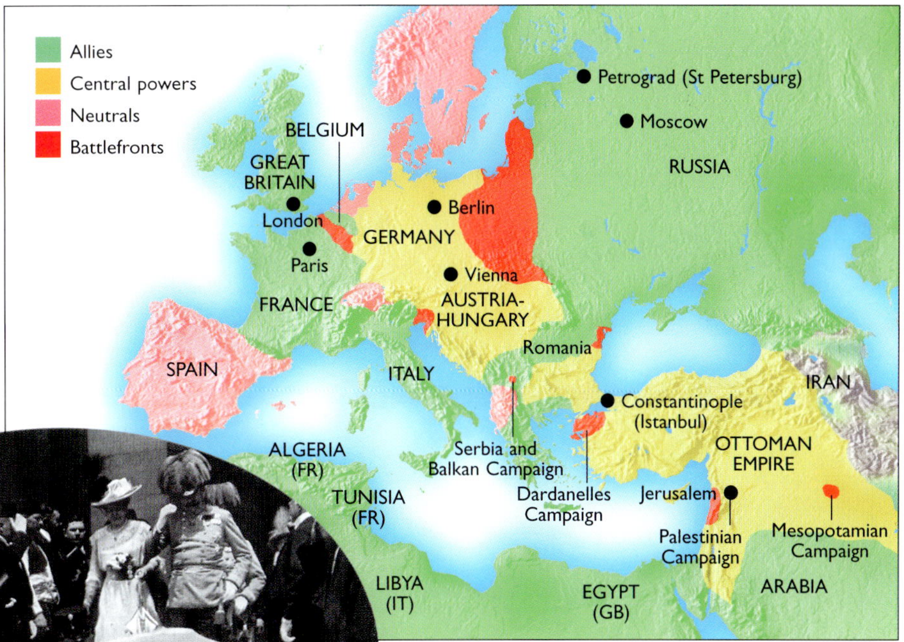

◁ ***Archduke Franz Ferdinand*** *on June 28, 1914, was paying an official visit to Sarajevo as inspector general of the imperial army, when a bomb was thrown at his car. It bounced off and exploded under the next car. As Franz Ferdinand and his wife were leaving to visit the wounded in hospital, they were shot dead by Gavrilo Princip.*

◁ ***In the trenches*** *soldiers on both sides were comparatively safe. There they ate and slept, while waiting for orders to go into battle. Dugouts, or underground shelters, offered some protection from enemy shells and the worst of the rain, but the trenches were usually cold, muddy and wet.*

throne of Austria-Hungary and the man who shot him was a Serbian protesting against Austro-Hungarian rule in Bosnia. Austria-Hungary declared war on Serbia, prompting Russia to mobilize its army to defend Serbia. Germany declared war on Russia and on France, Russia's ally. The following day the German army marched through Belgium to attack France. This drew Britain into the war, since, in 1830, it had made an agreement to defend Belgium if ever it was attacked.

People who lived through the war that followed called it the Great War, but it later became known as World War I (1914–1918) as it eventually involved many of the countries of the world. They were divided into two groups, known as the Allies and the Central Powers. The Central Powers were made up of Germany, Austria-Hungary and Turkey, while the Allies included France, Britain and its empire, Russia, Italy, Japan and, from 1917, the United States. The war was fought along two main lines, or fronts. These were the Western Front, which ran from Belgium, through France to Switzerland, and the Eastern Front which ran from the Baltic to the Black Sea. There was also fighting in the Middle East and along the border between Italy and Austria.

Sopwith Camel

WORLD WAR I PLANES

World War I (1914–1918) was the first war in which aeroplanes were widely used. Flimsy and unreliable, they were first used to spy on enemy trenches and troop movements. Later, they were used in aerial combat and in bombing raids. Two of the most famous aeroplanes to be used were the British Sopwith Camel, which was a biplane (which means it had two pairs of wings), and the German Fokker E1, which was a monoplane (single pair of wings). Fokker was a Dutch engineer, but he had built his factory in Germany in 1912 and so supplied planes to the Germans.

German Fokker E1 monoplane

Trench Warfare

What made World War I so different from any other war in the past was the fact that most of it was fought from two parallel lines of trenches separated by only a short stretch of ground known as "no-man's land".

Trench warfare was necessary because the power, speed and accuracy of the weapons used on both sides would have made it impossible to have fought a battle in the open. When soldiers did leave the trenches to launch an attack, often only a few metres of ground were gained and the cost in casualties was enormous. This led to a stalemate situation that lasted from the end of 1914 until the summer of 1918. Even the use of new weapons such as aeroplanes, tanks and poison gas did little to change the situation.

At the end of 1917, Russia started peace talks with Germany and German soldiers who had been fighting on the Eastern Front were able to join those fighting in the west. For a while they outnumbered the Allied forces, but by September 1918 over 1,200,000 well-trained and well-equipped soldiers from the United States joined the Allied forces in France. This made it possible for the Allies to start defeating the Central Powers. By the end of October, almost all German-occupied France and part of Belgium had been reclaimed, and Turkey and Austria had been defeated.

In Germany people were running short of food and fuel. The navy mutinied and there was widespread unrest. On November 9 the German ruler, Kaiser William II, abdicated and on November 11 an armistice was signed between Germany and the Allies, bringing the fighting in World War I to an end.

◁ ***T E Lawrence*** *(1888–1935), known as Lawrence of Arabia, worked for British army intelligence in North Africa at the start of the war. In 1916, he joined the Arab revolt against the Ottoman Turks, leading them to conquer Aqaba in 1917 and Damascus in 1918. With only a few thousand Arabs he took on the Turkish army.*

△ ***War leaders*** *US president Woodrow Wilson (left), French president Georges Clemenceau (centre) and British prime minister David Lloyd-George (right) lead their countries to victory.*

▽ ***On the Western Front*** *most of the fighting took place in northern France and Belgium. Mules were used to bring supplies to the front and heavy guns were horse-drawn. Dead horses and troops could not be moved quickly and the stench of their rotting flesh hung over the trenches.*

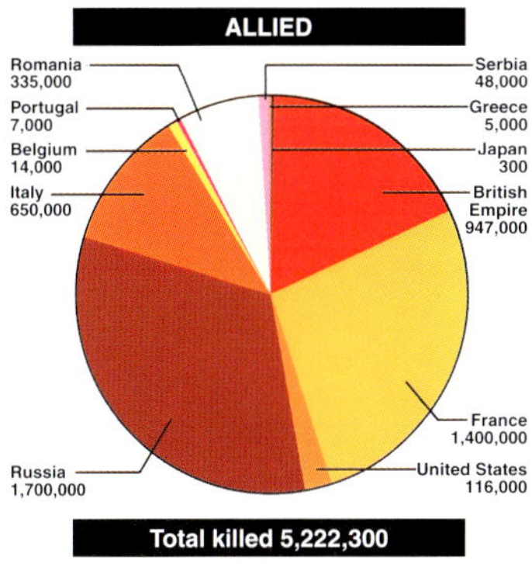

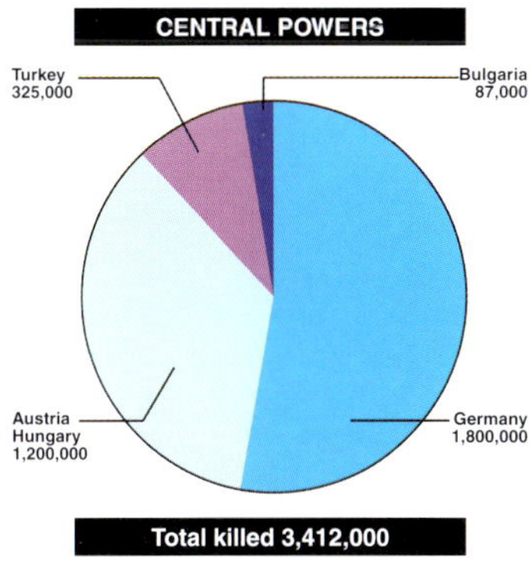

◁ ***These charts show*** *the numbers of Central and Allied soldiers killed during World War I for each of the countries that took part in the war. Germany sustained the greatest losses, followed by Russia, and then France. The number of civilian deaths was comparatively light.*

▽ ***Going over the top*** *of the trench was the most dangerous time for soldiers. First, they had to get through their own barbed wire before running through no-man's land to reach the enemy.*

In January 1919, the Allies met at the Paris Peace Conference, which formally ended the war. It drew up the Treaty of Versailles, which said that Germany was guilty of starting the war and that it had to pay vast sums of money in compensation to its former enemies. It also had to return Alsace-Lorraine to France and give up its overseas colonies. The same treaty established the League of Nations, which struggled to keep peace in the world throughout the 1920s and 1930s.

WORLD WAR I

1915 British naval blockade of Germany leads to a German submarine blockade of Britain.
April–May Germany uses poison gas for the first time at the second battle of Ypres.
May 22 Italy joins the Allies.
September British and French campaign at Loos fails.
1916 February Start of battle for Verdun, France, lasting for five months.
March Failure of the Gallipoli campaign by Australian, New Zealand and British forces to capture the Dardanelles and Constantinople.
May Only major sea battle at Jutland in the North Sea ends with both sides claiming victory.
June Russian offensive led by general Brusilov fails to defeat the Germans.
July 1 Start of the battle of the Somme (ends November).
1917 On April 6 the US joins the war on Allied side.
July Third battle of Ypres (Passchendaele), Allied offensive gains little.
October Italians are defeated at the battle of Caporetto.
1918 On March 3, Armistice signed between Russia and Germany.
July Germans launch offensive on the Western Front.
August Allies break through German defences and force them to retreat.
October After Italian victory at Vittorio Veneto, Austria-Hungary surrenders.
November Revolution in Germany. Armistice is signed on November 11 at 11 o'clock. World War I ends.
1919 Treaty of Versailles is signed.

The Russian Revolution

Following defeat in the Crimean War, Tsar Alexander II realized Russia was very backward compared with the rest of Europe. To modernize his country he freed the serfs (who were treated little better than slaves), improved government, education and the army and encouraged the development of industry and the railways. Many people, however, thought his reforms did not go far enough and in 1881 he was assassinated.

Alexander III succeeded him as tsar and promptly undid most of his father's reforms. Unrest began to grow and people such as Vladimir Lenin looked to the writings of Karl Marx, the founder of communism, for ways of changing Russian life. The first serious rebellion broke out in 1905 after troops fired on striking workers in the capital, St Petersburg. It was soon crushed and the leaders, including Lenin, went into exile. The new tsar, Nicholas II, promised more civil rights to his people, but this promise was soon broken.

When World War I started, life for most people in Russia went from bad to worse. The railways, which had been used to bring food, fuel and supplies for industry to the cities, were now used to take troops and weapons to the front. The economy almost collapsed and people started to go hungry. The government did nothing to improve the situation and in March 1917 riots broke out again. This time the troops joined the rioters. Nicholas abdicated and his advisers resigned.

A temporary government was set up, with Prince George Lvov as its chief minister. He was succeeded by Alexander Kerensky, but unrest continued. The Bolsheviks,

VLADIMIR ILYICH LENIN

Lenin (1870–1924) was a lawyer who was also involved in political activities. In 1897 he was exiled to Siberia for his political views and in 1898 he became leader of the Bolsheviks who wanted major reforms in the way Russia was governed. He was exiled again from January 1905 to March 1917, but on his return to Russia his strong personality and powerful speeches persuaded thousands of ordinary people to join the revolution.

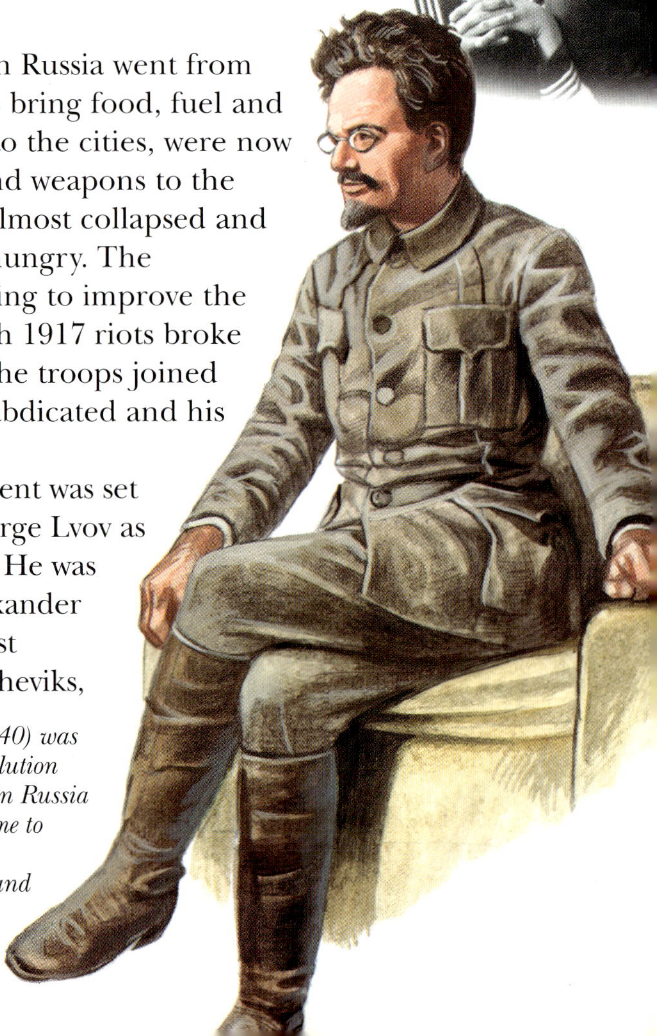

▷ ***Leon Trotsky*** *(1879–1940) was a leader of the Bolshevik revolution and the most powerful man in Russia after Lenin. When Stalin came to power in 1924, Trotsky was dismissed from office, exiled and eventually murdered.*

▽ ***Tsar Nicholas II*** *with his wife Alexandra and their five children. After the revolution, they were all imprisoned. In 1918 they were executed.*

led by Lenin who had returned from exile, began to plan a take-over of government. In November they attacked the Winter Palace in St Petersburg and seized power. (This is called the October Revolution because Russia used a different calendar at that time.)

The new government led by Lenin moved the capital to Moscow and made peace with Germany. It broke up the landowner's large estates and gave the land to the peasants who worked on it. The workers took control of the factories and the state took control of the banks. Not everyone agreed with this, however, and in 1918 civil war broke out between the Bolshevik Red Army and the anti-communist White Russians. This ended in victory for the Bolsheviks in 1921. The following year, the Union of Soviet Socialist Republics was formed. After Lenin's death in 1924, he was succeeded by Joseph Stalin. Stalin's rule was oppressive and many of his opponents were killed.

▽ ***Armed workers*** *led by the Bolsheviks stormed St Petersburg's Winter Palace in 1917, starting the revolution. They were joined by Russian soldiers, tired of fighting the Germans in World War I.*

RUSSIAN REVOLUTION

1887 Lenin becomes a Marxist after his brother is executed for trying to kill Tsar Alexander III.
1894 Nicholas II becomes tsar.
1898 Russian Social Democratic Workers' party is founded.
1904–1905 Russo-Japanese War over Russian expansion into Manchuria, a province of China under Japanese control. The Russians are driven out.
1905 Around 200,000 people march on the Winter Palace in St Petersburg. The rebellion is put down and Lenin goes into exile.

△ ***Rasputin*** *(1869–1916) was a priest who had great influence over the imperial family. He told the tsarina he could cure her sick son and persuaded the tsar to ignore the people's complaints.*

1917 Lenin returns from exile and goes to St Petersburg. Nicholas II abdicates and a republican government is formed. Revolutionaries attack the Winter Palace and the government falls.
1918 Russia withdraws from World War I after signing the Treaty of Brest-Litovsk. The imperial family is executed. Civil war between the Red Army (communists) and White Russians (anti-communists) lasts until 1920.
1922 The Russian empire is renamed the Union of Soviet Socialist Republics.

Irish Home Rule

At the end of World War I, the question of Irish independence from Britain became critical. Many Irish wanted self-government and were increasingly frustrated as two home rule bills put before the British parliament were defeated. Then, in 1912, a third home rule bill was approved, but it was prevented from coming into force by the outbreak of World War I.

Not all the Irish wanted home rule. Most people in the six counties of the north, known as Ulster, wanted to remain part of Britain and be governed from London, while in the south most wanted Ireland to become a completely independent republic. This division between north and south dated back to the 16th century, when a succession of English monarchs had used the planting of Protestant English and Scottish people on lands seized from Irish Catholics as a way of increasing loyalty to the British crown. Conflict between the two sides pushed Ireland to the brink of a civil war, also only prevented by the outbreak of World War I.

During the war, people who wanted Ireland to become a republic continued their campaign. They belonged to various organizations, including the political party Sinn Fein, the Irish Republican Brotherhood, the Irish Volunteers and the Irish Citizen Army. Led by Padraig Pearse and James Connolly, around 1,600 protesters rose up in armed rebellion on Easter Monday, 1916. They took control of several public buildings in Dublin and declared Ireland a republic. The fighting lasted for four days before they were forced to surrender.

In the British general election of December 1918, Sinn Fein candidates were elected to every Irish constituency outside Ulster. Instead of going to Houses of Parliament in London, however, they set up their

IRISH HOME RULE

1886–1893 Attempts to give Ireland its own parliament are defeated in London.
1896 James Connolly founds the Irish Socialist and Republican party.
1905 Sinn Fein, the Irish nationalist party, is founded.
1912 The third Irish Home Rule bill is introduced in the British parliament, but World War I starts in 1914 before it can be enacted.
1916 On Easter Monday in Dublin, Irish republicans rise in armed revolt against British rule. Although they are defeated, their cause gains much support when 15 of the rebels are executed.
1918 Newly-elected Sinn Fein MPs set up their own parliament in Dublin, rather than going to Westminster in London.
1919 Outbreak of bitter fighting between Irish republicans and British troops.

△ ***The Custom House*** *in Dublin was burned down in 1921 by republicans wanting to destroy the British records kept there. It was later rebuilt in its original style.*

1921 Anglo-Irish Treaty between the British government and the Irish Republican party separates Ulster from the rest of Ireland.
1922 Outbreak of civil war between supporters of the Anglo-Irish Treaty and those who oppose it. Michael Collins is assassinated.
1937 The Irish Free State becomes Eire.
1949 Eire withdraws from the British Commonwealth and becomes the republic of Ireland.

▷ ***The Easter rising*** *of 1916 saw fighting erupt on to the streets of Dublin. Barricades were set up with British soldiers on one side and Irish Republicans on the other. Both sides suffered casualties, with 100 British soldiers and 450 Irish Republicans and civilians being killed. Many public buildings in Dublin were destroyed or badly damaged in the conflict.*

own parliament, called the Dail Eireann, in Dublin. It had its own courts, tax system and postal service, and in 1919 it declared Ireland a republic. This led to three years of war between the military wing of Sinn Fein (later called the Irish Republican Army) led by Michael Collins, and the Royal Irish Constabulary, helped by British soldiers known as the Black and Tans. In July 1921 Michael Collins decided to negotiate with the British government, rather than continue fighting. In December he signed the Anglo-Irish Treaty, which made most of Ireland independent, but left Northern Ireland under British rule. This led to another outbreak of civil war, this time between the Free-Staters, who supported the Anglo-Irish Treaty, and the Republicans who wanted independence for a united Ireland.

The civil war lasted until 1923, when the Republicans decided to accept the division of Ireland for the time being. Their leader, American-born Eamon de Valera, founded a new political party, called Fianna Fail, in 1926, won the Irish general election in 1932, and served as head of government for many years.

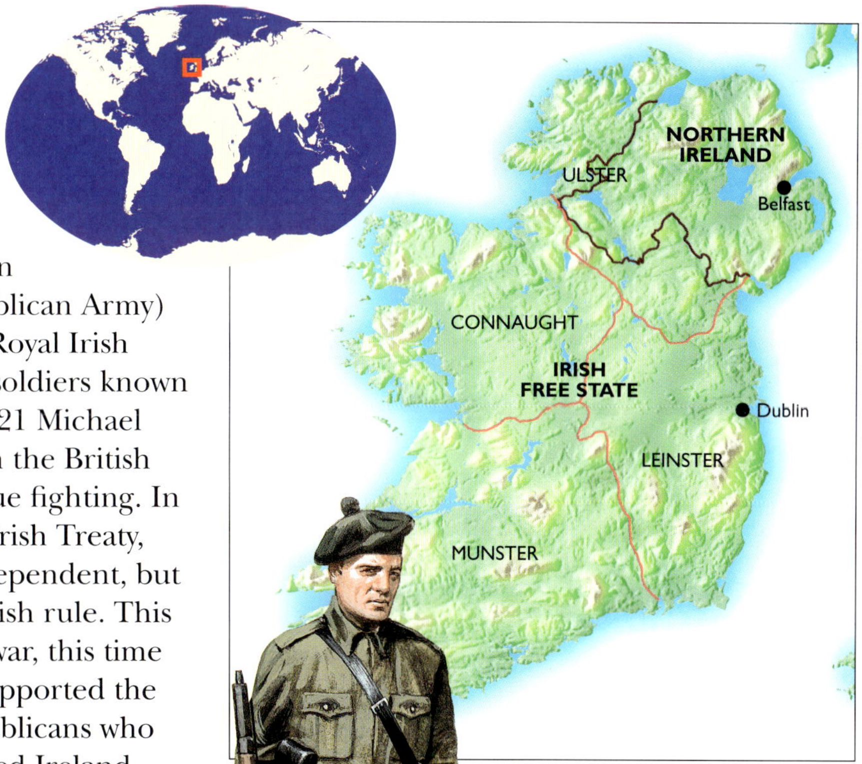

△ ***This map shows*** *Ireland after the settlement of 1923. Three of the nine counties of Ulster became part of the Irish Free State; the other six, stayed part of the United Kingdom.*

◁ ***Black and Tan*** *was the name given to British soldiers because of the colour of their uniforms. Specially recruited by the British government between 1920 and 1921, they were hated by the Irish.*

EAMON DE VALERA

Eamon de Valera (1882–1975) was born in the USA, but came to Ireland when he was just two years old. As a teacher he supported a campaign to revive the Irish language. He took part in the Easter rising but escaped execution because of his American birth. He was elected president of Sinn Fein and opposed the partition of Ireland in 1922. In 1926 he formed a new political party, Fianna Fail, and in 1932 he became prime minister of Ireland, becoming its president in 1959.

The Great Depression

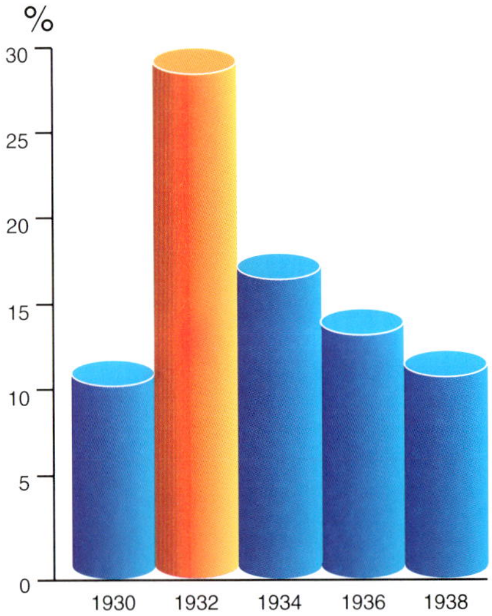

△ ***Unemployment figures*** *rose throughout the world during the Great Depression. The worst hit countries were the USA, Britain and Germany, whose economies were heavily based on industry.*

▽ ***Soup kitchens*** *serving free food were set up in many cities to feed the hungry. The Depression meant misery for millions who lost their jobs. It was estimated that over a quarter of the US's population had no income other than what they could get from begging, charity handouts and limited public welfare.*

After World War I, the economies of many European countries were in chaos. Germany had to pay reparations (large sums of money) to Britain and France for starting the war. This led its economy to collapse in the 1920s. Other nations also suffered as they tried to pay back money borrowed to finance their war effort.

Most of the money borrowed to finance the war came from the United States. There, many people were starting to invest in stocks and shares, pushing up the price of shares beyond their real value. Share prices reached a peak in August 1929, then started to dip. When they were still falling in October, investors began to panic and sold their shares for whatever they could get. Reckless selling made prices fall still further and thousands of investors lost all their money. This is called the Wall Street Crash and started an economic crisis as banks and businesses closed down, throwing people out of work.

▽ ***Panic in the streets of New York,*** *October 1929. As the value of shares dropped lower and lower, many investors rushed to the Wall Street Stock Exchange only to discover that they had lost all their money.*

THE NEW DEAL

Part of the New Deal introduced by President Roosevelt in 1933 included a programme to create more jobs. Young people were found work in the national forests, while a series of dams were built on the Tennessee River to provide electricity and prevent soil erosion. There were also welfare (social security) and labour laws to improve working conditions.

△ ***On the Jarrow Crusade*** *200 men set out in October 1935 from Jarrow in northern England to London to draw attention to unemployment in their home town. Helped by sympathizers, they marched all the way there on foot.*

The situation was made worse as a severe drought hit the agricultural states of the Midwest. The Dust Bowl was a vast area where the rich topsoil, worn away by droughts and over-farming, turned to dust and blew away in the wind. Nothing would grow, and many farms were abandoned as farmers and their families took what they could and went to start a new life in California.

The economic crisis in the US soon affected the whole world. The system of international loans depended on the US and collapsed as money loaned overseas was called back home. This brought economic problems to Europe, especially Britain and Germany, both of which had high unemployment. Many countries attempted to protect their own industries by passing laws placing import duties on foreign goods. At the height of the Depression in 1932, world exports of raw materials had fallen by over 70 per cent, ruining the economies of many colonies who depended on the export of food and raw materials for their income.

The US was particularly badly hit. Mass unemployment led to many being made homeless, reduced to living in shanty towns of tin and cardboard, called Hoovervilles after President Herbert Hoover. In 1933, however, a new government led by Franklin D Roosevelt introduced the New Deal. It included financial support for farmers and a construction programme to create more jobs. Banks were more closely regulated and savings better protected. Even so, unemployment remained high throughout the 1930s.

GREAT DEPRESSION

1929 In October the New York stock exchange on Wall Street crashes as people panic and sell their shares.
1932 At the height of the Depression there are 12,000,000 unemployed people in the US. Roosevelt is elected president.
1933 Roosevelt introduces the New Deal to protect people's savings and create jobs. In Germany there are 6,000,000 unemployed.
1935 In Britain 200 men march from Jarrow to London with a petition drawing attention to unemployment.
1936 The Depression ends in Germany as public works and munitions production bring full employment.
1939 Around 15 per cent of the US's workforce is still unemployed.
1941 Full employment returns to the US as it enters World War II.

The Rise of Fascism

△ ***Benito Mussolini** (1883–1945) impressed many Italians with his policies at first. After Italy's disastrous efforts in World War II, he was shot while trying to escape.*

Fascism is the name of a political movement that grew up between the wars. Fascist leaders promised strong leadership and were opposed to socialism. They gained massive support by promising to restore national pride and create jobs in countries humiliated by defeat in World War I and the misery of high unemployment.

Italy was the first country to have a Fascist government when Benito Mussolini marched his followers into Rome in October 1922 and threatened to overthrow the government by force if he was not made prime minister. The king agreed to his demand and asked Mussolini to form a new government. Gangs of armed Fascists then terrorized and killed members of other political groups who did not agree with them and by January 1923 Italy had become a one-party state. Two years later, Mussolini started ruling as dictator and became known as "Il Duce".

At that time, Spain was also ruled by a dictator by the name of Miguel Primo de Rivera. He tried to unite the people around the motto of "Country, Religion, Monarchy", but he did not succeed. He fell from power in 1930 and Spain became a republic the following year. But in 1933 Primo de Rivera's son founded the Falangist party, made up of Spanish Fascists.

△ ***In the Spanish Civil War** (1936–1939) the Spanish army led by Franco and supported by Germany, defeated the Republicans who were supported by USSR and many idealistic volunteers.*

▷ ***Hitler addressing a rally at Nuremburg, 1938.** Adolf Hitler (1889–1945) was a powerful speaker who knew exactly how to win the support of his audience. He turned Germany into a police state, persecuting his political opponents, trade unionists and Jews, whom he blamed for all Germany's problems.*

In 1936, under the leadership of General Francisco Franco, the Falangist party overthrew the elected government in Spain. A terrible civil war broke out in which Franco, supported by Italy and Germany, eventually defeated the Republicans supported by Russia. In 1939 Franco became dictator of Spain.

In Germany, the Nazi party and its leader Adolf Hitler rose to power in 1933. The Nazis won support by promising to build Germany into a great state again. Hitler started a programme of public works to create jobs and built up munitions and the armed forces. He imposed total control on the people, banning other political parties, introducing a secret police and persecuting minorities, especially the Jews. Hitler also wanted to take back lands Germany lost after World War I. These included the Saar area, which he reoccupied in 1935, and the Rhineland, reoccupied in 1936. In 1938, Hitler sent tanks into Vienna to persuade the Austrians to agree to a union with Germany and also threatened to take over the Sudetenland in Czechoslovakia. To try to keep the peace, the Munich Agreement of September 1938 gave the Sudetenland to Germany. The following March, however, Hitler's troops took over the whole of Czechoslovakia and began to threaten Poland.

△ ***Neville Chamberlain**, prime minister of Britain, waiving the Munich agreement in 1938. It was signed in an attempt to keep peace in Europe by recognizing Germany's claim to the Sudetenland.*

RISE OF FASCISM

1922 Fascists led by Mussolini as prime minister come to power in Italy.

1923–1930 Primo de Rivera rules Spain as dictator.

1925 From this date Mussolini rules Italy as dictator.

1929 Mussolini wins the support of the Roman Catholic church by making Vatican City an independent state.

△ ***Francisco Franco** (1892–1975) became chief of staff of the Spanish army in 1935. He sympathized with Hitler, but kept Spain neutral in World War II. He was a ruthless dictator and tolerated no opposition to his rule, which lasted until his death.*

1931 Spanish monarchy overthrown as Republican party wins the election.

1932 Sir Oswald Mosley forms the British Union of Fascists.

1933 Nazis led by Adolf Hitler come to power in Germany. In Spain, Primo de Rivera's son creates the Falangist (Fascist) party.

1934 Hitler gains total power as his rivals are assassinated on the Night of the Long Knives.

1935 Italy invades Abyssinia (Ethiopia).

1936–1939 Spanish Civil War between Republicans and Nationalists (Falangists). Nationalists win and Franco becomes dictator of Spain.

1937 German aircraft bomb the Spanish town of Guernica in support of the Nationalists.

1938 On March 13 the Anschluss unites Germany and Austria.

Revolution in China

By 1900, China's crumbling Manchu dynasty was losing control of government and large parts of the country were dominated by foreign powers. The Chinese Nationalist party, the Kuomintang, was founded by Sun Yat-sen to try and unify the country under a democratic government. In 1911, the Manchu dynasty was overthrown. China became a republic with Sun Yat-sen as provisional president.

Sun died in 1925 and Chiang Kai-shek then became president of China and leader of the Kuomintang. By that time the Chinese Communist party had been founded. Its first meeting was held in Shanghai in 1921. Mao Zedong was an early member of the party.

Throughout the 1920s, warlords in the north of China tried to gain control of the country. In order fight them, the Kuomintang and Communists united in 1926 and defeated the warlords. But the following year, in 1927, civil war broke out between the Kuomintang and Communists as Chiang Kai-shek carried out a lightning coup and executed hundreds of Communists. The Communists were forced out of Shanghai and took refuge farther south in the province of Jiangxi.

The Kuomintang then claimed to have united the whole of China under their government in Nanjing. But, in 1931, the Communists, led by Mao, set up a rival government in Jiangxi. In October 1933 Chiang Kai-shek sent his army to Jiangxi with the

△ ***The last emperor*** *of China was Pu Yi, who came to the throne in 1908 at the age of two. His father acted as regent and refused to allow any reforms in the country. Four years later, Pu Yi abdicated and China became a republic.*

▽ ***The Long March*** *from Jiangxi in the south to Shaanxi in the north claimed many lives. It took 568 days and, of the 100,000 who set out, about 80,000 died on the journey. The marchers were pursued by the Kuomintang.*

△ ***A Japanese armoured car*** *used in the war against China in 1937. The Japanese were much better equipped than the Chinese.*

▽ ***Mao Zedong*** *(1893–1976) was born into a peasant family in Hunan province. While fighting in the revolutionary army of 1911 he became interested in politics and in 1923 he became a member of the Chinese Communist party.*

intention of wiping out the Communists once and for all. After resisting the Kuomintang forces for a year, the Communists were forced to give up the province. In order to escape, Mao led 100,000 Communists on the "Long March" from Jiangxi in the south to Shaanxi in the north. Around 80,000 died on the year-long march. At its end Mao was confirmed as leader of the Communists.

During World War II, Japan invaded China and the two sides united to defeat them. When Japan surrendered in 1945, civil war broke out again. This time the Communists waged a successful guerilla war against the Kuomintang, helped by peasant uprisings throughout China. By January 1949 the Communists had taken control of Tianjin and Beijing from the Kuomintang. They continued moving south, forcing the Kuomintang off the mainland and on to the island of Taiwan. On October 1, 1949 mainland China became the People's Republic of China with Mao as its first president.

▽ ***This map shows*** *the route taken on the Long March from 1934 to 1935. It covered about 9,700 km and passed through 11 provinces. At the end of the march, with so many dead, Mao Zedong said "It proclaims to the world that the Red Army is an army of heroes."*

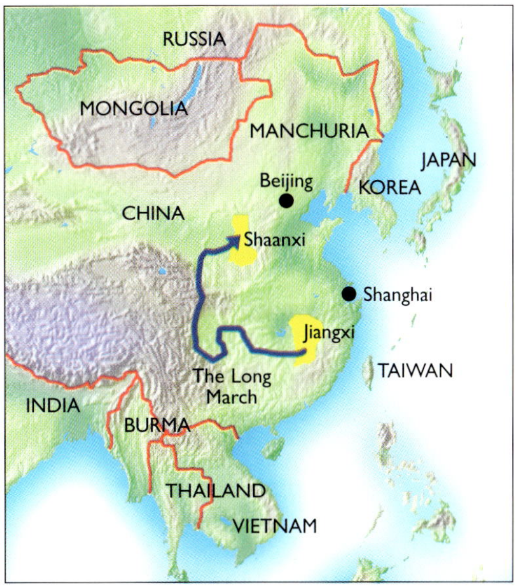

REVOLUTION IN CHINA

1905 Sun Yat-sen founds the Kuomintang (Chinese Nationalist party).

1911 Collapse of the Manchu empire. Sun Yat-sen becomes president.

1921 Foundation of the Chinese Communist party. Mao Zedong is one of its first members.

1925 Death of Sun Yat-sen. Chiang Kai-shek succeeds him as leader of China.

1926 With Communist help, Chiang Kai-shek defeats the northern warlords.

1927 Start of civil war between the Communists and the Kuomintang. Communists are forced out of Shanghai and into the Jiangxi hills.

△ ***Empress Dowager Cixi*** *was mother to one emperor and aunt to another and ruled as regent for both of them. She encouraged reactionary policies, however, and helped to bring about the downfall of the Manchu dynasty's empire.*

1931 Communists set up a rival government in the south.

1933 Chiang Kai-shek attacks the Communists in Jiangxi.

1934 Mao leads Communists on the "Long March".

1935 Mao becomes leader of the Communist party.

1937–1945 The Kuomintang and Communists unite to fight against Japan.

1938 Japanese controls most of the east. Mao's Communists control the northwest.

1939 The Soviet army stops the Japanese from advancing farther west in China.

1946 Civil war breaks out again.

1949 The People's Republic of China is proclaimed. Chiang and supporters escape to Taiwan.

World War II

World War II started on September 3, 1939, two days after Adolf Hitler had sent troops to invade Poland. Both Britain and France protested and when Hitler refused to withdraw, the two declared war on Germany. The war was fought between the Axis powers (Germany, Italy and Japan) and the Allies (Britain and the countries of the Commonwealth, France, the United States and the Soviet Union).

Initially, Hitler had signed a non-aggression pact with the Soviet Union and on September 17, Soviet troops invaded Poland from the east. By the end of 1939, the Soviet Union had also invaded Estonia, Latvia, Lithuania and Finland, while in the following spring German troops invaded Denmark, Norway, Belgium, the Netherlands and France. The tactics the Germans used became known as the Blitzkrieg, which means "lightning war", because they overcame any opposition so quickly. Using vast numbers of tanks, they made surprise attacks. Then, as the tanks moved ahead, bomber planes moved in behind to eliminate any remaining defences. The planes were then followed by infantry to complete the take-over. By June 1940, most of Europe had fallen and Britain stood alone.

WORLD WAR II

1939 Germany annexes Czechoslovakia. Italy annexes Albania. Italy and Germany agree an alliance.
August 23 Germany and USSR sign non-aggression pact.
August 25 Britain, France and Poland agree an alliance.
September 1 Germany invades Poland.
September 3 Britain and France declare war on Germany.

△ ***Many children were evacuated*** *from British cities and sent to live with families in the countryside away from the danger of bombs.*

September 17 USSR invades Poland.
December Battle of the River Plate, South America, is first real battle of the war.
1940 March USSR takes Finland. Germany submarines attack British merchant ships.
April–May Germany occupies Norway, Denmark, Belgium and the Netherlands.
June Germany occupies France. Allies evacuate from Dunkirk.
August–October Battle of Britain.
November Italy tries to invade Greece. Hungary, Romania and Slovakia join Axis powers.

▽ ***The battle of Britain*** *was fought in the skies above southeast England from August to October 1940. Although Britain had far fewer planes than the Germans it still managed to win. Over 2,600 planes were shot down in the battle.*

Europe by the end of 1941 *as almost completely under erman control. On the continent, ily neutral countries managed to main free. Axis troops had also panded into North Africa.*

Winston Churchill *(1874–965) was prime minister of ritain from 1940 to 1945. His rong leadership and rousing peeches encouraged people through e worst days of the war. Here he shown making a "V" for victory.*

World at War

The attack on Pearl Harbor marked the start of the war in the Pacific and by May 1942 Japan had taken control of all of Southeast Asia including Burma, Singapore, the Philippines and New Guinea, from where they threatened the north coast of Australia.

The Japanese also took control of many islands in the Pacific, but by August 1942 the USA had defeated their navy at the battles of the Coral Sea, Midway Island and Guadalcanal and stopped them invading any more territory. More victories for the USA followed, allowing them to take many Pacific islands out of Japanese control. This gave them bases from which they could now bomb Japan.

Meanwhile, British troops led by Field-Marshall Montgomery won a decisive battle at El Alamein, Egypt, in October and November 1942. Montgomery quickly advanced across Libya to meet Allied forces in Algeria and Morocco. The Axis armies, trapped between the Allies, were forced to surrender in May 1943.

German troops in the Soviet Union were also facing great difficulties. Although they had been within sight of Moscow by November 1941, the Russians had started to fight back and in 1943 they defeated the Germans at the battle of Stalingrad (now called Volgograd), but with the loss of many lives on both sides.

◁ ***Charles de Gaulle*** *(1890–1970) was a French general who escaped to Britain in 1940 when the Germans invaded his country. In London he quickly became leader of the free French who were determined to continue the fight against Germany. As the resistance movement grew in France, de Gaulle was recognized as its leader, too. After the liberation of France in 1944, he returned to Paris from Algeria and was elected president of France for only a few months. He was again president of France from 1959 to 1968.*

THE SIEGE OF LENINGRAD

German and Finnish forces besieged the Russian city of Leningrad (now St Petersburg) from September 8, 1941 to January 17, 1944. In that time the people of the city suffered terribly and around one million died of cold, hunger, disease and injury. They were determined not to let the Germans take control of their city and many of the children, sick and elderly were evacuated. The remaining population, together with 200,000 Soviet troops, fought back as best they could, until the siege was ended by a successful Soviet attack from outside the city.

◁ ***The US naval base at Pearl Harbor*** *in Hawaii was attacked without warning by the Japanese air force on December 7, 1941. Four battleships were destroyed, many more damaged and 3,300 people killed. This attack brought the USA into the war on the side of the Allies.*

It took until August 1944 to expel the last German troops from Soviet soil, by which time they were needed in the west to defend Germany itself from an Allied invasion.

The Allied invasion of Europe started on June 6, 1944 and by July 2 one million troops had landed in Normandy, France and started to advance towards Germany, via Belgium and the Netherlands. Reinforced by the troops returning from the Soviet Union, Germany was able to launch a counter-attack in December, but by January 1945 this had been defeated. In March 1945 Allied troops crossed the river Rhine and in the following month they reached the Ruhr, the heartland of German manufacturing and arms production. At the same time, Soviet troops were heading towards Berlin, where opposition to Hitler was growing rapidly. Realizing he was facing defeat, Hitler committed suicide on April 30. Soviet troops captured Berlin two days later and on May 7 the Germans signed a general surrender at Reims in France. This became official on May 9 when it was signed in Berlin.

△ ***Field-Marshall Montgomery*** *(1887–1976) was the commander of the 8th Army, which defeated Rommel's forces at El Alamein in Egypt, 1942. He also played an important role in the invasion of Italy and Normandy, accepting Germany's surrender in 1945.*

▽ ***The bombing of towns*** *and cities killed and injured many thousands of civilians on both sides. An Allied raid on Dresden in 1945 killed around 80,000 civilians in one night. Even those that escaped injury had their lives severely disrupted as fire destroyed their houses, factories, shops, offices and roads.*

WORLD WAR II

1941 February Allies capture 113,000 Italian soldiers in North Africa. German forces arrive to replace them.

April Yugoslavia and Greece fall to Germany.

May German invasion of USSR begins.

December 7 Japan attacks Pearl Harbor. The US declares war on Japan. Italy and Germany declare war on the US.

△ ***Heinrich Himmler*** *was the head of the SS, a military body created to defend Hitler. This also gave him control of the Gestapo (secret police service) and concentration camp guards.*

December Japan invades Malaya and Hong Kong.

1942 February Singapore falls to the Japanese; 90,000 British and Commonwealth troops are taken prisoner.

March Dutch East Indies (now Indonesia) fall to the Japanese.

May The Philippines and Burma fall to the Japanese.

August US victory at the battle of Guadalcanal finally ends Japanese expansion. In the Soviet Union the battle of Stalingrad begins.

October In North Africa, Allies defeat Axis forces at the battle of El Alamein, Egypt.

The War Ends

Although the war in Europe was at an end, fighting continued in Asia. In September 1944, US troops began to recapture the Philippines from the Japanese, while a campaign led by the British started to reconquer Burma. An Allied invasion of Japan was planned for late 1945, but before it could be put into operation, an atomic bomb was dropped on Hiroshima in Japan.

The bomb was dropped by the USA on August 6, 1945 and three days later a second atomic bomb was dropped on Nagasaki. Thousands of people died in the two explosions and many thousands more died later from radiation sickness, burns and other injuries. Five days later, the Japanese government under Emperor Hirohito surrendered and on August 14 World War II ended.

Almost six years of fighting had had a devastating effect on the world. There had been battles at sea, as well as on land and in the air, and the loss of life had been enormous.

▷ ***Roosevelt and Churchill** at the Casablanca Conference in 1943. The US president and British prime minister met to discuss the progress of the war and their plans for the invasion of Sicily and the defeat of Japan.*

WORLD WAR II

1943 February The battle of Stalingrad ends in defeat for the Germans.
May Axis troops in North Africa surrender.
July Allied troops invade Sicily. Mussolini's government is overthrown and Italy declares war on Germany.
1944 June Allied forces land in Normandy, France, to start invasion of Europe.
July An unsuccessful attempt to kill Hitler is made.

△ ***Hirohito** (1901–1989) was emperor of Japan, coming to the throne in 1926. After his country's defeat in World War II the US pressured Japan to have a constitution and the power of the emperor was diminished.*

October Allies invade Philippines.
December Start of battle of the Bulge, last German offensive.
1945 February At the Yalta Conference, Allies agree to divide Germany into four zones after the war.
March US captures Iwo Jima.
April Adolf Hitler takes his life.
May Soviet troops enter Berlin. Germany surrenders.
June US forces capture Okinawa.
July Division of Germany agreed at Potsdam Conference.
August Atomic bombs dropped on Hiroshima and Nagasaki. Japan surrenders.
October United Nations formed.

◁ ***The war in the Pacific*** *began when Japan bombed Pearl Harbor, in 1941. A year later, it held all the orange areas on the map. The crosses mark the ensuing battles.*

△ ***The atomic bombs*** *that were dropped on Nagasaki (above) and Hiroshima totally devastated the two cities. Heat from the blast destroyed buildings in a 7 km radius and over 155,000 people were killed in Hiroshima alone.*

Others died through ill treatment as prisoners of war. On both sides there had also been millions of civilian casualties, either through bombing raids or through illness, cold and hunger in cities such as Leningrad, which were besieged for many months. Probably the worst affected of all, however, were the Jews of occupied Europe. Hitler had been determined to wipe out the Jewish people and around six million died as a result of slave labour, torture, medical experiments and gassing in concentration camps throughout Germany and Poland.

After the war, Soviet troops occupied most of eastern Germany and other Allied troops the west. Its devastated capital, Berlin, was divided among the Allied powers. In November 1945, leading Nazis were put on trial at Nuremberg before an international military court. They were tried for war crimes and crimes against humanity.

NUREMBERG TRIALS

After World War II, the Allies set up an international military court at Nuremberg in Germany to try the Nazi leaders. They were accused on four counts: conspiracy to make war, war crimes, crimes against peace and crimes against humanity. Twelve were sentenced to death by hanging and six were sent to prison. Hermann Goering committed suicide before his sentence could be carried out and only two were acquitted. Lesser Nazi officials, such as concentration camp commanders, were also tried.

▽ ***The Allied invasion of Normandy*** *began on June 6, 1944 (D-Day). Around 156,000 troops were landed in the largest sea-borne attack ever mounted.*

Indian Independence

At the start of the 20th century, India was the largest colonial territory in the world. It included Pakistan and Bangladesh, as well as India and had been ruled directly from Britain since 1858.

The people of India wanted independence not only for self-government but also to build up their industries again, instead of having to supply raw materials to Britain and buy back manufactured goods at high prices. In 1885 a political party, the Indian National Congress, was founded and began to campaign for reforms. At first it wanted India to remain part of Britain, but from 1917 onwards, the National Congress began to campaign for Home Rule.

Britain saw India as the "jewel in the crown" of its empire and so was reluctant to let it go. Instead, mainly in gratitude for India's support during World War I, the British government passed a Government of India Act in 1919. This made some reforms, but most power remained with Britain. In the same year, British soldiers opened fire on a crowd at Amritsar protesting against British rule. Almost 400 people were killed and, as a result, the campaign for Indian independence began to grow.

By 1920 Mohandas Karamchand Gandhi had become the leader of the Indian National Congress and he launched a policy of non-cooperation with the British. This included encouraging Indians to boycott British goods, give up their jobs in local government and refuse to obey any British authorities. Many blocked the streets by sitting down and refusing to move even if they were beaten by the police. Gandhi himself was arrested several times and sent to prison, where he continued his campaign of civil disobedience by going on hunger strike. His biggest protest against British rule in India was in 1930 when he led thousands of people on the Salt March to the coast. There they made salt from sea water in protest against the law that made everyone

◁ ***Nehru (left) and Jinnah (right).*** *Jawaharlal Nehru was India's first prime minister and ruled until his death in 1964. His daughter, Indira Gandhi, was India's first woman prime minister from 1966. Mohammed Ali Jinnah (1876–1948) was the first governor general of Pakistan.*

▷ ***The partition of India*** *was followed by a mass migration of Muslims from India to Pakistan and of Hindus from Pakistan to India. Many travelled on foot or by ox-cart with all their possessions. Over one million people were killed as violence flared up between the two sides.*

buy heavily-taxed salt from the state, even though they could make it very cheaply themselves.

In 1945, the British government finally agreed to India's independence within the British Commonwealth. One of the greatest problems to independence was religion. The majority of India's people were Hindus, but there were also large numbers of Muslims who did not want to live under Hindu rule. Violence often broke out between the two sides, so Mohammed Ali Jinnah began to campaign for a separate state for the Muslims. This was finally agreed by the British government. On August 14, 1947, two areas to the northeast and northwest of India became the independent country of Pakistan, with Jinnah as their governor general. The following day the rest of India gained its independence with Jawaharlal Nehru as prime minister. Immediately violence broke out as a result of this partition. Millions of people found themselves living in the "wrong" country – Muslims in India and Hindus in Pakistan – and so mass migrations began. As the people fled, atrocities were inflicted on both sides and hundreds of thousands of people were killed.

◁ ***Mohandas Gandhi*** *(1869–1948), also known as Mahatma, which means "Great Soul". He was a peace-loving man who enjoyed a simple life. The violence of partition led to his assassination at a peace rally in Delhi by a Hindu extremist.*

▷ ***This map shows*** *how India was divided. East Pakistan became Bangladesh in 1971. Burma (now Myanmar) and Ceylon (Sri Lanka) gained their independence in 1948.*

INDIAN INDEPENDENCE

1885 Indian National Congress (INC) founded.
1887 Gandhi goes to London to study law and works in South Africa from 1893.
1905 Foundation of the Muslim League in India.
1915 Gandhi returns to India and turns down leadership of the INC.
1919 Government of India Act passed.
1919 Almost 400 Indians are killed by the British army in massacre at Amritsar.

△ ***Lord Mountbatten of Burma*** *was the last viceroy (British ruler) of India. In 1947 he oversaw the transfer of power from Britain to India and Pakistan. He then remained in India as governor general until 1948.*

1920 Gandhi, now leader of the INC, launches non-cooperation with British.
1930 Gandhi leads the Salt March.
1934 Mohammed Ali Jinnah becomes president of the Indian Muslim League.
1935 Second Government of India Act.
1945 British government decides to grant independence to India.
1947 On August 14, northeast and northwest India become the independent state of Pakistan.
1947 On August 15, the rest of India becomes independent.

Israel and Palestine

△ ***Golda Meir*** *(1898–1978) was a member of Israel's parliament from 1949, foreign minister from 1956–1966 and prime minister from 1969 until 1974. Born in Russia, she was taken by her parents to live in the US as a child and moved to Palestine in 1921. She always hoped to solve the problems of Israel and Palestine by peaceful means, but under her leadership Israel was involved in the Yom Kippur wars.*

The spiritual homeland of the Jews was in and around the ancient city of Jerusalem, but by the start of the 20th century most Jews lived elsewhere, especially in Europe, the USA and Russia. Jerusalem itself was in a country called Palestine, which was part of the Ottoman empire. Most of its people were Arabs, but from the 1880s small numbers of Jews began to go back there and settle.

In the Balfour Declaration of 1917 Britain promised its support for the establishment of a Jewish homeland within Palestine. At this time the Ottoman empire was facing defeat in World War I and was about to be broken up. When this happened, the League of Nations gave Britain its mandate (permission) to rule over Palestine until the country was able to govern itself.

At first, only small numbers of Jews arrived in Palestine. After the Nazi party came to power in Germany in the 1930s, German Jews were persecuted, imprisoned or even killed. Their businesses were destroyed and their families terrorized. Those who could began to leave.

△ ***Children in Palmyra, Syria.*** *Palmyra has been a Muslim city since 634, just two years after the death of Muhammad, the great prophet of Islam.*

▷ ***A kibbutz*** *in Israel in which all the land and property are owned or rented by the people who live there. All the work (usually farming) and meals are organized collectively.*

THE UNITED NATIONS

The United Nations Organization came into operation at the end of World War II on October 24, 1945. It took over from the failed League of Nations and its aim was to keep world peace and to solve international problems by cooperation rather than by fighting. This is reflected in its symbol, which shows a map of the world surrounded by olive branches.

Some went to other parts of Europe and the USA, but some started a new life in Palestine. As the numbers of Jewish immigrants increased, tension grew and fighting broke out. To keep the peace, Britain restricted the numbers of new settlers allowed in.

After World War II, many Jews wished to move to Palestine, their historical Jewish birth place, and so fulfil the Zionist dream. These Zionists were met with intense Arab opposition and whilst mainstream Jewry advocated "self restraint", underground Jewish groups advocated harsh retaliatory policies. Unable to solve the problem itself, Britain took the matter to the United Nations and in 1947 it was decided to split Palestine into two states, one Jewish and the other Arab. Jerusalem would become international, since it was equally sacred to Jews, Muslims and Christians. The Jews agreed to this, but the Arabs did not. Britain gave up its mandate on May 14 1948 and, on the same day, Jewish leader David Ben Gurion announced the founding of the state of Israel. The Arab League (Lebanon, Syria, Iraq, Transjordan and Egypt) instantly declared war on Israel and attacked it. Israel quickly defeated them, taking Palestinian lands that increased Israel's territory by a quarter.

△ ***Two of Jerusalem's holiest sites.*** *The Dome of the Rock (top) is sacred to Muslims while nearby is the Wailing Wall (above), a very important site to the Jews.*

ISRAEL AND PALESTINE

1840 After brief rule by Egypt, Palestine becomes part of Ottoman empire once more.
1882 First Zionist settlement established in Palestine.
1917 The Balfour Declaration supports a Jewish homeland in Palestine.
1920 The Treaty of Sevres ends Ottoman empire.
1922 Britain is given the mandate for Palestine.
1929 First major conflict between Jews and Arabs.
1933 Persecution of the Jews begins in Germany.
1939 Britain agrees to restrict the number of Jews allowed to emigrate to Palestine.

△ ***David Ben Gurion*** *(1886–1973) was born in Poland and emigrated to Palestine in 1906. Known as the Father of the Nation, he was Israel's first prime minister and renowned for his magnetic personality and informal approach.*

1946 British headquarters in Jerusalem blown up.
1947 The United Nations votes to divide Palestine.
1948 On May 14 the state of Israel is founded and Arab League declares war.
1949 UN negotiated cease-fire leaves Israel with the area allotted to it in 1947.

THE COLD WAR

1947 US-backed Marshall Plan gives financial aid to European countries.
1948 Blockade of West Berlin by the Soviet Union.
1949 North Atlantic Treaty Organization (NATO) formed. The Soviets explode their first atomic warhead. Communists come to power in mainland China.
1950–1953 The Korean War. North Korea, supported by the Soviets, invades South Korea, supported by the US.
1953 Death of Joseph Stalin.
1954 US helps overthrow leftist government in Guatemala.
1955 Warsaw Pact formed among countries of Eastern Europe.
1956 Soviets invade Hungary to preserve communist rule.
1958 Castro comes to power in Cuba and allies Cuba with the Soviet Union.
1960 A split develops between the Soviet Union and China.

△ ***The Berlin Wall*** *was built right across the city in 1961. The wall was built by the Soviets to divide the eastern part from the west and so prevent people escaping from the east. It was heavily guarded on the East German side.*

1961 The Berlin Wall is built. US supports an unsuccessful invasion of Cuba.
1962 Cuban missile crisis.
1963 The US and Soviet Union sign Nuclear Test-Ban Treaty.
1964 The US becomes involved in the Vietnam War.
1965 US invades the Dominican Republic.
1968 Invasion of Czechoslovakia by the Soviet Union to preserve communist rule.
1979 Afghanistan is invaded by the Soviet Union.
1983 The US invades Grenada.

The Cold War

The United States of America and the Soviet Union emerged from World War II as the world's dominant superpowers. Even though they had fought together against the Axis powers, they soon became enemies in what was known as the Cold War.

The Cold War started when the Soviet Union set up communist governments in the countries of Eastern Europe liberated by the Red Army. This effectively divided Europe by an "iron curtain". To stop communism spreading to the West, the US-backed Marshall Plan was set up to give financial aid to countries whose economies had been ruined by the war.

One of the first conflicts was the blockade of West Berlin in 1948. After the war Germany was divided between the Allies. The US, Britain and France controlled the western part of the country, while the east was controlled by the Soviet Union. The capital city, Berlin, lay inside Soviet-controlled territory, but was also divided. The Soviets tried to blockade West Berlin, forcing the Allies to airlift in supplies. Five months later, the blockade was defeated and the following year Germany was divided into West and East.

◁ ***This map shows*** *how Europe was divided after World War II. The boundary between the two halves of Europe was first named the "iron curtain" by Winston Churchill. Few people were able to cross this divide.*

NATO

The North Atlantic Treaty Organization (whose symbol is shown below) was set up on April 4, 1949, with its headquarters in Brussels, Belgium. It was a military alliance between several Western European countries, Canada and the United States, against aggression from any outside nation. In 1955, the Soviet Union formed an alliance of communist states, the Warsaw Pact.

Both sides distrusted each other and expected an attack at any time. To protect against this, the countries of Western Europe and North America formed the North Atlantic Treaty Organization (NATO) in 1949. In response, the Soviet Union set up the Warsaw Pact, an alliance of the Eastern European states under Soviet control, in 1955.

Both sides also began developing and stockpiling nuclear weapons. This led to another crisis in 1962 when Cuban dictator Fidel Castro allowed the Soviet Union to build missile bases in Cuba that threatened the USA. President John F Kennedy ordered the US Navy to blockade Cuba and eventually the Soviets agreed to withdraw. Both sides realized the danger of a nuclear war and the missiles were removed.

The USA and the Soviet Union encouraged many countries to take sides in the Cold War and, while they never fought against each other directly, the two superpowers became involved in many armed struggles in all parts of the world.

△ ***Soviet tanks rolled into Budapest, Hungary,*** *in October 1956, and crushed a rebellion, which started when police opened fire on a student demonstration. The army joined the people in rebelling against Communist rule.*

◁ ***Soviet tanks entering Prague,*** *Czechoslovakia's capital, in August 1968. Earlier that year, in the "Prague Spring" a liberal government had introduced many reforms, which worried the Soviets.*

▷ ***Churchill, Roosevelt and Stalin*** *at the Yalta Conference 1945, when, along with France, Britain, the US and the Soviet Union decided to divide Germany.*

△ ***In 1962 a crisis arose*** *when the Americans discovered Soviet plans to site rockets in Cuba. A clash of the superpowers was avoided only when Soviet ships carrying rockets turned back.*

The Space Race

During the 1930s, scientists in Germany experimented with making rockets. The first ones were used to launch guided missiles during World War II. When the war ended, many of the scientists left Germany and continued their research either in the United States or in the Soviet Union.

The scientists realized that their technology might make it possible for people to travel in space one day and, as the Cold War worsened, the "space race" started. Both countries wanted to be the first to send a rocket into space.

In 1957 the Soviet Union launched *Sputnik 1*, the first artificial Earth satellite. It weighed about 84 kg and took 96 minutes to orbit the Earth once at a maximum distance of 942 km. In the following year the US launched its first satellite *Explorer 1* and both sides started to spend vast amounts of money on space science and exploration.

The first person to orbit the Earth was Yuri Gagarin of the Soviet Union in 1961. This achievement prompted the president of the United States, John F Kennedy, to say that the United States would land a man on the Moon by 1970. This ambition was achieved when Neil Armstrong became the first person to walk on the Moon in 1969.

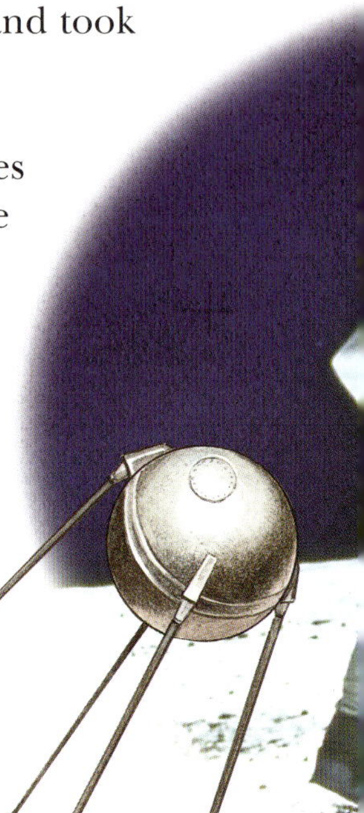

▷ **Sputnik 1** *was the first craft to go into space, launched on October 4, 1957. It travelled at 28,000 km/h, transmitting a radio bleep that was picked up around the world. Three months later it burned up.*

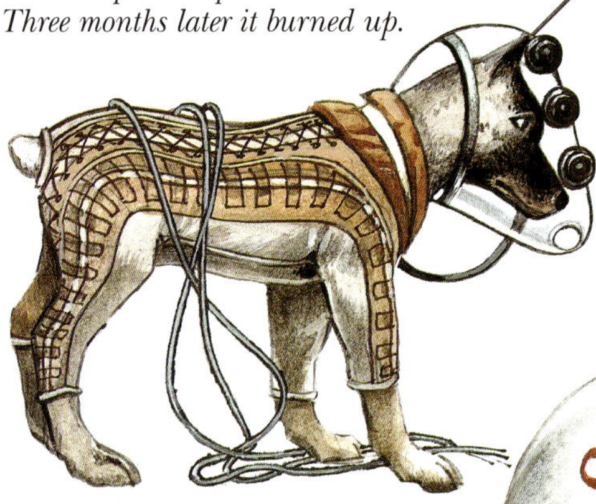

△ ***Laika the dog*** *on board* Sputnik 2 *was the first living creature to go into space. She wore a special suit, but as no one knew how to return the satellite to Earth, she died in space.*

THE SPACE RACE

1957 Soviet Union launches the first artificial satellite, *Sputnik 1.* Laika the dog is the first animal in space.
1958 US launches its first satellite, *Explorer 1.*
1959 *Luna 2*, a Soviet space probe, reaches the Moon.
1961 Soviets launch first manned spacecraft, *Vostok I.* A month later, US launches its first manned spacecraft, *Mercury.*
1962 Launch of the first communications satellite by the US.
1963 Russian cosmonaut Valentina Tereshkova becomes the first woman in space.
1965 Russian cosmonaut Alexi Leonov becomes the first person to walk in space.
1969 US astronaut Neil Armstrong becomes the first person to land on the Moon.
1970 A Soviet spacecraft lands on Venus.
1971 A Soviet spacecraft lands on Mars.
1972 US makes its last Apollo Moon landing.
1975 Soviet and US spacecraft link up in space.

▽ ***John F Kennedy*** *(1917–1963) was elected president of the US in 1960. The youngest man to hold the office, he took a firm stand against communism. His vision and vigour gave Americans the will to meet the challenges of a scientific age and his sudden assassination in Dallas, Texas, stunned the world.*

During the 1970s, Britain, China, France, India and Japan all joined in the space race and started launching their own spacecraft. Many of these were satellites, used for weather forecasting and for communications. At the same time the US and the Soviet Union continued to send craft deeper and deeper into space. Equipped with computers, these rival spacecraft were able to send back pictures and other information from planets as far away as Mars, Venus, Jupiter, Saturn, Uranus and Neptune.

With the easing of the Cold War, both sides began to share their ideas and worked together on projects, such as building and maintaining an orbiting space station. Improvements in computer technology and communications on Earth have made it possible for the US spacecraft *Pathfinder* to land a robot explorer on Mars in 1997, which was controlled from Earth. The pictures it sent back were not only seen by scientists in their laboratories, but also by ordinary people at home watching television.

△ ***The first space shuttle*** *lifted off in 1981. Launched like a rocket it lands back on Earth like a glider. In 1986 the Challenger shuttle exploded 73 seconds after takeoff. This disaster halted the shuttle programme for over two years.*

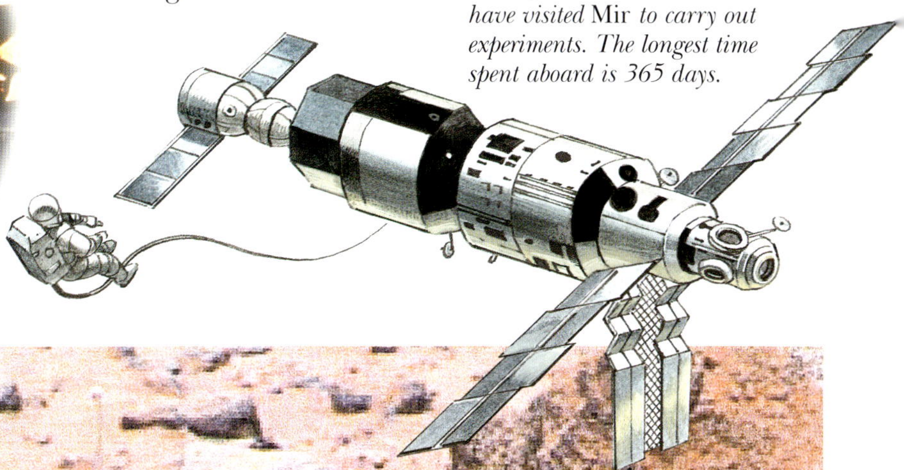

▽ ***The* Mir *space station*** *was launched by the Soviet Union in 1986. Astronauts from the Soviet Union, the US and other countries have visited* Mir *to carry out experiments. The longest time spent aboard is 365 days.*

△ ***Buzz Aldrin*** *became the second person, after Neil Armstrong, to walk on the Moon on July 21, 1969. The third crew member, Michael Collins, remained aboard* Apollo 11*'s Command Module orbiting the Moon.*

▷ **Pathfinder** *landed on Mars in August 1997. It sent out a small Earth-controlled rover called* Sojourner *to take photographs and examine the planet's surface.*

◁ ***Yuri Gagarin*** *aboard* Vostok 1 *orbited the Earth for 89 minutes on April 12, 1961. He reached a height of about 300 km above the Earth's surface.*

African Independence

After World War II, many of the countries of Europe found it difficult to maintain their overseas colonies. In Africa, as elsewhere, some achieved independence peacefully, but others had to use violence to regain the right to govern themselves.

Most African countries gained their independence in the 1960s and 1970s. Once they were independent, these countries had to work out their own systems of government, law, education and health services, which had previously been organized along European-style forms of government. They also had to run their own economies and their own armed forces.

What did not change at first, however, were the borders of the new countries. They remained as they had been set by the Europeans during the Scramble for Africa in the late 19th century. These borders did not reflect natural boundaries nor the ethnic groups of the peoples of Africa. This led inevitably to civil wars in several countries, notably in the Congo, Ethiopia and Nigeria, as people from one area within a country tried to become independent and form a new country of their own.

POVERTY AND FAMINE

Since independence, famine has become a great problem in parts of Africa. In places where the land has been over-farmed for too long, the soil is no longer fertile and, if the rains fail, crops cannot grow. Famine on a massive scale is made worse by over-population and civil wars. The people caught in the disaster have to rely on aid or face starvation and disease.

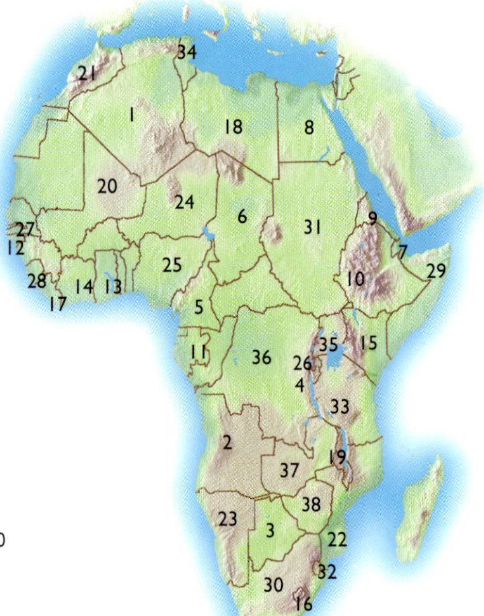

1 Algeria 1962
2 Angola 1975
3 Botswana 1966
4 Burundi 1962
5 Cameroon 1960
6 Chad 1960
7 Djibouti 1960
8 Egypt 1977
9 Eritrea 1993
10 Ethiopia
11 Gabon 1960
12 Gambia 1965
13 Ghana 1957
14 Ivory Coast 1960
15 Kenya 1963
16 Lesotho 1966
17 Liberia
18 Libya 1951
19 Malawi 1964
20 Mali 1960
21 Morocco 1956
22 Mozambique 1975
23 Namibia 1990
24 Niger 1960
25 Nigeria 1960
26 Rwanda 1962
27 Senegal 1960
28 Sierra Leone 1961
29 Somalia 1960
30 South Africa 1931
31 Sudan 1956
32 Swaziland 1968
33 Tanzania 1964
34 Tunisia 1956
35 Uganda 1962
36 Zaire (Congo) 1960
37 Zambia 1964
38 Zimbabwe 1980

◁ ***Kenneth Kaunda*** *(born 1924) founded the militant Zambia African National Congress in what was Northern Rhodesia in 1958. He was imprisoned for his political activities until in 1964 he became the first president of Zambia.*

△ ***This map shows*** *European colonies in Africa, which mostly gained their independence in the 1960s and 1970s. Only Ethiopia and Liberia were never colonized.*

△ ***Ghanaian chiefs*** *waiting for the first session of parliament to begin. Ghana, formerly known as the Gold Coast, gained full independence from Britain in 1957.*

In other countries, such as Angola, Rwanda and Burundi, civil wars broke out between rival ethnic groups, which wanted complete control of the whole country. In some countries the military overthrew the elected government, while others were ruled by dictators.

Problems also occurred in countries where the white settlers wanted to stay in control. This happened in Algeria, Rhodesia (now Zimbabwe) and South Africa and in each case cost many lives and much bitterness between the two groups. It was especially difficult in South Africa where, from 1948 to 1990, the white government used a system known as Apartheid to keep blacks out of power by not giving them the right to vote. Once Apartheid was abolished, free elections were held and in 1994 Nelson Mandela became the first black president of South Africa.

▽ ***Robert Mugabe*** *became prime minister of Zimbabwe in 1980. After independence, it took a long and bitter struggle for the black majority to gain power from whites.*

AFRICAN INDEPENDENCE

1951 Libya first country to gain independence (from Italy).
1952 Kenyan Mau Mau terrorists start campaign to gain independence from Britain.
1957 Ghana is first British colony to gain independence.
1956 Morocco and Tunisia independent from France.
1960 Zaire (now Congo) gains independence from Belgium. Nigeria and Somalia gain independence from Britain. Chad and Mali independent from France.
1961 Sierra Leone and Tanzania independent from Britain.
1962 Uganda independent from Britain. Algeria independent from France. Eritrea becomes part of Ethiopia. Burundi and Rwanda independent from Belgium.
1963 Kenya independent from Britain.
1964 Malawi and Zambia gain independence from Britain.
1965 Gambia independent from Britain. White government of Rhodesia (now Zimbabwe) declares itself independent from Britain.

△ ***Kwame Nkrumah*** *(1909–1972) was Ghana's first leader. He believed in African unity, but became increasingly dictatorial and was overthrown in 1966*

1966 Botswana and Lesotho independent from Britain.
1969 War breaks out as Biafra seeks independence from Nigeria.
1975 Angola and Mozambique independent from Portugal.
1976 Civil war in Angola.
1977 Djibouti independent from France. Civil war in Ethiopia.
1980 Zimbabwe becomes independent from Britain.
1993 Eritrea declares itself independent of Ethiopia.

A Social Revolution

At the start of the second half of the 20th century, many people throughout the world were still treated unequally because of their race, the colour of their skin, their religion, or sex.

Black people were especially discriminated against in education, employment, housing, transport and health care. Many also had to use separate facilities in public places such as restaurants, beaches, lavatories and cinemas. With few or no civil rights, they could not even vote to try and change their situation. All they could do was protest and campaign, even though this often led to fines, imprisonment or worse.

Some of the earliest protests were in the southern United States. They started in earnest in 1955 when Rosa Parks, a black American, was arrested for refusing to move from a seat reserved for whites on a bus in Montgomery, Alabama. This led to a boycott of the local bus service that lasted for over a year. It was followed by many more non-violent protests, often inspired by Dr Martin Luther King, a Baptist minister. The largest was a march to Washington, DC, in 1963 to demand equal justice for everybody. Over 250,000 people took part and, in the following year, the US government passed the Civil Rights Act, which made discrimination illegal.

At the same time, the white minority government in South Africa was tightening up on its policy of Apartheid (the separation of whites and blacks). In 1960 the police opened fire on a group of unarmed protesters in Sharpeville, killing 69 of them. This brought an end to peaceful demonstrations and led to the formation of a guerrilla army called Umkhonto we Sizwe (Spear of the Nation). One of its most

A SOCIAL REVOLUTION

1955 Rosa Parks is arrested in Montgomery, Alabama, for refusing to give up her seat on a bus.

1957 Many civil rights groups are brought together by the Southern Christian Leaders Conference, led by Martin Luther King. At Little Rock, Arkansas, troops are sent in to protect black students barred from high school.

1960 South African police fire on anti-Apartheid demonstrators at Sharpeville, killing 69 and ending peaceful protests.

1961 Amnesty International is founded to publicize violations of human rights and campaign for the release of political prisoners.

1962 Nelson Mandela is arrested and imprisoned for political activities. He remained in prison for 27 years.

1963 Martin Luther King organizes a march to Washington, DC, asking for equal rights for everybody.

1964 The Civil Rights Act is passed in the US to end all discrimination because of race, colour, religion or national origin.

1966 American feminists found the National Organization for Women.

1971 Swiss women are given the right to vote.

1980 Solidarity, an independent trade union, is set up in Poland (banned until 1989).

1985 Marriage between blacks and whites made legal in South Africa.

1986 Fighting in Black townships in South Africa by civil rights protesters.

1987 Half a million gay rights protesters march on Washington, DC.

1989 In Beijing, government troops crush a student demonstration for more democracy in China.

1993 Nelson Mandela and F W de Klerk win the Nobel peace prize for their work to end Apartheid.

1995 Fourth World Conference on Women, held in Beijing, is attended by women from 185 countries.

important members was Nelson Mandela, but in 1962 he was arrested and sent to prison. The following year he was accused of plotting to overthrow the government and sentenced to life imprisonment. This action drew attention to what was happening in South Africa and people all over the world started to protest against it. By 1990 the government, led by F W de Klerk, knew it had to change its policy and on February 11, Mandela was released from prison. After long discussions, Apartheid was abolished and in 1994 South Africa held its first election in which all adults had the right to vote.

△ ***Solidarity*** *was a trade union started in the shipyards of Gdansk, Poland, in 1980. It was formed to campaign for workers' rights and better conditions as well as freedom from communism.*

The struggle for black equality led others to protest against injustice. In the 1960s, women began to campaign for equal pay and job opportunities, better health care and the right to have abortions. New laws were introduced to ban sex discrimination in employment. In the late 60s, gay men and women also began to campaign for equal rights. Since then, in many countries there have been protests about lack of government action on gay issues, which include sexual freedom and equal rights of marriage and parenthood.

◁ ***Black townships in South Africa*** *were often disturbed by unrest and violence during the 1980s. Many people were killed or injured and vehicles and houses were set alight as a tide of protest arose against Apartheid.*

APARTHEID

Apartheid was a policy followed in South Africa from 1948 to 1990. The word means "apartness" and it was used to divide the country into separate areas for whites and blacks. There were different systems of education, employment, housing and health care, with the black majority always receiving inferior treatment. While whites usually had good jobs and lived in comfort, the blacks did all the heavy and dirty work and lived in crowded townships outside the cities. Township houses were often very basic and lacked facilities such as electricity and running water.

◁ ***Martin Luther King*** *(1929–1968) was an outstanding speaker whose belief in the non-violent resistance to oppression won him the Nobel peace prize in 1964. His most famous speech included the words "I have a dream". In 1968 he was shot dead in Memphis.*

◁ ***Nelson Mandela*** *was born in 1918 and trained as a lawyer. He remained in prison from 1962 until 1990 . He was able to vote for the first time in April 1994, when the country held its first free elections. Mandela's party, the ANC, won with a large majority and he became president.*

The Vietnam War

THE VIETNAM WAR

1946 Start of the war between Ho Chi Minh's Vietnamese nationalists and French colonial troops.
1954 Vietnamese communists defeat the French at Dien Bien Phu. The country is divided into North Vietnam and South Vietnam.
1961 South Vietnamese ask for military advice from the US to combat Viet Cong guerrillas.
1963 South Vietnamese government is overthrown. Viet Cong increase their activities.
1964 War breaks out between North Vietnam (backed by the Soviets) and South Vietnam (backed by the US).
1965 The US sends combat troops to South Vietnam.
1966 Australian troops arrive in Vietnam to fight with the Americans. The first anti-war demonstrations take place in the US.
1967 The first efforts are made towards peace, but they fail. Anti-war demonstrations increase and spread to other countries.
1968 North Vietnamese and Viet Cong launch an attack known as the Tet offensive against the South. Some Americans begin to realize that the Viet Cong cannot be crushed and the war will go on for many years.
1969 US withdraws 25,000 of its 540,000 troops. The fighting, and the anti-war protests, continue.
1970 US Army invades Cambodia to support an anti-communist government and prevent supplies reaching North Vietnam.
1971 Fighting spreads to Laos.
1972 Peace talks start again.
1973 A cease-fire is agreed and the US withdraws its troops by the end of the year. The Vietnamese continue to fight.
1975 The communists take control of the whole of Vietnam.
1976 Vietnam is reunited under a communist government.

Vietnam, together with Cambodia and Laos, was part of the French colony of Indochina. It was occupied by the Japanese in World War II and during this time the Viet Minh league, led by the communist Ho Chi Minh, declared Vietnam independent.

After the war, France refused to recognize Ho Chi Minh's government and war broke out between the French and Vietnamese. This war ended in defeat for the French at the battle of Dien Bien Phu in 1954. An international agreement then divided Vietnam into communist North and non-communist South.

Almost immediately civil war broke out between the two countries. From 1959, communist guerrillas in the South, known as the Viet Cong, were helped by North Vietnam. The US, worried about the spread of communism, sent military aid to help the South Vietnamese. As the conflict escalated, the US began sending troops to help the South from 1965. The Viet Cong's guerrilla tactics made it very difficult to defeat them. In an attempt to cut off their

△ ***Ho Chi Minh*** *(1892–1969) led Vietnam in its struggle for independence from France. As president of North Vietnam from 1954 he fought for a united Vietnam, achieved after his death.*

▽ ***Most Vietnamese*** *lived by farming, mostly growing rice in the fields around their villages. Many suffered greatly in the war as crops and villages were destroyed to flush out and kill the Viet Cong.*

▽ ***Most of the war*** *was fought in the jungles of South Vietnam. The Ho Chi Minh trail, from China through Laos into South Vietnam, was the Viet Cong's supply line from the North.*

supply lines, US planes began bombing North Vietnam. At the same time, whole villages in the south and vast areas of forest were sprayed with chemicals to destroy any Viet Cong hiding places.

By 1966, anti-war demonstrations had begun and in 1968, the Viet Cong's major Tet offensive on the South convinced Americans that the war could not be won. In 1969 the US began to withdraw its troops and a cease-fire was agreed in 1973. Fighting continued until 1975, when the North brought the South under its control.

◁ ***Viet Cong soldiers*** *used guerilla warfare to defeat the enemy. One tactic was to dig a maze of secret tunnels. Over 16,000 soldiers lived underground, attacking US troops from their hiding places.*

△ ***US soldiers*** *were expecting to fight a traditional war, with large scale battles between two sides. They had to adapt to the Viet Cong's guerilla tactics using small groups to mount surprise attacks.*

ANTI-WAR DEMONSTRATIONS

The Vietnam War was the first to be widely covered on television. People throughout the world, but especially in the US, were able to see events as they happened. As growing numbers of troops were killed or injured and large parts of Vietnam destroyed, people took to the streets in protest. By 1967, the protests had spread beyond the US and the strength of anti-war feeling helped persuade President Nixon to withdraw from the war.

The Cultural Revolution

When Mao Zedong came to power in 1949, many Chinese could not read or write. Many also suffered from ill health and hunger. To try and make life better for everyone, the new government improved health care and provided schools in which adults as well as children could be taught.

For the first time, women were given equal rights with men. Large farms were taken from wealthy landowners and divided up among the peasants. New roads and railways and power plants to generate electricity were built. But the problem of providing enough food for everyone remained. In 1958, Mao introduced the Great Leap Forward, to try and make each village self-sufficient, not only by growing its own food, but also by producing its own clothing and tools in small factories belonging to the whole village. The plan

▷ ***In the Cultural Revolution*** *schools and colleges were closed and teachers and students forced to work on the land. Opposition was brutally put down by the Red Guards.*

▽ ***Tiananmen Square, Beijing*** *full of students demonstrating for democracy in May 1989. The Chinese government sent in troops and tanks to clear the protesters and many people were killed.*

△ ***This poster of a triumphant Mao*** *appeared in 1949 when he first came to power. He took over a country where many could not read or write and civil war had left the country in financial disorder. Mao's initial reforms, called the Five Year Plan, helped to improve the economy.*

failed, because the government did not invest enough money in it, while bad weather led to poor harvests and even greater food shortages. Many people died of starvation and in 1959 Mao Zedong decided to retire.

Over the next seven years, Mao's successors tried to solve the economic problems caused by the Great Leap Forward. At the same time, tension grew between China and the Soviet Union. Mao thought the Soviet Union had lost its revolutionary spirit. Not wanting the same to happen to China, he swept back to power in 1966 and launched the Cultural Revolution. Its aim was to overthrow old traditional ideas and habits and rid the Communist party and the country of people who disagreed with Mao. Young people formed groups of Red Guards who criticized foreigners and their elders. Many artists, writers and teachers were forced to leave their jobs and go to work on the land. Schools, universities, factories and hospitals closed as older members of staff were forced out by students. Many people were killed and others were sent into exile for criticizing Mao.

When Mao died in 1976, the Cultural Revolution came to an end. His successor, Deng Xiaoping, began to open up China to trade and contact with the West.

CULTURAL REVOLUTION

1949 Mao Zedong's Communist party takes power in China.

1953 In the Five Year Plan peasants are encouraged to set up collective farms to increase their productivity.

1958–1960 The Great Leap Forward. It is abandoned when its policies result in widespread famine.

1959 Mao Zedong retires from his post as Chairman of the Chinese Communist party.

1960 A split occurs between China and the Soviet Union.

1966 Mao sweeps back to power and starts the Cultural Revolution. By 1968 factory productivity is 12 per cent lower than it was in 1966.

1973 Rivalry develops between the "Gang of Four" and Deng Xiaoping over who will succeed Mao.

1974 China tests its first nuclear weapons.

1976 Death of Mao. He is briefly succeeded by the Gang of Four who want to continue the Cultural Revolution.

1977 Deng Xiaoping comes to power and makes a state visit to the US.

1989 Tiananmen Square demonstration.

1995 Death of Den Xiaoping. China is gradually becoming more Westernized.

△ ***Deng Xiaoping*** *(1904–1995) ruled China from 1977 until his death. He set up trade links with the West and encouraged China's economy to grow by setting up privately owned factories.*

Crisis in the Middle East

An uneasy peace followed the defeat of the Arab League by Israel in 1948. Jordan had captured Israeli land on the West Bank of the River Jordan, including much of Jerusalem. At the same time, Israel continued to encourage large numbers of Jews to migrate from Europe, Russia and the United States. The Arabs who remained in Israel after the defeat of the Arab League by Israel in 1948 become full citizens of the state and continued to live in their villages. Those Arabs who fled Israel as the war broke out become know as Palestinian refugees. Palestinians did not recognize the legitimacy of the new state of Israel and began a campaign to defeat Israel and establish a state of their own.

The next crisis came in 1956 when Egypt took control of the Suez Canal. This led to a war, with Egypt on one side and Britain and France, who had previously controlled the canal, on the other. Feeling threatened by this, Israel invaded the Sinai Peninsula and destroyed Egyptian bases there. The third war between Israelis and their Arab neighbours broke out on June 5 1967 and lasted for six days. In this, Israel destroyed the Egyptian air force and also took control of the whole of Jerusalem, the West Bank, the Golan Heights, the Gaza Strip and Sinai. A fourth war broke out in October 1973 when Egyptian forces attacked Israel across the Suez Canal and Syrian forces attacked on the Golan Heights. Israel managed to defeat both forces.

▽ ***Ayatollah Khomeini*** *(1900–1989) was a revolutionary religious leader of Iran. He came to power in 1979 after the Shah of Iran was overthrown. Under Khomeini, Iran became a strictly Muslim state.*

▷ ***Beirut****, the capital of Lebanon, large parts of which were destroyed by fighting which broke out in 1976. By the time peace returned in the mid-1990s, many people had been killed and injured on all sides.*

1960 1970 1980 1990 2000

▽ ***Saddam Hussein*** *(born 1938) became dictator of Iraq in 1979 and the following year went to war with Iran. In 1990 he launched a war with Kuwait, but was heavily defeated by US-led troops. He managed to keep hold of power, but is deeply distrusted by the West.*

Three years later, fighting broke out in Lebanon, where many Palestinians lived in refugee camps. They joined forces with Lebanese Muslims who were in conflict with Lebanese Christians. Syrian and UN troops were also involved. In 1982, Israel invaded Lebanon to try and drive the Palestinians out, but failed.

From 1980 to 1988 another large-scale war broke out between Iraq and Iran, both of which were major oil-producing countries. Then in 1990 Iraqi troops invaded oil-rich Kuwait. UN forces freed Kuwait in 1991.

Since then, peace agreements have been signed between Israel, Egypt and Jordan. Israel has granted limited Palestinian self-rule, but tension and conflict continue to disrupt the peace process.

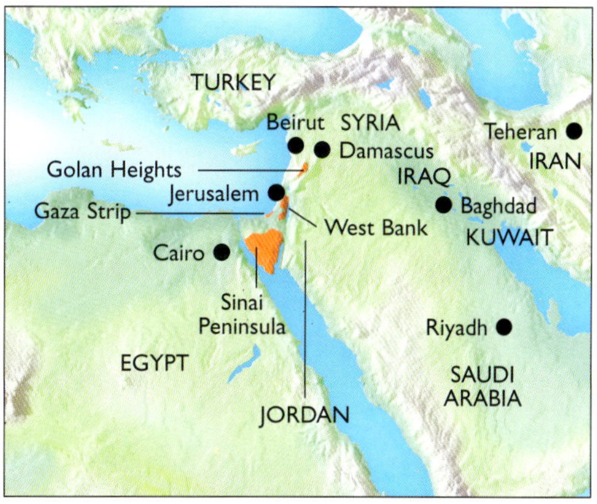

MIDDLE EAST CRISIS

1956 Egypt takes control of the Suez Canal.
1964 Formation of the Palestinian Liberation Organization (PLO).
1967 Six Day War, between Israel and Egypt, Jordan and Syria, is won by Israel.
1973 The Yom Kippur War between Israel and Egypt and Syria.
1976 Fighting breaks out in Lebanon.
1979 Peace treaty between Israel and Egypt. Shah of Iran is overthrown and Islamic republican government set up.

◁ ***Wars in the Middle East.*** *The shaded area shows land taken by Israel in the Six Day War.*

1980–1988 Iran-Iraq War.
1982 Israel invades Lebanon.
1987 Violent fighting starts between Palestinians and Israeli troops in the West Bank and Gaza Strip.
1990–1991 In the Gulf War, Iraq invades Kuwait, but is repulsed by UN troops.
1993 Israeli prime minister Yitzhak Rabin, and PLO leader Yasser Arafat, meet in Washington, DC.
1994 Israel and Jordan sign a peace agreement.
1995 Israel signs an agreement to extend self-rule to the Palestinians.

▽ ***At peace talks*** *in 1993, Israeli prime minister Yitzhak Rabin (left) and Yasser Arafat, leader of the Palestinian Liberation Organization (right) under the guidance of President Clinton (centre), agreed in principle to Palestinian self-rule in Gaza and Jericho.*

The Rise of Asia

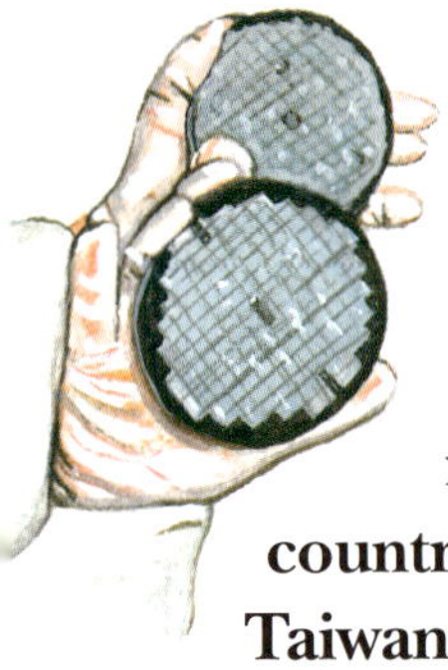

After decades of lagging behind the industrialized West, or being controlled by European powers, many Asian countries began developing their own industries from the 1950s. With stable governments, modern factories and a well-educated labour force, countries such as Japan, Singapore, South Korea and Taiwan have seen living standards rise dramatically as their economies have prospered.

The first to succeed was Japan, whose economy had been ruined by defeat in World War II. Business and industry had both suffered badly and most of the country's raw materials had to be imported. In a effort to stop the spread of communism, the United States helped Japan to rebuild its economy. Japanese factories supplied military equipment for the Korean War, which kick started the economy, helping it to revive. By the 1970s, Japan was the second-largest economic power in the world after the US. Its exports now include cars and trucks, office machinery, consumer electronics such as cameras, televisions, radios, video recorders and personal computers, chemicals and scientific equipment. Most of these items have a sale value that is far greater than the cost of the raw materials and labour

▽ ***Tokyo**, the capital of Japan, is the centre of the Japanese business world. With the port of Yokohama and the industrial area of Kawasaki, Tokyo is one of the world's largest cities. Its industrial growth has brought problems of pollution and congestion.*

△ ***Hong Kong**, whose name means "favourable water" or "good harbour", is a major centre for banking and finance, as well as industry, in China. It also has many small, family-run businesses, often involved in tailoring and dress-making directly for individual customers and not mass-production.*

DECLINE OF INDUSTRY IN THE WEST

Until the mid-1900s, Western industry dominated the world. Britain was the first industrialized nation, followed by France and Germany, which in turn were overtaken by the United States. During World War II, much of Europe's industrial heartland was destroyed or damaged. That which did survive relied on out-of-date equipment in old and often inadequate factories, since there was little money to invest in anything new. The countries of Asia, without a background of old, heavy industries, were able to design and build factories as new industries, such as electronics, began to develop. Some Asian countries also developed heavy industries, such as shipbuilding and steel production, again with modern equipment and cheap labour, against which the West could not compete.

used to manufacture them. This has added to Japan's success and since 1976 the value of its exports has exceeded that of its imports.

Other successful industrial nations include Taiwan, Malaysia and South Korea, all of which send about one third of their exports to the US. Like the Japanese, they have well organized workforces and have invested a great deal of money in equipment, such as computers and robots. Places such as Singapore and Hong Kong have grown wealthy on international trade and banking. In the mid-1990s, however, these countries started to experience serious economic problems and property values, stocks and shares all fell.

The success of countries such as the Philippines is due to industries that employ many people to do monotonous work, such as making clothes and footwear and assembling electronic equipment, largely for export. China has modernized its industry. Strict restrictions on private ownership have been relaxed and China today has one of the world's fastest growing economies.

▽ ***In India*** *many people, especially women and children, are employed in low-paid jobs such as making shoes and clothes for export. Some work in good conditions, but many work in cramped, dark or dangerous surroundings.*

THE RISE OF ASIA

1960s Japan starts selling cars on the world market.

1970s Taiwan starts to develop high-technology industries.

1975 Japanese launch the first VHS (Video Home System) on to the market.

1976 From this date, Japan has a balance of trade surplus, which means its exports are more valuable than its imports.

1979 Compact discs are co-developed by a Dutch and a Japanese company.

1980s Japanese become world leaders in the manufacture of motor vehicles.

1995 By this date, over half of China's industrial output comes from privately owned businesses.

1997 Britain returns Hong Kong to Chinese control.

▽ ***Automated robots*** *are widely used in Japan, especially in the manufacture of cars and computers. Japanese businesses were among the first to use modern methods of assembly. Robots can do repetitive jobs all day without breaks or pay.*

The End of the Cold War

EUROPEAN UNION

The European Union is an organization of European states. It was founded by the Treaty of Rome in 1957 when it had six members: France, West Germany, Italy, Belgium, the Netherlands and Luxembourg. It was known then as the European Economic Community (EEC) or the Common Market, since one of its main aims has been to encourage free trade between member countries. By 1998 it had 15 members, each of which sends elected representatives to a European parliament that meets at Brussels in Belgium and Strasbourg in France. Bills that affect the whole Union are voted on and passed in parliament. They include policies on fishing, farming and food, as well as on transport and finance. European Union money is often provided to help redevelop former industrial sites, derelict areas and poorer communities in member countries.

By the beginning of the 1960s, the division between the Soviet Union and the United States was becoming less clear. China and the Soviet Union had split apart, while Western Europe, after recovering from the effects of World War II, was no longer as dependent on the US. In spite of this, both the US and the Soviet Union remained deeply suspicious of each other.

Tension between the two superpowers eased a little in the late 1960s. After a great deal of negotiation, known as the Strategic Arms Limitation Talks (SALT), two agreements were signed. This was an attempt to reduce the arms race, payment for which was ruining the economies of countries in Eastern Europe. The situation worsened after 1980, however, when Ronald Reagan became president of the US. He was extremely anti-communist and increased military spending. One project began looking at the possibility of defending the US from nuclear attack by building a defence system in space. At the same time, both the US and the Soviet Union tried to extend their influence in developing countries and continued to increase stockpiles of weapons.

Then, in 1985, the Soviets elected a new leader, Mikhail Gorbachev, as their general secretary. Unlike his predecessors, he tried to introduce political, social and economic reforms. This lessened the tension

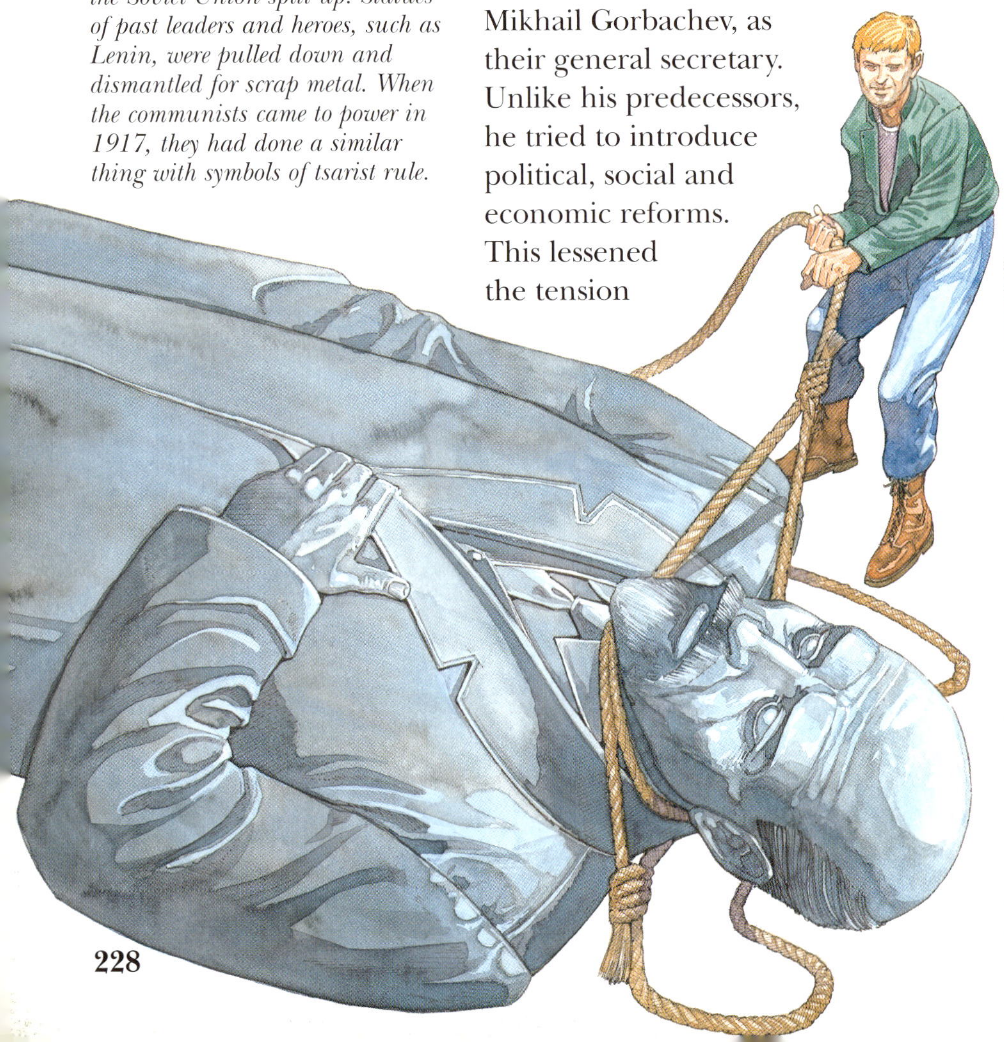

▽ ***Many symbols of communism*** *were destroyed after the Soviet Union split up. Statues of past leaders and heroes, such as Lenin, were pulled down and dismantled for scrap metal. When the communists came to power in 1917, they had done a similar thing with symbols of tsarist rule.*

△ ***The hated Berlin Wall*** *was demolished in 1989 after the collapse of communism in East Germany. It had divided the city since 1961 and many had been shot trying to cross it. As the wall came down and the guards left, people from both sides chipped off pieces to take away as souvenirs.*

between the two superpowers once more. Two years later, Gorbachev and Reagan signed an agreement to ban all medium-range nuclear missiles.

Gorbachev's reforms in the Soviet Union had led to demands for free elections in the countries of Eastern Europe and by the end of 1989, communism had collapsed in Poland, Hungary, East Germany, Czechoslovakia and Romania. In the following year, East and West Germany were reunited for the first time since 1945 and free elections were held in Bulgaria. In August 1991 an attempted coup in the Soviet Union led to the downfall of Gorbachev's government and the banning of the Communist party. By December the Soviet Union had been abolished and its former members split up into 15 independent nations. Its superpower status vanished as each nation tried to set up new systems of administration and rebuild their economies under private ownership. After more than 40 years, the Cold War had finally come to an end.

▷ ***Czechoslovakians demonstrate*** *in the capital Prague in 1989. Throughout that year, people in Eastern Europe began to demand greater democracy without fear of recriminations.*

▽ ***McDonald's first restaurant*** *in Moscow. Gorbachev, realizing the Soviet economy was in a mess, began opening his country to Western enterprise. Despite McDonald's reputation for quick service, long queues soon built up as so many people wanted to try the food.*

END OF THE COLD WAR

1967 The US, Britain and the Soviet Union sign a treaty banning the use of nuclear weapons in outer space.

1969 President Johnson of the US initiates the Strategic Arms Limitation Talks.

1972 The first SALT agreement is signed by President Nixon of the US and Brezhnev of the Soviet Union.

1979 Second SALT agreement is signed by President Carter and Brezhnev.

1981 Ronald Reagan becomes president and increases military spending.

1985 Mikhail Gorbachev comes to power in the Soviet Union and starts to make reforms.

1989 Free elections are held in Poland. Communism collapses in Hungary, East Germany, Czechoslovakia and Romania. The Berlin Wall is demolished.

1990 East and West Germany are reunited. Free elections are held in Bulgaria.

1991 A multiparty government is set up in Albania. The Soviet Union is abolished and replaced by 15 independent nations.

▽ ***Mikhail Gorbachev (left) and Ronald Reagan (right)*** *got on remarkably well together despite their different ideologies. In 1987, they signed a treaty banning all medium-range nuclear missiles.*

Global Awareness

FAMINE IN AFRICA

Although famine had long been a problem in many parts of Africa, television pictures of famine in Ethiopia in 1984 shocked the world. Money poured in to charities to help provide food and medicine. This only solved the problem in the short term. Now aid agencies realize they must support long-term projects that will help prevent famine in the future.

One of the greatest changes in the 20th century has been in the speed at which news and other information can travel around the world. Radio, television and computers now make it possible to see or hear events all over the world as they take place.

This revolution in communications, together with faster and more convenient ways of travelling, has helped scientists and others to become aware of what is happening at a global level, rather than just in their own town or country.

One of the biggest concerns of the late 20th century has been for the environment. Until the 1960s, very few people believed that Earth was in danger. During the 1970s, however, pressure groups, such as Greenpeace and Friends of the Earth, were formed and started to campaign on many different environmental issues. These included the dumping of nuclear and toxic waste, the protection of endangered wildlife and the destruction of the rain forests in Africa, Asia and South America. At the same time, scientists began to study the effects of pollution, especially the increasing amounts of carbon dioxide in the air. Carbon dioxide is a gas that comes from the burning of fossil fuels, such as coal and oil. These fuels are used to provide power for factories and transport, as well as for heating homes, shops and offices. At one time the amount of fossil fuel that was burned was much smaller and could be safely absorbed

△ ***Recycling** is one way in which the Earth's resources may be saved. Items such as paper, glass, metal and some plastics can be reused again and again. These items would otherwise be burned in incinerators or buried in landfill sites.*

▷ ***Burning fossil fuels releases carbon dioxide** into the atmosphere where it dissolves in rainwater, making acid rain that can destroy trees and kill fish.*

◁ ***Computers** linked to television, telephone and satellite services now let people exchange or obtain information almost immediately. Tiny microchips have revolutionized home and work life.*

▽ ***The nuclear reactor at Chernobyl** in Ukraine exploded in 1986, releasing about 8 tonnes of radioactive material into the atmosphere. Traces of it spread as far as Italy, France, Scandinavia and Britain. The incident turned many firmly against building more nuclear power stations.*

by trees and plants all over the world. Now the amount is much larger, but there are fewer trees as forests are cut down to make way for more farms. This means that the carbon dioxide stays in the air where it can trap the heat of the Sun and cause the temperature of the Earth to rise. In turn, the rising temperatures cause more land to turn to desert which leads to more frequent droughts. Carbon dioxide in the air also dissolves in rainwater, making acid rain that can destroy trees and kill fish.

Many governments have now taken action to try and limit the amount of carbon dioxide released into the air, by encouraging the use of public transport instead of private cars, funding research into alternative sources of energy, such as solar power and wind power, and encouraging people to recycle items such as paper, glass and metal. In parts of the developing world, many people's only chance of supporting their families or of making income is by cutting down the forests and selling the timber, then growing crops on the cleared land. Cutting down the forests may also be leading to climatic changes and to increased flooding and soil erosion.

GLOBAL AWARENESS

1962 Rachel Carson's *The Silent Spring* creates an awareness of the dangers of pollution.

1971 Founding of Greenpeace, the international organization concerned with protecting the environment.

1972 Government concern for the environment starts when the US bans DDT, a powerful pesticide.

1976 US scientists voice the first fears about damage to the ozone layer. .

1980 Computers are now widely used in business and industry.

1985 In New Zealand, French agents blow up Greenpeace's ship *Rainbow Warrior*, which is protesting against nuclear testing in the Pacific. Live Aid concerts are organized in Britain and the US to help famine victims in Ethiopia.

1986 A serious explosion and fire at the nuclear power station at Chernobyl, Ukraine (then part of the Soviet Union) releases large amounts of radioactivity into the surrounding area.

1987 Scientists discover a hole in the ozone layer above the Antarctic.

1991 The world's population is estimated to be 5.3 billion. A gigantic tidal wave kills at least 100,000 people in Bangladesh.

1992 All nations send representatives to the Earth summit in Rio de Janeiro, Brazil, organized by the UN to discuss the future of the planet.

1995 A year of natural disasters. An avalanche in the Himalayas traps over 5,000 people in their cars; at least 200 of them die. In the US a heatwave in June kills over 1,000 people. In August flash floods in Morocco kill over 200 people with 500 missing. In December over 350 people die in a period of intense cold that spreads across Europe and Asia.

	10,000–2000 BC	2000–1000 BC	1000–500 BC	500–200 BC	200 BC–AD 0
POLITICS	***c.* 3500 BC** Sumerians set up city-states in Mesopotamia ***c.* 3100 BC** King Menes unites Upper and Lower Egypt ***c.* 2500 BC** Indus Valley civilization in ancient India is at its height	***c.* 1800 BC** Babylon begins to build new empire in Mesopotamia ***c.* 1600–1100 BC** The Mycenaeans dominate ancient Greece ***c.* 1200 BC** Beginning of Olmec rule in western Mexico	***c.* 1000–960 BC** David rules united kingdom of Judah and Israel **883–859 BC** Ashurnasirpal II rules kingdom of Assyria in Mesopotamia **753 BC** Traditional date of the foundation of the city of Rome	**479–431 BC** Athens dominates ancient Greece **336–323 BC** Alexander the Great of Macedonia rules Greece, Persia and Egypt **221 BC** Qin Shi Huangdi unites China, calls himself the First Emperor	**147–146 BC** Romans invade and conquer Greece **49–44 BC** Julius Caesar rules Rome as dictator **27 BC** Octavian become Rome's first emperor, taking the title Augustu
EXPLORATION	***c.* 3000 BC** Phoenician ships are sailing around the Mediterranean Sea ***c.* 2300 BC** Egyptian Harkhuf explores up the river Nile	***c.* 1492 BC** Egyptians travel to the Land of Punt (possibly Ethiopia) ***c.* 1001 BC** People from Southeast Asia begin colonizing Polynesia	***c.* 650 BC** Greek sailors discover the Strait of Gibraltar ***c.* 600 BC** Phoenicians sail into Atlantic and may have sailed round Africa ***c.* 515 BC** Greek geographer Scylax explores the river Indus	***c.* 470 BC** Carthaginian navigator Hanno founds settlement in West Africa **449–444 BC** Greek historian Herodotus explores the Near East ***c.* 330 BC** Pytheas of Marseille sails around the British Isles	**138–125 BC** Chang Ch' of China explores centr Asia and India **120 BC** Eudoxus of Gre travels from Egypt to In **55–54 BC** Roman gener Julius Caesar twice inva Britain
TECHNOLOGY	***c.* 4000 BC** Boats on the river Nile are the first to use sails ***c.* 3500 BC** Sumerians in Mesopotamia invent writing and the wheel ***c.* 3000 BC** Egyptians build irrigation system to water their fields	***c.* 2000 BC** Tobacco is grown in Mexico and South America ***c.* 2000 BC** Babylonians began counting in 60s – hence 360° in a circle ***c.* 1450 BC** Ancient Greeks begin using shadow clocks	***c.* 1000 BC** Phoenicians introduce purple dye made from murex snails **876 BC** First known use of a symbol for zero on an inscription in India ***c.* 700 BC** Assyrians begin using water clocks	***c.* 500 BC** Indian surgeon Susrata performs eye operations for cataracts ***c.* 500 BC** Steel is made in India **406 BC** Dionysius of Syracuse, Greece, makes the first war catapult	***c.* 200 BC** Gear wheels invented ***c.* 110 BC** The Chinese invent the horse collar, which is still in use
ARTS	***c.* 2800 BC** Building begins at Stonehenge in England ***c.* 2600 BC** Work begins on the Great Pyramid in Egypt ***c.* 2000 BC** In Sumeria the *Epic of Gilgamesh* is written down	***c.* 1500 BC** Tapestries are made in Egypt, China and Babylonia **1339** In Egypt, king Tutankhamun is buried with hoard of treasure ***c.* 1100 BC** First Chinese dictionary is compiled	At this period: Music flourishes in Babylonia, Greece and Israel ***c.* 950 BC** Solomon's temple is built in Jerusalem ***c.* 850 BC** Chavin people of Peru make many clay pots and sculptures	***c.* 450–387 BC** Greek playwright Aristophanes is at work **447–438 BC** Greeks build the Parthenon temple in Athens **351 BC** Tomb of Mausolus, one of the Seven Wonders of the World, is built	***c.* 140 BC** The *Venus of Milo* is carved in Greece ***c.* 112 BC** Pharisees sec develops in Palestine **47 BC** The great library Alexandria, Egypt, is destroyed by fire
RELIGION	During this period: Sumerians worship mother-goddess Tammuz During this period: Egyptians worship their pharaoh as a god-king	***c.* 2000 BC** Babylonians begin worship of the god Marduk ***c.* 1500 BC** Probable date of the development of the Hindu religion ***c.* 1364–1347 BC** New religion based on Sun worship flourishes in Egypt	**700s BC** The Hebrew prophet Isaiah is active ***c.* 563 BC** Birth of the Buddha (Siddhartha Gautama in Nepal) ***c.* 551 BC** Birth of the Chinese philosopher Confucius (Kong Qiu)	***c.* 400 BC** The first five books of the Bible reach their final form **260 BC** Emperor Ashoka Maurya makes Buddhism India's state religion ***c.* 255 BC** Greek version of the Old Testament is compiled	**168 BC** Antiochus IV of Syria persecutes the Jew and sacks Jerusalem ***c.* 165 BC** The Book of Daniel in the Old Testament is written **4 BC** Probable birth da of Jesus of Nazareth
DAILY LIFE	***c.* 8000 BC** farming first practised in Near East and in Southeast Asia ***c.* 5000 BC** Aboriginal Australians begin using boomerangs During this period: copper is first used in Asia and North America	***c.* 1500 BC** First glass vessels used in Egypt and Mesopotamia ***c.* 1450 BC** Explosion of Thera volcano in Mediterranean wipes out Cretan civilization	***c.* 950 BC** Poppies are grown in Egypt ***c.* 900 BC** Noble Egyptians and Assyrians begin wearing wigs **776 BC** The first Olympic Games are held in Greece	**430–423 BC** Plague breaks out in Athens ***c.* 250 BC** Parchment is first made in Pergamum (now Bergama, Turkey) **214 BC** The building of the Great Wall of China is started	***c.* 170 BC** Rome has its first paved streets **46 BC** Romans adopt th Julian Calendar and the idea of leap years ***c.* 50 BC** Basic Hindu medical book, the *Ayurveda*, is compiled

AD 0–600	AD 600–700	AD 700–800	AD 800–900	AD 900–1000
D 100s Kingdom of xum ses to power in what is ow Ethiopia **D 350–550** The Gupta npire dominates India **D 476** Collapse of the estern Roman empire	***c.* AD 600** Huari empire begins to develop in Peru **AD 655–698** Arabs dominate North Africa and spread Islam **AD 687** Pepin of Herstal becomes leader of the Franks in Gaul	**AD 732** Charles Martel of France defeats Muslims at battle of Poitiers **AD 786** Harun al-Rashid becomes Caliph of Baghdad **AD 800** Frankish king Charlemagne is crowned Emperor of the West	**AD 800s** Ife kingdom rises to power in Nigeria **AD 802** Khmer empire is founded in Cambodia **AD 878** Alfred the Great defeats Vikings and divides England with them	**AD 926** Welsh, Picts and Scots submit to King Athelstan of England **AD 936** Otto I of Germany is crowned as Holy Roman emperor **AD 968** Toltecs in Mexico build their capital city, Tula
D 14–37 Hippalus of ome sails from the Red a to the Indus **AD 50** Greek scientist olemy publishes *Guide to ography* **D 399** Chinese monk Fu-sien begins journey to dia, Sri Lanka and Java	**AD 629–645** Chinese monk Hsüan-Tang goes to India to obtain Buddhist texts **AD 698** Willibrord of Utrecht (Netherlands) discovers Heligoland	**AD 787** First Viking raid on Britain ***c.* AD 800** Vikings colonize Shetland Islands, Orkneys, Hebrides and Faeroes	**c. AD 850** Arab merchant Soleiman sails to Melaka, now in Malaysia **c. AD 860** Irish saint Brendan of Clonfert is said to have sailed to America and back	**c. AD 982** Viking Erik the Red explores Greenland coast **c. AD 986** Viking Bjarni Herjolfson lands in North America **c. AD 1000** Viking Leif Eriksson sails to Vinland, North America
AD 100 Scientist Hero of exandria makes the first eam engine **AD 150** The Chinese ake the first paper **D 271** Chinese invent the st form of compass; it ints south	***c.* AD 600** Earliest known windmills are built in Persia (now Iran) ***c.* AD 650** Greek fire, which burns in water, is invented in Egypt ***c.* AD 670** Hindu works on mathematics are translated into Arabic	***c.* AD 725** Native Americans build Casa Grande fort, Arizona **AD 765** Japanese print first pictorial books **AD 782** In England, Offa's Dyke (a barrier against the Welsh) is started	**c. AD 850** Earliest reference in China to gunpowder	**c. AD 940** Astronomers in China produce a star map **c. AD 960** French priest Gerbert introduces Arabic numerals to Europe **AD 984** Canal locks are invented in China
AD 164 The oldest Maya onuments are built **386** Ambrose, bishop Milan, introduces hymn ging **478** First Shinto shrines ected in Japan	**AD 650** Art of weaving develops in Byzantium **AD 650** Neumes, early form of music notation, are developed **AD 700** Rock-cut temples are begun at Ellora, India	***c.* AD 750** Wind organs begin to replace water (hydraulic) organs	**c. AD 850** Building of Great Zimbabwe, now in modern Zimbabwe	**AD 942** Arabs introduce trumpets and kettledrums into Europe **AD 961** Emperor Li Yü of China establishes an academy of painting at Nanking
D 30 Probable date of the ucifixion of Jesus of zareth **D 45** St Paul begins his ssion to the Gentiles **313** Roman Emperor nstantine decrees eration of Christians	**AD 622** Arab prophet Muhammad flees from Mecca to Medina **AD 632** Abu Bakr, the first Caliph, begins to spread Islam through Arabia ***c.* AD 680** St Wilfrid converts people of Sussex to Christianity	**AD 730** Venerable Bede works on his *History of the English Church* **AD 782** Alcuin of York goes to Aachen to teach in Charlemagne's school	**AD 845** Persecution of Buddhists in China is rife **AD 879** The oldest mosque in Cairo, Ibn Tulun, is built	**AD 959** In England, St Dunstan becomes Archbishop of Canterbury **AD 963** First monastery is established at Mount Athos, Greece **AD 966** The Poles are converted to Christianity
D 79 Vesuvius erupts, stroys Pompeii and erculaneum **AD 200** The Chinese ent porcelain **AD 300** Maya of Central nerica invent a calendar		**AD 750** Hops are first used to make beer in Bavaria, Germany **AD 789** Charlemagne introduces his foot as a unit of measurement	**AD 812** China issues the earliest paper money **AD 851** The crossbow first comes into use in France **AD 870** Calibrated candles are used in England to measure time	**AD 942** Weaving of linen and wool is established in Flanders (Belgium) **AD 962** Hospice is established at St Bernard's Pass, Switzerland **AD 1000** The Danegeld (a tax to buy off Viking raiders) levied in England

	1000–1050	1050–1100	1100–1150	1150–1200	1200–1250
POLITICS	**1016** Canute II of Denmark becomes King of England **1040** Macbeth murders Duncan of Scotland and becomes king **1042** Saxon Edward the Confessor becomes King of England	**1066** Harold II becomes King of England; he defeats an invasion from Norway, but is killed at the battle of Hastings and William of Normandy becomes king **1076** Pope Gregory VII excommunicates German emperor Henry IV	**1120** Heir of Henry I of England is drowned in the *White Ship* disaster **1135** Henry I dies; his nephew Stephen takes the throne; he is challenged by Henry's daughter Matilda and civil war breaks out	**1154** Henry Plantagenet becomes King of England as Henry II **1155** Pope Adrian IV "gives" Ireland to Henry II of England **1187** Muslim leader Saladin captures Jerusalem	**1206** Tribal chief Temuji is proclaimed Genghis Khan, ruler of Mongolia **1215** King John of Engla is forced to agree to Magna Carta **1228** Emperor Frederick of Germany leads the Six Crusade to Palestine
EXPLORATION	**1004–1013** Vikings try unsuccessfully to settle in Vinland, North America	**1096–1099** Members of the First Crusade travel to Turkey and Palestine	***c.* 1150** Rabbi Benjamin of Tudela, Spain, travels to Mesopotamia and Iran	***c.* 1154** Al-Idrisi's map muddles the Nile and the Niger rivers **1183–1187** Ibn Jubayr, a Spanish Moor, travels to Mecca, Baghdad and Damascus	**1245–1247** Franciscan fr John of Pian del Carpin visits Mongolia
TECHNOLOGY	**1035** Spinning-wheels are in use in China ***c.* 1050** Arabs introduce the decimal system into Spain ***c.* 1050** Chinese begin printing books from movable type	**1066** Halley's Comet is seen, and is feared in Europe to portend evil **1100** Italians find out how to distill brandy from wine	**1107** Chinese use multi-colour printing for paper money **1129** Flying buttresses are first used in building churches in Europe **1142–1154** Books on algebra and optics are translated from Arabic	**1150** The Chinese make the first rockets **1189** First European paper mill is built in Hérault, France	**1202** Italian Leonardo Fibonacci introduces 0 (zero) to Europe **1221** Chinese use bomb containing shrapnel
ARTS	***c.* 1050** Polyphonic (many voiced) singing is introduced in the Christian Church	**1067** Monte Cassino Monastery, Italy, is rebuilt **1078** Work begins to build the Tower of London	**1110** Earliest known miracle play is performed in England **1147** Geoffrey of Monmouth writes his *History of Britain*	**1151** Golden age of Buddhist art in Burma (now Myanmar) **1174** Bell tower of Pisa, Italy, is built and at once begins to lean	***c.* 1220** Italian poets develop the form of the sonnet **1225** *Sumer is icumin in* i the earliest known Engli round song
RELIGION	**1012** Persecution of heretics begins in Germany **1030** Norway is converted to Christianity **1042** Edward the Confessor begins to build Westminster Abbey	**1084** Carthusian order of monks is founded **1098** First Cistercian monastery is founded at Cîteaux, France	**1119** Military Order of Knights Templars is founded **1123** First Lateran Council in Rome forbids priests to marry	**1154** Adrian IV becomes the only English pope (Nicholas Breakspear) **1155** Carmelite Order of monks is founded in Palestine **1170** Archbishop Thomas à Becket is murdered in Canterbury Cathedral	**1215** Spanish priest Dominic founds the Dominican Order **1229** The Inquisition in Toulouse, France, forbi laymen to read the Bibl **1233** Pope Gregory IX a the Dominicans to carry out the Inquisition
DAILY LIFE	***c.* 1009** Persians introduce 7-day week to China, which had 10-day weeks	**1086** *Domesday Book* is first complete survey of England **1094** Gondolas come into use in Venice	**1124** Scotland has its first coins **1133** St Bartholomew's Hospital, London, founded **1133** St Barthlomew's Fair begins in London (closed 1855)	**1151** Game of chess is introduced into England **1189** Silver florins are first minted at Florence, Italy	**1230** Returning Crusad bring disease of leprosy Europe **1233** Coal mining at Newcastle, England, beg **1244** First competition f the Dunmow Flitch for married couples is held

1250–1300	1300–1350	1350–1400	1400–1450	1450–1500
272 Edward I becomes ing of England **274** Kublai Khan, nperor of China, tries to nquer Japan, but fails **286** Margaret, the Maid Norway, becomes ueen of Scotland, aged ree; she dies in 1290	**1301** Edward I of England creates his son Prince of Wales **1306** Robert Bruce is crowned King of Scotland **1337** Hundred Years War between England and France begins	**1363** Mongol ruler Tamerlane begins the conquest of Asia **1368** Ming dynasty in China ousts the Mongol Yuan dynasty **1375** Truce halts Hundred Years War (until 1378)	**1413** Henry V becomes King of England and claims large areas of France **1428–1430** Joan of Arc leads the French armies against England **1438** Inca rule begins in Peru	**1453** Hundred Years War ends **1453** Turks capture Constantinople; end of the Byzantine empire **1455** Wars of the Roses break out in England; end with accession of Henry VII (Tudor) in 1485
253–1254 Guillaume of ubruquis, a French friar, avels to Mongolia **271–1295** Venetian trader arco Polo spends 24 ears at the court of Kublai han in China	**1325–1349** Moroccan explorer Ibn Battuta visits Mecca, India and China	***c.* 1352** Ibn Battuta explores African empires of Songhai and Mali **1391** Venetian brothers Niccolo and Antonio Zeno set off to Iceland and the Faeroe Islands	**1420** João Zarco of Portugal discovers Madeira	**1488** Bartolomeu Dias rounds Cape of Good Hope, at the tip of Africa **1492** Christopher Columbus explores the Caribbean **1498** Vasco da Gama makes the first sea voyage to India
267 English scientist oger Bacon proposes the se of spectacles **1290** Cable bridges are uilt over deep valleys in e Andes **299** Florence, Italy, bans e use of Arabic numerals	***c.* 1310** First mechanical clocks are made in Europe **1327** Grand Canal in China, begun AD 70, is completed **1336** University of Paris insists that students study mathematics	***c.* 1380** Cast iron becomes generally used in Europe **1391** Geoffrey Chaucer of England writes on how to make and use an astrolabe ***c.* 1400** Ethiopians start making a drink from wild coffee	**1408** The Dutch use a windmill for pumping water ***c.* 1440** Johannes Gutenberg of Germany begins printing with type	**1454** Gutenberg produces the first printed Bible **1476** William Caxton prints the first book in English **1480** Italian artist Leonardo da Vinci designs a parachute
257 Persian poet Saadi rites *The Fruit Garden* **285** French composer dam de la Halle writes omic opera *Le Jeu de Robin de Marion*	**1325** Aztecs of Mexico build their capital city, Tenochtitlan **1341** Italian poet Petrarch is crowned as poet laureate in Rome **1348** Italian poet Giovanni Boccaccio begins writing the *Decameron* (to 1353)	**1369** Geoffrey Chaucer writes *The Book of the Duchesse* **1375** First appearance of Robin Hood in English legends **1387–1400** Chaucer writes *The Canterbury Tales*	**1414** German monk Thomas à Kempis writes *The Imitation of Christ* **1426** Netherlands becomes the centre of music in Europe **1444** Cosimo de' Medici founds a library in Florence, Italy	**1463** French poet François Villon sentenced to death for brawling, but escapes **1473** Sheet music printed from wood blocks is produced in Germany
256 Order of Augustine ermits, or Austin Friars, founded **268–1271** Quarrels keep e papacy vacant until regory X is elected **276** Popes Gregory X, nocent V and Adrian V e in turn; John XXI cceeds them	**1309** Pope Clement V moves his office from Rome to Avignon, France **1322** Pope John XXII bans the singing of counterpoint in churches **1349** Persecution of Jews breaks out in Germany	**1377** Gregory XI returns the papacy to Rome **1378** Gregory dies: Great Schism begins when two popes are elected, one in Rome, one in France	**1415** Bohemian reformer Jan Hus is burned at the stake for heresy **1417** End of the Great Schism: Martin V is elected pope in Rome	**1453** St Sophia Basilica, Constantinople, becomes a mosque **1484** Papal bull is issued against witchcraft and sorcery **1492** Roderigo Borgia becomes pope as Alexander VI
278 In London, 278 Jews e hanged for clipping ins **284** Legend of the Pied per of Hamelin begins; it ay be founded on fact	**1332** Bubonic plague is first heard of in India **1347–1351** The Black Death (bubonic plague) kills 75 million Europeans **1348** Edward III of England founds the Order of the Garter	**1360** France issues its first francs **1373** English merchants are made to pay tunnage and poundage taxes	**1416** Dutch fishermen begin using drift nets **1433** Holy Roman emperors adopt the double-eagle as an emblem ***c.* 1450** Mocha in southern Arabia (now in Yemen) begins exporting coffee	**1467** Scots parliament bans football and golf **1485** Yeomen of the Guard formed in England **1489** The symbols + and – come into general use

	1500–1520	1520–1540	1540–1560	1560–1580	1580–1600
POLITICS	**1509** Henry VIII becomes King of England, marries Catherine of Aragon **1517** Ottoman Turks conquer Egypt **1519** Charles I of Spain becomes Holy Roman emperor, uniting Austria and Spain	**1531** Protestants in the Holy Roman empire form a defensive alliance **1533** Henry VIII divorces his wife and marries Anne Boleyn **1536** England and Wales are united by the Act of Union	**1541** Ottoman Turks conquer Hungary **1553** Mary I, a Roman Catholic, becomes Queen of England **1558** Elizabeth I, a Protestant, succeeds Mary as Queen of England	**1562** Huguenots (French Protestants) begin emigrating to England **1567** Mary, Queen of Scots, abdicates after her husband's murder **1571** Christian fleet defeats a Turkish fleet at battle of Lepanto	**1581–1582** Livonian Wa Poles take Livonia and Russian access to sea **1587** Mary, Queen of Scots, imprisoned in England, is executed **1588** The Spanish Arma an attempt to invade England, fails
EXPLORATION	**1502–1508** Ludovico de Varthema is the first Christian to visit Mecca **1519–1521** Hernando Cortés conquers Aztec empire in Mexico **1519–1522** Sebastian del Cano is the first captain to sail round the world	**1527–1536** Cabeza de Vaca explores southern North America **1531–1532** Francisco Pizarro explores Peru and conquers the Incas **1535** Jacques Cartier explores the St Lawrence River for France	**1541** Spanish soldier Hernando de Soto discovers the Mississippi **1553–1554** Richard Chancellor opens up trade between England and Moscow, which he reaches by way of the White Sea	**1577–1580** Francis Drake of England sails round the world	**1584** Sir Walter Raleigh begins colonization of Virginia **1596–1597** Dutch navigator Willem Barer dies trying to find the Northeast Passage
TECHNOLOGY	**1502** Peter Henlein of Germany makes the first pocket watch **1507** The name America is used on maps for the first time **1520** First turkeys are imported to Europe from America	**1523** Anthony Fitzherbert writes the first English manual on agriculture **1528** Michelangelo designs fortifications for the city of Florence, Italy **1530** Swiss physician Paracelsus writes book on medicine	**1543** Nicolas Copernicus declares that the Earth revolves around the Sun **1551** Leonard Digges invents the theodolite, used for surveying **1557** Julius Scaliger of Italy discovers the metal platinum	**1569** Gerhardus Mercator invents his projection for maps **1570** The camera obscura, or pinhole camera, is invented **1576** Danish astronomer Tycho Brahe begins sensational discoveries	**1589** William Lee in England invents a knitt machine **1592** Galileo of Italy invents a primitive thermometer **1600** William Gilbert of England proposes that Earth is a giant magnet
ARTS	**1503** Leonardo da Vinci paints the *Mona Lisa* **1508–1512** Michelangelo paints the ceiling of the Sistine Chapel, Rome **1513** Niccolo Machiavelli writes *The Prince* on the theory of government	**1532** François Rabelais of France writes the comic book *Pantagruel* **1538** The first five-part madrigals are published	**1543** Benvenuto Cellini makes golden salt cellars for the King of France **1545** First ever book fair is held in Leipzig, Germany **1548** Building of the Pitti Palace, Florence, begins	**1570** Andrea Palladio writes influential work on architecture **1572** Luis de Camöens of Portugal writes his epic poem *Os Lusíados* **1576** First theatre in England opens in London	**1587** Christopher Marl of England writes play *Tamburlaine the Great* **1590–1594** William Shakespeare of Englan begins writing his plays
RELIGION	**1507** Church begins selling indulgences to pay for St Peter's Basilica, Rome **1517** Martin Luther begins the Reformation in Europe **1519** Ulrich Zwingli reforms the Church in Switzerland	**1526** Sweden converts to Protestantism **1534** English Church breaks from Rome, with the monarch as its head **1534** Ignatius Loyola of Spain founds the Jesuit order	**1545** Council of Trent begins the Counter Reformation **1549** Jesuit missions are sent to Brazil and Japan **1555** In England, persecution of protestants begins; many are burned	**1560** Scotland breaks with the Roman Catholic Church **1570** Pope Pius V excommunicates Queen Elizabeth of England **1572** Massacre of St Bartholomew: French Protestants are killed	**1590–1592** Three pope die in a period of three months **1593** Attendance in ch on Sundays is made compulsory in England
DAILY LIFE	**1504** First shillings are minted in England **1517** The first coffee is imported into Europe **1519** Hernando Cortés reintroduces horses to North America	**1525** Hops are introduced to England from France **1528** Severe outbreak of bubonic plague hits England **1531** Halley's Comet returns, causing great alarm	**1547** Fire destroys Moscow **1550** People begin playing billiards in Italy **1555** Tobacco is imported to Spain from America	**1560** Madrid becomes the capital of Spain **1565** The first potatoes arrive in Spain from America **1568** Bottled beer is first produced in London	**1582** Most Roman Cath countries adopt new Gregorian calendar **1596** Tomatoes are introduced into Europe from America **1596** Sir John Haringto of England invents the water closet (lavatory)

1600–1620	1620–1640	1640–1660	1660–1680	1680–1700
603 James VI of Scotland ecomes King of England s James I, uniting crowns **514** French Estates eneral (parliament) ispended until 1789 **618–1648** Thirty Years /ar engulfs most of urope	**1624** Cardinal Richelieu becomes all-powerful in France **1629** Charles I of England quarrels with Parliament, rules without it until 1640 **1637** Manchu rulers of China turn Korea into a vassal state	**1642** Civil War breaks out in England between King Charles I and Parliament **1649** Charles I is beheaded and England becomes a republic under Cromwell **1660** Monarchy is restored under Charles II	**1662** England sells city of Dunkirk to France **1664** England seizes New Netherland (now New York) from the Dutch **1665–1674** England is at war with the Dutch Republic	**1686** France annexes the island of Madagascar **1688–1689** Peaceful revolution in England drives the Catholic James II off the throne; Protestants William II and Mary II are offered the throne
605 Samuel de hamplain of France xplores Nova Scotia coast **615** Luis Vaez de Torres iscovers strait between ustralia and New Guinea **620** Pilgrim Fathers sail to merica in *Mayflower* and ound Plymouth Colony	**1613** Pedro Paez of Spain discovers source of the Blue Nile in Ethiopia **1627** Thomas Herbert of England explores Persia (now Iran) **1637–1639** Pedro Teixeira of Portugal explores the river Amazon	**1642** Abel Tasman of the Netherlands discovers New Zealand and Tasmania **1650** Franciscan missionaries explore the upper river Amazon **1651** Dutch pioneers begin to settle at the Cape of Good Hope	**1673** Jacques Marquette and Louis Joliet of France explore the Mississippi **1679** Louis de Hennepin and René Cavalier of France reach the Niagara Falls	**1686** William Dampier of England explores northern coast of Australia **1689** Louis de Lahontain of France reaches the Great Salt Lake in Utah
508 Hans Lippershey of e Netherlands invents e microscope **510** With a telescope alileo of Italy discovers ıpiter's moons **513** Galileo agrees with e theory that the Earth oes round the Sun	**1622** William Oughtred, English mathematician, invents the slide-rule **1624** Flemish chemist Jan van Helmont invents the word "gas" **1637** Pierre Fermat and René Descartes of France develop analytic geometry	**1642** Blaise Pascal of France designs an adding machine **1642** Evangelista Torricelli of Italy invents the barometer **1650** Otto von Guericke of Germany invents an air pump	**1665** Isaac Newton of England develops calculus **1675** Greenwich Royal Observatory is founded in England **1679** Denis Papin of France invents the pressure cooker	**1682** Edmund Halley of England observes comet now named after him **1684** Robert Hooke of England invents the heliograph **1698** Thomas Savery of England invents the first steam pump
505 Miguel de Cevantes f Spain writes the first art of *Don Quixote* **507** Composer Claudio onteverdi is working in antua, Italy **611** Royal mosque at fahan, Persia (Iran) is uilt	**1623** The *First Folio* prints most of Shakespeare's plays **1624** Frans Hals of the Netherlands paints *The Laughing Cavalier* **1633** John Milton of England writes poems *L'Allegro* and *Il Penseroso*	**1642** Rembrandt van Rijn of the Netherlands paints *The Night Watch* **1652** Vienna opens its first opera house **1660** Samuel Pepys, English civil servant, begins his diary	**1662** Work begins on Louis XIV's Palace of Versailles in France **1667** The colonnaded square of St Peter's, Rome, is completed **1677** John Dryden is England's leading poet	**1688** Aphra Behn becomes first English woman novelist **1692** Henry Purcell of England composes opera *The Fairy Queen*
504 England's rulers amp down on Roman atholics and Puritans **511** The Authorized ersion of the Bible is ıblished in Britain **516** Protestants in ohemia are oppressed	**1633** The Catholic Church forces Galileo to say Sun revolves around Earth **1634** First Oberammergau Passion Play is put on as thanks for avoiding the plague **1637** Japan bans Christian missionaries	**1645** Presbyterianism is made England's official religion **1648** George Fox founds the Society of Friends (Quakers) **1650** Archbishop James Ussher of Ireland says the Creation was in 4004 BC	**1662** England forbids Nonconformist priests to preach **1678–1684** John Bunyan of England writes *The Pilgrim's Progress*	**1684** Increase Mather becomes a leading preacher in Massachusetts **1692** At witch trials in Salem, Massachusetts, 19 people are hanged **1699** Roman Catholic priests face life in jail in England
507 Table forks come into se in England and France **510** The first China tea is ıported into Europe by e Dutch **519** First black slaves are nployed in Virginia	**1625** England has its first fire engines and hackney coaches **1626** The Dutch buy Manhattan Island from Native Americans for $24 **1630** The card game cribbage is invented	**1650** England has its first coffee house (in Oxford) and starts drinking tea **1654** Paris has its first letter-boxes **1658** Sweden's state bank issues the first banknotes in Europe	**1665** Plague ravages London, killing 68,596 people **1666** Fire destroys most of London and ends the plague there **1677** Ice cream becomes popular in Paris	**1683** Wild boars become extinct in Britain **1692** Lloyd's Coffee House, London, becomes marine insurance office **1697** Fire destroys most of the Palace of Whitehall, London

	1700–1720	1720–1740	1740–1760	1760–1780	1780–1800
POLITICS	**1702** Anne, daughter of James II, succeeds to the English throne **1707** England and Scotland are united as Great Britain **1715** Stuart rebellion in Britain against new king, George I, fails	**1721** Robert Walpole is Britain's first prime minister (to 1742) **1727–1728** War between England and Spain over Gibraltar	**1745–1746** British Jacobite rebellion, led by Bonnie Prince Charlie, fails **1756** Seven Years War begins in Europe **1760** George III becomes British king (to 1820)	**1763** Seven Years War ends: Britain gains French lands in India and America **1775–1783** American War of Independence from Britain **1776** The 13 Colonies declare independence from Britain	**1789** The French Revolution begins **1789** George Washingto elected as US president **1800** Napoleon Bonapa assumes power in Franc
EXPLORATION	**1708** Alexander Selkirk, the original "Robinson Crusoe", is rescued from an island off the coast of Chile **1719** Bernard de la Harpe of France explores North American rivers	**1722** Jacob Roggeveen of the Netherlands discovers Easter Island and Samoa **1736** Anders Celsius leads French expedition to Lapland **1740** George Anson of Britain begins round the world voyage (to 1744)	**1741** Vitus Bering explores Alaskan coast for Russia **1748** American Pioneers cross the Cumberland Gap in the Appalachian	**1766** Louis de Bougainville of France discovers Tahiti and New Guinea **1768–1771** James Cook of Britain makes his first round the world voyage	**1790** George Vancouver England explores north west coast of America **1793** Alexander Macker of Scotland explores northwest Canada **1795** In Africa, Mungo Park of Scotland explor the river Niger
TECHNOLOGY	**1707** Johann Böttger of Germany discovers how to make hard porcelain **1709** Abraham Darby of England begins using coke to smelt iron **1714** Gabriel Fahrenheit of Germany makes a mercury thermometer	**1733** John Kay of Britain invents the flying shuttle **1735** John Harrison of Britain builds first accurate chronometer **1737** Georg Brandt of Sweden discovers cobalt	**1742** Anders Celsius of Sweden invents the centigrade thermometer **1751** Carl Linnaeus of Sweden publishes his landmark book on botany **1752** American Benjamin Franklin invents the lightning conductor	**1769** James Watt of Scotland invents the steam condenser **1769** Nicolas Cugnot of France builds first steam road carriage **1773** First cast iron bridge built at Coalbrookdale, England	**1783** Montgolfier broth of France make first ho balloon ascent **1792** Claude Chappe of France invents the mechanical semaphore **1793** Eli Whitney of the United States invents th cotton gin
ARTS	**1709** Bartolommeo Cristofori of Italy invents the piano **1710** Building of St Paul's Cathedral in London is completed **1719** Daniel Defoe writes first part of the story of *Robinson Crusoe*	**1721** J. S. Bach of Germany composes the *Brandenburg Concertos* **1735** Imperial ballet school in St Petersburg, Russia, opens **1737** England begins censorship of plays	**1741** German George Frederick Handel composes *Messiah* in England **1747** Samuel Johnson of Britain begins work on his dictionary **1751–1772** French scholars compile the *Encyclopédie*	**1768** The Royal Academy of Arts is founded in London **1773** Johann von Goethe of Germany writes first version of *Faust* **1778** In Milan, Italy, La Scala Opera House opens	**1786** In Scotland Robei Burns publishes his firs book of poems **1790** In Austria, Mozart composes the opera *Co. Fan Tutte* **1793** Building of the Capitol in Washington, D.C., begins
RELIGION	**1716** Chinese emperor bans the teaching of Christianity **1719** Dunkards, German Baptist Brethren, settle in Pennsylvania	**1730** John and Charles Wesley establish the Methodist movement **1734** The Koran is translated into English **1737** Alexander Cruden of Britain compiles his *Concordance to the Bible*	**1759** Jesuits are expelled from Portugal and its colonies	**1766** Catherine the Great of Russia grants her people freedom of worship **1767** Jesuits are expelled from Spain **1776** Mystic Ann Lee forms the first Shaker colony in America	**1781** Religious toleranc proclaimed in Austria **1785** State of Virginia passes a statute of religi freedom **1790** Jews in France are granted civil liberties
DAILY LIFE	**1711** South Sea Company takes over £9 million of Britain's National Debt **1712** The last execution of a witch in England takes place **1720** South Sea Company crashes; thousands of people are ruined	**1722** Thomas Guy, British bookseller, helps found Guy's Hospital, London **1725** New York City gets its first newspaper, the *New York Gazette* **1727** Brazil sets up its first coffee plantation	**1744** First official cricket match in Britain (Kent versus All England) **1752** Britain adopts the Gregorian calendar, dropping 11 days **1755** Earthquake kills 30,000 people in Lisbon	**1768** Publication of the *Encyclopaedia Britannica* in weekly parts begins **1770** Paris has its first public restaurant **1779** First running of the Derby horse race at Epsom, England	**1787** United States ado the Stars and Stripes fla **1792** Denmark abolishe the slave trade **1792** Scot William Murdoch is first person light his home with gas

1800–1820	1820–1840	1840–1860	1860–1880	1880–1900
01 Act of Union unites 'eat Britain and Ireland **03** USA buys Louisiana ›m France **04** Napoleon becomes ıperor of France and is ally defeated in 1815	**1821** Simón Bolívar liberates Venezuela from Spain **1822** Brazil becomes independent of Portugal **1837** Queen Victoria comes to the British throne, aged 18	**1845** The United States annexes Texas **1848** Year of Revolutions: Austria, France, Germany, Italy, and Hungary **1853–1856** The Crimean War: Britain, France, and Turkey against Russia	**1861–1865** American Civil War: 11 states secede from the Union **1865** President Abraham Lincoln is assassinated as Civil War ends **1867** The United States buys Alaska from Russia for $7,200,000	**1881** President James Garfield of the USA is assassinated **1883** The scramble for European colonies in Africa starts **1899** The Boer War in South Africa starts (to 1902)
03–1806 Lewis and Clark pedition finds a route to e Pacific from the east **12** William Moorcroft of ıgland explores Tibet **22–1825** Denham Dixon d other Britons cross the hara	**1829** Charles Sturt finds the Murray River in Australia **1831** James Clark Ross of Britain reaches the North Magnetic Pole **1840–1841** Edward Eyre crosses the Nullarbor Plain of Australia	**1852–1856** David Livingstone of Scotland explores the Zambesi River **1854** Richard Burton explores East Africa, including Ethiopia **1858** John Speke and Richard Burton discover Lake Tanganyika	**1871** Henry Stanley is sent to look for Livingstone and finds him at Ujiji **1872** *HMS Challenger* begins a world survey of the oceans **1879** Nils Nordenskiöld of Sweden sails through the Northeast Passage	**1882** Adolphus Greely explores Greenland and the Arctic **1888–1892** Emin Pasha of Germany explores central Africa **1893** Fritjof Nansen of Norway tries to reach the North Pole, but fails
14 George Stephenson uilds first successful steam comotive **15** Humphrey Davey vents the miners' safety mp **16** René Laennec of ance invents the ethoscope	**1825** First passenger railway opens in northern England **1827** Joseph Niépce of France takes the world's first photograph **1834** Cyrus McCormick of the United States invents a reaping machine	**1844** Artist Samuel Morse of the USA demonstrates the use of the Morse Code **1847** James Simpson of Britain uses chloroform as an anaesthetic **1860** Christopher Scholes of the USA invents a practical typewriter	**1873** Joseph Glidden of the USA invents barbed wire **1876** Alexander Graham Bell invents the telephone **1879** Electric lamp bulbs are invented	**1885** Karl Benz of Germany builds the first motor-car **1895** Guglielmo Marconi of Italy invents wireless telegraphy **1900** Graf von Zeppelin (Germany) invents the rigid airship
01 Joseph Haydn of ıstria composes oratorio *'ie Seasons* **13** Franz Schubert of ıstria writes his first mphony **14** Walter Scott writes s first novel, *Waverley*	**1822** Royal Academy of Music is founded in London **1835** Hans Christian Andersen publishes his first fairy tales	**1843** Richard Wagner of Germany writes opera *The Flying Dutchman* **1846** Adolphe Sax of Belgium invents the saxophone **1860** George Eliot (Mary Anne Evans) of Britain writes *The Mill on the Floss*	**1868** Louisa M. Alcott writes *Little Women* **1874** Impressionist movement in painting starts in Paris **1875** Gilbert and Sullivan produce their first light opera, *Trial by Jury*	**1883** Royal College of Music in London founded **1884** Mark Twain writes *Huckleberry Finn* **1895** Promenade Concerts begin in London
04 British and Foreign ble Society is formed in ›ndon **08** Napoleon abolishes e Inquisition in Italy and ain **12** Restrictions on ›nconformists in ıgland are relaxed	**1826** Jesuits are allowed to return to France **1827** John Nelson Darby founds the Plymouth Brethren **1830** Joseph Smith founds the Church of Latter-Day Saints (Mormons)	**1846** Mormons in the USA begin migrating to the Great Salt Lake, Utah **1853–1868** Johann Herzog writes *Encyclopedia of Protestant Theology* **1854** Pope Pius IX proclaims Immaculate Conception as dogma	**1865** William Booth founds the Salvation Army in Britain **1871** Charles Russell founds the Jehovah's Witnesses **1879** Mary Baker Eddy founds the Christian Science Church	**1890** James Frazer of Britain writes *The Golden Bough: A Study in Magic and Religion* **1896** Theodor Herzl of Austria proposes a Jewish state in Palestine
07 Britain ends the slave ıde **15** Tambora Volcano in donesia erupts: 50,000 ›ople are killed **19** Freedom of the press guaranteed in France	**1829** First Oxford and Cambridge Boat Race is held on the Thames **1834** Fire destroys Britain's Houses of Parliament **1840** Penny Postage and adhesive stamps are introduced	**1844** First co-operative society is formed in Rochdale, England **1851** The Great Exhibition is held in Hyde Park, London **1855** Britain abolishes stamp duty on newspapers	**1864** Louis Pasteur of France invents pasteurization **1868** The first Trades Union Congress meets in Britain **1874** Walter Wingfield invents Sphairistiké – now called lawn tennis	**1887** Victoria celebrates her Golden Jubilee as Britain's queen **1900** The Labour Party is founded in Britain

	1900–1910	1910–1920	1920–1930	1930–1940	1940–1950
POLITICS	**1901** Edward VII succeeds Victoria as British monarch **1902** The Boer War ends **1904–1905** Russo-Japanese War; Japan wins	**1911** China becomes a republic after 2,000 years under emperors **1914–1918** World War I: nearly 10 million soldiers die **1917** October Revolution in Russia: Lenin and the Bolsheviks seize power	**1922** Benito Mussolini forms a Fascist government in Italy **1924** Joseph Stalin becomes ruler of the Soviet Union **1924** Britain has its first Labour government	**1933** The Nazi leader Adolf Hitler becomes dictator of Germany **1936–1939** Spanish Civil War **1939** World War II begins as Germany and the Soviet Union invade Poland	**1941** The US enters Wo War II, following Japan' attack on Pearl Harbor **1945** World War II ends with German and Japan surrender **1945–1951** Labour retu to power in Britain; ma industries nationalized
EXPLORATION	**1901–1903** Erich von Drygalski of Germany explores Antarctica **1907–1909** Ernest Shackleton of Britain nearly reaches the South Pole **1909** Robert Peary of the USA reaches the North Pole	**1911** Roald Amundsen of Norway leads first party to reach the South Pole **1912** Briton Robert Falcon Scott also reaches the South Pole, but perishes **1919** Alcock and Brown make first non-stop flight across the Atlantic	**1926** Richard Byrd and Floyd Bennett of the USA fly over the North Pole **1926** Umberto Nobile of Norway makes airship flight over North Pole **1929** Richard Byrd flies over the South Pole	**1931** First submarine ventures under the Arctic Ocean ice **1932** Auguste Piccard ascends 28km in a stratospheric balloon	**1946–1947** Operation Highjump maps coast o Antarctica from the air **1947** Thor Heyerdahl o Norway sails the raft *Ko Tiki* from Peru to the Tuamoto Islands
TECHNOLOGY	**1903** In the USA, the Wright Brothers make the first powered flights **1907** Louis Lumière of France develops colour photography **1909** Louis Blériot of France flies across the English Channel	**1917** Ernest Rutherford of Britain splits the atom **1919** First mass spectrograph machine is built **1920** First public broadcasting station in Britain opens	**1922** Insulin is first given to diabetics **1925** John Logie Baird invents a primitive form of television **1928** Alexander Fleming accidentally discovers penicillin	**1935** Radar is developed for use in detecting aircraft **1937** Frank Whittle builds the first jet aero engine **1940** Howard Florey develops penicillin as a working antibiotic	**1942** Magnetic recordir tape is invented **1946** ENIAC, first fully electronic digital computer, is built **1948** Peter Goldmar invents the long-playing record
ARTS	**1901** Ragtime music becomes popular in America **1905** First regular cinema opens in Pittsburgh, Pennsylvania **1909** Sergei Diaghilev's Ballets Russes starts performing in Paris	**1914** Charlie Chaplin creates his film character in *The Tramp* **1916** Artists and poets start the Dadaist movement in Switzerland **1917** The Original Dixieland Jazz Band is formed in New York	**1926** A. A. Milne writes *Winnie the Pooh* **1927** Theremin, the first electronic musical instrument, is invented	**1935** American George Gershwin writes *Porgy and Bess* **1937** First full-length cartoon film, *Snow White and the Seven Dwarfs* **1938** Radio play *War of the Worlds* causes panic in the United States	**1947** *The Diary of Anne Frank* is published **1949** George Orwell wr the satire *Nineteen Eight Four* **1950** United Nations building in New York C is completed
RELIGION	**1904** Germany partly lifts its ban on Jesuits **1909** First Jewish kibbutz is founded in Palestine	**1912** Church of Scotland issues a revised prayer book **1917** Balfour Declaration: Britain backs homeland for Jews in Palestine **1920** Joan of Arc is canonized (declared to be a saint)	**1924** Mahatma Gandhi fasts in protest at religious feuding in India **1929** Presbyterian Churches in Scotland unite	**1932** Methodist Churches in Britain reunite (split since 1797) **1933** All Protestant Churches in Germany unite **1937** Protestant parson Martin Niemöller is interned by Hitler	**1946** Pope Pius XII cre 32 new cardinals **1947** The Dead Sea Scr are discovered in caves Qumran, Jordan **1948** The World Counc Churches is established
DAILY LIFE	**1902** Eruption of Mt Pelée in Martinique kills 38,000 people **1903** The first teddy bears are made in Germany **1906** An earthquake destroys most of San Francisco; 3,000 people die	**1912** Liner *Titanic* sinks on her maiden voyage; more than 1,500 people drowned **1918** British women over the age of 30 gain the vote **1918** First airmail service is established in the United States	**1920** Women in the USA gain the vote **1929** Wall Street crash: biggest world economic crisis begins **1930** Youth Hostels Association founded	**1932–1934** Pontine Marshes in Italy are drained **1934** Dionne Quintuplets are born in Canada **1936** King Edward VIII abdicates to marry divorcee Wallis Simpson	**1941–1949** Clothes rationing in force in Britain **1945** Bebop form of jaz comes into fashion **1947** First microwave o go on sale

1950–1960	1960–1970	1970–1980	1980–1990	1990–2000
56 Egypt's ruler Gamel sser seizes Suez Canal **50** Seventeen African onies gain lependence from ropean powers	**1961** Communists build the Berlin Wall **1963** US President John F. Kennedy is assassinated **1965–1973** The Vietnam War **1967** Six Day War between Israel and Arab nations	**1974** US President Nixon resigns over Watergate scandal **1979** Margaret Thatcher becomes Britain's first woman prime minister **1980** Marshal Tito, leader of Yugoslavia since 1953, dies	**1982** Argentina's invasion of the Falkland Islands fails **1989** Communist rule ends in East Germany; Berlin Wall is demolished	**1991** Collapse of the Soviet Union: republics become independent **1991** Breakup of Yugoslavia: civil war breaks out **1997** In referendums, Scots vote for a parliament and Welsh for an assembly
57–1958 Vivien Fuchs of itain makes first crossing Antarctica **58** US nuclear omarine *Trieste* travels der the North Polar ice **50** A Bathyscaphe scends 10,910m into the riana Trench	**1961** Yuri Gagarin of the Soviet Union makes the first manned space flight **1968** US space craft *Apollo 8* first orbits the Moon **1969** Neil Armstrong of the USA is the first person to walk on the Moon	**1971** Space probes orbit Mars and send back photographs **1979–1989** Space probe *Voyager 2* flies past and photographs Jupiter, Saturn, Uranus, and Neptune	**1981** The first space shuttle, *Columbia*, orbits the Earth **1982** Soviet space probes land on Venus and send back colour pictures **1984** Two US astronauts fly in space untethered to their spacecraft	**1993** Two Britons complete the first foot crossing of Antarctica **1997** US robot, controlled from Earth, explores surface of Mars
51 Heart-lung machine nvented **56** Albert Sabin invents l vaccine against polio **57** Soviet Union nches the first Earth ellites, *Sputniks 1* and *2*	**1967** Christiaan Barnard performs the first human heart transplant **1963** Theory of continental drift is proved by two British geophysicists **1969** First flight of the supersonic airliner *Concorde*	**1972** *Apollo 17* crew make last manned visit to the Moon **1978** Louise Brown, the first "test tube baby", is born **1980** Smallpox is eradicated world wide	**1984** The first Apple Macintosh microcomputer goes on sale **1986** The Dutch complete their flood protection scheme after 33 years **1988** Undersea tunnel linking Honshu and Hokkaido, Japan, opens	**1993** Astronauts repair the Hubble Space Telescope (launched 1990) **1994** Channel Tunnel is completed at a cost of £10 billion
50s Rock and Roll velops **51** John Osborne's *Look k in Anger* is staged in ndon **50** New buildings npleted in Brasilia, ital of Brazil	**1965** Op Art, based on optical illusions, becomes popular **1966** New Metropolitan Opera House opens in New York City **1968** Four Soviet writers are jailed for "dissidence"	**1971** *Fiddler on the Roof* closes after record New York run of 3,242 performances **1980** Former Beatle John Lennon is murdered in New York	**1983** Symphony written by Mozart aged nine is discovered **1985** Live Aid rock concert raises $60 million for African famine relief **1986** Wole Soyinka is the first black African to win the Nobel Prize for Literature	**1992** Classic FM radio station begins broadcasting in Britain **1993** Missing treasure from Troy found in 1873 is rediscovered in Russia
58 John XXIII becomes pe **58** Supreme Religious ntre for World Jewry is ened in Jerusalem **0** Swedish Lutheran urch admits women nisters	**1968** In Northern Ireland, Catholics and Protestants clash over civil rights **1969** Pope Paul VI removes 200 saints from the liturgical calendar **1970** Jewish and Roman Catholic leaders confer in Rome	**1978** Deaths of Pope Paul VI and his successor Pope John Paul I; succeeded by Pope John II, a Pole and fist non-Italian pope for 456 years	**1981** John Paul II becomes the first pope to visit Britain **1986** Desmond Tutu becomes the first black archbishop of Cape Town **1990** First Anglican women priests are ordained in Northern Ireland	**1992** Ten women become Anglican priests in Australia **1996** Strict Islamic law is imposed in Afghanistan
53 Mount Everest is nbed for the first time **4** Roger Bannister runs mile in under four nutes **8** First life peerages are ated in Britain	**1966** Miniskirts come into fashion **1967** Francis Chichester completes single-handed voyage around the world **1970** Storms and floods kill 500,000 people in East Pakistan (Bangladesh)	**1976** Earthquakes shake China, Guatemala, Indonesia, Italy, the Philippines and Turkey: 780,000 people die **1978–1979** Union troubles close *The Times* of London for nearly a year	**1982** Disease kills 20 million elm trees in Britain **1987** World stock market crash on Black Monday **1989** World ban on ivory trading is imposed	**1992** Betty Boothroyd becomes the first woman Speaker of the British House of Commons **1997** Hong Kong is returned to China

IMPORTANT BATTLES OF HISTORY

Marathon (490 BC) The armies of Athens crushed an attempt by Persia to conquer Greece

Salamis (480 BC) Greek ships defeated a larger Persian fleet and thwarted an invasion

Syracuse (414–413 BC) During a long war between the city states of Athens and Sparta the Athenians besieged Syracuse but lost power after a heavy defeat

Gaugamela (331 BC) Alexander the Great of Macedonia defeated the Persians and conquered the Persian Empire

Metaurus (207 BC) A Roman army defeated a Carthaginian attempt to invade Italy

Actium (30 BC) A Roman fleet destroyed the Egyptian fleet of Mark Antony and Cleopatra, ending Egypt's threat to Rome

Teutoburg Forest (AD 9) German tribes led by Arminius ambushed and destroyed three Roman legions

Châlons (451) Roman legions and their Visigoth allies defeated the Huns, led by Attila

Poitiers (732) The Franks led by Charles Martel defeated a Muslim attempt to conquer western Europe

Hastings (1066) Duke William of Normandy defeated the Saxons under King Harold II and conquered England

Crécy (1346) Edward III of England defeated Philip VI of France, using archers to shoot his opponents

Agincourt (1415) Henry V of England defeated a much larger French army and captured Normandy

Orléans (1429) The French under Joan of Arc raised the siege of Orléans and began liberating France from England

Constantinople (1453) Ottoman Turks captured the city and ended the Byzantine (Eastern Roman) Empire

Lepanto (1571) A Christian fleet defeated a Turkish fleet in the Mediterranean and halted Muslim designs on Europe

Spanish Armada (1588) England fought off a Spanish attempt to invade and conquer it

Naseby (1645) Parliamentary forces defeated Charles I, leading to the end of the English Civil War

Blenheim (1704) During the War of the Spanish Succession, British and Austrian forces stopped a French and Bavarian attempt to capture Vienna

Poltava (1709) Peter the Great of Russia fought off an invasion by Charles XII of Sweden

Plassey (1757) An Anglo-Indian army defeated the Nawab of Bengal, beginning England's domination of India

Quebec (1759) British troops under James Wolfe defeated the French and secured Canada for Britain

Bunker Hill (1775) In the War of Independence, British troops drove the Americans from hills near Boston, Mass.

Brandywine Creek (1777) British troops forced American forces to retreat

Saratoga (1777) American troops surrounded a British army and forced it to surrender

Savannah (1778) Britain captured the port of Savannah from the Americans and gained control of Georgia

King's Mountain (1780) Americans surrounded and captured part of a British army

Yorktown (1781) A British army surrendered to a larger American force, ending the American War of Independence

The Nile (1798) A British fleet shattered a French fleet in Abu Kir Bay, ending Napoleon's attempt to conquer Egypt

Trafalgar (1805) A British fleet defeated a Franco-Spanish fleet, ending Napoleon's hopes of invading England

Austerlitz (1805) Napoleon I of France defeated a combined force of Austrian and Russian soldiers

Leipzig (1813) Austrian, Prussian, Russian and Swedish armies defeated Napoleon I, leading to his abdication the following year

Waterloo (1815) A British, Belgian, and Dutch army supported by the Prussians defeated Napoleon I, ending his brief return to power in France

Fort Sumter (1861) In the opening battle of the American Civil War, Confederate forces captured this fort in the harbour of Charleston, South Carolina

Merrimack and Monitor (1862) This inconclusive battle was the first between two ironclad warships

Gettysburg (1863) Union forces defeated the Confederates, marking a turning point in the American Civil War

Vicksburg (1863) After a long siege Union forces captured this key city on the Mississippi River

Chickamauga (1863) At this town in Georgia the Confederates won their last major battle

Chattanooga (1863) A few weeks after Chickamauga Union forces won a decisive victory over the Confederates

Tsushima (1905) A Japanese fleet overwhelmed a Russian one, ending the Russo-Japanese War

Tannenberg (1914) At the start of World War I two Russian armies invaded East Prussia, but a German army under Paul von Hindenburg crushed them

Marne (1914) The French and British halted a German invasion of France at the start of World War I

1st Ypres (1914) A series of German attacks on this Belgian town were beaten back with heavy losses on each side

2nd Ypres (1915) The Germans attacked again with heavy shelling and chlorine gas, but gained only a little ground

Isonzo (1916–1917) This was a series of 11 inconclusive battles on the Italo-Austrian front

Verdun (1916) French forces under Philippe Pétain fought off a German attempt to take this strong point

Jutland (1916) This was the major naval battle of World War I; neither Germans nor British won

Brusilov Offensive (1916) A Russian attack led by General Alexei Brusilov nearly knocked Germany's Austrian allies out of the war

Somme (1916) A British and French attack was beaten back by German machine-gunners; total casualties for both sides were more than 1 million

3rd Ypres (1917) British and Canadian troops attacked to drive the Germans back, fighting in heavy rain and mud

Passchendaele (1917) This village was the furthest advance of 3rd Ypres; casualties of both sides totalled 500,000

4th Ypres (1918) This was part of a general German offensive, which died down after heavy fighting

Marne (1918) French, American, and British forces halted the last German attack of World War I

Britain (1940–1941) In World War II, German attempt to eliminate Britain's air force failed

The Atlantic (1940–1944) Germany narrowly lost the submarine war against Allied shipping

Pearl Harbor (1941) In a surprise air attack Japan knocked out the United States fleet at Hawaii

Coral Sea (1942) In the first all-air naval battle, Americans thwarted a Japanese attack on New Guinea

Stalingrad (1942–1943) The German siege of Stalingrad (now Volgograd, Russia) ended with the surrender of a German army of 100,000 men

El Alamein (1942) The British Eighth Army finally drove German and Italian forces out of Egypt

Midway (1942) An American fleet defeated a Japanese attempt to capture Midway Island in the Pacific

Normandy (1944) American and British troops landed in occupied France to begin the defeat of Germany; the largest ever seaborne attack

Leyte Gulf (1944) In the biggest naval battle of World War II, an American fleet thwarted a Japanese attempt to prevent the recapture of the Philippines

Ardennes Bulge (1944–1945) A final German attempt to counter the Allied invasion failed

Hiroshima/Nagasaki (1945) Two US atomic bombs on these cities knocked Japan out of World War II

Falklands (1982) A British seaborne assault recaptured the Falkland Islands following an Argentine invasion

Desert Storm (1991) An American, British and Arab attack ended Iraq's invasion of Kuwait

CHINESE DYNASTIES

Hsia Dynasty	c. 2000–1500 BC
Shang or Yin Dynasty	c. 1766–1027 BC
Zhou Dynasty	1027–256 BC
Qin Dynasty	221–206 BC
Former Han Dynasty	202 BC–AD 9
Xin Dynasty	AD 9–22
Later Han Dynasty	25–220
Three Kingdoms	221–265
Six Dynasties:	
Western Chin	265–316
Eastern Chin	317–420
Liu Sung	420–479
Southern Ch'i	429–502
Liang	502–557
Southern Ch'en	557–587
Tatar Partition:	
Bei Wei Dynasty	486–554
Northern Ch'i Dynasty	550–557
Northern Chou Dynasty	557–581
Sui Dynasty	581–618
T'ang Dynasty	618–906
Partition (rulers were mostly non-Chinese):	
Hou Liang Dynasty	907–936
Hou T'ang Dynasty	923–936
Hou Chin Dynasty	936–948
Hou Han Dynasty	946–950
Hou Chou Dynasty	951–960
Northern Song Dynasty	960–1126
Southern Song Dynasty	1127–1279
Yuan (Mongol) Dynasty	1279–1368
Ming Dynasty	1368–1644
Qing (Manchu) Dynasty	1644–1912

ROMAN EMPERORS

Augustus	27 BC–AD14
Tiberius	14–37
Caligula	37–41
Claudius	41–54
Nero	54–68
Galba	68–69
Otho	69
Vitellius	69

Vespasian	69–79
Titus	79–81
Domitian	81–96
Nerva	96–98
Trajan	98–117
Hadrian	117–138
Antoninus Pius	138–161
Marcus Aurelius	161–180
Lucius Verus	161–169
Commodus	180–192
Pertinax	193
Didius Julian	193
Septimius Severus	193–211
Caracalla (jointly with Geta)	211–217
Geta	211–212
Macrinus	217–218
Elagabalus	218–222
Alexander Severus	222–235
Maximin	235–238
Gordian I	238
Gordian II	238
Pupienus	238
Balbinus	238
Gordian III	238–244
Philipp "Arabs"	244–249
Decius	249–251
Hostilian	251
Gallus	251–253
Aemilian	253
Valerian	253–259
Gallinus	259–268
Claudius II	268–270
Quintillus	270
Aurelian	270–275
Tacitus	275–276
Florian	276
Probus	276–282
Carus	282–283
Numerian	283–284
Carinus	283–285
Diocletian (in the east)	284–305
Maximian (in the west)	286–305
Constantius I (in the west)	305–306
Galerius (in the east)	305–311
Severus	306–307
Maximian (again)	306–308
Maxentius (in the west)	306–312
Maximinus Daia	308–313
Licinius (in the east)	311–324
Constantine I, the Great	311–337
Constantine II	337–340
Constantius II	337–361
Constans	337–350
Julian the Apostate	361–363
Jovian	363–364
Valentian I (in the west)	364–375
Valens (in the east)	364–378
Gratian (in the west)	375–383
Valentinian II (in the west)	375–392
Theodosius the Great	379–395
Maximus	383–388
Eugenius	393–394
Arcadius (in the east)	395–408
Honorius (in the west)	395–423
Constantius III	421
Johannes	423–425
Theodosius II (in the east)	408–450
Valentinian (in the west)	425–455
Marcian (in the east)	450–457
Petronius (in the west)	455
Avitus (in the west)	455–456
Majorian (in the west)	457–461
Leo I (in the east)	457–474
Severus (in the west)	461–465
Anthemius (in the west)	467–473
Olybrius (in the west)	472
Glycerius (in the west)	473
Julius Nepos (in the west)	473–475
Leo II (in the east)	473–474
Zeno (in the east)	474–491
Romulus Augustulus (in the west)	475–476

Some emperors overlapped because they were set up by one army or another, and were then deposed, or murdered by their own troops; from 282 there were often two emperors, one ruling the west from Rome, the other ruling from Constantinople (formerly Byzantium). There were no Roman emperors after 476.

EASTERN ROMAN (BYZANTINE) EMPERORS

(The Eastern Roman Empire outlasted that of Rome; it is often called the Byzantine Empire from the old name for Constantinople, its capital – now Istanbul.)

Zeno	474–491
Anastasius I	491–518
Justin I	518–527
Justinian the Great	527–565
Tiberius II	578–582
Maurice	582–602
Phocas I	602–610
Hercalius I	610–641
Constantine III	641
Heracleon	641
Constans II	641–668
Constantine IV	668–685
Justinian II	685–695
Leontius	695–698
Tiberius II	698–705
Justinian II (restored)	705–711
Philippicus	711–715
Anastasius II	713–715
Theodosius III	715–717
Leo III	717–741
Constantine V	741–775
Leo IV	775–780
Irene (empress)	797–802
Nicephorus I	802–811
Stauracius	811
Michael I	811–813
Leo V	813–820
Michael II	820–829
Theophilus I	829–842
Michael III	842–867
Basil I	867–886
Leo VI, the Wise	886–912
Alexander II	912–913
Constantine VII	912–959
Romanus I	920–944
Romanus II	944–963
Basil II (a minor until 976)	963–1025
Nicephorus II	963–969
John I	969–976
Constantine VIII	1025–1028
Zoë (empress)	1028–1050
Romanus III (husband of Zoë)	1028–1034
Michael IV (husband of Zoë)	1034–1041
Michael V (usurper)	1041–1042
Constantine IX (husband of Zoë)	1042–1055
Theodora (empress)	1042–1055
Michael VI	1056–1057
Isaac I	1057–1059
Constantine X	1059–1067
Romanus IV	1068–1071
Michael VII	1071–1078
Nicephorus III	1078–1081
Alexius I	1081–1118
John II	1118–1143
Manuel I	1143–1180
Alexius II	1180–1183
Andronicus I	1183–1185
Isaac II	1185–1195
Alexius III	1195–1203
Isaac II (restored)	1203–1204
Alexius IV	1203–1204
Alexius V	1204
Latin (Crusader) Emperors	
Baldwin I	1204–1205
Henry	1205–1216
Peter of Courtenay	1216–1217
Yolande (Peter's wife, regent)	1217–1219
Robert of Courtenay	1219–1228
Baldwin II	1228–1261
John of Brienne (co-emperor)	1231–1237
The Palaeologus family	
Michael VIII	1261–1282
Andronicus II	1282–1320
Michael IX (co-emperor)	1295–1320
Andronicus III	1328–1341
John V (a minor)	1341–1347
John VI	1347–1354
John V (restored)	1355–1376
Andronicus IV	1376–1379
John V (restored)	1379–1391
John VII	1390
Manuel II	1391–1448
Constantine XI	1448–1453

The Ottoman Turks captured Constantinople in 1453, ending the Byzantine empire

NOTABLE POPES

(Up to 1998, 246 men have held the office of Pope, the supreme head of the Roman Catholic Church; these have been among the most influential.)

St Peter (the Apostle)	33–*c.* 67
St Clement I (wrote an important epistle to the Church)	*c.* 88–*c.* 97
St Leo I (asserted papal supremacy)	440–461
St Gregory I (sent missionaries to England)	590–604
St Leo IX (split with the Eastern Church)	1049–1054
Nicholas II (decreed that only cardinals could elect popes)	1059–1061
St Gregory VII (quarrelled with Emperor Henry IV of Germany)	1073–1085
Adrian IV (only English pope; "gave" Ireland to Henry II of England)	1154–1159
Innocent III (influenced European politics)	1198–1216
Boniface VIII (decreed that all human beings should submit to papal authority)	1294–1303
Alexander VI (member of the ruthless Borgia family; fathered many children)	1492–1503
Paul III (summoned the Council of Trent)	1534–1549
Gregory XIII (reformed the calendar)	1572–1585
Benedict XIV (encouraged education)	1740–1758
Pius IX (longest reign; called himself a "prisoner" after Italian unification)	1846–1878
Pius XII (led humanitarian work in World War II)	1939–1958
John XXIII (led a revival of religious life)	1958–1963
Paul VI (carried on the work of John XXIII)	1963–1978
John Paul II (first Polish pope, and the most widely travelled)	1978–

PRIME MINISTERS OF AUSTRALIA

Name and Party	*Held office*
Edmund Barton (Protectionist)	1901–1903
Alfred Deakin (Protectionist)	1903–1904
John C. Watson (Labor)	1904
George H. Reid (Free trade)	1904–1905
Alfred Deakin (Protectionist)	1905–1908
Andrew Fisher (Labor)	1908–1909
Alfred Deakin (Fusion)	1909–1910
Andrew Fisher (Labor)	1910–1913
Joseph Cook (Liberal)	1913–1914
Andrew Fisher (Labor)	1914–1915
William H. Hughes (Labor)	1915–1917
William H. Hughes (Nationalist)	1917–1923
Stanley M. Bruce (Nationalist)	1923–1929
James Scullin (Labor)	1929–1932
Joseph A. Lyons (United)	1932–1939
Earle Page (Country)	1939
Robert G. Menzies (United)	1939–1941
Arthur Fadden (Country)	1941
John Curtin (Labor)	1941–1945
Francis M. Forde (Labor)	1945
Ben Chifley (Labor)	1945–1949
Robert G. Menzies (Liberal)	1949–1966
Harold E. Holt (Liberal)	1966–1967
John McEwen (Country)	1967–1968
John G. Gorton (Liberal)	1968–1971
William McMahon (Liberal)	1971–1972
Gough Whitlam (Labor)	1972–1975
Malcolm Fraser (Liberal)	1975–1983
Robert Hawke (Labor)	1983–1991
Paul Keating (Labor)	1991–1996
John Howard (Liberal-National coalition)	1996–

20TH CENTURY BRITISH PRIME MINISTERS

Marquess of Salisbury (Conservative)	1895–1902
Arthur Balfour (Conservative)	1902–1905
Sir Henry Campbell-Bannerman (Liberal)	1905–1908
Herbert Asquith (Liberal)	1908–1915
Herbert Asquith (Coalition)	1915–1916
David Lloyd-George (Coalition)	1916–1922
Andrew Bonar-Law (Conservative)	1922–1923
Stanley Baldwin (Conservative)	1923–1924
James Ramsay MacDonald (Labour)	1924
Stanley Baldwin (Conservative)	1924–1929
James Ramsay MacDonald (Labour)	1929–1931
James Ramsay MacDonald (Coalition)	1931–1935
Stanley Baldwin (Coalition)	1935–1937
Neville Chamberlain (Coalition)	1937–1940
Winston S. Churchill (Coalition)	1940–1945
Winston S. Churchill (Conservative)	1945
Clement Attlee (Labour)	1945–1951
Sir Winston S. Churchill (Conservative)	1951–1955
Sir Anthony Eden (Conservative)	1955–1957
Harold Macmillan (Conservative)	1957–1963
Sir Alec Douglas-Home (Conservative)	1963–1964
Harold Wilson (Labour)	1964–1970
Edward Heath (Conservative)	1970–1974
Harold Wilson (Labour)	1974–1976
James Callaghan (Labour)	1976–1979
Margaret Thatcher (Conservative)	1979–1990
John Major (Conservative)	1990–1997
Anthony Blair (Labour)	1997–

CANADIAN PRIME MINISTERS

Sir John MacDonald (Conservative)	1867–1873
Alexander Mackenzie (Liberal)	1873–1878
Sir John MacDonald (Conservative)	1878–1891
Sir John Abbott (Conservative)	1819–1892
Sir John Thompson (Conservative)	1892–1894
Sir Mackenzie Bowell (Conservative)	1894–1896
Sir Charles Tupper (Conservative)	1896
Sir Wilfred Laurier (Liberal)	1896–1911
Sir Robert L. Borden (Conservative)	1911–1917
Sir Robert L. Borden (Unionist)	1917–1920
Arthur Meighen (Unionist)	1920–1921
W. L. Mackenzie King (Liberal)	1921–1926
Arthur Meighen (Conservative)	1926
W. L. Mackenzie King (Liberal)	1926–1930
Richard B. Bennett (Conservative)	1930–1935
W. L. Mackenzie King (Liberal)	1935–1948
Louis S. St Laurent (Liberal)	1948–1957
John C. Diefenbaker (Progressive Conservative)	1957–1963
Lester B. Pearson (Liberal)	1963–1968
Pierre E. Trudeau (Liberal)	1968–1979
Charles J. Clark (Progressive Conservative)	1979–1980
Pierre E. Trudeau (Liberal)	1980–1984
John E. Turner (Liberal)	1984
Brian Mulroney (Progressive Conservative)	1984–1994
Kim Campbell (Progressive Conservative)	1994
Jean Chrétien (Liberal)	1994–

PRESIDENTS OF FRANCE SINCE 1947

Fourth Republic	
Vincent Auriol (Socialist)	1947–1953
René Coty (Republican)	1953–1958
Fifth Republic	
Charles de Gaulle (Gaullist)	1959–1969
Georges Pompidou (Gaullist)	1969–1974
Valéry Giscard d'Estaing (Independent Republican)	1974–1981
François Mitterand (Socialist)	1981–1995
Jacques Chirac (Conservative)	1995–

CHANCELLORS OF GERMANY SINCE 1949

(West Germany to 1990, united Germany from then)

Konrad Adenauer (Christian Democratic Union)	1949–1963
Ludwig Erhard (Christian Democratic Union)	1963–1966
Kurt Kiesinger (Christian Democratic Union)	1966–1969
Willy Brandt (Social Democrat)	1969–1974
Helmut Schmidt (Social Democrat)	1974–1982
Helmut Kohl (Christian Democratic Union)	1982–

PRIME MINISTERS OF INDIA SINCE 1950

Jawaharlal Nehru (Congress)	1950–1964
Lal Bahardur Shashtri (Congress)	1964–1966
Indira Gandhi (Congress)	1966–1977
Morarji Desai (Janata)	1977–1979
Indira Gandhi (Congress-I)	1979–1984
Rajiv Gandhi (Congress)	1984–1991
Narasimha Rao (Congress)	1991–1996
Atal Vajpayee (BJP)	1996
Deve Gowda (United Front Coalition)	1996
Inder Kumar Gujral (United Front Coalition)	1996–

NEW ZEALAND PRIME MINISTERS

Richard Seddon (Liberal)	1893–1906
William Hall-Jones (Liberal)	1906
Sir Joseph Ward (Liberal)	1906–1912
Thomas Mackenzie	1912
William F. Massey (Reform)	1912–1925
Francis Bell (Reform)	1925
Gordon Coates (Reform)	1925–1928
Sir Joseph Ward (United)	1928–1930
George Forbes (Coalition)	1930–1935
Michael J. Savage (Labour)	1935–1940
Peter Fraser (Labour)	1940–1949
Sidney J. Holland (National)	1949–1957
Keith Holyoake (National)	1957
Walter Nash (Labour)	1957–1960
Keith Holyoake (National)	1960–1972
Sir John Marshall (National)	1972
Norman Kirk (Labour)	1972–1974
Wallace Rowling (Labour)	1974–1975
Robert Muldoon (National)	1975–1984
David Lange (Labour)	1984–1989
Geoffrey Palmer (Labour)	1989–1990
Michael K. Moore (Labour)	1990
James Bolger (National)	1990–1996
James Bolger (Coalition)	1996–

SOUTH AFRICAN LEADERS

(Prime Ministers up to 1984, thereafter Presidents)

Louis Botha (South African Party)	1910–1919
Jan Smuts (South African Party)	1919–1924
James Hertzog (Pact Coalition)	1924–1939
Jan Smuts (United Party)	1939–1948
Daniel Malan (National)	1948–1954
J. G. Strijdom (National)	1954–1958
D. H. Verwoerd (National)	1958–1966
B. J. Vorster (National)	1966–1978
P. W. Botha (National)	1978–1989
F. W. de Klerk (National)	1989–1994
Nelson Mandela (African National Congress)	1994–

PRESIDENTS OF THE UNITED STATES

George Washington (no party)	1789–1797
John Adams (Federalist)	1797–1801
Thomas Jefferson (Democratic-Republican)	1801–1809
James Madison (Democratic-Republican)	1809–1817
James Monroe (Democratic-Republican)	1817–1825
John Quincy Adams (Democratic-Republican)	1825–1829
Andrew Jackson (Democrat)	1829–1837
Martin Van Buren (Democrat)	1837–1841
William H. Harrison (Whig)	1841
John Tyler (Whig)	1841–1845
James K. Polk (Democrat)	1845–1849
Zachary Taylor (Whig)	1849–1850
Millard Fillmore (Whig)	1850–1853
Franklin Pierce (Democrat)	1853–1857
James Buchanan (Democrat)	1857–1861
Abraham Lincoln (Republican) *	1861–1865
Andrew Johnson (National Union)	1865–1869
Ulysses S. Grant (Republican)	1869–1877
Rutherford B. Hayes (Republican)	1877–1881
James A. Garfield (Republican) *	1881
Chester A. Arthur (Republican)	1881–1885
Grover Cleveland (Democrat)	1885–1889
Benjamin Harrison (Republican)	1889–1893
Grover Cleveland (Democrat)	1893–1897
William McKinley (Republican)*	1897–1901
Theodore Roosevelt (Republican)	1901–1909
William H. Taft (Republican)	1909–1913
Woodrow Wilson (Democrat)	1913–1921
Warren G. Harding (Republican)	1921–1923
Calvin Coolidge (Republican)	1923–1929
Herbert C. Hoover (Republican)	1929–1933
Franklin D. Roosevelt (Democrat)	1933–1945
Harry S. Truman (Democrat)	1945–1953
Dwight D. Eisenhower (Republican)	1953–1961
John F. Kennedy (Democrat)*	1961–1963
Lyndon B. Johnson (Democrat)	1963–1969
Richard M. Nixon (Republican)	1969–1974
Gerald R. Ford (Republican)	1974–1977
Jimmy Carter (Democrat)	1977–1981
Ronald Reagan (Republican)	1981–1989
George Bush (Republican)	1989–1994
William Clinton (Democrat)	1994–

** Assassinated*

SECRETARIES-GENERAL OF THE UNITED NATIONS

Trygve Lie (Norway)	1946–1953
Dag Hammarskjöld (Sweden)	1953–1961
U Thant (Burma)	1961–1971
Kurt Waldheim (Austria)	1972–1982
Javier Pérez de Cuéllar (Peru)	1982–1991
Boutros Boutros-Ghali (Egypt)	1991–1997
Kofi Annan (Ghana)	1997–

BELGIAN MONARCHS

Leopold I	1831–1865
Leopold II	1865–1907
Albert I	1909–1934
Leopold III	1934–1951
Baudouin	1951–1993
Albert II	1993–

BRITISH RULERS

RULERS OF ENGLAND

Saxons	
Egbert	827–839
Ethelwulf	839–858
Ethelbald	858–860
Ethelbert	860–866
Ethelred I	866–871
Alfred the Great	871–899
Edward the Elder	899–924
Athelstan	924–939
Edmund	939–946
Edred	946–955
Edwy	955–959
Edgar	959–975
Edward the Martyr	975–978
Ethelred II (the Redeless)	978–1016
Edmund Ironside	1016
Danes	
Canute	1016–1035
Harold I (Harefoot)	1035–1040
Hardicanute	1040–1042
Saxons	
Edward the Confessor	1042–1066
Harold II	1066
House of Normandy	
William I (the Conqueror)	1066–1087
William II (Rufus)	1087–1100
Henry I (Beauclerk)	1100–1135
Stephen	1135–1154
House of Plantagenet	
Henry II	1154–1189
Richard I (Coeur-de-Lion)	1189–1199
John (Lackland)	1199–1216
Henry III	1216–1272
Edward I (The Hammer of the Scots)	1272–1307
Edward II	1307–1327
Edward III	1327–1377
Richard II	1377–1399
House of Lancaster	
Henry IV	1399–1413
Henry V	1413–1422
Henry VI	1422–1461
House of York	
Edward IV	1461–1483
Edward V	1483
Richard III	1483–1485
House of Tudor	
Henry VII	1485–1509
Henry VIII	1509–1547
Edward VI	1547–1553
Jane	1553
Mary I	1553–1558
Elizabeth I	1558–1603

RULERS OF SCOTLAND

Malcolm II	1005–1034
Duncan I	1034–1040
Macbeth	1040–1057
Malcolm III (Canmore)	1057–1093
Donald Bane	1093–1094
Duncan II	1094
Donald Bane	1094–1097
Edgar	1097–1107
Alexander I	1107–1124
David I	1124–1153
Malcolm IV	1153–1165
William (the Lion)	1165–1214
Alexander II	1214–1249
Alexander III	1249–1286
Margaret (the Maid of Norway)	1286–1290
Interregnum	1290–1292
John Balliol	1292–1296
Interregnum	1296–1306
Robert I (Bruce)	1306–1329
David II	1329–1371
House of Stuart	
Robert II	1371–1390
Robert III	1390–1406
James I	1406–1437
James II	1437–1460
James III	1460–1488
James IV	1488–1513
James V	1513–1542
Mary, Queen of Scots	1542–1567
James VI	1567–1625

RULERS OF GREAT BRITAIN

House of Stuart	
James I and VI	1603–1625
Charles I	1625–1649
Commonwealth	
Oliver Cromwell (chairman, Council of State)	1649–1653
Oliver Cromwell (Lord Protector)	1653–1658
Richard Cromwell, (Lord Protector)	1658–1659
House of Stuart	
Charles II	1660–1685
James II and VII	1685–1688
William III (joint ruler with Mary)	1689–1702
Mary II	1689–1694
Anne	1702–1714
House of Hanover	
George I	1714–1727
George II	1727–1760
George III	1760–1820
George IV (Prince Regent 1811–1820)	1820–1830
William IV	1830–1837
Victoria	1837–1901
House of Saxe-Coburg-Gotha	
Edward VII	1901–1910
House of Windsor	
George V	1910–1936
Edward VIII	1936
George VI	1936–1952
Elizabeth II	1952–

DANISH MONARCHS SINCE 1808

Frederik VI	1808–1839
Christian VIII	1839–1848
Frederik VII	1848–1863
Christian IX	1863–1906
Frederik VIII	1906–1912
Christian X	1912–1947
Frederik IX	1947–1972
Margrethe II	1972–

FRENCH KINGS SINCE 987

(Before this date the kings of France were rulers of various lands, and some of them were German emperors.)

Hugh Capet	987–996
Robert II	996–1031
Henri I	1031–1060
Philippe I	1060–1108
Louis VI (the Fat)	1108–1137
Louis VII (the Young)	1137–1180
Philippe II	1180–1223
Louis VIII	1223–1226
Louis IX (St Louis)	1226–1270
Philippe III (the Bold)	1270–1285
Philippe IV (the Fair)	1285–1314
Louis X	1314–1316
Jean I	1316
Philippe V	1316–1322
Charles IV	1322–1328
Philippe VI	1328–1350
Jean II	1350–1364
Charles V	1364–1380
Charles VI	1380–1422
Charles VII	1422–1461
Louis XI	1461–1483
Charles VIII	1483–1498
Louis XII	1498–1515
François I	1515–1547
Henri II	1547–1559
François II	1559–1560
Charles IX	1560–1574
Henri III	1574–1589
Henri IV	1589–1610
Louis XIII	1610–1643
Louis XIV	1643–1715
Louis XV	1715–1774
Louis XVI	1774–1792
The First Republic	1792–1804
Napoleon I (Emperor)	1804–1814
Louis XVIII	1814–1824
Charles X	1824–1830
Louis Philippe	1830–1848
The Second Republic	1848–1852
Napoleon III (Emperor)	1852–1870
The Third Republic	1870–1940
(Vichy Régime	1940–1945)
The Fourth Republic	1944–1958
The Fifth Republic	1958–

MONARCHS OF THE NETHERLANDS

Willem I	1815–1840
Willem II	1840–1849
Willem III	1849–1890
Wilhelmina	1890–1948
Juliana	1948–1980
Beatrix	1980–

Kingdom of the Netherlands became independent in 1815

NORWEGIAN MONARCHS SINCE 1905

Haakon VII	1905–1951
Olav V	1951–1991
Harald V	1991–

Danish kings ruled Norway from 1450, and Swedish kings from 1814

SPANISH RULERS SINCE 1874

Alfonso XII	1874–1885
Maria Cristina	1885–1886
Alfonso XIII	1886–1931
Republic	1931–1947
Francisco Franco, Caudillo and Chief of State	1936–1975
Juan Carlos	1975–

SWEDISH RULERS SINCE 1818

Carl XIV Johan (Jean-Baptiste Bernadotte)	1818–1844
Oscar I	1844–1859
Carl XV	1859–1872
Oscar II	1872–1907
Gustav V	1907–1973
Carl XVI Gustav	1973–

Jean-Baptiste Bernadotte was one of Emperor Napoleon I's marshals, and was adopted as heir by the childless King Carl XIII

Index

Page numbers in bold refer to main entries. Italic numbers refer to the illustrations and their captions.

I

J

K

N

O

P

Acknowledgements

The publishers wish to thank the following artists who have contributed to this book:

Martin Camm, Richard Hook, Rob Jakeway, John James, Shane Marsh, Roger Payne, Mark Peppé, Eric Rowe, Peter Sarson, Roger Smith, Michael Welply and Michael White.

The publishers wish to thank the following for supplying photographs for this book:

Page 9 (TL) Bridgeman Art Library; 11 (CR) (AFF/AFS Amsterdam, the Netherlands, (BR) Mary Evans Picture Library; 13 (BR) Rex Features; 17 (BR) The Stock Market; 19 (BR) AKG London; 20 (TR) Novosti; 24-25 (C) The Stock Market; 27 (BL) The Stock Market; 28 (CL) Dover Publication; 31 (CL) AKG London; 32-33 (C) ET Archive; 34 (BR) AKG London; 36 (BL) AKG London; 38 (TL) AKG London, 38 (CB) ET Archive; 43 (TL) ET Archive; 49 (TL) Dover Publications; 50-51 (CT) AKG London; 51 (C) MacQuitty International Collection; 52 (BL) ET Archive 53 (BR) Skyscan Photo Library; 54 (BL) AKG London; 56-57 (CB) Dover Publications; 60 (BL) Robert Harding Picture Library; 64 (TR) ET Archive; 67 (B) ETArchive; 68-69 (C) Rex Features; 72 (B) ET Archive; 75 (CR) AKG London; 76-77 (C) ET Archive; 77 (BR) AKG London; 86-87 (C) Bridgeman Art Library; 93 (CT) AKG London; 100-101 (C) ET Archive; 106-107 (C) Mary Evans Picture Libary; 107 (CB) ET Archive; 111 (BL) AKG London; 114-115 (CB) AKG London; 115 (CB) AKG London; 117 (CR) Robert Harding Picture Library; 118 (CL) AKG London; 118-119 (BC) ET Archive; 120 (CR) AKG London; 121 (BR) ET Archive; 122-123 (TC) AKG London; 127 (C) Bridgeman Art Library; 132 (BL) AKG London; 133 (TR) AKG London; 148 (C) ET Archive; 149 (BR) ET Archive; 150 (BR) ET Archive; 154-155 (CB) AKG London; 155 (CR) AKG London; 160-161 (C) ET Archive; 164 (B) AKG London; 165 (B) AKG London; 170 (TL) ILN, (BL) ET Archive; 170-171 (C) ET Archive; 171 (CB) ILN; 172 (TR) ILN; 173 (C) ILN; 177 (C) ILN; 177 (C) ILN; 179 (TC) AKG London; 180 (TL) ILN; 182 (BL) ILN; 183 (TR) ILN; 186 (TR) ILN; 187 (CR) ILN; 188-189 (C) ILN; 189 (CL) ILN; 190-191 (B) ILN; 191 (C) ILN; 192-193 (C) ILN; 193 (CR) ILN; 196-197 (C) Corbis; 198 (TL), (CL) ILN; 199 (CR) ILN; 201 (CL) ILN; 203 (C) ILN; 204 (BL) ET Archive, (TR) ILN; 205 (TC), (CR) ILN; 206 (CL), (CR) ILN; 206-207 (CT) ILN; 207 (CR) ILN; 208 (TR) ILN; 209 (CR) ILN; 212-213 (C) Rex Features; 213 (BC) ILN, (BR) Rex Features; 215 (BR) The Stock Market; 216 (BL) Rex Features; 217 (BR) Rex Features; 219 (CR) Rex Features, (CL) Panos Pictures; 221 (CL), (CR) Rex Features; 222 (BL) ET Archive; 222-223 (BC) Panos Pictures; 224-225 (CB) Panos Pictures; 225 (TL) Rex Features; 227 (C) Panos Pictures; 229 (C), (BR) Rex Features, (BL) Panos Pictures; 230 (CL) The Stock Market, (TL) Panos Pictures; 230-231 (C) Rex Features.

All other photographs from Miles Kelly Archives.